How to Live in the New America

How to Live in the New America

by
WILLIAM KAYSING

PRENTICE-HALL, Inc., Englewood Cliffs, N.J.

Acknowledgment is also made for permission to reprint excerpts from the following: *Steal This Book*, Abbie Hoffman; courtesy Abbie Hoffman and Pirate Editions, Inc., New York. *How to Build Cabins*, courtesy Popular Science Pub. Co. *Food Is Your Best Medicine*, Henry G. Bieler; Random House, Inc., New York, © 1966. *Intelligent Motorcycling*, Bill Kaysing; courtesy Parkhurst Publishing Co. "Quick Hard Summary on How to Start a New School" from *Big Rock Candy Mountain*. "County Power," Ted Radke, from *Clear Creek*.

Many of the line illustrations which appear in this book are through the courtesy of Dover Publications, Inc., New York.

Portions of this book were published previously in pamphlet form from 1966 to 1971.

CONTENTS

APPRECIATION AND ACKNOWLEDGMENTS

JOHN BROWN.

He made a start. . . . .
Others followed.
Others will follow.

FIRST AND FOREMOST, MY EVERLOVING WIFE RUTH DESERVES (AND earnel) the credit for meeting the deadlines and lending much warm encouragement.

Dozens of American firms and chambers of commerce sent data and illustrative material, which is used with credit and which I gratefully acknowledge.

Among the people within and without the movement who contributed ideas and assistance in the preparation of this book are:
Jon Goodchild
Wendy Kaysing
Jill Kaysing
Albert Hodge
Robert Allen
Dan Clark
Tom Cole
Charles Eastman
W. H. Ferry
Leonard Gross
Alan Rinzler
Bill Schuler
J. B. James
Joseph Parkhurst
Paul Doerr
John Shuttleworth
Albert Mitchell
Vernon Johnson
Michael Hunter
H. A. Smolinski
Kathi Maben
My thanks to all...

Preface

THIS BOOK CONTAINS WHAT I'VE LEARNED IN ALMOST FIVE DECADES of performing a balancing act between a sellout to the establishment and living like Robin Hood.

I've been an establishment minion, taking the king's shilling each Friday for work on a defense project that would blow most of the Russians and at least half the Chinese into radioactive bits. On other jobs I've received fees to help convince people that they should buy things they didn't really need or want.

The reason for taking a "business trip" for a good part of my life can be found in my schooling. I was taught to shut up, sit still, learn to read, and after twelve years or so of serving time in several educational prisons, I would be ready for a "good" job. Then after forty years or so of paper shuffling, I'd get the gold watch and the man's permission to do anything I wanted for the rest of my life.

I started wondering why people had to work 96 percent of the time...why everyone, regardless of his income, seemed to be constantly struggling and most of all, why a man was given just the tail end of his life — the physical dregs — to do his own thing.

The writings of Thoreau, Whitman, and Muir extolling the benefits of the outdoor life turned me away from the city. Next, my children opened my eyes to another world. Instead of wall-to-wall payments and a once-a-year vacation that seemed to last ten minutes, here was a much larger world of sharing, of doing, of loving. So I quit my job and began living the financially precarious life of a free-lance everything — writer, salesman, huckster. As Thoreau promised, the rewards of being your own man came. First a series of articles for a national magazine, next a book on the back-to-the-land movement, and then an invitation from Mike Hunter of Prentice-Hall to put together this book. Whether you like it or not, it's as real and as true as I could make it. It's purpose is clear...to help you, the reader, become as free as you want to be.

Why limit yourself to something that'll kill your mind when the whole world's a storehouse of possibilities?
— SYLVAN HART, LAST OF THE MOUNTAIN MEN

Introduction

What is the "New America" going to be like? Here are a few predictions from a variety of sources:

"U.S. citizens will enjoy a standard of living far beyond present-day levels…the average wage earner will make $10,000 per year." (No mention is made that bread might be a buck a loaf.)

"Within ten years or sooner, cities will be armed camps, with race wars, everyone armed, shoot-outs daily, private armies." (This from an ex-police officer.)

"We are headed for the micro-dollar," says economist Pink, "worth 25 percent of the pre-war dollar. Then we'll go to the maxi-dollar and screw all the people who are stupid enough to buy government bonds and tax-exempt bonds and privilege all the people who owe money."

In *The Coming Devaluation and How to Profit from It*, Harry Browne says: "We will not have a rerun of 1929. We will have something more severe. There is nothing that can avert it…after 30 years of continuous inflation." He argues that Washington's more sophisticated techniques of prolonging inflationary prosperity make more painful liquidation periods unavoidable." Coupled with economic distress, more severe forms of governmental repression seem likely.

Climb the mountains and get their good tidings. Nature's peace will flow into you as sunshine flows into trees. The winds will blow their own freshness into you, and the storms their energy, while cares will drop off like summer leaves.

JOHN MUIR ON THE SIERRA NEVADA

ix

Then there are wars that aren't wars but kill just as dead, rising unemployment, minority oppression, a mounting credibility gap in our leadership, campus unrest, and the immediate threats to health from pollution.

Wouldn't it be great if you could climb aboard an intergalactic spaceship and bug out for another, more peaceful and intelligently operated planet? Since none is running, the next best thing is to make out the best you can with what's at hand. The several wilderness areas still left in the U.S. should give anyone hope. After all, the Indians lived long and healthful lives in just such surroundings. They had no taxes, no traffic jams, and no preservatives in their foods. Instead, they lived completely with nature —enjoyed listening to the rustle of leaves, the splash of cascades, took pleasure in the sight of vivid sunsets and, in the evening, of orange flame patterns in their campfires. Though living naturally is the major theme of this book, we aren't going to completely abandon the useful and worthwhile amenities of civilization...rather we're going to consider a more careful, discriminating selection. Also, we're going to get into some judgments on what is really valuable and what is not. As Thoreau put it..."Most of the luxuries and many of the so-called comforts of life are not only not indispensable, but positive hindrances to the elevation of mankind."

In a letter to an underground paper, one man wrote: "Cities are death...will split by next freeze." If you now live in a city or have visited one recently, there's no need to labor the point about how impossible they have become as places to enjoy a healthy, hassle-free way of life. The opportunity to enjoy life and be a productive member of humanity is still offered throughout America in its small towns, its countryside, communes, and wilderness. All you really need is knowledge. We believe that the only life worth living will be in the rural areas...that will be the New America. This book will provide some of the know-how you'll need and point out sources which can give you more.

You've heard many people ask, "How can I make a living in the country?" There are literally thousands of ways to earn your bread in sylvan surroundings. One chapter even shows how to cut the umbilical to the U.S. Mint —how to live with virtually no cash at all. This chapter also suggests some alternatives to one of the biggest leaks in anyone's budget —insurance. Food and housing together comprise the largest drain on everyone's income. Each of these subjects rates a chapter of its own. If you'd like to cut your food costs to less than a dollar a day and be healthier than you are now, you'll find the answers here. We'll also show you a forest home costing $65 in cash plus a couple of months of labor, and give you some instructions on how to build your own. The age of individuality has dawned. People can dress the way they like instead of the way society would like to have them dress. Since the omnipresent, omnipotent automobile-petroleum industry is suffocating the entire country, there are lots of words about how to save money on transportation while simultaneously improving the quality of the air that you breathe.

Education is the real key to fulfillment. That's why we're presenting a chapter that describes several methods of getting a relevant, useful education without going through conventional educational channels (ruts?).

If traveling light is your bag, then the chapter titled "Nomad" will be of deep interest. There are details on how to live without a permanent address…how to enjoy outdoor America for most of the year…how to have a vacation almost as long as a conventional person's working year.

It's difficult to enjoy life in America new or old, if you are being hassled by the authorities. With more and more repressive legislation coming into the statute books, it is imperative that everyone learn to avoid legal trouble. Mark Twain once said that many things are easy to get into but difficult to get out of, and this includes American jails and prisons.

The compendium contains everything that we'd like to tell you about in greater detail but only have space to catalog briefly. This is a hodgepodge, a Pandora's box with odds and ends of information which should be valuable to you.

1 How to Escape the Rat Race

A substantial number of Americans have already left the confusion and hassle of the big cities. They now live a more relaxed and happier way of life in the rural regions of this beautiful country. Instead of sulphur dioxide, they now breathe the aroma from alfalfa fields. The crash-bang of superhighways has given way to the sound of birds and the croak of frogs. The hectic, nine-to-five struggle for a paycheck has been traded for a leisurely paced life that's worth living amid nature.

> Today 140 million people, or seven in every ten Americans, are crowded onto just one percent of the land. The result is strangled cities, slapdash suburbs, and rush-hour nightmares.
> Rural America has breathing space ... room for people to work, to live, to enjoy recreation ... to be a part of the land.
>
> —Orville Freeman, former Secretary of Agriculture

This chapter is a guide. No easy solutions or quick panaceas. However, for those who have had it up to here with city life, this information will present ideas, information, and encouragement concerning the many unique and interesting ways that a resolute individual can make a better life in more beautiful surroundings for himself and his family.

This land was given the Gillette Razor treatment before they dropped those cookie-cutter houses out of a 747. (USDA)

What a place to get your head together! Grow your own food, go swimming in that big pond in the summertime, and in the evening sit out on the porch and listen to those big bullfrogs. (Ontario Travel & Publicity

Why You Should Leave

We can be brief on this subject, because if you live in the city you already know how terrible it is. Overcrowding, polluted air, heavy traffic, violence, and the atmosphere of an armed camp all make for a thoroughly unpleasant way of life for you and your entire family.

There is every indication that urban conditions will become even worse. More and more people are crowding into major cities to take the jobs created by the ever-expanding business community. With each new wage earner and his family in the city, there must be an equivalent increase in services. More police, more utility employees, more hospital rooms—in short, more of everything urban becomes necessary to accommodate the inexorable increase in population.

Can you stand more smog, more traffic, more congestion, and more of what makes life chaotic and unhealthy? If you can't take it any longer, then you are ready for the many benefits of country life:

1. You will be surrounded by fresh air, pure water, greenness.

2. It costs less to live—lower taxes, lower rent or payments.

3. Furnishings can be less expensive. Your cabin in the pines can be a showplace with some rustic tables, chairs, and bunks that you built yourself.

There's a deep satisfaction that comes from working close to the earth. The flow of irrigating water is music . . . the green leaves of new bean plants are like poetry. (Nevada State)

4. Clothing costs are less. You can wear informal, leisure garb and you'll feel and be at home. Kids can wear what they want, including bare feet!

5. You can build your own home or add on to an existing one. Restrictions on architecture and building codes are more lenient in the country.

6. Since electric power is available in almost all rural areas, you can enjoy any city conveniences you want, including toasters, washers, dryers, even a color TV. Electricity makes much rural work fun. It pumps your water, hoists your hay, lights up your patio and barbecue. Or you can do without it and maybe get even more satisfaction.

7. Buying by mail makes living in the boondocks as convenient as city life. There's Sears and Wards, *The Whole Earth Catalog*, or just about any magazine. There's almost nothing that you can't buy if you just send in an order.

8. Good highways make it easy to get to the city, if and when you have to go. You and your family don't need to feel as isolated as farm and country families once felt.

Instead of walking into your office tomorrow morning at about nine o'clock, how would you like to amble out on this pier and take the paddle-wheeler around the lake—as the captain!

9. All that is worthwhile recreationally is located in the country. Lakes, deserts, mountains, rivers ... the best of everything worth seeing is out in the great outdoors.

10. You can grow your own food. The USDA has a tremendous stock of information on home gardens, canning, animal husbandry, and everything else you need to know about supplementing a small income with your home-produced vittles. Besides, have you ever tasted anything as wonderful as the tomato, squash, or cucumber that you planted yourself?

Backing from Your Family

Your wife will be the first to agree that the health of the family must come before anything else and that her entire family will be better off in the fresh air and invigorating surroundings of open country.

Convincing your children, large or small, is no problem at all. If they're small, simply tell them about the chickens and rabbits. If older, remark on the feasibility of keeping a horse or two ... most useful for bounding over the nearby meadowlands.

Most people hate change because they fear the unknown. Many people will vicariously fear for your future welfare. Close your ears to all of the naysayers, toughen your resolve to live your own life in your own way. Use any popular two-word sentence that you wish in response to the people who tell you that you'll fail.

While it is true you can fail (we don't guarantee anything except that the air is fresher in the country), at least you'll be able to say that you tried, which is a lot more than the doom-criers can.

In summary, make up your mind that you're going to realize your dream regardless of what any outsiders have to say.

Why Buy a Farm?

Some men buy farms for a livelihood, some for preservation of investment capital, and some for speculation. Other men want farms because of a strong desire to return to a modernized version of the environment they lived in and enjoyed as a boy. Some feel an instinctive desire to return to the basics, to work for their own food and shelter, and they want to give this experience to their children.

Others buy farms because they are tired of the grime and noise of the city, too close association with uninteresting and irritating neighbors, high taxes, too many restrictions, or the regulated and regimented pace of city living. Some people buy their farms as retreats, so that when business headaches pile up through the week they can picture the weekend ahead when they will be able to walk across their own fields, fill their lungs with good clean air, enjoy the pride of possession, and plan for the future.

What to Sell and What to Keep

Those who want fewest things are nearest to the gods.
—SOCRATES

Fortunately there are many things that you will no longer need when you leave the city. For example, you can get rid of that big hunk of Detroit iron that you've been making payments on just to impress the neighbors. Buy yourself a solid little Jeep or International pickup which will serve you very handily in the boondocks. Among the other things that you can eliminate are all of your fancy clothes: dress shirts, suits, those eight pairs of shoes, and all the other expendable trappings of "civilization."

Cashing in on big things like a house and boat, if you have them, will give you the nest egg you need to support yourself in the wilderness for quite some time. Your treasured pieces of furniture and appliances can go with you if you want, along with family heirlooms, relics, pets, etc. These will make your rustic dwelling seem more homelike right away.

If you are going to travel a long distance, forego buying anything major for your new fresh air home until you arrive there. However, there are some items that you can purchase cheaply in the city that would be of great value in the country. This would include pumps, generators, and various tools, such as axes and saws. Although these items can be

acquired at your destination, it is fun to buy ahead. If it gives you moral support and encouragement, then by all means acquire a .30-.30 carbine, a saw, jacket, wool hat, and fishing tackle.

How to Liquidate Your Assets to Get the Most from Them

> Most of the luxuries of life are hindrances to the elevation of mankind.
>
> —THOREAU

Probably the most advantageous way of liquidating your things is to have a garage sale. In the unlikely event that you aren't familiar with this term, it simply means moving everything you wish to sell into your garage or any other convenient place, labeling each item with a price, and then, after placing suitable ads in your local newspaper, waiting for customers. This type of sale has become so popular that it attracts both professional and nonprofessional buyers. If your prices are right, you'll sell everything out the first day.

Don't overlook the possibility of offering some of the items for trade. You might get a two-and-a-half-ton stake truck for your "Firespitz V-8." Thus, without any cash changing hands, you've obtained what could be the most useful item in your country-living inventory.

As far as the big-tag items are concerned, these will be no problem if you consult the many books written on the subject. For example, there are fine publications available on how to sell your own home. Despite what real estate brokers tell you it's really quite simple to put your home up for sale, find a buyer through newspaper ads or a sign out front, and then let a qualified escrow firm handle the details. In fact, this is what a salesman or broker will do amid the smoke screen of so-called services that he provides.

For all other items from boats to airplanes, ads on your company bulletin board or in the local newspaper will suffice. However, if you find yourself with a lot of unsalable items, consider the possibility of an auction—with either you or a professional auctioneer presiding.

Cutting the Costs of Living to the Bone and Beyond

> It is life near the bone where it is sweetest.
>
> —THOREAU

Although you might have to take a severe cut in pay to enjoy the bountiful benefits of woodland living, you have something very strong going for you: If you play all the angles, you can live for a lot less in the country.

For example, did you know that the average family wastes about 20 percent of its food? All you have to do to cut your food bill (the largest expense except for housing) a fat 20 percent is cut out waste. Obviously you don't need to move anywhere to do this, but where it becomes doubly important to save, food conservation would be an excellent place to start!

As another example, did you know that 60 percent of the cost of fruits and vegetables is for transportation and handling? We've all seen produce sold from rural roadside stands for about half the city wholesale price. This is a great advantage to the rural dweller—not only does he get tree-ripened fruit and garden-fresh vegetables, he gets them for much less money. (Don't forget the possibility of canning and preserving, which permit you to buy in quantity lots and hold them over the winter or off-season.)

Here are some positive steps you can take when you reach the countryside:

1. Raise your own food. About one-half acre is sufficient to grow all the vegetables and small fruits a medium-sized family can eat, with surplus for sale or canning. This is a fact established by the USDA. Be sure to send for their list of bulletins on growing your own food, both vegetables and meats. Most of the bulletins are free. Just write USDA, Washington, D.C. 20250.

2. Buy from neighbors when it's cheapest. Many times you can work a trade-off . . . help the neighbor harvest his orchard of peaches for a payment of several dozen boxes. Then you can eat them fresh, can them for winter use, or dry them for indefinite storage.

3. Learn how to recognize wild plants to add to your family's larder. Many millions of people are totally unaware that there are dozens of plants throughout the U.S. that can be picked free and used as food. Some examples are piñon nuts, mushrooms, all kinds of wild berries, including blackberries, raspberries, and blueberries, rose hips, wild cranberries, black walnuts, and innumerable other wild fruits, nuts, barks, roots, flowers, pods, saps, gums, herbs, leaves, greens, and tubers.

There are a number of books on the subject of living off the country. One good example is Bradford Angier's *How to Stay Alive in the Woods*, published originally as *Living Off the Country* by Collier Books, New York, N.Y. Your local library probably has a copy. The U.S. government has some books on survival published for members of the armed services. They are very inexpensive (one dollar for a book on survival published for the USAF). Just write Superintendent of Documents, U.S. Government Printing Office (GPO), Washington, D.C. 20402.

On this same subject, don't forget that when you live in the country, all kinds of game become fair game for you during fishing and hunting season. Many people in northern states enjoy such delicacies as smoked salmon, barbecued

If you've always picked up a carton of impersonal eggs at the supermarket, you'll really enjoy the fun of finding them under a friendly chicken. (Ohio Chamber of Commerce)

Fathers and sons, mothers and daughters, can really enjoy being together when there's as much room for play as you see here. (Las Vegas News Bureau)

bear, deerburgers, and roast elk. One large animal shot and dressed during the winter can provide food for months for an average family. In addition to cutting food costs, you can live cheaply in the country if you:

1. Rent, lease, or buy an old farmhouse and fix it up to suit.

2. Buy a mobile home and have it towed to a suitable piece of view property.

3. Build your own lodge, cabin, houseboat, dome, or whatever.

4. Wear nothing but leisure clothes—Levis, lumberjack shirt, and a Stetson in the north country, T-shirt and shorts in the great air-conditioned southwest.

5. Drive vintage cars . . . no need to put on the dog in the boondocks. A heavy-duty pickup truck will serve you well as an all-around piece of transportation.

You'll find hundreds of ways to cut your needs to the bone once you land in the paradise of your choice. And don't forget, the tax collector will be hard-pressed to find a way to collect much revenue from those in the low-income brackets and there are many beautiful deductions for the self-employed.

Let's say you are now making $15,000 a year. If you can stand ten more years of hassling the boss, you will make $150,000, of which you may save a percentage . . . perhaps $15,000. But here's the rub. After ten years of hassle, your ulcers are having ulcers and it looks like a long siege with the doctors. That $15,000 will melt away like Jell-O under a blowtorch. Then where are you? Broke, old, unable to get another job, and with a bad stomach.

So what's the alternative to the ten years at 15 thousand? Well, let's put you in a low-stress position in the country. Let's make you a teacher and counselor in a rural school. This school is so far back in the boondocks that they don't ask any questions about advanced degrees. As long as you keep the kids occupied during class period, the school board and the parents are happy. The pay? It's a mere $6,000, but that is enough to keep your family in shoes and beans. There's no expense for movies because the nearest movie is fifty-five miles away. You hunt and fish and add quite a lot of protein to the family diet while having fun. The family doesn't need fancy clothes; Levis and a lumberjack shirt serve for both boys and girls. A car? You are happy with an old Jeep wagon that keeps running and running. With all the fresh air sweeping out of the tall mountains, there's little need for doctors and medicines.

So at the end of ten years you'll look years younger than your age; your family will eat well, enjoy nature, and think Dad is a great fellow since he's a respected member of the rural community and not a gray cog in some ugly industrial machine.

Not much money saved after ten years, but at least you're ready and willing to go another ten years . . . and another ten after that.

If one advances confidently in the direction of his dreams and endeavors to live the life which he has imagined, he will meet with a success unexpected in common hours. . .

—BIG HANK THOREAU

The simplest pleasures—a drink of cold water from the well—can mean more (and cost less) than anything obtainable along Main Street. (USDA)

Summary

Here are a few tips on what you can find. We've included a bibliography to help you get started. . .

1. Mining is one of America's greatest industries. You can become a part of this with virtually no investment. Most of the mining activity is in desirable areas such as the gold placers of Alaska. In addition, the U.S. government will grubstake you for a percentage of the take. Write to the Department of Interior, Washington, D.C. 20240, for further information. You might also send for a publication that covers western states' mining activities: *California Mining Journal*, P.O. Drawer 628, Santa Cruz, Calif. 95060.

2. Want to buy eighty acres of farmland for just $7,500? With it you get a three-bedroom house, barn, shed, poultry house, smokehouse, all-year spring, drilled well, one-quarter acre of strawberries, assorted fruit trees, ten acres of fenced pasture, fifty-five acres of woodland, and the balance in open country with sites for small lakes. They'll also toss in a tractor, milker, and two cultivators. Amazing? Hardly. This was a typical listing in a recent issue of a rural property catalog. Oh, yes, the down payment was $1,750. Most city dwellers have the full price as the equity in their homes.

3. Did you know that you can get into the fish-farming business and that the U.S. government will help you get started with both capital and know-how? Just write the USDA, Washington, D.C. 20250, and ask for the bulletins on this subject. It's a brand-new field that's just opening up. In a recent article, the USDA pointed out that a twenty-acre lake could easily produce 31,000 pounds of fish—all fifteen-plus tons delicious and salable at about fifty cents a pound. Multiply this out and see how it compares with your present gross income!

4. There are hundreds of magazines that are published for the benefit of farmers and other rural dwellers. As a part of your escape plot, subscribe to several of them, and get a preview of what it will be like to live where a lung full of air won't give you emphysema. Here's a sampling:

Arizona Farmer-Rancher, 434 W. Washington Street, Phoenix, Ariz. 85003

Arkansas Farmer, Box 246, Little Rock, Ark. 72201

Big Farmer, 534 N. Broadway, Milwaukee, Wis. 53202

California Farmer, 83 Stevenson Street, San Francisco, Calif. 94105

California Rancher, 2900 Rio Linda Boulevard, Sacramento, Calif. 95815

Doane's Agriculture Report, 8900 Manchester Road, St. Louis, Mo. 63144

The Farm and Garden, 260 Washington Street, Watertown, N.Y. 13601

Farm Journal (this is the big one, with three million circulation), 230 W. Washington Street, Philadelphia, Pa. 19106

New Mexico Farm and Ranch, 421 N. Water, Las Cruces, N.M. 88001

Successful Farming, 1716 Locust Street, Des Moines, Iowa 50505

Western Farm Life, P.O. 201 Elliot Avenue, West Seattle, Wash. 98119

Special Tip: For information on cheap land write the Superintendent of Documents, U.S. Government Printing Office, Washington, D.C. 20402, and ask for "Our Public Lands" (single copy, twenty cents). From a recent issue. . .

NEW MEXICO

7 tracts, 40 A to 120 A, 13 to 15 miles southwest of Kenna, east-central portion of Chaves Cty. Moderately rolling with sand hummocks. Thin to moderate depth of sandy soil covered with moderate density of vegetation. Best suited for livestock grazing. Power transmission line passes through 2 tracts. App. $10 to $13 per A. 2 tracts 160 A each, 12 to 13 miles south of Deming, Luna Cty. Level with sandy loam soils. Suitable for rural homesites; tel and elec. App. $50 per A.

Despite all of the bad press that the United States receives with about its declining environment, there are still some great places to live. Here's a review of just a few.

1. SAN JUAN ISLANDS

Although somewhat overrated as far as sunshine is concerned, the 172 islands of this region have less rain than damp Vancouver and soppy Seattle. There's lots of room, since some of the islands have no residents and others only a few.

2. WENATCHEE, WASHINGTON

This land of blue skies, apple blossoms, and the biggest and best Delicious apples you've ever eaten is tucked away on the eastern side of the Cascades. If it's true that an apple a day eliminates the doctor, then this spot can be your combination Shangri-La and health resort.

3. WILLAMETTE VALLEY, OREGON
This fertile region bordering the placid and picturesque Willamette River provides an outasite home for people who don't mind quite a bit of rain but enjoy the feeling of being close to nature. Living is inexpensive because of the abundance of food grown here.

4. CAVE JUNCTION, OREGON
Low-cost land, fresh air, and the beautiful Illinois River make this a paradise. However, don't look as if you're having too much fun or the local rednecks will find some excuse to run you out. Cool it, lay low, keep a sharp watch, and you'll be able to enjoy a place that looks like pioneer America.

5. THE MOTHER LODE COUNTRY, CALIFORNIA
This region, from Mariposa in the south to Grass Valley in the north, was once the scene of a vigorous rush for gold. Today, with the yellow-metal fever abated, people enjoy tall pines, lovely rivers, and a way of life little changed from 1871.

6. BIG SUR, CALIFORNIA
A magnificent region of steep hills and cliffs all terminating in the lashing breakers of a chilly Pacific. Mecca of libertarians and free-thinkers, Big Sur provides permanent homes for few, but for a nomad it would be a marvelous place for an extended (or even permanent) visit.

7. WHITE PINE COUNTY, NEVADA
Nevada is really a sleeper state because most people see only its barren deserts through the windows of a speeding Impala. However, places like this rugged and beautiful mountain region may be reached by slowing down a bit and taking a side road or two. With no industry nearby, this county has some of the best air left in the U.S. (When you arrive, throw away the keys to your smog-generator and help keep it that way.)

8. SAWTOOTH MOUNTAINS, IDAHO
Evergreen-clad peaks, rushing rivers lined by quaking aspen, and huge green fields of bright wildflowers are only a few of the inviting characteristics of this as yet untroubled region. With enough money to live anywhere, Ernest Hemingway chose this spot. Once you see it, you'll know why.

9. GLACIER COUNTY, MONTANA
Most of the people who visit this county, made famous by A.B. Guthrie in "The Big Sky," want to cut all ties with their previous home. If you can figure out a way to make a living there during the summer and fall, it could well be the best place to live in America. But as the name implies, winters are very severe.

10. JACKSON HOLE, WYOMING

Everyone has seen photographs of the striking Grand Tetons. If that kind of scenery turns you on, you'll also enjoy the blue lakes, fish-filled, flashing streams, placid mountain meadows, and thick green forests.

11. FLAGSTAFF, ARIZONA

Here in Coconino County is a land of contrasts—12,000-foot peaks descending to warm sands shaded by desert cedar. Nature lovers will enjoy the western scenery and have the clear water and fresh air as a bonus.

12. MONTEZUMA COUNTY, COLORADO

If you like a combination of mountains and desert, this region will appeal to you. Land is inexpensive, the climate is dry, the people few and far between ... a great place to escape jangling telephones and the drone of freeways.

13. THOMAS COUNTY, NEBRASKA

Few people think of Nebraska as a place to enjoy the new America. Most tourists recall only elephant-eye-high corn. However, forests, hills, and numerous bodies of water, plus low-population small towns make this area an attractive consideration.

14. DOOR COUNTY, WISCONSIN

With certain types of farming on the decline, land has become very inexpensive in many parts of this state. Although close to some urban centers, this county is one of the cleanest rural regions in America. Sturgeon Bay on mighty Lake Michigan has a small population, and if that's too crowded, you can tool on up to little villages like Valmy and Jacksonport.

15. THE OZARKS

Many lakes (some of them huge), nearly a dozen major rivers, and hundreds of streams and creeks make this a water lover's paradise. Good land with water frontage is inexpensive. With wild game plentiful and a vegetable garden in your backyard, you can live like Huckleberry Finn.

16. CULPEPER, VIRGINIA

For some strange reason, the two major rivers in this area are still clean and unpolluted. Even stranger is the fresh air. For a part of the densely populated East to be such a delightful island in the midst of chaos is most surprising. Prepare to devote your time to growing things.

17. COOS COUNTY, NEW HAMPSHIRE

This region near the Canadian border has been called one of the healthiest spots in eastern America. If you would enjoy a wilderness life (with or without a permanent piece of property under you), you could be there in a flash. With a tipi, a crossbow, and a supply of flint, you could easily make out like a happy Mohawk.

18. HANCOCK COUNTY, MAINE

This area, not too far from the congestion of Manhattan, contains some of the most beautiful and untouched pioneer country in the eastern United States. It includes the verdant mountainlands of Acadia National Forest. If you know how to be self-supporting, you can live a long and healthy life free from urban pressures.

Epilogue

If you are thinking in terms of bright sunlight on dark green pine needles and brisk winds rippling the surface of a hidden pool in some out-West desert canyons, then study this chapter carefully, make your plans boldly, and execute them with courage and determination. The results will be most rewarding for you and your family.

We guarantee . . .

Long life and much happiness where the air is fresh and the sun shines brightly on the same kind of people who advanced the frontiers down through history.

2 OK, But How Do I Make a Living?

If you live in the city, it probably takes all of your salary just to stay even, to support the life you are accustomed to: $2,400 for house payments, another $2,000 to pay for and support a new car, expensive food, entertainment, medical and dental bills, and all the other urban expenses leave little if any savings. But with *careful management*, every single one of your expenses in the city can be cut drastically if you live either in a resort area or in the country. (More detailed information on this in later chapters.)

Get a Job

A man in his late thirties decided that Los Angeles was too much for both him and his family. He pulled up stakes completely—sold his house, furniture, everything—and drove to a resort in the wine country of California. There, in a town catering to local folk as well as tourists, he became the manager of the only tourist hotel in town. Lucky? Perhaps, but remember that no matter what the economic situation, there are jobs opening up constantly due to death, sickness, and disagreements. In fact, it has been established that about 15 percent of all jobs are "available" at any given time. Thus, your chance of finding a job, even in a job-poor rural area, are reasonably good, provided you are there at the right time.

   With quarters thrown in as part of the management job, a substantial part of our man's income was no longer needed. If you don't have to spend it, you don't have to earn it . . . it's as simple as that. Also, the hotel kitchen frequently has leftover spaghetti and meatballs or the end of a prime rib, so dinner is often free. The man acts as his own maintenance man for which he is paid extra by the owner. His children help with the dining room chores. His wife doubles as waitress and bookkeeper. No longer does he have to rush through breakfast to dash down the freeway to a dull job shuffling bits of paper. Instead, he enjoys the challenging problems of dealing with the traveling public, in the environment that people travel many miles to see.

Buy a Job

If you are fortunate enough to have saved some money, perhaps you can do what one ex-insurance broker did, although not in quite the same way. This man crashed his plane trying to land at a resort town on the Snake River in Idaho. While recovering in the local hospital, he mused, "The business is running without me and look at the view out of that window. I wonder if. . . ." He stopped wondering and sold his insurance business, which was located in a city full of congestion and airborne chemicals. With the proceeds he bought a small boat-supply and repair shop on the banks of the Snake. He now spends as much time fishing and boating as "working" . . . the so-called work consisting of bantering with the locals and the summertime tourists. There are enough sales to keep things together economically; beyond this, he doesn't care and neither does anyone else.

Creating Your Own Job

Even if there are no jobs and you don't have the means to buy a business, there are still thousands of potentially profitable enterprises that you can start with little capital or none at all.

One man who tired of the urban rat race found a modest ranch that had become unprofitable from the standpoint of raising cattle. He was able to buy it for a small down payment with low monthly payments. He revamped one of the barns to accommodate his business, which was making small metal parts with automatic machines. Now he ventures down into the city only to pick up and deliver orders. Although he nets less money than before, he actually lives at a higher standard of living. Furthermore, his family is in much better health, with fewer trips to the doctor. Entertainment is no problem for his boy and girl, who ride their own ponies along the miles of trails that adjoin his ranch. His wife would never consider returning to the city . . . clothes stay cleaner, she has fresh fruits and vegetables from her garden, and most of all she enjoys the great natural beauty of the ranch and its environs.

This account involved a previously existent business, but it is possible to begin a rural business with even less, as the following story indicates. There is an ever-present problem in casting small parts to remove the "flash" or small bits of metal remaining after the parts are removed from the mold. Most of the work is done by hand, with ordinary knives or files. An enterprising man who wanted to live where the air was fresh and the trees were thick rented a large old building near his country home. He then made a tour of factories in a nearby city and offered to perform the flash removal service at a very low price. He brought home several jobs, and then hired local women to do the work on their own time on a piecework basis. By hiring people on this basis, he has no burden or overhead problems . . . no work, no employees to pay. He has cut his costs down to where he can compete with city prices and still cover the increased travel expense. He can expand at any time to include other types of small parts work, but for the present, the business brings a satisfactory return and he has much time for simply enjoying life.

Opportunities exist in rural America for men and women of any age. We've found boys of sixteen who make $200 a month cutting firewood while still attending school. We've encountered two retired women schoolteachers who own and successfully operate a tourist store specializing in rocks and relics.

Here are a number of do-it-yourself ideas that are appropriate for *anyone*! Keep in mind that if your enterprise does not produce enough revenue for your needs, simply add another business until income is sufficient.

Furniture Refinishing   After housing, food, and clothing, furniture is one of the largest items in anyone's budget. A very comfortable living can be made by buying and reselling furniture, either with or without a certain amount of restoration.

Restoring furniture is actually quite simple. It entails removing the old finish by either abrasive or chemical means and applying a new one. Almost anyone can do it, and there are many books in the library that cover the subject very well. Here's the general plan that will permit a young couple to have a comfortable part- or even full-time living in a rural area.

1. First acquire a suitable work area. This could be something simple like a shed or garage. In fact, the less fancy it is the more buyers will think they are going to get bargains.

2. Acquire some simple tools, such as scrapers, sandpaper blocks, etc. This plus your varnishes, lacquer, shellacs, and other finishing materials complete the basic requirements.

3. Find old furniture. This is usually a lot easier than you may think. One easy method is to read the classified ads in any paper, whether a large or small town. People are always moving, dying, or in some way getting rid of their household belongings. If you can get to the suburbs of a big city, you can pick up truckloads of low-priced furniture at

garage sales. Another source of furniture is the abandoned house. It's surprising how many old houses there are in America that have no owners and no tenants. They are often full of odds and ends of furniture which anyone who happens along can have for nothing as long as there are no Keep Out signs posted. On a recent trip through central California, the author found four homes jammed with various items of furniture, including some pieces that when refinished would bring two to three hundred dollars in an Early American-type antique shop. So keep an eye out as you drive through the countryside. A third source is the direct approach to home-owners. All you have to do is push a doorbell and ask the resident if he's got any old furniture he'd like to sell or give away. Here's where your bargaining instincts come into play, because obviously you want to acquire the items as cheaply as possible. Sometimes you'll find an owner with a garage or barn just stuffed with old pieces that he'd love to have someone cart away.

Other sources are the Salvation Army, Goodwill Industries, or other charitable organizations. They frequently have an "as is" yard where the furniture that's brought in is just dumped. Since they have very little money invested, they are willing to sell very cheaply to dealers and refinishers. You will discover other sources of furniture if you use your imagination.

From here on out, it's strictly up to you . . . it's hard work, but it can be done outdoors and can be quite enjoyable. To watch an old scratched, worn piece of furniture emerge glistening and beautiful is a most satisfying way to earn a living.

Finding customers is really easy. One of the best ways is to put one of your refinished pieces out on the side of the road with a For Sale sign. It won't be long before a car full of tourists will screech to a stop and then the fun starts. You ask your price and then they'll offer theirs and somewhere in the middle you'll get together. Being paid for a job that you did yourself on your own time is really one of the most satisfying ways of earning a living.

Winemaking Think of the market you could generate for homemade wine made from wild grapes. If you run into the revenooers, make a quick switch to homemade jelly.

Vinyl Repairs One young college student has set up a fine business that has no real limits. He has mastered the art of repairing vinyl upholstery fabrics or plastics. He learned this from a book which he obtained from a plastics company. Since most bars, restaurants, and other public places are furnished with vinyl upholstered pieces that are subjected to a great deal of wear and tear, the repair of these pieces becomes a very vital needed service. He has learned how to repair cigarette burns and tears and even make extensive repairs where the seats or chairs have become worn.

His charges are far less than the cost of upholstering the entire piece, so restaurant and bar owners are always anxious to have him take care of their latest damage.

For information, you can subscribe to some magazines that deal with the plastics field. You can look over the following in your nearby library or else write to the editors for sample copies:

Modern Plastics
1301 Avenue of the Americas
New York, N.Y. 10019

Plastics World
221 Columbus Avenue
Boston, Mass. 02116

Progressive Plastics Magazine
481 University Avenue
Toronto 2, Ontario

Automobile Electrical Repair   Here's an ingenious business that was originated by a man who taught himself how to repair automobile horns. For some reason, when a car is a few years old the horn stops working. This can be caused by loose switches or water in some of the electrical mechanisms, but whatever the reason, when a horn stops functioning, the owner of the car becomes liable for a ticket.

A young student capitalized on this fact by putting out a sign in front of his home "Any Car Horn Fixed, $3.00." While this price is quite modest and he occasionally lost money on a tough job, there was usually enough additional electrical repair work to more than offset any losses.

Getting into this kind of business requires a little training and know-how. However, there are plenty of books in the library on this subject, and you can practice on your own car. Since there are over 100 million motor vehicles in the United States, there won't be any lack of work for quite some time . . . at least until we find a good substitute for those polluting vehicles.

No-Investment Tire Business   Here's another automotive-related enterprise that anyone can get into with practically no investment. A man on the East Coast earns $12,000 a year from this unique method of getting customers.

First he had some cards printed showing the four tires on a car sketched in diagram form. He then went around to parking lots and places of business and inspected the tires of parked cars, placing his written inspection on the windshield of each car. On the back of the card was a note advising the car owner to contact him for wholesale prices on tires. If they did, he would drive out to their homes and give a quotation on equipping the car with one or more tires. He then had his crew of tire changers go to the home and install the new tires and collect the money. Therefore, the man really did no work himself . . . his was simply a contact job.

The tires were purchased at the lowest possible wholesale price from a large distributor in the state and shipped to him on a 30-day charge basis.

This is the type of business that involves selling somebody else's product but without having the overhead of a store or employees. In addition, you can work whenever you please. All it takes is a little bit of imagination and some walking around town.

This type of business might be expanded to seat covers, paint jobs, body and fender repair. No matter what the item or service, you can always line up the work to be done by an existing facility; you, in effect, become a broker.

Water Sports If you can find an unused lake, try leasing it. Then, stock it with game fish, as the basis for a profitable business. Besides charging for fishing privileges, you can rent boats and equipment, sell bait and tackle, or provide guide service.

Pictures from Remnants A young college girl has helped pay her way through school by making unusual pictures from cloth and fabric remnants. Here's how it works. She first canvasses upholstery and fabric stores for scraps. Many of these stores are only too happy to get rid of their small remnants to someone who will make good use of them. Thus she is able to get most of her material free. Occasionally she is able to buy large quantities of old clothing and drapery and upholstery material from the Goodwill or Salvation Army type stores for practically nothing.

Once she gets all of these remnants and scraps home, she takes a rectangular piece of masonite. She then cuts out the fabric scraps in the form of an interesting picture. For example, one of her best sellers is a picture of a big city skyline where each building is cut from a different pattern or different colored fabric. The cut-out pieces are glued to the backing board in an interesting design or picture pattern with ordinary contact cement or other adhesive.

When the picture is done, she frames it with a simple and inexpensive frame which she has previously refinished, and the entire product takes on a most artistic and striking appearance. She has no trouble selling these colorful fabric pictures through craft shops, and to interior decorators and gift stores. She has always been able to sell all she makes, and since the cost of her materials is low and the labor negligible,

the profits are as high as almost any type of home business can be.

This business could be a joint effort for a couple, the man collecting the samples and doing some of the heavy cutting out and the girl pasting the pieces on. In addition, the man can take care of cutting out the boards, framing, and delivering the finished product.

Relics   Gathering up abandoned artifacts from lonely ghost towns can produce a modest income. Resell to tourists or shops that cater to tourists.

The Remnant Store   There is one kind of business that is always popular in good times or bad. But when times get less than affluent, this store really comes into its own. It's called a remnant store and simply sells pieces of cloth that are purchased cheaply from wholesalers. The fabrics can be discontinued patterns, mill ends, all kinds of woven goods that can be obtained for very little. For sources of supply, check the Yellow Pages of big directories under fabrics, cloth, weavers, clothing manufacturers, upholsterers.

Your store can be about as simple as a store can get. Just have some tables and shelves where the boxes and bolts of fabric can be displayed. You'll find that very little advertising is necessary since people who make their own clothes are always on the lookout for inexpensive fabrics. The beauty of this business is that it requires very little attention and sales are continuous. Keep in mind that more and more American women are making their own clothes and home decorator items. You are advancing into a rapidly expanding market.

This store could be located at the extreme outskirts of a small town, in the low-rent district where people naturally go to find bargains. If you need to advertise at all, pick out some of your low-cost fabrics and offer them at just about what you paid for them. This "loss leader" will bring people into your store and your other merchandise will sell itself.

As an adjunct to this business, you might stock thread, needles, zippers, and other sewing accessories which again may be obtained through wholesalers and distributors by mail from the big ugly cities you've left behind.

Be a Tourist Guide   This little business requires virtually no capital. At the very most you will have to buy a few posters to place around the town where you live. The only requirement is that the town have some point of tourist interest. It might be a mine, a historical monument, a battlefield, a group of interesting buildings, or one of the old traditional hanging trees that appear all over the Mother Lode country in California. Once you have located such an item of interest, prepare a poster to place at different points around town which tourists might frequent. The poster will point out that you are available at a certain place or telephone number to act as a guide. Or it can specify that tours leave at specific hours.

Let's say that you found an old mine near a ghost town. Tourists who come to these areas always enjoy learning as much historical information as they can. In the case of a mine, you not only have the historical data to draw from, but you can add a lot of technical information. It should be as accurate as possible, but a few embellishments here and there wouldn't hurt a bit.

However you arrange the tour, the process itself is very simple. Meet your tourist group, greet them, and simply ask them to follow you on foot or in their cars. Once at the mine you start your spiel: tell when it was started, how much gold was taken out, how deep it is, how many men worked there, and why it closed down. People will ask you a lot of questions, so you should be well prepared to answer them.

In addition to your talk, you might pass out leaflets or brochures describing your tour and ask people to pass them along to others who are interested. At the conclusion, you could open a display case and offer to sell samples of the quartz ore that came from the mine.

This kind of business would be great for the person who likes walking and talking with people. With only an investment in the posters and your time, it can make you a very handsome income during the summer season. If you wish, you can move on to other places as the season changes. For example, you could go on into snow country and give a lecture on some interesting aspects of that region.

Tourist Entertainment Business   On the Atlantic seaboard there are many abandoned canals. One enterprising man has made a section of a canal into an easy source of income for himself. He acquired an authentic-looking canal boat and a couple of horses to pull it, and now he tows tourists along the canal while he gives a little speech about the historical aspects. This is similar to the guide service except that it requires a little more in the way of investment. However, if you are as enterprising as one man out West, the amount of money you would have to put into it can be very small. This man found a stagecoach in a barn located in an old gold-mining town. He arranged to lease it from the owner and rented a couple of horses on a weekly basis. Practically no investment was required, and he nets from $50 to $100 a day giving kids and their parents rides around this forty-niner community.

There's really no end to the potential here. Let's say that you live near an old logging town where there is a flume. . . . the type of trough that carried lumber from the logging area to where it was milled. Installing one of these units, filling it with water, and giving the tourists the thrill of their lives would be both exciting and profitable. A more restful and relaxed way of earning money would be to find a nice section of stream bed somewhere in the old gold country of the West. Posters would direct the tourists to your gold-panning instruction business. The tourists would pay you a modest sum to show them how to pan gold.

A sideline to this business would be the sale of gold-mining pans and perhaps a simple mimeographed booklet on just how it's done and some of the historical background of the area.

There are literally unlimited opportunities at any location where tourists congregate. Consider the possibilities of just taking a Polaroid camera and photographing couples at scenic spots. You buy the film for about twenty-five cents a shot and you charge a dollar. This should do well at honeymoon spots or ski resorts.

Winter sports grow more popular every season. By rigging a homemade rope tow on a beginner's ski slope, you can probably make enough money to go south for the winter. The tow shown produces a gross income of $2,500 per week for the owners—the result of five hundred visiting skiers spending an average of $5 each for use of the tow.

The Tourist Newspaper   Since we're on the subject of tourists, I'd like to mention here a simple business for those with experience in graphic arts, printing, or writing. First a word of background.

In the California Mother Lode country is an authentic restoration of an early forty-niner gold-mining community called Columbia. Distributed in various stores around town is a very cleverly produced old-fashioned newspaper. It doesn't contain too much of great interest, but it's printed in old Barnum type and has the look and feel and appearance of a 100-year-old newspaper freshly printed. The paper is about eight or twelve pages long and retails for twenty-five cents. It probably didn't cost more than two to three cents a copy to print, and even when you give about a 30 to 40 percent discount to the retailer, you're bound to make money.

This idea could be put into operation in almost any community that attracts tourists. There are infinite variations; for example, you can pay for your printing costs by having the local merchants take ads in your paper.

The best thing about this venture is that the newspaper doesn't have to come out daily or even monthly. Just put it out whenever the sales seem to be weakening. Incidentally, there is a newspaper in existence that will tell you how to live better for less. It's called the *Better World News* and I publish it myself. If you'd like to have a sample copy and information on how you can become a dealer, write to Paradise Publishers, Better World News Division, P.O. 88, West Point, Calif. 95255.

To learn more about the fascinating field of publishing, go to your local library and get some books on graphic arts, printing, journalism, and related subjects. If you study them you will soon be knowledgeable enough to tackle this interesting and profitable type of business.

Poster Printing   Take a look at any U.S. town of any size and you'll see posters. These printed pieces of cardboard are as common as Coca-Cola signs. Think about it a moment . . . someone had to set these up in type and print them. Someone had to pay for them. Poster printing can be done simply, with a very small investment, through silk-screening. Without going into the technicalities of silk-screening here, suffice it to say that it is a simple process which uses a piece of very fine silk material in conjunction with a stencil which allows the user to produce as many vari-colored posters as he wishes. You can obtain further information about silk-screen printing from your local library. Two publications that are valuable sources of information are *Graphic Arts Product News*, 6725 Sunset Boulevard, Los Angeles, Calif. 90028, and *Graphic Arts Supplier News*, 134 N. 13th Street, Philadelphia, Pa. 19107.

Once you obtain your outfit, there is no limit to what you can produce. You can do reproductions of old-fashioned posters using old-fashioned type and artwork, or you can prepare modern psychedelic and far-out posters that could bring one or two dollars retail in head shops.

A constant source of living money for you will be in providing posters for club meetings, conventions, and all types of public events. Simply write the president or secretary of organizations located in your town and offer your services.

You can also get into the advertising field, making signs and displays for stores of all types. If you live midway between two moderate-sized communities, you can draw business from both. This allows you to live in a country area and get your money from a larger town.

The best part of all is that it's really fun. Printers probably have more fun in their trade than almost any other type of professional. You'll find this is true the first time you sit down and produce a colored poster.

Painting Curb Numbers   During the great depression of the thirties people wracked their brains to try to earn enough money for food. One of the better ideas that emerged was providing curb numbers for homeowners. Although this practice has died out to some extent, it can easily be revived. Most homeowners would like to have their houses identified clearly with numbers so that they can be found by friends. This requires that a neat set of numbers be painted on the curb and occasionally be renewed with fresh paint.

With paint and brush in hand, it's just a matter of house-to-house canvassing. You merely ask the homeowner if he would like to have his house number painted on the curb in front of his house, the charge being as low as fifty cents or perhaps as high as a couple of dollars, depending on the neighborhood. Be sure that you canvass from one side of the street to the other, so that the neighbor across the street will be able to see the freshly painted number on the curb directly across from him. If one house accepts your service, others will be likely to go along as well. Try a strategic ploy. Paint the first number on a curb whether the house owner pays you or not. Point it out to the next customer, and you could go on down the street picking up every homeowner on the block. If you worked steadily all day long, you could do 100 or more houses, and at a dollar each, this is very "heavy" bread.

Tree and Hedge Trimming There's one good thing about trees and hedges ... they keep right on growing through depressions, good times, wars, or revolutions. Anyone who owns a tree or a hedge is a likely customer for a tree or hedge-trimming service. To go into this business requires only that you buy a long-handled saw and a pair of hedge clippers. To get customers you merely go down the street and find somebody with a droopy looking tree or an unkempt hedge and punch the doorbell. Then you're on your own. You can set the price at any level you wish. If you're really hungry, make it low; if you're fairly affluent, you can dicker with the owner. Often you may be asked to do other work of a similar nature. In time you might acquire a regular route.

None of this work requires living in a city. You can live in the furthermost reaches of a rural region and commute into a moderate-sized town whenever you need money. There are a number of publications on the subject. Two sources of general information about landscaping are *Western Landscaping News*, 1623 S. La Cienega, Los Angeles, Calif. 90035, and *Brown's Maintenance*, 1014 Wyandotte Street, Kansas City, Mo. 64105.

Bottled Water A recent investigation revealed that one out of four Americans is drinking water unfit for human consumption. How about providing this 25 percent segment of the American population with delicious, fresh, chemical- and pollution-free spring water in bottles?

This operation is easier than it sounds. Here's the story of a couple who started a bottled water business in a medium-sized community. They first located a small, steadily producing spring in the mountains above the town. They rigged a simple funnel-filling device and then began acquiring large one- and five-gallon bottles from secondhand stores and other sources.

They owned an old but sturdy pickup truck, which they converted into a delivery wagon by installing racks to hold the bottles of water.

They then designed and had printed an attractive label showing water gushing out of a beautiful mountain spring, with the caption, "pure, fresh mountain spring water."

With the help of an interesting leaflet, selling was simple. They canvassed the neighborhood; the person who answered the door was offered a drink of mountain spring water and asked to compare it to the water they were drinking from the tap. It wasn't long before they had hundreds of steady customers, with the number still growing.

It would be possible to operate this business strictly in the country. Simply find a spring, bottle the water, and hire somebody else to haul it into the polluted city for you.

Soft Water Service One of the fastest growing services in America provides soft water to homeowners. Many large companies such as Culligan and Rayne have dealers in every major city who rent, sell, or lease water-softening equipment. One man takes advantage of the fact that it requires real selling to place this equipment with the homeowner. Every time he needs money, he goes to a nearby city and makes arrangements with a water-softening company to solicit customers for them. He then canvasses various neighborhoods, delivering a regular spiel to the homeowners and showing them samples of fabrics, some of which have been washed in soft water and others in ordinary tap water. He is an affable young man who knows how to rap with the housewives. He averages about one sale out of every five calls and gets a substantial commission . . . so large that he only has to sell three or four clients per day to make enough money to last him for a long time in the country.

There are many products and services that could be sold on commission in the same way: service station equipment to service station operators, advertising for various media, solicitation of accountants for financial institutions, all types of food products to individuals and institutions, and so on.

All you have to do to get started in a business like this is contact the wholesalers or distributors of the company and tell them that you would like to sell for them on commission. If you're good at it, there's no limit to what you can earn, and the best part of it is that you can take off from the city scene as soon as you have enough bread to make it back to the country. You don't even have to leave the country if you happen to live in an area where there are a series of small towns.

Following the Harvest When John Steinbeck wrote his famous *Grapes of Wrath*, he portrayed the people who harvested as woebegone, oppressed, and bedraggled individuals. Of course this is true in many parts of the country. However,

there has emerged a new type of crop follower. These people, most of them young, know exactly where to go to make the most money for the least effort. Here's an example. Thousands of tons of almonds are grown in the central valleys of California. When this nut is ready to be harvested, the pay is high for anyone who can put out a heavy day's work. Recently a young friend of mine went to the outskirts of Paso Robles to pick almonds and was averaging between $50 and $60 a day for shaking the nuts out of the trees and sacking them.

Actually, when crops are ripe the farmer is at a great disadvantage. He must harvest his foodstuffs or suffer a loss. For this reason, any group of crop harvesters is in a good position to bargain with the farmer for their work. Cesar Chavez counted on this when he went into negotiations with grape growers.

Regardless of your union affiliations, there will always be an opportunity to make good money harvesting crops. And there are other benefits. You're out in the fresh air, you get to eat all you want of whatever you're harvesting, and if you get tired of one place, you just travel wherever you wish. To me this would be an ideal way for a young couple to live in and off the country. Just buy an inexpensive trailer and a pickup truck to tow it and you can be your own boss, following the crops wherever it strikes your fancy.

There may well come a time when you'd like to settle

down. If so, you could settle in an area where there is some crop like Bartlett pears or freestone peaches to be harvested at least once a year. Then you'd be sure of some seasonal employment and all the fruit you could eat.

Did you know that 70,264,320 acres in Nevada are under federal jurisdiction? Consult the local Bureau of Land Management and see if you can't lease some of it for dry farming of hay and grain.

Ranch Work Many young people are totally unaware that there's a lot of work on the great farms and ranches of America; others just don't know how to get started. There are a number of ways to get into ranch work. First of all, you can subscribe to magazines that deal with ranching. One good one is *Western Livestock Journal*, 1730 S. Clementine, Anaheim, Calif. This publication lists jobs on farms and ranches all over the West. There's a much larger magazine called the *Farmer Stockman* (P.O. 25125, Oklahoma City, Okla. 73125) with a circulation of almost a half million. An ad seeking a position in either of these publications is almost certain to get results.

If these don't do it, go to a library and get a copy of *Standard Rate and Data*, the issue that deals with American periodicals. There you will find listings of hundreds of farm magazines. Another source of these listings is the *Publicity Checker*, published by Bacon's, 14 E. Jackson Boulevard, Chicago, Ill. 60604.

Once you have made contact by mail, the next step is to visit the farm or ranch and see if your talents fit the job. Most farm work is quite simple, and a student with his wife or girl friend will find it easy to fit right in.

Knowledge of animals, tractors, and welding are three good skills to have for a farm job. Usually a home or trailer comes with the job, along with unlimited amounts of whatever the farm or ranch produces. Freaks may have to reduce the length of their hair to avoid conflicts with WASPish owners, but that's a small price to pay for fresh air and water, blue sky, and the relaxation that comes after a hard day in the fields.

Carnival Concessions   It is surprising how many small carnivals are still traveling the byways of America. Few people know that it's possible to join up and be a carny. If you can acquire a good secondhand popcorn machine, for example, you can ask if they need a popcorn concession. The terms vary from show to show, but they usually ask a percentage of your take plus a fixed fee to pay traveling expenses.

Carny people are a clannish lot, and you may or may not like this aspect. However, they are loyal to one another and many of them have followed their profession for decades.

There's always room for new concessions ... rides, foods, novelties, games. Let your imagination roam and if you come up with a new idea, you could make enough in one season to support yourself in the country for a year or two.

If you write to the editors of *Variety* (154 W. 46th Street, New York, N.Y. 10036) and *Billboard* (165 W. 46th Street, New York, N.Y. 10036), they'll probably tell you how to get information on traveling carnivals, shows, and circuses.

Recently, the *Mother Earth News*, P.O. Box 38, Madison, Ohio 44057 had a fine article on how a group of young people made considerable money by preparing fresh lemonade for a traveling show. Write to John Shuttleworth, the editor, and tell him Bill sent you for a copy ... it will cost you about one buck, but it's well worth it.

The Roving Welder   One young college couple make it every summer (and could make it all year too) by traveling around in a pickup camper with a trailer full of welding equipment. The man is skilled with both gas and arc welding ... a trade that doesn't require a college degree or 150 IQ.

To get money from this rig is ridiculously simple. All you have to do is to pull up to any outlying ranch, farm, or home and ask if there is any welding to be done. Some farms have welding rigs but many do not. There is always some metal part to be repaired. This is a business much like that of the old scissors grinders and tinkers who, sadly, have just about disappeared from rural America.

Much money can be made by joining the giant harvest crews who follow the wheat harvests north each year. Also, there is always work around water sports regions . . . lakes, seaports, and rivers. All of these places are likely to be rural and inviting . . . a portable welding rig could be your passport to freedom, independence, and enough money to take care of all your needs.

Advertising by Mail   Here's a business that can be operated from any point in the world, providing it has a place to mail and receive letters.

First obtain an assortment of magazines. Look through the ads and find a few that really reveal a lack of talent on the part of the advertiser and/or his agency. Cut out the ad and mount it on a piece of plain paper. Then sketch your version of a much-improved ad on a separate piece. Mail both items with a cover letter to the advertiser, telling him that you'll prepare a finished version of the ad for a fixed fee.

There is a lot of competition, but considering how many bad ads are produced each day in the U.S., you don't need an overabundance of art and copy talents. If you have some creative imagination and a flair for layout, design, and snappy copy, you should have no trouble in obtaining steady clients for your "Ad Agency by Mail" enterprise.

For more information on the advertising field in general, you might subscribe to *Advertising Age*, 740 N. Rush Street, Chicago, Ill. 60611.

Writing   Very few people are writing nonfiction in a country that offers a tremendous market for it. While 99 percent of would-be writers are grinding out bad fiction for a saturated market, the remaining one percent are living fairly high on the hog by writing nonfiction for a market of more than 4,000 magazines, many more house organs, not to mention syndicates, newspapers, and other publications.

Get a copy of *Writer's Market* (22 E. 12th, Cincinnati, Ohio 45210). It's published annually and contains a fabulous amount of information on how a person can earn a living by writing nonfiction.

For example, there is *Country Living Magazine* (4302 Indianola Avenue, Columbus, Ohio 43214), which will pay you three cents a word for new ideas on how electricity can save time and labor on the farm or in the home.

No matter what your interest or specialty, you'll find a publication that covers it. Start by writing a letter to the appropriate magazine and tell them what you can do for them. This is called a query and is much appreciated by editors who enjoy working with writers who will endeavor to fill the magazine's needs rather than wasting paper, postage, and the editor's time.

Motorcycle Rental Many vacationers find themselves bored with the countryside after a few hours or days. They might be potential customers for a cycle rental business, which can be started with a modest investment. One young man started his enterprise with just one secondhand cycle and a sign. He put up the sign near a popular tourist stopping place and soon found that his one machine was out most of the time. With the proceeds he bought another and then another. He now has five that keep him in good bread all year. Best of all, at the end of the season, he sells the machines for almost what he paid for them and "retires."

This same technique could be applied to snowmobiles, skis, sleds, and all sorts of other recreational equipment. What's more, you get to use them whenever you want.

Free Wood Few people are aware that it is possible to obtain free or nearly free wood from national forest preserves. Forest rangers welcome individuals to come into the forest and remove fallen or dead trees. All you need is a chain saw and a truck. Contact the supervisor of the nearest national forest and ask him how you can perform this service.

The operation is simple . . . drive your truck into the forest, cut up the trees and fallen branches into convenient logs, load them on the truck, and drive them to a busy thoroughfare. Here you place signs and offer to fill the trunk of any car with logs for, say, ten or fifteen dollars. Alternatively, you can sell the logs to firewood wholesalers.

At Christmastime tie a big red ribbon around the better-looking logs and sell them through the markets, liquor stores, and gift shops as traditional yule logs.

A sideline would be gathering interesting gnarled pieces of wind-worn wood to be made into lamps or other decorative interior furnishings.

This business can even be conducted with zero capital by renting a chain saw and truck by the day. A young man in Ojai started this way and now earns $300 a week by buying wood from the Santa Barbara Los Padres Forest for $2 a cord and selling it for $30 a cord.

As another possibility, here's a display showing a few of the varieties of woodland materials that can be sold to wholesale florists. You also have the option of creating finished decorative items for sale to tourists or by mail.

Repainting Existing Signs Two girls worked their way across the country by noting the condition of signs in any small town or village they came to. If the sign was peeling and weathered, they offered to repaint it for about one-fourth of what a regular sign painter would charge. This operation was easy because it's simple to repaint an existing sign . . . the difficult part is in laying it out the first time.

The girls carried a small kit of brushes and purchased the weatherproof sign paint from local hardware stores as needed. Working only a few hours a day, they were able to earn enough to finance a trip by Volkswagen camper from coast to coast.

It is suggested that you practice a little bit before you attempt this part-time avocation. Just take an old real estate sign (these people make great customers) and see how well you can repaint it.

Old Bottle Collecting One of the newest collecting rages in America today is acquiring all kinds of bottles. The strangest thing about this craze is that the bottles don't necessarily have to be old. There are hundreds of collectors of Jim Beam whiskey bottles in the United States. However most bottle collectors are seeking bottles manufactured in the 1800's. These are easy to spot because many of them have thick bottoms, air bubbles, and other imperfections.

Like gold, bottles are where you find them. Here are some suggestions. As you travel through the countryside on foot or aboard your camper, make it a point to stop at desrted buildings, old barns, or farmhouses. There will usually be a trash pile somewhere in the vicinity and these could be the mother lode for a find of rare and valuable old bottles. As a historical note, the present-day town of Jackson, California, used to be called Botillas (Spanish for "bottles") because of the thousands of empty whiskey bottles that were found there after the forty-niners left.

This is a simple and fun sideline business that can be conducted anywhere anytime. Your local antique dealers and interior decorators can help you find buyers of old bottles. You might also contact some collector magazines, such as *Antiques* (55 Fifth Avenue, New York, N.Y. 10017) or *Western Collector* (P.O. 0166, San Francisco, Calif. 94129).

Bulk Health Food Sales   This country is gradually turning away from the worthless junk foods purveyed by the big supermarkets. Health food stores are booming all over. However, most health food stores overcharge their customers by packaging organic grains and other goodies in such small quantities that the price is out of sight.

So here's the plan. Go to a feed store or even better, a feed and grain wholesaler. Arrange to buy wheat, corn, rice, and other staples in 100-pound sacks or even by the truckload. Then resell in smaller but still bulk quantities at a modest and fair profit. I visualize this business being conducted on a route basis, much as fruits and vegetables used to be sold four or five decades ago.

You can buy wheat for three or four dollars per 100 pounds from the ranchers, repackage and resell it for six to eight cents a pound, and make a handsome profit. Once the news that you are selling good food for pennies a pound gets around, you'll build a big trade through word-of-mouth advertising.

Encourage your customers to use bulk foods by telling them about *The Natural Foods Cook Book*, a paperback available at most bookstores and drugstores for $.95. This wonderful guide shows how to use whole grains in thousands of healthful and tasty ways. (To get new customers, give this booklet away as a premium.)

Craft Work   Springing up all over America are thousands of new craft stores, featuring handcrafted wood, metal, cloth, leather, and ceramic goods made in the home. Baskets are one of hundreds of handmade things to sell. If you're not a basket weaver, import them from Hong Kong where many people are weavers. Look up dealers under "Importers" in the San Francisco Yellow Pages. This is such a vast field and such a great opportunity that it would require a complete book to describe even a small part of it. Therefore, we will just describe one small aspect—leather.

You can buy leather in wholesale quantities by checking the Yellow Pages of a phone directory. Write the dealers for prices and quantities. Leather sources can also be obtained by sending for a copy of *The Leather Manufacturer*, a trade magazine, 683 Atlantic Avenue, Boston, Mass. 02111. Another good publication that deals in the leather trade is *Luggage and Leather Goods*, 111 Fourth Avenue, New York, N.Y. 10003.

Once you have a supply of wholesale leather, let your imagination run wild ... make jackets, belts, sandals, hats, coats, vests, billfolds, boots, and saddles. Souvenir items are especially salable when stamped or embossed with a local name or tie-in.

The best thing about this business is that your tools are as simple as those of the earliest leather craftsmen . . . knives, punches, and carving instruments. There is a store in Santa Barbara called "The Little Beaver" which does a booming business in this field.

There are hundreds of other ways to earn money in the country. Check your local library for books on self-employment and home income. An excellent one is *The Home Income Guide: Over 600 Ways to Make Money at Home*, by John D. Martin of Vocational Education Enterprises. It's one of the best books on this subject in print—far superior to several similar volumes on the market—and contains a bibliography for further information. The book is divided into ten sections so that no matter what your interests, capabilities, or age, you'll probably be able to find something suitable:

Arts, crafts and home manufacturing
Home service business
Cash from your kitchen
Typing your way to the bank
Making it with your needle
Shoot pictures for bread
Telephoning brings income
Plants, herbs and flowers
Birds, fish, pets and small animals
Miscellaneous opportunities

Recently I encountered a young couple who live in a small High Sierra town. They earn all the money they need by caning chairs. Once a month they make a tour of furniture stores, antique shops, hotels, and other businesses in neighboring communities. They pick up new work and drop off the completed furniture.

In this way they enjoy the pleasures of a rural life but make it into urban areas often enough to avoid cabin fever and to verify their belief that they live in the best possible environment.

3 Rural Land and How to Buy It

There are millions of people like yourself who yearn to get back to the land. Like you they want to leave our big cities behind and enjoy the peace, quiet, independence, and security that can come from ownership of fertile land in rural America. Fortunately, the opportunities to do this today are greater than ever. There is a lot of public land coming up for sale every month and there are literally thousands of small farms being abandoned each year. There are many reasons why a farm is abandoned; it is not necessarily a bad farm. A new owner could step in and operate it on a part-time basis, obtaining his ready cash through mail order, writing, or some other financial tie with the urban area he left behind.

In this chapter we describe both public and private land opportunities selected from many sources. Whatever property you select, it is advisable to visit it and live in the vicinity for a time before you buy it. This is the soundest piece of advice that anyone could give a would-be rural dweller.

How to Get Land from the U.S. Government

Uncle Sam has lots of land. More than 464 million acres are classed as public lands and can be acquired by private citizens under certain conditions. Here's what the Department of the Interior says about the subject in one of their "question-and-answer" booklets.

What is Public Land?   While there are all kinds of "public" land—Federal, state, county, municipal—as used here it means land owned by the Federal Government and administered by

This tranquil view of rolling fields with scattered copses of evergreens and deciduous trees is typical of much of the western United States. With water and electricity, all urban conveniences can be yours without the urban disadvantages. Imagine getting up in the morning and taking a long walk over these hills, enjoying the fresh, brisk air, birdsongs, and the natural and friendly scents of wild grasses and flowers. This region is in Latah County, Idaho. (Idaho Department of Commerce and Development)

the U.S. Department of the Interior's Bureau of Land Management. For the most part, this is original public domain land which has never left Federal ownership. "Public land" as described here does not mean National Forests or National Parks.

The following question-and-answer series was abstracted from the latest government publication on the subject:

In what states is most public land for sale located?
Almost all of it is in the public land states of the West—Arizona, Montana, Wyoming, Colorado, New Mexico, Oregon, Nevada, Idaho, Utah, California, and Washington. For information about public land in Alaska, write Bureau of Land Management, U.S. Department of Interior, Washington, D.C. 20240, and ask for Information Bulletin No. 2.

What kind of lands are they?
Those in the West range from the flat terrain of the low desert country to deep, multicolored canyons and towering buttes and mountains. The gamut of cover runs from cacti to sagebrush and piñon pine to majestic redwoods and Douglas fir of the Pacific Northwest. Together, they offer some of the most dramatically sweeping vistas of the untamed West. The lands of Alaska are mostly timber or tundra, but also include mountains and swamps, even desert areas.

Characteristics of the sweeping plains of Kansas, Nebraska, and Wyoming, this view shows what much of America still looks like, although this particular scene is from Virginia. If your vision has been barred by the four walls of an office, you'll find relaxation in being able to see clear to the horizon. (USDA)

Watersheds of the public lands are the source for a large portion of the West's water supply. Mostly arid or semiarid, very little acreage is suitable for farming; but they have great value for livestock grazing, mineral development, timber, wildlife, and outdoor recreation. They also include many areas of scientific value. Most lands are distant from population centers, and many are not accessible by all-weather roads.

What about lands in the east and elsewhere?

Small amounts of public land still remain in Alabama, Arkansas, Florida, Louisiana, Michigan, Minnesota, Mississippi, and Wisconsin, but land sales in these states are very rare. There are no public lands in Delaware, Georgia, Hawaii, Illinois, Indiana, Iowa, Kentucky, Maine, Maryland, Massachusetts, Missouri, New Hampshire, New Jersey, New York, North Carolina, Ohio, Pennsylvania, Rhode Island, South Carolina, Tennessee, Texas, Vermont, Virginia and West Verginia.

How is public land sold?

By public auction sale through sealed or oral bidding.

Where are the sales held?

In Land Offices of the Bureau of Land Management [as listed on page 46].

Is any of this land free or cheap?

Every parcel is appraised by the Government at fair market value. You cannot buy it for less than the

You can almost touch the rough wood of this old log fence on a ranch in southern Utah. In the fall, aspen and oak put on a brilliant show of color from vivid crimson to subtle shades of yellow and orange. Terrain in this region varies from low-cost sagebrush land to aspen and pine—often the two are ten or fifteen miles apart. (Utah Tourist and Publicity Council)

appraised price. Don't be deceived by promoters who advertise "free" or "cheap" public land.

If I want to buy some public land, what is the first thing I should do?

Get the very best information available. "Our Public Lands," a quarterly magazine published by the Bureau of Land Management, carries a listing of public lands to be sold in the near future. The magazine's "Public Sale Bulletin Board" gives a thumbnail description of these lands, including their general location, appraised price, and other information. If you live in the West, you may visit the nearest BLM Land Office and ask for information.

How do I subscribe to this magazine?

Send one dollar to Superintendent of Documents, U.S. Government Printing Office, Washington, D.C. 20402, and ask for a year's subscription to "Our Public Lands." Be sure that your name and address, including zip code, are typed or printed clearly.

If a parcel listed in the magazine interests me, what is my next move?

When you have looked over the "Public Sale Bulletin Board" and found listed a parcel of public land that interests you, you should get additional information about the parcel. To do this, write the BLM Land Office for the state in which the parcel is located.

To show how unpopulated America still is, try flying over it. This view of Amador County in California, taken from 10,000 feet. shows only a few roads, rivers, and creeks, and virtually no signs of human habitation. Vertically, the view encompasses three miles and there are probably fewer than fifty people living in the region. (USDA)

Touring by air is an excellent way to get the "feel" of a region. You are looking down on the Carpinteria Valley, south of Santa Barbara, California. (William Kaysing)

What do I ask the land office?
Ask for a prospectus describing in detail the tract you saw listed in "Our Public Lands." The prospectus will include date of sale, facts about preference rights for adjoining landowners, a more complete description of the parcel than given in the magazine, and other things you should know before buying. You can also ask for a bid form on which to make your bid.

If I decide I want to buy the parcel, what is the next thing I should do?
From the prospectus you obtain from the Land Office, you will be able to decide if you really want to bid. If you still aren't sure, you can write for additional details. If at all possible, inspect the property yourself or engage someone to do so for you.

Can land listed in "Our Public Lands" be taken off the market before sale?
Yes. For unexpected technical and legal reasons some tracts listed for sale must be taken off the market. Such action is unfortunate, but it happens from time to time. If this happens in your case, the BLM Land Office can tell you why it was necessary.

Can I actually buy a parcel of public land by mail?
Yes, you can actually purchase Government land by mail. But, there is a distinct advantage in being present for the sale or sending a representative. Bids sent in by mail cannot be raised unless the bidder, or his representative, is present at this sale.

Are transactions cash, or may I buy this land on a time plan?
All public land sold by the Bureau of Land Management must be paid for in full at the time of the sale. Mailed bids must be accompanied by certified check, Post Office money order, bank draft, or cashier's check made payable to the Bureau of Land Management. Personal checks or cash are accepted from bidders present at the

Seasonal changes transform a countryside into a wilderness. Here, the Tahoe forest wears its winter coat. This region was called by Mark Twain "the fairest sight the world affords." (USDA)

No parking meters or jangling telephones in this plains state. (USDA)

auction. All bids must be for not less than the advertised appraised value.

Are there any other fees required of the purchaser?

Yes, the land buyer must also pay the cost of publishing legal notice of the sale in a newspaper. These costs vary depending upon the parcel. The Land Office will tell you the amount you must pay.

Are there any preference rights for veterans?

No.

Are there any preference rights that I should know about?

The law under which most parcels are sold specifies that an adjoining landowner may acquire a parcel offered for sale by (1) matching the highest bid, or (2) paying three times the appraised price, whichever is less. The right of preference must be asserted within 30 days after sale is held. If more than one adjoining landowner wants the same parcel, a division of the tract becomes necessary. The Land Office has complete information. However, under some of the land sales laws, no preferential rights are provided.

Can I buy only part of a tract that is advertised for sale?

No. You must bid on the entire tract as offered for sale.

What about size of the tracts?

Most of them range from 40 to 120 acres. But they may

A state of astounding contrasts, Oregon offers good bargains in rural land. (USDA)

be as small as a fraction of an acre or as large as 5,000 acres.

Will it be possible for me to farm a tract of this land?
Farming opportunities are very slim. Some parcels are suitable for grazing. Occasionally, a parcel is advertised as having "some agricultural potential."

While the gummint isn't too encouraging on this score, there are ways of making marginal agricultural land productive. This subject is well covered in chapters on compost and water in a book called *The Ex-Urbanite's Complete and Illustrated Easy-Does-It First-Time Farmer's Guide.* It's by some character by the name of Kaysing who spent twenty years on some kind of farm . . . probably a county honor farm. But nevertheless, it's full of the latest and best information on what to do with badlands, how to get water where there is no apparent water, and how to grow great crops where none have grown before. With it, your chances of making a go of even marginal land and very nervous water conditions are sharply increased. Write to Straight Arrow Books, 625 Third Street, San Francisco, Calif. 94107, if you can't find a copy locally: $7.95. Another excellent source of information on all aspects of first-time farming: *How to Make It on the Land* ($4.95) by Ray Cohan. Order it from Prentice-Hall, Inc., Englewood Cliffs, N.J. 07632.

Not all of California is heavily populated, as this near-ghost town substantiates. (USDA)

Are some parcels inaccessible?

Some are completely surrounded by private holdings. This means, if you buy such a tract, you would probably need an access agreement with your neighbors, or else you may be unable to reach your land. Many of the parcels are far from public roads, utilities, and water. The Government does not guarantee access.

What about taxes?

After buying public land, you will be required to pay local taxes on it. Your deed from the Bureau of Land Management should be recorded at the County Court House as soon as possible after the purchase. The fact that you bought the land from the Federal Government does not exempt it from local taxation.

Are there any age limits involved in buying public lands from BLM?

This depends upon the law under which the particular parcel is offered. Under the Public Land Sale Act of 1964, a purchaser must be at least 21 years old. Under other laws, a bidder of any age capable of entering into a binding contract is eligible.

How do I buy "tax land" or land sold for tax delinquency?

The Federal Government has no jurisdiction over lands on which local taxes have become delinquent and does not sell such lands. Just how to purchase "tax lands" would depend upon the laws of a particular state. Full information should be sought from the Tax Assessor in the county in which such land is located.

What about leasing instead of buying public land?

The Bureau of Land Management leases rights for grazing and mineral development but does not normally lease land for homesites. It leases none for agricultural purposes.

Does BLM ever have land for sale in Texas or Hawaii?

No. There are no public domain lands in either state. For information about state-owned lands in Texas, write Commissioner, General Land Office, Austin, Texas 78701; for Hawaii, write Department of Land and Natural Resources, Box 621, Honolulu, Hawaii 96809.

Does the sale of public land have anything to do with homesteading?

Nothing at all, if you are referring to the Homesteading Act of 1862. Homesteading is an entirely different matter. It is almost a thing of the past, even in Alaska.

What about "surplus land"?

Sale of so-called "surplus lands," or "surplus property," is handled by regional offices of the General Services Administration, Washington, D.C. 20405. BLM has no "surplus land."

If I buy public land, do I get the minerals, too?

Ordinarily, public lands valuable for minerals are not sold. However, in some instances such lands are sold and certain minerals are reserved to the Government. The notice of sale from the Land Office will clearly state whether minerals relating to a particular parcel are to be reserved.

Does the Government require me to make any special use of land I buy?

No. When you buy land from the Bureau of Land Management, the Federal Government does not tell you what use you can make of it. However, in some areas local zoning regulations and building codes apply.

Can I buy more than one parcel of public land?

Yes, except under the Small Tract Act which allows only one tract per person under ordinary circumstances.

What about "Public Land for Sale" ads by private promoters?

The Bureau of Land Management is the only official and authentic source of information about lands it sells. In the past, innocent citizens have paid thousands of dollars for questionable services and information about public land. Official information is readily available without charge from BLM addresses listed below. Before answering advertisements promoting the sale of public land at bargain prices, it would be wise to contact the Bureau of Land Management.

BUREAU OF LAND MANAGEMENT OFFICES
ALASKA:
555 Cordova Street, Anchorage, Alaska 99501
516 Second Avenue, Fairbanks, Alaska 99701

ARIZONA:
Federal Building, Room 3022, Phoenix, Ariz. 85025

CALIFORNIA:
Federal Building, Room 4017, Sacramento, Calif. 95814
1414 University Avenue, Riverside, Calif. 92502

COLORADO:
14023 Federal Building, Denver, Col. 80202

IDAHO:
323 Federal Building, Boise, Idaho 83701

MONTANA (NORTH DAKOTA, SOUTH DAKOTA):
Federal Building, 316 N. 26th Street, Billings, Mont. 59101

NEVADA:
Federal Building, 300 Booth Street, Reno, Nev. 89502

NEW MEXICO (OKLAHOMA):
Federal Building, Santa Fe, N.M. 87501

OREGON:
729 N.E. Oregon Street, Portland, Ore. 97208

UTAH:
8217 Federal Building, 125 S. State Street, Salt Lake City, Utah 84111

WASHINGTON:
729 N.E. Oregon Street, Portland, Ore. 97208

WYOMING (NEBRASKA, KANSAS):
2120 Capitol Avenue, Cheyenne, Wyo. 82001

ALL OTHER STATES:
Robin Building, 7981 Eastern Avenue, Silver Spring, Md. 20910

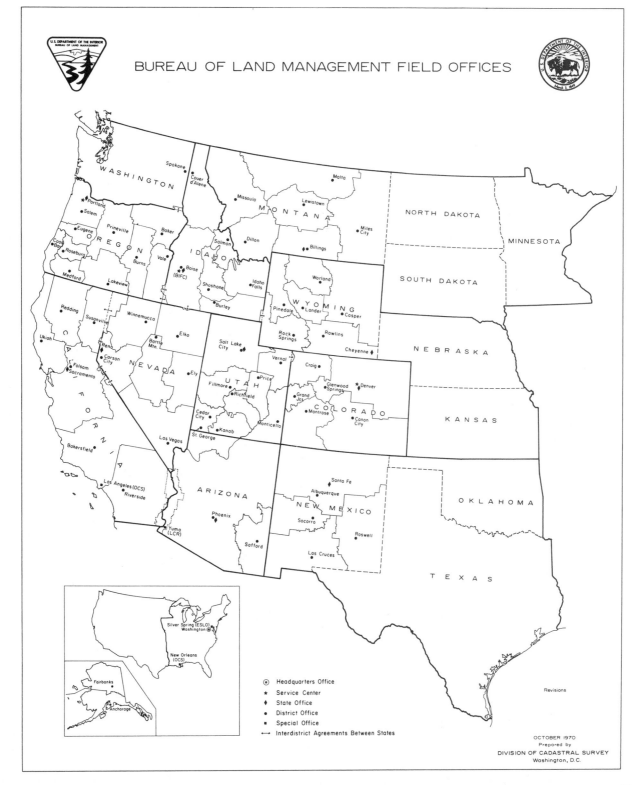

BUREAU OF LAND MANAGEMENT FIELD OFFICES

U.S. DEPARTMENT OF THE INTERIOR
BUREAU OF LAND MANAGEMENT

WASHINGTON

Spokane
Coeur d'Alene
Portland
Salem
Eugene
Prineville
Baker
OREGON
Coos Bay
Roseburg
Burns
Vale
Medford
Lakeview
IDAHO
Salmon
Dillon
Boise (BIFC)
Shoshone
Idaho Falls
Burley

MONTANA
Missoula
Lewistown
Malta
Miles City
Billings

NORTH DAKOTA
MINNESOTA

SOUTH DAKOTA

Redding
Susanville
Winnemucca
Elko
Ukiah
CALIFORNIA
Reno
Battle Mtn.
Carson City
Folsom
Sacramento
NEVADA
Ely
Bakersfield
Los Angeles (OCS)
Riverside
Yuma (LCR)

Salt Lake City
UTAH
Vernal
Price
Fillmore
Richfield
Cedar City
Kanab
St. George
Las Vegas

WYOMING
Worland
Pinedale
Lander
Casper
Rock Springs
Rawlins
Cheyenne

Craig
Glenwood Springs
Denver
Grand Jct.
COLORADO
Montrose
Canon City
Monticello

NEBRASKA

KANSAS

ARIZONA
Phoenix
Safford

NEW MEXICO
Santa Fe
Albuquerque
Socorro
Roswell
Las Cruces

OKLAHOMA

TEXAS

Silver Spring (ESLO)
Washington
New Orleans (OCS)

Fairbanks
Anchorage

⊙ Headquarters Office
★ Service Center
♦ State Office
● District Office
■ Special Office
→ Interdistrict Agreements Between States

Revisions

OCTOBER 1970
Prepared by
DIVISION OF CADASTRAL SURVEY
Washington, D.C.

Twenty Acres of the Outdoors for $100 Worth of Work a Year

In old movies of the West, someone was always "claim jumping." Usually collecting a .45 slug for his malefaction, the claim jumper generated a little excitement in what might have been a dull movie. But for real excitement, think of this. Available to every U.S. citizen is the opportunity to find a valuable mineral on public land and stake a claim. The claim, properly filed, gives the individual the right to work the land, remove and sell the valuable minerals, and generally enjoy an outdoor life with no outlay for property. Furthermore, the land can ultimately be owned by going through a "patenting" procedure.

Here are some basic facts which will give you a working knowledge of this fascinating way to live on, work at, and ultimately own your own piece of some pine-studded mountainside.

Staking a Mining Claim on Federal Lands

A mining claim is a particular piece of land, valuable for specific minerals, to which an individual has asserted a right of possession for the purpose of developing and extracting discovered minerals. This right is granted the miner if he meets the requirements of the mining laws, and these same laws guarantee him protection for all lawful uses of his claim for mining purposes.

In 1872 Congress passed "An Act to Promote the Development of the Mining Resources of the United States." If you wish to file a mining claim on public domain land open to location under the mining laws, this is the law giving you the right to do so. It also sets the limits of your rights. This mining law, together with the regulations and court decisions which have interpreted them, are collectively called the General Mining Laws. The law itself is in United States Code, Title 30, Sections 21-54. The regulations can be found in Code of Federal Regulations, (CFR) Title 43, Parts 3400-3600, which are available from BLM in circular form (BLM, USDA, Washington, D.C. 20250).

The minerals you can look for are divided into three types:

1. Locatable. Both metallic (gold, silver, lead, etc.) and nonmetallic (fluorspar, asbestos, mica, etc.) minerals may be located under the mining laws.

2. Salable. By law, certain materials may not be located under the mining laws but may be purchased under the Materials Sale Act of 1947. These include the common varieties of sand, stone, gravel, pumice, pumicite, cinders, and clay. These may be purchased for their fair market value, either at competitive or noncompetitive sales. Petrified wood is not subject to location under the mining laws. Small

This is a compilation of the most up-to-date information possible on up-coming sales of public lands by land offices of the Bureau of Land Management. For details of land descriptions, prices, and other information pertinent to sales, you must write the individual land office concerned. In most cases, there are adjoining land-owners who have statutory preference rights and may wish to exercise them to buy the land. Sales notices will point out, insofar as possible, problems relating to (1) access, (2) adjoining owner preference rights, (3) small-tract sales limitation of one per customer, and other pertinent information. When possible, all sales are scheduled far enough in advance so ample notice can be given in Our Public Lands. Sales listed can be canceled on short notice for administrative and technical reasons. A listing of BLM land offices with addresses is found on the opposite page.

ALASKA

Public lands in Alaska are not available for sale at this time. Future public land sales will be announced in this space when scheduled.

ARIZONA

29.30 A, 2.7 miles north of Safford. Moderately level to steep; partially suitable for rural residential. El 2,900 feet. Utilities available. Paved county highway traverses tract. Est val $70 per A.

40 A, 2.25 miles northwest of Safford. Moderately level to steep; suitable for rural residential. Paved county road nearby. Est val $70 per A.

40 A, 1½ miles northeast of Duncan. Flat to rough and broken; suitable for rural residential. El 3,770. Utilities within one-half mile. Est val $3,600.

80 A, 10 miles north of Duncan. Rough and broken; suitable for livestock grazing and possibly for residen-tial on a portion. El 3,775. No legal access. Utilities within one-half mile. Est val $3,200.

40 A, 9½ miles north of Duncan. Suitable for rural residential; utilities within one-half mile. El 3,750 feet. No legal access. Est val $2,400.

CALIFORNIA

80 A, 10 miles southwest of Lake Berryessa resort area. No public road access; surrounded by privately owned lands. Poor soil; heavy brush; no water. To be sold at auction November 19, 1970. Write Sacramento L.O. for details.

SOUTH DAKOTA

40 A, 10 air miles southeast of Hot Springs, Fall River Cty. Gently to moderately rolling grassland range. Sandy soils are subject to severe wind erosion if tilled. Veg is mostly blue gama and sand dropseed with some threadleaf sedge. No stock water; no legal access. App $1,720 plus pub.

NEW MEXICO

40 A, 28 air miles northeast of Roswell, Chaves Cty. Relatively flat with thin to moderate depth of sandy loam soil. Moderate density of veg; best suited for grazing. No utilities. Est val $11 to $14 per A.

WYOMING

80 A, 32 miles north of Lingle, Goshen Cty. Moder-ately to steeply rolling rangeland. Surrounded by pri-vately owned lands; no legal access. Write Wyoming L.O. for details. Sale after November 1, 1970.

WASHINGTON

20.83 A, 2 miles from Columbia River, near North-port, Stevens Cty. Level to steep. Native grasses, forbs, and young timber. No legal access; no water. Write Oregon-Washington L.O. for details.

MONTANA

40 A, 10 miles southwest of Brockway, McCone Cty. Gently to moderately rolling grazing land; generally silty soils. Good stand of native grass; no stock water.

This is an actual page from Our Public Lands *showing the public lands available for sale at the time of publication. The* government *is selling lots of land since this places it back on the tax rolls.*

amounts may be removed free of charge by hobbyists for noncommercial use. Larger amounts may be purchased.

3. Leasable. A few other minerals and fuels may be leased from the Government and may not be claimed under the mining laws. These are oil and gas, oil shale, potash, sodium, native asphalt, solid and semisolid bitumen, bituminous rock, phosphate, coal, and in Louisiana and New Mexico, sulphur. All minerals on certain lands, such as acquired lands and areas offshore, are subject to special leasing laws and regulations.

In order for a mining claim to be validly located and held, there must be an actual physical discovery of the mineral on each and every mining claim and this discovery must satisfy the "prudent man" rule. Traces, isolated bits of mineral, or minor indications are not sufficient to satisfy the "prudent man" rule.

If you establish a valid claim, perform and record annual assessment work required by state law, and meet all other requirements of Federal and state mining regulations, you establish a possessory right to the area covered by the claim for the purpose of developing and extracting minerals. This possessory right may be sold, inherited, or taxed according to state law. No one else can mine, without your consent, the minerals which you have claimed. To maintain your claim, it is required that at least $100 worth of labor or improvements be performed on or for the benefit of a claim each year. This is called annual assessment work. It must be completed on or before 12:00 noon on September 1 of each year. This proves your active interest in the claim and must be done to maintain your right to the claim against "jumping" or location by others.

A mining patent or deed received from the Government gives you the exclusive title to the locatable minerals. In most such cases, you will also obtain full title to the land surface and all other resources. The local BLM or Forest Service office will tell you whether you may receive full title of both surface and mineral rights.

Mining claims are of four types:

1. Lode claims. Deposits subject to lode claims include classic veins or lodes having well-defined boundaries. They also include other rock containing valuable minerals and may be broad zones of mineralized rock. Examples include quartz or other veins bearing gold and other metallic minerals and low-grade disseminated copper deposits.

2. Placer claims. Deposits subject to placer claims are all those not subject to lode claims. These include the "true" placer deposits of sand and gravel containing free gold and also include many nonmetallic deposits.

3. Mill site. A mill site is a plot of unappropriated public domain land of a nonmineral character, suitable for the erection of a mill, or reduction works. Mill sites may be located under either of the following circumstances:

A. When used or occupied distinctly and explicitly for mining and milling purposes in connection with the lode or placer location with which it is associated.

B. For a quartz mill or reduction works unconnected with a mineral location.

4. Tunnel sites. A tunnel site is located on a plot of land where a tunnel is run to develop a vein or lode, or to discover a vein or lode. Tunnel sites cannot be patented.

There are large areas, mostly in the Western States, where you may prospect for minerals, and if you discover a deposit of valuable minerals you may stake a mining claim. These areas are in Alaska, Arizona, Arkansas, California, Colorado, Idaho, Montana, Nebraska, Nevada, New Mexico, North Dakota, Oregon, South Dakota, Utah, Washington, Wyoming, and certain parts of Florida, Louisiana, and Mississippi. Such areas are mostly on open (not withdrawn) public domain land administered by the Forest Service, Department of Agriculture, or by the Bureau of Land Management, Department of the Interior. You may also locate mining claims on certain patented lands in which the Government has reserved the mineral rights but you may mine and patent only the reserved minerals in such lands.

According to the Wilderness Act of September 3, 1964, the mining laws and mineral leasing laws apply to the National Forest lands designated by the Act as "wilderness" until the end of 1983, to the same extent as they applied prior to September 3, 1964. Mining on these lands is subject to the provisions of the law and the wilderness regulations of the Secretary of Agriculture and the Secretary of the Interior. These regulations may be obtained from local forest officers or BLM offices.

Regulations issued May 31, 1966, prescribe access to valid mining claims as well as to prospecting and mining operations. You should contact the local forest officer (District Ranger) before entering a wilderness. He will also provide you with a copy of the regulations and discuss them with you.

To locate a claim, first visit the local land office of the Bureau of Land Management, Department of the Interior, to determine if the land you wish to claim is open to mining location. The local forest officer may also assist you in determining the land's status on National Forest land.

The Bureau of Land Management keeps up-to-date land status maps and records at its land offices. These maps and records of all public domain lands and minerals are available for inspection by the public, and a BLM employee will show you how this information is recorded. The office will inform you of the status of any individual tract of land upon request.

After determining that the land is open to location, and after doing sufficient prospecting to determine that it contains a valuable mineral, the essential elements in locating a mining claim are:

1. The physical exposure or "discovery" of a valuable mineral.

2. Distinctly and clearly marking the boundaries of the claim on the ground so that it can be readily identified.

3. Posting the notice of location on the claim in a conspicuous place, usually at the place of discovery.

4. Recording an exact copy of the location in the appropriate office, usually the County Recorder's office in the county in which the claim is located.

The requirements vary from state to state. Usually a location notice must contain the following information:

1. Date
2. Name of locator(s)
3. Name of the claim
4. Whether claim is lode or placer type
5. Mineral claimed
6. The distance claimed along the course of the vein each way from the discovery point and the direction (for lode claims and placer claims located by metes and bounds), or the acreage claimed and the legal description by particular parts of the section, township, and range (for placer claims located by legal subdivisions).
7. A connection by distance and direction as accurately as practicable from the discovery point to some well-known permanent and prominent natural object or landmark such as a hill, mountain, bridge, fork of a stream, or road intersection. Where a placer claim is located by legal subdivision, no other tie-in is required.

Federal law specifies only that a claim should be marked distinctly enough so it can be readily identified. However, to permit easy identification, each state usually has its own detailed requirements for marking boundaries. Generally, as a minimum, all four corners of lode or placer claims, not located by legal subdivision, should be marked with posts or stone monuments. For placer claims located by legal subdivision, corner monuments are usually unnecessary.

The point of discovery of both lode and placer claims should be marked by a post or monument. The location notice, giving information about the claim, should be placed in or on this monument.

This procedure identifies and establishes the boundaries of your claim and is notification to others of your claim. The more clearly the boundaries are marked and state laws adhered to, the less chance your claim will be "jumped."

Each state has established detailed procedures for receiving and recording location notices. These notices usually are filed with the County Recorder's offices in the county in which the claim is located and in Alaska with the District Magistrate.

Location notices are not filed with the Bureau of Land Management except in a few instances where specifically required by law. In these situations, copies must also be filed in the usual place of recordation, as required by state law.

The Forest Supervisor or District Ranger having jurisdiction over the land must be notified in writing of any claim located in a National Forest Wilderness within thirty days after the date of location.

You should also record in the County Recorder's office each year a statement that you have performed the annual assessment work. Annual assessment work is not recorded with the Bureau of Land Management, except where specifically required by law.

Supplementing the United States mining laws are state statutes which specify the manner of locating a claim, marking the boundaries, recording notices of location and annual assessment work, the size of "discovery" pits or shafts, and many other requirements.

There is no limit to the number of claims you may hold as long as you have made a discovery of a valuable mineral on each one and meet other requirements. Only one discovery of mineral is required to support a placer location, whether it is of 20 acres by an individual or of 160 acres or less by an association of persons.

Anyone who is a citizen of the United States, or who has declared his intention to become a citizen, may stake or locate a mining claim. This includes minors who are bona fide locators and corporations organized under the laws of any state.

You may build a house or cabin or other improvements such as tool sheds or ore storage bins, etc., on a mining claim if they are reasonably necessary for your use in connection with your mining operations (That leaves it wide open!).

More information and a copy of the United States mining regulations may be obtained from the Bureau of Land Management Land Offices listed earlier in this chapter.

Eventually you may want to obtain a "patent" or ownership of your claim. This can be done through the procedure outlined in a booklet produced by the U.S. Department of the Interior. Just write them in Washington,

D.C., attention Bureau of Land Management, and ask for the free booklet titled "Patenting a Mining Claim on Federal Lands."

In summary, the way to a rural life with an income built in may be through the mining claim method. One thing's for sure . . . it would be a fun way to make it. (The great part of this is that if large corporations can do it, then you can do it too. It's lots of fun to see a bureaucracy squirm when they have to recognize the rights of the solo operator as well as Anaconda Copper.)

There are several other possibilities for obtaining government land, although you had better be as ready for a fight as the Indians were when they tried to get Alcatraz. One is to qualify for free surplus land. This is quite a hassle but if you have a nonprofit school of some kind, it can be done. Old Army and Navy bases are sometimes turned over to organizations that have a good use for them. Your first step is to contact General Services Administration, Washington, D.C. 20405, and get the rundown. They will refer you to the local office in all probability. If you enjoy wading through miles and miles of red tape, try this route. It could pay off, although you will probably have to form a genuine nonprofit group to qualify. However, if it means that you end up with a 640-acre base with buildings, water systems, roads and infinite possibilities, then it's worth it, isn't it?

Although this is not strictly a U.S. Government thing, you can see the tax assessor of any county and ask him about lands that have been sold to the state for taxes. If you pay up the back taxes and wait a certain period . . . up to about five years . . . you may be able to claim the land as your own. There are myriad catches . . . more than twenty-two for sure. Many people are hip to this so there's competition to start with. In addition, the land is often rather poor, which is what caused the tax default in the first place. But all things considered, it could be a way to acquire a usable piece for just the tax money. Check with the local assessor where you live just to get the hang of it.

Private Land Acquisitions

As many experts in real estate advise, you may be much better off buying an already developed piece of land. The reason for this is clear. Much of the land that comes up for public sale has been passed over by many generations as being inferior. Thus, even though the initial price for land is low, you might spend more in bringing in water, electricity, and roads than you would have spent for an already existing farm.

Furthermore, dealing with the Federal, state, or county government is generally nothing but hassles. By the time you fill out lebenty-leben forms, declare yourself an untainted

WASP, and present yourself for a USDA stamp in purple ink, you just *may* want to buy the land from some human being. Of course, it won't be as much of a bargain, but then again, freedom from bureaucratic problems is worth something.

With taxes going up, city planners cooking up new assessments, and the cost of developing land pyramiding daily, there's lots of land on the market all over the U.S. As farming becomes mechanical and gross with the tag of agribusiness, many small farms come on the market weekly. Then too, as little towns die, the young people move away and even town property along Main Street in villages is available in plentiful supply. Here's a selection of rural properties from the catalogs published by the following large country land brokers:

United Farm Agency, 612 W. 47th, Kansas City, Mo. 64112

Strout Realty, P.O. 2757, Springfield, Mo. 65803

Statewide Realty Co., Pyramid Life Building, Little Rock, Ark. 72201

The catalogs are free, so get on the mailing list for a continuous supply.

Now, if you see anything in the catalogs you like, the next step is to conduct an analysis to see if living in rural Kentucky or 78 miles east of Duluth is really what you want to do. List the particular requirements that would be important to you, such as type of climate, number of people in the community, availability of shopping areas and schooling, nearby recreational opportunities, and employment or business opportunities. To find out about these characteristics in an area you are considering, here are some handy information sources:

Local Newspapers Subscribe as soon as possible. The true picture of the politics, social life, and economics are revealed quickly and accurately by the local fish wrapper. For example, if the editorial talks about how Nixon ought to drop an H-bomb and you've been on all the peace marches, scratch that podunk off your list. If there's evidence that the rednecks would feel offended if you didn't attend their combination church social and weekly lynching party, and you are, also black, skip that burg. Finally, if the only Help Wanted ad reads like this:

> Needed, boy, girl, man, or woman to
> sell Cloverbloom Salve on commission

and you are used to a weekly paycheck, dump that particular country crossroads.

On the other hand, if there seem to be points of agreement between you and the local weekly . . . things like news about an apple pie eating contest and you weigh 320 pounds, then it would be desirable to pursue the matter further.

STREAM & WATERFALL

No.1015—30 acres, $5,900. A feeling of complete solitude and privacy pervade when you watch this beautiful mountain stream tumble into

picturesque waterfalls, cascades, pools and rushing waters. Secluded setting on old logging road, 1/2 mile to a hardtop highway and 2 miles to a nearby town, 10 to college town. 30 acres, all wooded, natural habitat for deer and birds. Many choice building sites overlooking the s t r e a m, excellent camping sites. Borders thousands of acres of forest land that abound with wildlife and give added privacy. Capture a piece of nature for only $5,900, low down payment. UNITED, Lyndonville, Vt.

EARLY-DAY RANCH HUMBOLDT RIVER FRONTAGE!

No.624—1,684 acres, $90,000. Old-time ranch at an old-time price! Portion of place was homesteaded by present owner's family in the 1880's! 1,684 DEEDED acres, mostly all fenced. Also under fence is BLM land, which used in conjunction with deeded land, allows the ranch, under proper management, to run 300 head of cattle. 325 acres hay meadow and 75 acres irrigated pasture all irrigated with FREE water from river which flows through for 2 miles. Some mineral rights included. Fronts blacktop highway for 1/2 mile, easy drive Elko. 3 older, but usable buildings including garage, barn, equipment shed, located at old headquarters. Excellent building site with domestic well. Rare opportunity for the man with an eye to the future

at $90,000, under one-fourth down. UNITED, Elko, Nev.

"ROD & GUN" FARM ON BUFFALO RIVER!

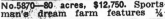

No.5870—80 acres, $12,750. Sportsman's dream farm features 1/4-

mile frontage on fabulous Buffalo River noted for its float trips and bass fishing. Surrounding area abounds with deer, squirrel, fox, mink and other wild game. 80 acres, 25 tillable bottomland acres,

45 wooded, 20 acres native pasture, 15 acres improved pasture. Older 3-room house, small log barn, storage building. Buildings of little value. Choice building site on high bluff that overlooks winding river, road leading to river's edge. On gravel road, 10 miles to town, 125 to Little Rock. Sportsman's secluded haven—only $12,750, excellent terms. UNITED, Marshall, Ark.

LITTLE COTTONWOOD RANCH

No.630—400 acres, $56,500. Seclusion surrounds you in this peaceful valley setting, far from the hustle and bustle of today's world! 10 miles to quiet ranching village, 45 miles to hub city of northeast-

ern Nevada for good shopping, churches and transportation, in-

grazing land, fenced in and combined with privately owned property, allows this little dandy to run 50 mother cows year-round. Older outbuildings and corrals, in need of repair. Many choice building sites to choose from. Ideal for retirement or just to "get away from it all" . . . good deer, upland game, rabbit, chukar hunting and fishing—all within minutes in surrounding hills or nearby Ruby Mountains. Not too big and not too small. Just enough to keep busy, enjoy those leisure hours and have that Nevada ranch you've always wanted. Inquire and retire . . . only $56,500, excellent terms. UNITED, Elko, Nev.

ABANDONED FARM

No.158—111 acres, $42,000. Located in quiet remote area. Well suited for cattle raising, game preserve or tree farm. 111 acres, 30 tillable, 40 native pasture, 80 woodland. 3 44/100-acre tobacco allotment. 40 acres barbed wire fencing. 1,500-ft creek frontage, well, 2 springs large lake site. Game galore with deer, rabbit, squirrel, quail. Stucco over log 2-story 6-room house, 3 bedrooms, 2 FIREPLACES. 2-story 5-room log cabin. 2 tobacco barns pack barn, stable with 4 stalls, crib with attached tool shed. On gravel road, 1 2/5 miles to hardtop, 4 miles town, 15 college town. Fix this farm up to be a real showplace for only $42,000, excellent terms. UNITED, High Point, N. C.

HOMESTEAD DAYS RETURN!

No.5850—800 acres, $38,500. Years ago this land was thriving with homesteads but is now abandoned and grown over—many deer and wildlife now make it their home! 800 wooded acres, could reportedly carry 150 head of stock if cleared, many good building sites, scenic views. Springs. On private road for utmost in seclusion, 12 miles to town. Create a future land rush of your own. Now only $38,500, low $8,500 down. UNITED, Marshall, Ark.

TOP LAND INVESTMENT!

No.770—480 acres, $28,000. Could be used for either farming or grazing. 480 acres, 300 tillable. 350 acres improved pasture, very good fencing. Reservoirs for stock water. Excellent mountain views, deer right on property. Only 4 miles to town, close to all big game hunting and fishing. Priced for action

at only $28,000. UNITED, Cortez, Colo.

CRAMPED FOR SPACE?

No.1502—2 1/4 acres, $1,600. Move out to the wide open spaces of Oregon! Build your dream home or just a vacation retreat on these 2 1/4 acres, plenty of room to move around and act like a kid again! Has pretty timber, pine and juniper trees. Secluded, close to good fishing, 5 miles to highway, 8 miles town, 40 Klamath Falls. Spend some time in the country close to nature—have plenty of "elbow room" right here for $1,600, low down payment! UNITED, Klamath Falls, Oreg.

cluding airline service. 400 acres, 316 tillable. 2 miles frontage on sparkling stream which provides free irrigation water for 107 acres of lush meadow hayland. BLM

2 STREAMS, LAKE FRONTAGE!

No.1017—105 acres, $31,000. Picturesque property with 300-ft. frontage on excellent trout fishing lake! Borders vast wilderness area. Old apple orchard provides romping grounds for deer, 2 fine brooks that

cross property. 105 acres, 10 acres open, 95 acres are wooded with both hard and soft woods, pond, springs, maple sugar orchard,

Christmas trees. An old road winds through and leads to a old field where there is an old homesite, view of lake. Many fine building or camping sites. Fronts town gravel road, 5 miles to town. Won't

last long at $31,000. UNITED, Lyndonville, Vt.

Look for the famous oval orange-and-black UNITED sign.

ROUGH AND RUGGED

No.6598 — 80 acres, $12,500. This rough 80-acre mountain property is easily reached by government road to look-out on mountaintop. Excellent timber cover represents many kinds of trees. Canyon through one part is a natural habitat for deer, bear and quail. Natural spring. Many cabin sites. Close to highway within 5 miles of store. Perfect for hunting lodge or family

retreat. Yours for only $12,500, $2,000 down. UNITED, Redding, Calif.

LEARN NATURE'S WAYS

No.948—10 acres, $3,000. Stream flows through full length of this isolated woodland with pine, hemlock, maple and birch trees. Springs. Excellent deer and other wild game hunting. 10 acres, 8 woodland. Lots of wild cherries, raspberries and blackberries. Only 2 miles to hard-top highway, 5½ miles town, 18 college town. Say good-bye to the city, hello to peace and quiet found

with nature—ONLY $3,000. UNITED, Stevens Point, Wis.

Security, the goal of all Americans today, can best be assured on the farm.

UNSPOILED NATURAL BEAUTY

No.1390—160 acres, $24,000. This 160-acre rolling - to - mountainous natural beauty features ½-mile frontage on year-round stream teeming with salmon, steelhead and trout. Deer, quail and small game abound on the timbered hillsides. 20 acres grassland, balance in pine, fir, madrone and other native trees and shrubs. Everlasting springs provide free gravity-flow water to several good building sites. Power

and phone lines at hand. Fronts U.S. 101, 12 miles to town. Hunt, fish, swim, relax and enjoy life here. Yours for only $24,000, low down payment. UNITED, Laytonville, Calif.

LONESOME OUTPOST

No.319 — 80 acres, $8,000. Enjoy nature in all its glory! Serene silence, blue skies pillowed with white cotton clouds, unobstructed view of distant mountain ranges. 80 acres covered with blue sage, mountain grasses and alpine flowers. Ideal for building that summer cabin or hunting camp. Plenty of grass to summer a few head of horses or beef cattle. Bordered by government BLM lands. Great for exploring, enjoy snowmobiling in the area during winter. Hunt sage hens and grouse right on property. Area is noted for fine deer hunting, short distance to elk hunting on many thousands of BLM acres. 12 miles to town, only 26 miles to Blue Mesa Lake. Put on your boots and bust on over to see this one now at only $8,000, excellent terms. UNITED, Gunnison, Colo.

RIVERFRONT RETREAT

No.1501—5 1/5 acres, $13,500. Enjoy many days of fun and relaxation resting beside the waters of this good fishing river! 200-ft. frontage! Comfortable 5-room home has 2 large bedrooms, bath, built-in

kitchen cabinets, carpeted living room with picture window, handy utility room, front porch. View of river and small valley. 16x32-ft. garage and wood shed. Outdoor fireplace. 5 1/5 acres, well, many shade trees, yellow pines. Good hunting area. Borders state highway for easy access, only mile to town, 26 miles Klamath Falls. Immediate possession for low $13,500, $3,000 down! UNITED, Klamath Falls, Oreg.

PRICE SLASHED!

No.3968—290 acres, $11,150. Price reduced for quick sale of this rugged Ozark acreage. 290 acres, isolated, wild and primitive, elevations vary from 1,500 to 2,000 ft. affording panoramic Ozark Mountain views, land most all wooded with oaks and other hardwoods. Spring and branch reported. Old logging trails many years ago have since grown up to brush, trails could be reactivated. Lots of wildlife including deer. 6 miles to town. Start your own camping or private hunting domain—only $11,150, good terms. UNITED, Jasper, Ark.

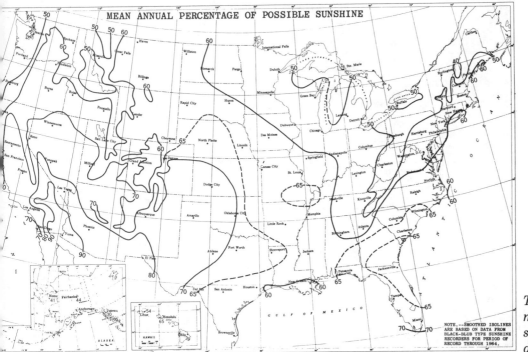

MEAN ANNUAL PERCENTAGE OF POSSIBLE SUNSHINE

NOTE.—SMOOTHED ISOLINES ARE BASED ON DATA FROM BLACK-BLUB TYPE SUNSHINE RECORDERS FOR PERIOD OF RECORD THROUGH 1964.

Typical government climate map. This one shows where the sun shines and where it doesn't.

Incidentally, the ads for property in the local papers will give you a fine opportunity to compare values against those of other localities.

The Chamber of Commerce   Most towns of any size have something comparable to a Chamber of Commerce. The usual objective of these organizations is to bring in more people to help alleviate the tax burden. Thus, it is necessary to view everything they say with much skepticism. For example, if they talk about an average temperature of 70 degrees, they might well have it . . . 140 all summer and zero all winter. Further, the local C of C is likely to boast about the opportunities to start a business, hoping that someone will arrive with some new capital. Of course, the Chamber can't be too far out in their allegations since most of the brochures have a sufficient number of photos to give the lie to completely erroneous statements. It's a good idea to check up on the glowing statements by referring to the following totally unprejudiced sources of information.

Government Climate Descriptions and Weather Maps   Write to the Superintendent of Documents, U.S. Government Printing Office, Washington, D.C. 20402 and ask for weather history and other related data for the location that you've tentatively selected. With these in hand (they look like this), you'll be able to check up on the C of C. This material may also be available from the capital of the state in which you

CLIMATE IN CALIFORNIA

The climates in California are notable for extreme variation. Highly diversified topography and proximity to the ocean are combined to bring about a climate pattern that is unique. There is no sharply defined four-season climate except in the mountain regions. In general, the weather is relatively cool and moist along the coast, increasing in warmth from north to south. The Great Central Valley climate is characterized by long, hot summers and moderate winters. Mountain areas above 6,000 feet have cold weather and moderate to heavy snowfall in winter. The southeastern desert is very hot during long summers and mild the remainder of the year. Precipitation is heaviest in the north coastal area decreasing to merely a trace in certain desert regions. Fog is frequent in coastal and closely adjacent foothill areas decreasing from north to south. Relative humidity is moderately high throughout the year on the coast; in the interior valleys it is low in the summer and high in the winter, and in the desert area it is extremely low.

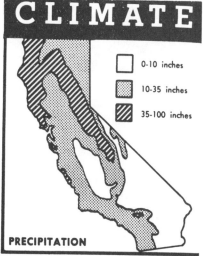

CLIMATE

- ☐ 0-10 inches
- ▨ 10-35 inches
- ▨ 35-100 inches

PRECIPITATION

	J	F	M	A	M	J	J	A	S	O	N	D	Yearly Avg.
COASTAL AREAS													
EUREKA (43')													
Precipitation	7	6	5	3	2	.8	.1	.2	.9	3	5	6	39
Avg. Max. Temp.	53	54	54	56	57	59	60	61	61	60	58	54	57
Avg. Min. Temp.	41	42	43	45	48	50	52	52	51	48	45	42	46
Humidity AM	86	87	87	87	89	90	91	92	91	90	88	86	89
Humidity PM	78	78	76	76	77	77	79	81	80	80	80	79	78
SAN FRANCISCO (52')													
Precipitation	5	4	3	2	.7	.2	0	0	.3	.9	2	4	22
Avg. Max. Temp.	55	58	61	62	63	65	65	65	68	68	63	56	63
Avg. Min. Temp.	45	47	48	49	51	52	53	53	55	54	51	47	50
Humidity AM	85	84	83	83	85	88	91	92	88	85	83	83	86
Humidity PM	71	68	66	67	69	70	75	77	70	67	65	70	70
LOS ANGELES (312')													
Precipitation	3	3	3	1	.4	.1	0	0	.2	.6	1	3	15
Avg. Max. Temp.	65	66	67	70	72	76	81	82	81	76	73	67	73
Avg. Min. Temp.	46	47	49	51	54	57	60	61	59	55	51	48	53
Humidity AM	65	72	76	80	84	87	87	86	81	74	61	61	76
Humidity PM	57	58	58	59	61	60	58	59	59	61	55	57	59
SAN DIEGO (19')													
Precipitation	2	2	2	.7	.3	.1	0	.1	.1	.4	.9	2	10
Avg. Max. Temp.	63	64	65	66	67	70	73	75	74	71	69	65	68
Avg. Min. Temp.	47	48	50	53	56	59	63	64	62	57	52	48	55
Humidity AM	73	78	80	82	82	85	87	87	86	81	71	71	80
Humidity PM	66	67	65	67	70	71	72	72	71	70	66	66	69
COASTAL VALLEYS													
SANTA ROSA (167')													
Precipitation	6	5	4	2	1	.3	0	0	.4	2	3	5	30
Avg. Max. Temp.	57	62	66	70	74	80	83	83	82	77	68	58	72
Avg. Min. Temp.	36	38	39	41	44	47	49	49	47	44	38	36	42
SAN JOSE (95')													
Precipitation	3	3	2	1	.5	.1	0	0	.3	.7	1	2	14
Avg. Max. Temp.	58	61	65	69	73	78	81	80	79	74	66	58	70
Avg. Min. Temp.	39	42	44	45	48	51	54	54	52	48	43	40	47
Humidity PM	66	61	59	54	52	50	50	52	51	53	58	67	56
SANTA MARIA (224')													
Precipitation	2	2	2	.8	.2	0	.1	0	0	.4	1	2	11
Avg. Max. Temp.	62	63	64	67	68	70	72	72	74	73	69	64	68
Avg. Min. Temp.	38	40	41	44	47	49	52	52	51	47	43	40	45
Humidity AM	81	83	86	90	91	91	93	94	91	86	80	80	87
Humidity PM	61	60	61	62	62	60	64	65	63	63	62	64	62

Northeast California looks pretty wet after checking this state climate map.

are interested. Another source is the state historical society, but watch these closely for skipped years.

Local People You can write the local postmaster, sheriff, newspaper editor, realtor, or other town personage and simply ask them specific questions. Most people will answer and give you straight information . . . they know that if you showed up when the snow was 73 feet deep, they'd get the snowball. Another advantage here is that you'll be making a contact even before you arrive on the scene, which statement brings us to the next consideration . . .

Try It There's nothing like living in a place for a week or two to see if you could be happy there. Here are some suggestions on how to do it:

1. Simply go there and live in a hotel or motel.
2. Tow a trailer and set up in a nearby park.
3. If you're low on cash, hitchhike over and set up housekeeping by the local river.

No matter what method you use, you'll be seeing the place in all its glory or all its squalor . . . what could be better for making that all-important decision to live somewhere?

Alaska Want lots of elbow room? Then try this, our largest state. It has only about three people per square mile as against some sixty-odd for the balance of the U.S.

Here are the sources of all of the relevant information you'll need about Alaska.

General Information:
Department of Economic Development and Planning, Juneau 99801

Forest Resources:
Forest Service, Juneau, 99801
Division of Lands, 344 6th Avenue, Anchorage, 99501

Chambers of Commerce:
Anchorage, Bethel, Cordova, Dillingham, Douglas, Fairbanks, Haines, Homer, Juneau, Ketchikan, Kodiak, Nenana, Nome, Palmer, Petersburg, Seldovia, Seward, Sitka, Skagway, Valdez, Wrangell

Land:
Bureau of Land Management, Box 1481, Juneau 99801
Division of Lands, 344 6th Avenue, Anchorage, 99501

National Park Service, McKinley National Park, Alaska 99755
National Park Service, Box 1781, Juneau 99801
National Park Service, Box 1781, Juneau
Division of Lands, 344 6th Avenue, Anchorage, 99501
Alaska Travel Bureau, Juneau, 99801

One of the best ways to see Alaska is by boat. Less expensive than air travel, it lets you to get the feeling of this vast and virtually uninhabited land. As your ship cruises the quiet inland waterways, you'll see many places where you want to build that log cabin in the wilderness. (Alaska Economic Development)

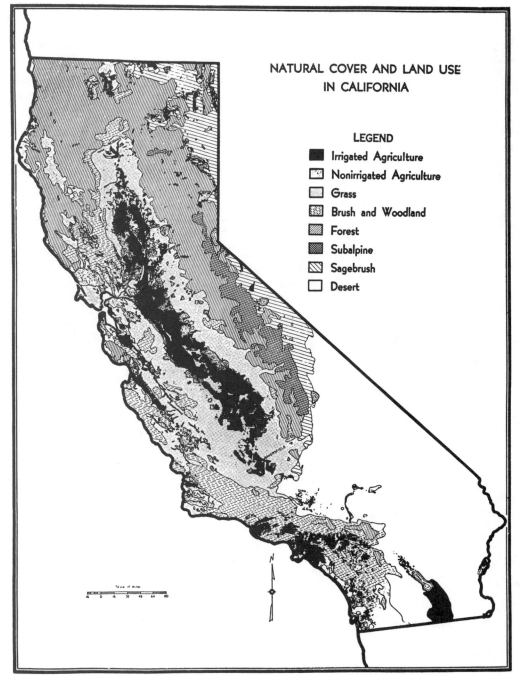

NATURAL COVER AND LAND USE IN CALIFORNIA

LEGEND
- Irrigated Agriculture
- Nonirrigated Agriculture
- Grass
- Brush and Woodland
- Forest
- Subalpine
- Sagebrush
- Desert

State sources often produce valuable data such as this natural cover map of California.

SAM SNEAD REAL ESTATE

P.O. BOX 117
WEST POINT, CA. 95255
PHONE (209) 293-7979

P.O. BOX ~~
RA~~
PHO~~

RESIDENT SALESMEN IN BOTH OFFICES

Two bedroom home with new ~~
house on 1 level VIEW
well for family ~~
$22,000/ ~~
Large ~~

GOT TWO HUNDRED AND FIFTY BUCKS?
If you haven't, go out and earn it honestly. It will then be the
complete down payment on a piece of the California High Sierras that's '48
described like this:

One and a half acres with a little stream and big trees.
Total price, $2150 with $250 down and $50 a month

This is a listing that belies the legend that it costs a great bundle he
to get a start in the boondocks. Here are several others from the
same (For more information on this particular one, write to Sam Snead,
P. O. 117, West Point, Ca. 95255)

(End of paragraph)

~~ &
~~ usion.
~~ per mo.
~~ for another horseman,
~~es. Close to county road.
~~ue watering hole. Small town
~~ly 2 miles. $8000/$1500/$65 mo.

6 acres, TOWERING PINES. Just off
county road in town water district.
VIEW parcel. Easy walk to town.
$9500/ $1500 down/ $85 mo.

EIGHT-PLUS ACRES bordering the
shore line of new reservoir. You
can't fish here, but you CAN ENJOY
the peace & quiet. Camp today --
build later. $12,500/$3500/$100.

10 acres for plenty of elbow room,
FREE FRESH AIR & country living.
Good insurance in case you might
divide and sell some later. County
road frontage. Area of new homes.
$9500/ $2000 down/ $75 mo.

10 acres of THICK cedars; seclusion
deluxe. No power or phone yet, but
PLENTY OF PRIVACY! Only $6500 on
very easy terms.

18 acres on top of the world.
HIGHEST POINT AROUND. 360° view.
Plus 278 walnut trees (count 'em)
County road frontage. Just waiting
for a nice country home & gentleman farmer. $29,500. Asking half
cash and balance in ten years.

20 acres on year-round trout
stream. Beautiful trees, level
land. Blacktop road. Power and
phone. $18,500/ $3500 down.

40 acres for the guy who wants to
get away. Tree covered hilly land
at 2400 ft elev. Joins 300 acres
of unpatented USA LAND. $13,500

T ~~
$~~
RE.
dou~~
wor.
$11.~~
Fish ~~ ~~nth.
cabir ~~ ~~eat little
for y~~. $ ~~urnished, waiting
~~ $700 down,down,down.

3/4 acre wooded site for camping or
cabin. $2000/ $350 down/ $35 mo/

3/4 acre building site on county rd
and electric line. Quarter mile to
creek. Joins 100 acres USA LAND.
$3250/ $400 down/ $40 per month.

CREEKS! Yes, we have creeks!!
1½ acres with little stream, big
trees. $2150/$250/$50 month.

Another 1½ acres with spring-fed
water system. Level site. Good road.
$9500/ $750 down/ $65 per month.

3½ acres bordered by 600 feet of
year-round stream. Half of this is
LEVEL. Only two miles to town.
$7500/ $1000 down/ $75 per mo.

A full acre hilltop parcel, Great
view of Blue Mtn. Excellent WELL
with pump and electric power. Area
of newer homes near river. All goes
for $2950/ $950 down/ $40 mo.

4 acres on good road. Power in.
A perfect mobile home site, or
camp here until you build.
Four miles east of town. Secluded!
$5500/ $1000 down/ $60 mo.

Take your choice of 3½ or 4½ acres
atop the hill. A great spot for

Although Canada has large cities, they quickly trail off into picturesque rural regions like this farm south of Napanee, Ontario. (Ontario Department of Tourism and Information)

Maps:
Alaska Distribution Unit, U.S. Geological Survey, 520 Illinois Street, Fairbanks 99701
Regional Forester, U.S. Forest Service, Juneau, 99801

Prospecting and Minerals:
Bureau of Mines, Box 2688, Juneau 99801
Division of Mines and Minerals, Box 1391, Juneau 99801

Canada An entire book could be devoted to this friendly country . . . a place we like to think of as a more peaceful extension of America. Canada offers an alternate life for those whose needs preclude even the New America. Here are sources of information:

General Information:
Alberta—Travel Bureau, Edmonton
British Columbia—Government Travel Bureau, Victoria
Canada—Canadian Government Travel Bureau, Ottawa, Ontario
Manitoba—Bureau of Travel and Publicity, Winnipeg
Ontario—Department of Travel and Publicity, Toronto
Quebec—Province of Quebec Tourist Bureau, Quebec
Saskatchewan—Department of Travel and Information, Regina
Yukon—Canadian Government Travel Bureau, Ottawa, Ontario

Land:

Alberta—Dept. of Lands and Forests, Edmonton

British Columbia—Lands Branch, Dept. of Lands and Forests, Victoria (A groovy province!)

Manitoba—Dept. of Mines and Natural Resources, Winnipeg

Ontario—Dept. of Lands and Forests, Toronto

Quebec—Dept. of Lands and Forests, Quebec

Saskatchewan—Dept. of Natural Resources, Prince Albert (Good vibes!)

Yukon—Dept. of Northern Affairs and National Resources, Ottawa, Ontario

When you write, you can expect to receive information in the neat, no-nonsense form as shown.

The following data was abstracted from a most complete and courteous presentation by the people in Regina, Saskatchewan.

Canadian Land Opportunities: Saskatchewan, with its generous and friendly invitation to all non-Canadians, is typical of many of the provinces of Canada. The Tourist Branch of its Industry Department will tell you that it is permissible for a non-Canadian to lease or purchase property in Saskatchewan. There are three general topographical regions from which to choose:

(1) South of Meadow Lake, Prince Albert, and Hudson Bay. This is largely farmland with prices ranging from $48 to $100 per acre. For information write to Regina Real Estate Board, 1149 8th Street East, Saskatoon.

(2) North of the above area, to the Churchill River. Here the topography is mixed woods and coniferous forest land. South of that the land is undulating, wild and of a sandy nature, interspersed with lakes, rivers, and muskegs. The area is virtually all Crown (Government or Public) owned and suitable for private cottage as well as resorts, fishing camps, restaurants, service stations, etc. Standard size lots of approximately 75 x 150 feet are readily available on a lease basis. Lease fees start at $25 per year. The land agent for the northern forest belt is the Northern Affairs Branch, Department of Natural Resources, Provincial Office Building, Prince Albert.

(3) Between the Churchill River and the Northwest Territories border. This is primarily wild, fly-in country with coniferous forest on pre-Cambrian rock interspersed with many lakes and rivers. It can accommodate fly-in fishing camps and similar commercial developments. Contact the Northern Affairs Branch in Prince Albert if interested in this Crown land.

It should be noted that while region No. 2 lends itself

PROVINCE OF BRITISH COLUMBIA
LANDS SERVICE

DEPARTMENT OF LANDS, FORESTS,
AND WATER RESOURCES
VICTORIA, BRITISH COLUMBIA

HON. R. G. WILLISTON
Minister of Lands, Forests, and Water Resour

The

Disposition
Crown L

in

British Co

Land Series
Reprinted

Printe
in ri

The
Disposition of Crown Lands
in British Columbia

•

PART A.—GEOGRAPHY

I. GEOGRAPHIC BACKGROUND

British Columbia is the westernmost and, in terms of both area and population, the third largest of the 10 provinces of Canada. The 366,255-square-mile area of British Columbia exceeds that of the three Pacific States of the United States (Washington, Oregon, and California) combined. Similarly, the area of this Province is greater than the combined extent of Great Britain, Ireland, France, Belgium, and The Netherlands. When population is considered, however, British Columbia has only 2,200,000 people, compared with 24,000,000 for Washington, Oregon, and California, and 128,000,000 for the above European countries.

The surface of the Province is dominantly rolling to mountainous, the chief exception being the north-eastern corner, which is an almost featureless plain. Extending in a northwest-southeast direction through the Interior of the Province is a series of high rolling plateaux notched by deep valleys and broken by several large mountain ranges. These plateaux are bordered by two very large mountain systems—the Rocky Mountains on the east and the Coast Mountains on the west.

The existence of rugged terrain over much of British Columbia is of considerable geographic importance. Among its influences has been to greatly reduce the area suitable for agriculture and to increase the importance of the natural forest-cover.

Almost 60 per cent, or 214,000 square miles, of British Columbia's area has been classed as forest land, most of which bears trees of commercial quality. An additional 78,000 square miles is barren, consisting of land above timber-line, glaciers and snowfields, rockslides, and the like. Non-productive tree cover accounts for 54,000 square miles. Lakes, rivers, and swamps occupy 14,000 square miles. Another 3,800 square miles is in natural meadows and grassland. *The remaining 2,200 square miles, or little more than one-half of 1 per cent of the total area of British Columbia, is in urban use and crop land.*

The distribution of population within British Columbia is very uneven, a condition which has been emphasized by mountainous terrain and by wide

eace River region encourages this
he fruit-growing industry is an
farm income in certain sections
actically all of the tree fruits
rom irrigated orchards in the
ie Southern Interior. Much
te from the Kootenay Lake
hompson Valley. Most of
it (e.g., strawberries, rasp-
blueberries) is found in the
uthern Vancouver Island,
and Okanagan have the

field crops, wheat, oats,
ains. The Peace River
region for grain grown
ages at Creston (south
)kanagan. The Lower
Island are important
ed grain. Seed and
a field crop in all
Potato-growing is
iry- or beef-cattle

egetables is pro-
r Fraser Valley,
Thompson Val-
eading regions.
he specialized
hich originate
ompson, and
s and bulbs
the Lower
d horticul-
ms, holly,
ly in the
d, where
erprises.

zed by
xtreme
gnized
Mean
uary
pita-

ler
re
s

5

66

A typical Canadian land access bulletin.

well to the location of summer cottages, one cannot "live off the land" on a year round basis. Fishing season is open from early May until mid-April of the following year, but hunting seasons last for just a few weeks in fall and winter and trapping is restricted to northern residents, with native Indians having first priority on trapping rights. Farming would be out of the question that far north due to late spring and early autumn frosts.

Immigration regulations are too voluminous to incorporate here. It is suggested that those who are interested in becoming citizens of Canada write to:

Officer in Charge
Immigration Branch
Department of Manpower & Immigration
Financial Building
Regina, Saskatchewan

or contact the Canadian Government Immigration Service Office in the area in which you are interested.

Summary

So there are some land facts about rural U.S.A., our biggest state, and even an alternate America. With all this territory from which to choose, you have no excuse to hang around the local drugstore breathing exhaust gas.

In a word . . .

GO!

4 How to Reduce Your Need for Money

We all have certain money "habits"—not needs, just habits—most of them created by the Establishment for their profit. The man who makes and spends $800 a month has an $800 a month "habit." If he could suddenly cut down on his *need* for $800, he wouldn't be forced to earn it.

Here's a good example from the author's own early experiences. My wife and I both held full-time jobs and had the two-paycheck habit. The biggest expense was for two cars to make it to work each day. In addition, there was an outlay for a baby-sitter for one-year-old Wendy. I sat down one evening and made a close accounting of income versus outgo and I discovered that the *net* from my wife's job was about $18 a week. This was a meager return for the daily hassle of getting to and from work, making quick meals, permitting someone else to care for our child, and suffering from everything else that anyone who has done it knows! What we had produced was that phenomenon peculiar to America . . . one of us was really working for the "privilege" of working.

As a result of this bit of economic soul-searching, we decided to split the city and drop one job. We bought an unfinished cabin in the Santa Monica mountains . . . no inside plumbing, no heat, and nothing but studs for walls. However, the down payment was negligible and so were the monthly payments. I traded one car for a motorcycle and instituted some of the saving methods described in this chapter. Ultimately, though we only had one paycheck, we found our-

selves with a higher net at the end of each month. Here were some of the additional benefits:

1. Our daughter was home with her mother instead of with an insensitive baby-sitter.

2. My wife had time to grow a garden and work on the place, making it into a real home.

3. There was more time for preparation of money-saving dishes like slow-simmered stew, big pots of soup, and home-baked bread.

4. Meals were ready when I got home from work.

5. Our money went into a home that we finally owned instead of into rent receipts.

6. We were living in a more healthful environment . . . far from the city.

Most books on saving money talk about things such as using an old light bulb as a darning egg. This is hogwash direct from the Insidious Advice Department (IAD) of the Establishment. The things on which to *really* save money are the big items . . . insurance, housing, transportation, medical and dental fees. It's a cop-out to reuse a paper towel when you keep getting quarterly insurance bills for $116.26 or a statement from your pill-pushing doctor for $207.89.

Here are some basic pointers for living on little:

1. Buy nothing new if at all possible.

2. If you really need something, check all used item outlets first.

3. Get as much as you can from free sources.

4. Turn off Madison Avenue completely . . . don't read ads, put a free rock through the "eye" of your TV set.

5. Abide by this wise old aphorism . . . "Make do or do without, use it up or wear it out."

Establishment-Type Expenses and How to Cut Them

John Steinbeck once wrote an essay in which he described how many American men actually contribute to their premature deaths by carrying a heavy load of insurance premiums. I've seen this in my own experience . . . it happened to my brother-in-law. He had such a huge policy on his life that he worked himself into an early grave paying for it. Now this is one way to provide for your family but it's rather hard on the little ones who don't yet realize that in the U.S., dollars are often thought more important than fatherly affection.

There's no question that some insurance serves a useful purpose, such as creating an instant estate for a young family man. However, as with anything, there are upper limits on how much anyone should pay. It's ridiculous to saddle yourself with enormous, long-term obligations and then slowly die, both mentally and physically, at a stupid, nerve-wracking, nowhere job making the money to meet these obligations.

Alternative Life Insurance Plan   Here's a logical alternative to heavy insurance premiums. Buy a small place in the country . . . one that your survivors can pay off with whatever you leave them . . . social security, *small* mortgage insurance policy, or savings. As an example, in Calaveras County, a California High Sierra region, a five acre parcel of nearly level land with many oaks and pines and a flowing spring was offered for $7,500 with $1,000 down and $60 a month payments. Instead of buying an insurance policy, suppose you saved up the grand, put it down on the land, and

Here are a couple in Illinois . . .

No. 392. Nice 1-bdrm, bath brick home in town. Separate garage. Short walk to shopping & river. 120x125 corner lot.$2900

No. 393 - 4-1/2a along creek, at edge of sm country vlg. 3-story grist mill w/sturdy oak frame, 2 wheels & shaft. 7-rm hse. Gar-type bldg. 2 wells. Tms.$3560

One in sunny Florida . .

LOOK WHAT $4500 BUYS!

No. 266. Deep lot fronting paved road in residential neighborhood. School bus service; mile to shopping, 3 miles from lake. Cottage of 4 rooms with bath, gas heat, city water & attached carport. Price $4500; easy terms. STROUT, Belleview, FL

Many abandoned farms cost as much to buy outright as you would pay for a down payment on a city crackerbox. (USDA)

71

Two in the boondocks of California . . .

No. 1002 - $3800. Comfy little retirement home with lovely view of mountains & Goose Lake! 2 bedrooms, small sewing room...and some furnishings stay! Easy-care lot; block to stores. Price $3800; good terms too! STROUT, Alturas, CA

LOW PRICE NEWS!
No. 224 - $4250. Shaded corner lot in good neighborhood, within walking distance of complete shopping center & schools. Only a mile to Sacramento River. 4-room house needs some repairs to put it in A-1 condition; has bath, refrigeration cooling. Poultry house. ALL for $4250; LOW down. STROUT, Los Molinos, CA

And look at these fantastic buys in Arkansas . . . a state of growing popularity with rural land lovers . . .

No. 1200 - 5a retirement spot. Town 4 mi. Acre for truck crops; some pasture. Gd 6 rms, mostly paneled. 2 outbldgs. Tms.$4750

No. 1294 - 35a pt-tillable pastureland; spring, pond water. Saleable timber, fruit & nuts. Only 3-1/2 mi out. Tms.$3100

No. 1317 - 1/2a cornering pvd st, in town; mi to lake. Fruit. 4 rms with screened porch, carport. Smokehouse...$4000

No. 1310. 110x220 shady hillside lot. Mi to schools; walk to lake! Furn'd, well-kept 1-room paneled cabin. Storage bldg.$3890

No. 1318 - 2a retirement/truck farm on st hwy at townedge. Partly paneled 4-rm dwelling; utility shed. Part down....$3500

No. 1124 - 40a timberland; spg brook. Scenic bldg sites! Just off U.S. Hwy. Tms.$4000

No. 200 - 4a at edge of sm city. Gd soil & views. Pear, apple trees. Gd tms. $4500

No. 101 - 4-1/2a; level & tillable. Beautiful bldg sites; well. Town 5 miles. $1200

Every single property shown here and described is under $5,000 total. (Strout and United Realty)

then made the payments as though they were insurance premiums. Then, if you die prematurely, your family can go live on the land, grow their own food, and pay off the mortgage with your social security benefits. If that $7,500 price tag is too rich for your blood, here are some selected rural properties from a recent issue of the Strout catalog . . . both with and without houses.

Insure Yourself or How to Beat the Car Insurance Racket at Its Own Game In addition to providing for your survivors through purchase of a small land parcel, you can do something tangible about the high cost of insuring a vehicle. First, drive the smallest, cheapest car you can. VW's and similar long-lasting bugs make minimal insurance demands. If the car is old enough, carry your own collision insurance: just set aside the money that you would pay for damage premiums, to cover any accident.

Many people have found, to their dismay, that collision insurance is a bad joke. Here's a typical example. A man buys a new car for $4,000 and is about halfway through the payment book when the car is totally demolished after rolling down an embankment when the parking brake fails. Since no one is hurt and there is no other car involved, it looks like a very simple case—and it is . . . for the insurance company. They follow the fine print in the contract and decide to provide the "actual cash value" to the owner. They call around to used car lots and determine the average price of the demolished car. Let's say it's worth $2,000. There's one little problem, though . . . the car has depreciated faster than it was paid off. The owner of the wreck owes $2,345.67! Does the insurance company feel sympathetic? Tut, tut. Not only do they lack sympathy, they take off the $100 deductible from the actual cash value price and deliver a check for $1,900 to the (get this) *holder of the car's mortgage.* This means that our friend is not only out of a car, *he has to pay the difference* between the insurance payoff and the balance owed!

Now for the final shaft. By paying off the car, the insurance company owns it legally. Let's say the owner wants it for a possible rebuild or just for parts. He has to buy it back from the insurance company for whatever they choose to sell it for. Usually they offer it to several wrecking yards and if the bid of a yard is higher than that of the former owner, too bad.

Is this an isolated example of what you can expect from a car insurance company? Hardly; that's why they are so unbeloved by most of the drivers of the old America.

So, as we said in the beginning . . . buy a small, old car that can be easily repaired and provide your own insurance.

But what about public liability and property damage, you say. That's easy. If you're feeling unlucky, buy the smallest amount you can. Keep in mind that no matter what the amount is, the insurance company will fight like a wounded tiger to retain it. Thus, you usually have as much protection with a small coverage policy as you have with a large one.

An even better solution is to simply drive carefully and never let yourself be at fault for any accident.

About the only automobile insurance coverage presently offered that is moderately worthwhile are medical payments. After all, it is impossible to predict when some stoned idiot is going to come over that double line on a narrow bridge.

In summary, look upon all auto insurance as a gambling game where the odds are stacked heavily in favor of the companies that do the insuring. When and if you do buy a policy, sit down and read all the fine print. You'd be amazed at how the contract is arranged to favor the company regardless of what occurs. The best person to talk to before you buy is an ex-insurance adjuster. He knows all the loopholes through which the company walks out of their end of the "bargain."

Other Legally Approved Insurance Frauds   Eliminate fire insurance from your budget by simply becoming your own fire department. First, prevent fires from starting by removing all the possible causes. You can get a list of fire hazards from your local fire department or write to any fire insurance company and get their booklets . . . after all, they make even more money when nobody's house burns down. Once your house has been made as fireproof as you can make it, provide means to put out fires while they are small . . . buckets of sand around the stove, hoses coiled in handy places ready to turn on.

There's no disagreement that keeping your pad from burning is far better than hassling with a fire insurance company over the payoff. In addition, no check from any insuror can compensate you for the loss of personal articles.

Theft insurance is easily eliminated. Give all your goodies to the poor and donate the premiums that would have been used to cover them to your favorite charity.

As far as medical and accident insurance is concerned, forget it. Just move to the country, live on natural foods, and don't climb ladders or play with loaded guns. In that way, you can ignore the local AMA member.

Create Your Own Medical Protection Plan   No question that this is a big item for city-dwellers, and with good reason . . . sulfur and nitrogen dioxide, asbestos and rubber particles, plus just about every other industrial chemical compound can be found floating around in the air of big cities. Then there's the psychological pressure of a big city . . . confusion, congestion, office politics complete with the knife in the back. But worst of all, there's little that's edible, healthful, or nutritious in the supermarkets. Once you've made your move to rural America, you'll be able to breathe fresh air, dump urban pressures, and obtain good food as your best medicine. This combination will eliminate almost 100 percent of the medical bills you once had to pay. You will become, in effect, your own doctor with the emphasis on staying well rather than having to be cured after you become ill.

Incidentally, the Chinese have a highly effective medical plan . . . the doctor gets paid a small fee while you are well. When you're sick, the payment stops. Obviously, this keeps the Oriental medicine man heavily interested in your continued well-being, unlike in our system, where your current disease is your physician's next Cadillac.

For some pertinent facts on why an American doctor could be the worst person to see when you are sick, write for a copy of *Autopsy on the AMA*, An Analysis of Health-Care Delivery Systems in America. It's $1.50 from the good brothers at Student Research Facility, 1132 The Alameda, Berkeley, Calif. 94707.

With permission from the good Dr. Henry G. Bieler, here are some principles from his book, *Food Is Your Best Medicine.* (Random House, 457 Madison Avenue, New York, N.Y. 10022. If it's not available in your local library or bookstore, write the publisher.) Their beautiful logic makes any further comment unnecessary.

> . . . throughout the centuries many men of medicine have pointed to the importance of food and to the relative incompetence of drugs when considering health and disease. The greatest physicians have used the fewest and simplest of drugs, because they were fully aware of the role of nature in health; they knew that all the forces of nature in man, beast, and the plant world are dedicated to obtaining and keeping a perfect state of health. They knew that many diseases are "self-limited," that is, they cure themselves whether you do anything or nothing for them.

If you had to summarize the good physician's book in four sentences, these would suffice:

> This is the dark age of medicine.
> There is *no special medicine* which is a remedy for any chronic disease.
> Nature does the real healing.
> Improper foods cause disease; proper foods cure disease.

If you never used any of the material in this book except our strong recommendation to read Dr. Bieler's book, you would still be doing yourself and those around you the greatest service.

Dental Care That You Can Provide for Yourself An extremely capable dentist once commented that people will insure a $3,000 car but spend virtually nothing to protect their invaluable set of teeth. "Even when they know that courts attach a dollar value to teeth ($1,000 each in case of loss due to negligence of others) they still will not spend enough money to keep their natural $32,500 homegrown teeth in good repair." He also said that healthy teeth are basic to a healthy body since one cannot prepare food for digestion without proper mastication. "False teeth are no answer, since they are an extremely poor substitute for even poor real ones. That is why many dentists are making extreme efforts to save any naturally rooted tooth or to implant them in the gum when they are lost," he concluded.

In a book which should have been a best seller but wasn't (*Your Teeth* by D. A. Collins, D.D.S., Doubleday & Company, Inc., N.Y.), some facts are pointed out that can help you "insure" your own teeth by preventive maintenance and proper diet. Dr. Collins gives these three general rules for oral health:

1. Do not eat refined sugar or sweets.

2. Follow a regular program of home care. This includes brushing the teeth after every meal, the use of dental floss, toothpicks and water-flushing instruments (ordinary baking soda or salt makes a satisfactory dentrifice).

3. Make regular visits to your dentist for a checkup.

More teeth are lost due to gum disease than decay. Massaging the gums with rounded toothpicks or rubber stimulators or the eating of hard-crusted bread or other chewy foods is highly desirable. Incidentally, natives throughout the world who don't have the money for a toothbrush (even if they could find the local drugstore) use the end of a small green stick or twig. They chew it until it is fuzzy and then brush their teeth and massage their gums with this natural woodland dental aid.

As with any aspect of physical care, prevention is the real key to continued reliability.

How to Make Ends Meet at the (Inevitable) End Another grave consideration for the urban dweller is burial expenses. Whether you save for it through insurance or a "pay-now-die-later" plan, it's still another heavy burden on your back. Recently, I toured an area where the community has its own graveyard and takes care of it on a communal basis. The plots are free ... the land was donated many years ago and the only stipulation is that the survivors help with maintenance. Containers for the dead are simple pine boxes made by friends of the deceased. Services are in the local church or in a home or not at all, dependent on the terms of the will. Even if you don't find this handy arrangement in your rural community, you can write:

Continental Association
39 E. Van Buren Street
Chicago, Ill. 60605

Send them a dollar for a copy of a manual on how to conduct the services and another quarter for a list of associated members who will provide standard interments at low prices. (The author is a member of a society which will provide pickup, cremation, and ash scattering for less than $150).

Transportation   As they say in the ads, MAKE THIS COMPARISON YOURSELF! A man lives eight miles from work. He can get behind the wheel of a new Cadillac with an 8,000 cubic centimeter mill under the hood or he can swing a leg over an 80 cubic centimeter motorcycle. The cost per mile is about twenty cents for the big Detroit canoe while the little two-wheeler can get around for about two cents! Not only is it one-tenth of the cost, think of the polluting characteristics . . . the big Cad spews forth 100 times the exhaust gas of the bike.

Just imagine how the air in big cities would improve in one day if everyone switched from an oversized car to an undersized motorcycle. It can be done if everyone does it. Why not start with yourself . . . *now*. (We've gone into the purchase and use of cycles in depth in Chapter 9.)

If you live in an area where the climate precludes the use of motorcycles for a good part of the year, then by all means buy the smallest car you can. Not only do they cost less from an insurance standpoint as we've already pointed out, they cost less to gas up and repair. There's a good reason why the parking lots of most high schools and universities in present-day America look like the display yard of a large VW dealer. People of all ages are coming to realize that the air they pollute is the same as that they must breathe. In addition, the status symbol games that Detroit once played with the car buyers of this country no longer have much appeal, especially to the younger generation. It's becoming obvious that Detroit has little intention of producing a nonpolluting vehicle in the near future. Thus, the only recourse of a citizenry oriented to individual transportation is to use the smallest, most efficient vehicles. In addition, doubling up whenever you drive cuts the use of petroleum products by 50 percent.

If you've been fortunate enough to make it out of the Big City, then you can possibly eliminate your need for a car completely. Raising your own food, operating a cottage industry, buying your needs by mail order, and finding your recreation in the fields, streams, and meadows around your country place can totally end your dependence on a four-wheeled smoky monster. As they used to say in the days before cars took over the country, "get a horse." And why

Enjoyed anything like this lately? (USDA)

Just in case you've forgotten the alternative. (USDA)

not? A horse costs little initially, eats grass and hay, returns valuable manure to the land, and has got to be just about the most fun way to get around the countryside.

Freaky Furniture In Abbie Hoffman's *Steal This Book*, there is an illustration of a room furnished with furniture, most of which could be obtained free. For example, the coffee table is an old cable drum available all over the U.S. There are many other things that you can obtain free that will:

1. Serve you well as interesting and useful furniture
2. Help reduce the amount of trash and junk in America
3. Cut down on the amount of lumber and other raw materials needed to supply the heavy furniture industry

Here are some specific ideas for your home.

* By connecting plain wooden boxes together, an infinite number of attractive storage combinations can be created.

Popular Science *magazine has lots of literature on making your own rustic furniture.*

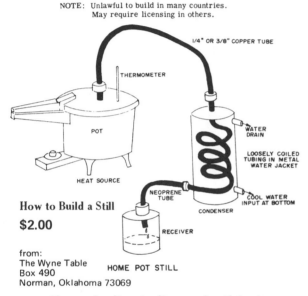

NOTE: Unlawful to build in many countries. May require licensing in others.

How to Build a Still

$2.00

from:
The Wyne Table
Box 490
Norman, Oklahoma 73069

If you don't get a license for this piece of "furniture," just put it in the cellar or the woodshed. (Whole Earth Catalog)

* Old refrigerators that no longer get cold can have their locks removed (to prevent children from suffocating) and be used to hold all manner of good things like wheat, brown rice, and peach preserves.
* Often, perfectly good but out-of-fashion dressers, bureaus, cabinets, and chests can be salvaged from junk piles and dumps. Transformed with paint and fabric, they'll amaze your visitors who just signed a long-term contract to pay for some kitschy store-bought ensembles.

The Devil's Trumpet or How to Escape the Tyranny of the Telephone If you're average, you've made this statement upon looking at the bill from Ma Bell . . . "I'm going to cut down on phone calls" . . . and then you never do. You go right on paying from $20 to $40 or more for an instrument that, like fire, is great when under control but terrible when out of control.

The basic charge for a phone is quite reasonable . . . what makes the bill go outasite is long distance use . . . even when the distance is under 100 miles. First, take a look at these average prices for long distance phone calls:

3,000 miles—$1.85 for first three minutes
2,000 miles—$1.75 for first three minutes
1,000 miles—$1.35 for first three minutes

Add to these charges the natural talkativeness of just about everyone, and it's no mystery why you get a bill for $26.78 every month. Here are some pointers on what you can do about it, ranging from mild to extreme:

1. Buy an egg timer. Turn it over when you start to talk . . . start winding it up when the sand gets low. In the old days, the operator would break into toll calls and warn you that your three minutes were up. They don't do this anymore, but the timer will.

2. Prepare your conversation carefully. Talk from notes if necessary so that you can transmit the maximum information in the shortest time. Here's what some sharp operators do if they must say a lot on a regular basis. They tape record the message at the low inch-per-second 1-7/8 rate on a three-speed tape recorder. Then they transmit this recording over the phone to another tape recorder but at a speed of 7-1/2 IPS. The other recipient can play back this Donald Duck-sounding transmission and hear the voice at normal speed.

3. A simpler version of the above is to use a prearranged code where certain words stand for entire sentences. For example, the word *save* could stand for the exchange of *how are you fine how are you fine.*

4. If you overdo it the phone company might get unhappy but the oldest one in the book still works. Just call for yourself on a person-to-person basis to let your loved ones know that you arrived in Montana safely. An infinite variety

of tunes can be played with this theme. For example, the name you use can be a code as follows:

Ask for	This means
Elmer Perkins:	Tell the kids to wear their pajamas
Dodsworth Lewis:	Don't loan out my copy of the Anarchist's Cookbook
Abbie Hoffman:	Send me bail money

5. Weigh every phone call carefully. Decide whether an eight-cent letter or ten-cent airmail missive might not do the same job for one-tenth the cost.

6. Have the phone taken out (or don't even start with one in the country) and get yourself a ham radio outfit or a pair of carrier pigeons. Don't freak out . . . many people use amateur radio to great advantage. For example, you can call someone by radio and then have the respondee use a local phone to complete the call. Pigeons can travel great distances in a relatively short time. If you often call someone twenty-five or fifty miles away, this could be a fun way to go, besides having the pleasure of observing this gentle and interesting bird.

To wind up this discussion of money saving, try this test . . . it will let you know if the telephone is really an asset or a liability in your life:

Rate all incoming calls with "grades":

Calls that were most welcome	A
Calls that were blah	B
Calls that I could have lived without	C
Calls that really turned me off	D
Calls that made me want to rip the phone out with my bare hands	F

If you are getting mostly calls with B to F ratings, try having the phone disconnected for a month or two. The luxury of undisturbed meals, baths, and sessions in bed may surprise you. You may end up with either an unlisted number or total freedom from the tyranny (not to mention the expense) of the devil's electronic trumpet.

Entertainment Costs Less in the Boondocks

City dwellers often hire a baby-sitter for a dollar an hour, pay four to seven dollars for even a modest dinner out, and the lowest-priced movie hovers around two or three dollars. Thus, an evening for two, not counting parking fees, can run from twenty dollars up. Everything the city dweller does has a price tag on it. Contrast this with taking the evening meal down by a fast-flowing mountain river and cooking it over the hot coals of a driftwood fire. Then as the moon rises, everyone slides into the cool, turbulent water for a moonlit swim. Cost? Since the dinner was the usual fare sparked by riverside preparation and appetites and there's no admission to most rivers—nothing.

Why should the animals have all the fun?

One of the big drains on an urbanite's income is eliminated when he moves to an area that he would normally only visit as a tourist. Just think of all the fortunate people who live in resorts the year round—the Adirondacks, Warm Springs, Taos, Aspen, Sun Valley and the fabulous High Sierra country of California. Then there are places, thousands of them, which don't qualify as resorts or resort areas but still possess all of the advantages. These would include many parts of wild and uninhabited Nevada, Idaho north of Ketchum, much of the forested regions of Oregon and Washington, backwoods New Hampshire, Vermont, and Maine . . . in fact, almost anywhere *outside* of a large city would have the one basic and mandatory requirement of a tourist attraction—purer air. We can't honestly say pure air, since practically all of the U.S. is inundated with some degree of air pollution. However, you'll have much less chance of getting emphysema in northeast Nevada than you will in Anaheim, California.

Standard fare on the recreation menu in country areas includes swimming, riding, hiking, picnicking, skiing, and boating. However, there are many more unique, unthought-of entertainments that can be enjoyed only where there is room to roam. Here's just a sampling:

River Rafts Although you can purchase a commercial rubber raft, it's much more exciting to buy some canvas and a little rope and make your own Tom Sawyer "floating palace." Flotation can be provided by inner tubes (free from many gas stations) or empty cans or drums. If your budget is really low, then fasten some logs together. Next step is to find a good long river with not too many rapids. With sleeping bags, a bag of brown rice, and a slingshot or two, you can enjoy what early settlers did in the name of "exploration." (Actually, most early "explorers" were just escapists from the urban rat race.)

Motorcycling Ever since the motorcycle explosion in the early Sixties, there have been millions of low-priced motorcycles and scooters on the market, both new and used. Everyone who has tried them agrees that there's nothing quite so much fun as bouncing along some old logging road on a trail bike with a tasty lunch securely strapped to the luggage rack. You don't have to be rich to enjoy this sport. Here's a little 80 cc machine that was purchased for under $100. It runs and runs with a minimum of maintenance and hassle. It's so light that you can toss it in the trunk of a car and carry it with you to the scenic places you'd like to explore.

If you've never revved up the engine of a swift motorcycle and gone off around a track with several companions in friendly competition, you really haven't been exposed to all that life affords. Sailing down the straights at a modest fifty

Words can't describe the joys of touring on a motorcycle. (William Kaysing)

That goes for this sport too. (William Kaysing)

MPH, diving into the corners with your foot down for stability, taking the checkered flag as you dart across the finish line first are thrills that cannot be described.

Around major cities are found a scattering of motorcycle race courses. But because cycling still has hoodlum connotations in some areas, these courses are often in far from desirable locations. Furthermore, they are usually only activated on weekends. Just imagine the fun that a small group of cycle fans could have on a small country track of their own. It could be established on land belonging to one of the group or on some unused leased or rented parcel out of sight and hearing of possible complainers. Incidentally, by using adequate mufflers, the chance of complaint is negligible.

Races themselves can be as simple or as complex as the riders desire. The easiest way to get into dirt track racing is simply to lay out a course yourself with plenty of right and left turns and perhaps a "jump" or two. A jump is merely a dirt ramp two or three feet high that is used to launch the cycles on a short but exciting flight. In a race, everyone starts at once and the first one to complete three or four laps wins. A variation of this form of "scrambles" is "motocross." In the latter form, each group of riders competes three times. By a point system the winner is the one who turns in the most consistently "up-front" performance. For example, two firsts and one third would win him the trophy. There is another form of motorcycle competition called "trials." No speed contest (and thus safer), this involves riding a tough up-and-down-hill course without putting a foot down, stalling, or otherwise exhibiting less than top skill. A trials course can be laid out by an experienced rider and the others can take their turns one at a time. Trials demand the utmost in motorcycle-handling skill rather than sheer guts, and so they are frequently used to perfect the riding ability of racers.

There are many other games and contests for two-wheeled machinery. One popular form is the Hare and Hound. Here, an expert rider lays out a course over difficult terrain, leaving a trail of lime or ribbons tied to bushes. The object is to complete the entire course in the shortest time. This sport can be quite hairy and dangerous, but the people who pursue it wouldn't have it any other way.

For riders with less of a desire for super thrills, there are such games as standing on the seat while riding a specified course, running up narrow planks, the Australian pursuit wherein riders chase each other in an ever-diminishing circle, and the rollicking "slow race" in which the object is to see who can take the longest time to go twenty-five feet. You'll learn a lot about the various forms of cycling fun if you'll subscribe to or buy a sample copy of *Cycle World*, Joe Parkhurst's with-it cycle magazine (1499 Monrovia Avenue,

Newport Beach, Calif. 92660). More on motorcycles in Chapter 9.

Water Sports   During a conventional vacation there is usually only enough time to pursue the routine swimming sports. However, living in an area that has a plentiful supply of canals, rivers, ponds, lakes, or the ocean itself offers infinite variations on the theme of water fun. For example, a simple length of one-inch rope swinging from an overhanging branch above a slow-moving river can give you and your friends all of the delights enjoyed by Tom and Huck. The longer the rope and the higher the tree, the more fun it can be. As a variation, the rope can be tied to the branches of two tall trees so that it spans the river, the object being to go across hand over hand. Even though you don't make it, look at that beautiful plunge into refreshing water.

Let's assume that you've been fortunate enough to purchase a piece of country property that has some source of water on it . . . a small stream or creek or possibly the fork of a larger river. There are myriad possibilities for great times. Put up a small dam and you've got your own back yard swimming pool. (Incidentally, the law on rivers usually permits damming the water as long as you let it continue to flow when your pond is full.)

If you have fairly extensive frontage on the creek, tap its flow upstream and run some water down a canal or trough (called a flume) into a mill pond. Now you're ready to construct your own mill or water wheel . . . as small or large as you wish. What do you do with the power it creates? Well, how about grinding your own grain and corn like our ancestors did. Or, you can use it to drive an electric generator through a system of gears or pulleys to increase speed. The power could also be used for a home workshop . . . lathes, drill presses, or saws. Probably the greatest thing about a mill of your own is the picturesque scene that it makes—the water splashing off the wood, the sound of its great bulk slowly turning in its bearings.

Nature Study as Recreation   John Muir spent most of his life in the mountains contemplating their grandeur and studying the flora and fauna that inhabit them. Hundreds of books have been written since his time on the subject of mountain wildernesses. Here are a few unique books to illustrate the tremendous outdoor opportunities available to those who would like to study nature firsthand:

> *Survival, Evasion and Escape*, Field Manual, Headquarters, Department of the Army
> *The Last of the Mountain Men*, Harold Peterson, Charles Scribner's Sons, N.Y.
> *The Herbalist*, Joseph E. Meyer, Sterling Publishing Company, Inc., N.Y.

How to Go Live in the Woods on Ten Dollars a Week,
Bradford Angier, Stackpole Books, Harrisburg, Pa.

Good Investments

The Establishment is much in favor of everyone's saving some money. They have a number of reasons for fostering this procedure, most of them profiting the people who hold your money. There is no argument that a pile of money in the bank gives a person a secure feeling, but then there are other places to put it. For example, an investment in a small piece of land and some garden tools could return much more than the equivalent amount of money in the bank. Take a look at this chart, which shows how much food you can grow on a single acre:

Estimated Value of 1-Acre Vegetable Garden

Vegetable	No. of 100-ft. rows	Yield per 1/100-ft. row	Total Yields	Unit Price	Wholesale Value
Asparagus	8	50#	400#	.20	$ 80.00
Beets	4	50#	280#	.09	25.20
Broccoli	4	50#	200#	.17	34.00
Cabbage	8	135#	1,080#	.04	43.20
Cauliflower	4	120#	480#	.12	57.60
Collards	4	75#	300#	.05	15.00
Sweet Corn	12	85#	1,020#	.10	102.00
Cucumbers	4	180#	720#	.05	36.00
Green Pea (pods)	8	20#	160#	.14	22.40
Kale	4	75#	300#	.07	21.00
Lettuce	4	50(hds)	200(hds)	.10	20.00
Lima Beans	8	25#	200#	.12	24.00
Muskmelon	4	150#	600#	.11	66.00
Onions	8	75#	600#	.08	48.00
Peppers	4	70#	280#	.13	36.40
Potatoes	12	150#	1,800#	.04	72.00
Pumpkins	4	300#	1,200#	.03	36.00
Radishes	4	45(bun)	180(bun)	.05	9.00
Snap Beans	8	30#	240#	.13	31.20
Spinach	4	40#	160#	.05	8.00
Squash	4	160#	640#	.04	25.60
Sweet potatoes	8	100#	800#	.09	72.00
Tomatoes (staked)	8	160#	1,280#	.10	128.00
Turnips	4	65#	260#	.06	15.60
Watermelon	4	200#	800#	.04	32.00
TOTALS	148				1,060.20
Retail Value					1,378.26

Besides land, all you need to grow this much food is seed and a collection of simple garden tools ... items like shovels, hoes, rakes, and springtooth cultivators. You don't need the big ugly gasoline-engined stuff, since once the ground has been loosened up by adding compost, it will stay as soft and workable as a child's sandbox.

Investment in Recycling

1. Locate an empty store building in your area ... even an old shed or barn would do.

2. Ask the owner to donate the use of it to a good cause. Tell him he can use it as an income tax deduction ... that should convince him.

3. Now take that pitiful sum of money that's really too small to invest conventionally and buy a stack of big fancy posters that say: "Grand Old Rummage Sale! Please Donate Your Castoffs and Junk. Proceeds to Charity. Bring to ___. Date ____." (You may be able to get the printer to do these free.)

4. Put these posters on the general store bulletin board, at the local filling station, on most of the local trees, fence posts, and telephone poles.

5. Now you can donate some time instead of money. Open the store on Monday to receive the goodies in person. In that way you can get to know the people in the community.

6. As time is available, sort through the stuff and put it into categories ... children's blouses, old double-bitted axes, fine old overstuffed furniture from the Thirties, somewhat scratchy Glenn Miller records, Waring blenders, refrigerators with the big round cooling towers on top, granny rockers, and tons of stuff that is always junk to the person who gives it and a treasure to him or her who buys it.

7. If you see something you really like, well, you know what to do.

8. On the appointed day ... according to the poster, Saturday ... open the shop and prepare to be inundated with curiosity seekers, meddlers, rednecks, people who donated coming to see how you priced their toaster, and just about everyone else in the county, not to mention tourists, second-hand store owners from 100 miles away and, last but not least, the pushy matrons from Rich City who expect to buy heirloom sterling for fifteen cents a pound. What you are seeing is the current mania in America for things that are from an earlier and gentler era ... a period when the most deadly weapon was a blockbuster.

9. At the end of the day, count up the money, sweep up the candy wrappers and commuter tickets and enjoy the heady feeling of success. You are now ready for the fun phase.

10. Write to the Women's Club of the nearest large city. Ask them to send you a list of underprivileged children ... black, white, yellow, or red. Don't take any excuses—they can get it for you.

11. Write the parents of the children and ask them if their child would like to spend the day or weekend in your charming resort village as your guest.

12. If you must, spend some of that rummage sale money to procure the following:

A. Rental of a large station wagon or bus

B. Healthful foods—fruits, vegetables, homemade bread

C. Game equipment—table tennis, croquet, volley balls.

13. On the appointed day drive down and pick up the children and drive them to your village. Give them a tour of the town and a nature walk. Let them breathe the fresh air, feed them the good food at lunchtime, turn them loose in a grassy meadow with the recreational equipment, and finally, take them for a swim in the local river, pond or lake. Be casual, let them set their own pace. You just stand by to comfort the bruised and settle arguments. At the end of the day, you'll not only feel, but be at least ten feet tall. Now that's what's known as making good investment in the New America. Repeat dose as needed.

An especially fine investment that pays great recollection dividends for many years is the barbecue party and river swim. Here's a good recipe. First purchase a side of beef or a whole hog. Dig a large hole in the ground and fill it with hardwood like oak, hickory, or cherry. Burn the wood down to coals and lay the meat directly on the glowing embers, hide side down. Now cover it with a large clean canvas, and top with earth. Let it slowly roast for a day or so while you frolic with your guests in the river. Just before opening the barbecue pit, boil a lot of fresh corn, turn sourdough French bread into slices of absolute heaven by adding plenty of butter and grated cheese, toss a gigantic salad, cut open the watermelons and then—fanfare! Serve out the juicy, tender totally outasite barbecued beef or pork in big chunks. Your friends who attend this event will return much more than mere interest on your investment and you'll keep the memory of good vibes for a long, long time.

Among the other good investments you can make are:

1. Fifty dollars worth of fruit trees to be planted along village streets. Years after you're gone, this investment will be paying appreciated dividends.

2. Four dollars worth of perennial flower seeds for the village square or the strip along the front of your house.

3. Fifteen dollars for a pet-watering trough somewhere near the village center.

4. Three dollars for some green paint to brush on to a collection of old fifty-gallon drums. These are placed around town to collect and recycle all kinds of throwaways.

5. One hundred dollars for unique and unusual books (like this one) and unique records (*J.C. Superstar*) that you can donate to the local library.

The list is obviously endless, but one thing is for sure ... these investments in the New America won't be subjected to spectroscopic examination by the IRS. Furthermore, you'll find the interest payoff more rewarding than plain money.

5 How to Eat Well on Less Than a Dollar a Day

Where to Get Food

Recently when we were on a short trip, my wife went into a grocery store to get some food for lunch. When she returned empty-handed a few minutes later, I asked her why.

"*Everything* in that store was wrapped in *plastic*. Two slices of phony meat in a vinyl saucer for eighty-nine cents! I just couldn't bear to waste our money on it."

This brought home the realization that it's becoming more difficult daily to buy something in a grocery store that's worth *buying*, let alone worth *eating*. The trend is increasing, unfortunately. Artificial, heavily processed foods sealed in plastics or metal is food for robots, not people.

However, there is a way out—stop going to the supermarket! Where do you shop instead? Any place *but* a supermarket. Here are some possibilities:

Hay, feed, and grain stores
Ranches and farms
Fields, gardens and orchards—yours or someone else's
Rivers, streams, lakes and oceans
Woods, forests, marshes and meadows

Where to Find Great Foods for Just Six Cents a Pound

An increasing number of smart people have discovered that their local hay, grain, and feed store is a fabulous storehouse of healthful, low-cost food. Here you'll find bulging sacks of whole wheat, bins full of rolled oats, bushels of whole or cracked corn.

Ten pounds of wheat in its most beautiful form—the whole grain—will probably cost you about ten cents a pound . . . the price would drop to about six cents a pound or less if you bought a hundred-pound sack. Take it home, put a handful in the blender, and turn the switch. Within twenty seconds you'll have something that looks mighty like the expensive hot cereals you've been buying. If you leave your blender on longer, you'll end up with a robust-looking flour. But stop short of that. Let the wheat remain somewhat crunchy looking.

Now boil a pint of water and add a little salt if you wish. Add the freshly ground meal (4 ounces) while stirring. Turn down the heat and let it cook slowly for about ten minutes, stirring occasionally. You now have two large bowls (over a half-pound each) of the tastiest, freshest cereal you've ever eaten. Add some chopped walnuts, a few raisins, a handful of dates or any other dried fruit, plus milk and honey and you have a great breakfast. You are now off and running on a brand new health track!

What did this cost you? The wheat was (at the most) just 1.5 cents or three-quarters of a cent per serving! How's that for chopping the food budget to an all-time low? And making your own breakfast cereal is just the start of the fun you can have with whole grain wheat. With this basic grain you can prepare nutritious pancakes and biscuits, big crunch-crusted loaves of bread, huge trays of healthful cookies, and

THE "RIPE" TEST   KNEADING   PUNCHING DOWN THE DOUGH

STEPS IN SHAPING A LOAF OF BREAD

Steps in shaping a loaf of bread.

FAN TANS   CLOVERLEAF

CRESCENTS   PARKERHOUSE

Variations on a roll.

your own homemade noodles and ravioli ... all for a few cents a serving.

Are there other grains in your friendly feed store that promise the same rewards? You can bet your new and healthy life there are. Rolled oats, corn, and barley are just the start of what's in store for you in this rock-bottom *real* health food shop.

A Review of Basic Food Costs

Prices quoted in books risk being obsolete before the volume leaves the presses. But if you know what basic foods cost as

FAMILIA: SURVIVAL FOOD

JUD EAGLE/WILLAMETTE BRIDGE, 522 W. Burnside, Portland, Oregon 97209

Familia is a grain, fruit and nut combination developed by the Swiss. Some friends living in the Bay Area gave me the recipe and I, in turn have passed it on to others—most of whom had never heard of the mixture.

Doing some research on Familia, I have found that a few large grocery and health food stores stock it already packaged. But some ingredients are left out, and it's also so expensive, that many of us couldn't afford it. It's much more inexpensive, and more enjoyable to make your own.

Supplemented with fresh vegetables and fruits Familia is a perfect survival food, containing everything your body needs to stay healthy. You may use it cooked as a hot cereal, uncooked as a cold cereal, in breads, cookies, or eat it as it is.

Originally, I intended to use Familia as a nutritious supplement to a city diet, but if you're into backpacking trips and mountain living, it's the answer for a perfect, light-weight compact food.

Here is the recipe for a 15 lb. batch.

1 lb. oats	1 lb. sunflower seeds
2 lb. wheat flakes	1/2 lb. pumpkin seeds
2 lb. rye flakes	1 lb. sesame seeds
1/3 lb. soy flour	1 pkg. chia seeds
1 lb. wheat germ	2 lb. raisins
1 oz. rice polish	1 lb. dried fruit
1 lb. soy lecithin	1 lb. nuts

You can purchase the sunflower seeds, pumpkin seeds, rice polish, soy lecithin and chia seeds at one of the health food stores downtown. The other ingredients are carried by large markets. If you live in Portland, I would suggest Jimmy Corno and Sons, across the Morrison Bridge on Union.

The cost for 15 pounds? Around 12 or 13 dollars. Happy eating.

this book goes to press, you'll at least have a jumping-off point. For example, if you read that soft red wheat was going for about $3.20 per hundred pounds wholesale at the farm when this book was printed and six months later you see it at $4.20, you'll know which way the price went, what to expect in the future, and more important, how the price compares with what you have to pay retail for a comparable product.

Take a look at the current commodity level. By commodity we mean the basic price per hundred pounds as quoted in the business sections of most papers. These prices were taken from a recent bulletin of a commodity newsletter.

Barley #2 Western	$3.00
Blackeye Beans	$12.00
Corn, Yellow #2	$3.00
Rice, Milled #1 head	$12.50
Wheat #2 Soft Red Winter	$3.20

You can often buy at these prices or close to them if you locate a grain wholesaler. Check the Yellow Pages.

Some Other Basic Foods That Will Save You Many Dollars

Barley   Barley is a really great grain. It's a basic ingredient in beer as barley malt and it forms the bulk of a popular soup. The soup is labeled *beef* but from where I stand the can is about three-fourths barley with the balance water and a few bits of stew meat.

Barley is available at most feed stores and is as cheap as or cheaper than any other grain. It's wonderful in soups, can be added to cooked cereals, makes a fine bread, and generally can be used anywhere you would use rice, millet, or similar basic grains.

Rice There's only one kind of rice to buy and that's organic brown rice. Brown rice has all of the valuable minerals and vitamins that make it an almost perfect food. As you will recall, hundreds of millions of people throughout the world do heavy work every day of their lives on a diet of little more than boiled brown rice.

The custom in America is to "polish" the rice to make it white and more attractive. The part that is polished off—the outer hull—is then used (and what a travesty this is) to absorb the oil on service station floors!

In addition to buying your rice in its natural brown state, buy it in the largest quantity that you can afford or store. A sack of brown rice purchased at the ranch or from a wholesaler will bring the cost down to ten or fifteen cents a pound.

Rice is such a versatile food, it can be used in anything from soups to desserts. You might want to try cooking it as a cereal for breakfast, adding raisins, dates, chopped apples, and nuts and serving it with milk and a little honey. We guarantee you'll have energy and good spirits the like of which you've never known before.

Millet Everyone has handled millet if he has ever had a pet bird; it's one of the main ingredients in "bird seed." It consists of little round globes about one-sixteenth of an inch in diameter. It's a grain food that has been used since antiquity, and tens of thousands of people all over the world still depend on it. It is eaten with gusto in Greece, Russia, India, China, Germany, Austria, and Italy. In Africa it's a staple food.

Millet is easily grown and in many parts of the world grows wild. You can purchase it from almost any feed store or pet store and the cost is very low—most often under ten cents a pound.

To bring out the flavor of millet, you would usually mix it with other foods. For example, it can be simmered until tender and then added to meat loaf or stew. It can be added to soup as is or cooked up in stock and served as an accompaniment to meat or fish. Try it in waffles and pancakes or as a substitute for cornmeal in any recipe, using a cup of millet for a cup of cornmeal. The author has made a delicious candylike snack by slowly cooking millet with honey and letting it harden into bars.

Corn In its basic form, corn is sold in many feed stores. For maximum nutritional benefit, buy it in undegerminated form. Making your own cornmeal is simple. Just pour about a cupful in your blender and turn it on to high speed. Keep an eye on it and remove when you have the desired grind. This

freshly ground cornmeal can be used in many ways, most of which may already be familiar to you, such as cornbread, muffins, pancakes, Indian pudding, and tamale pie.

Corn is an important food throughout the world, since it requires a relatively short growing period. Only a little more than two months is needed to bring a crop to harvest. Primitive man depended largely on corn crops for survival and we find legends and mythology concerning corn in the history of many ancient cultures.

Grinding Your Own Flour and Meal

The old stone flour mills of our forefathers produced flours and meal retaining all the important elements of each kernel of wheat and grain of corn, including the vital germ oils. There was no heat problem during milling that caused rancidity and spoilage of flours. There were no processing problems that resulted in loss of vital nutrients.

That's why breads, biscuits, and other baked goods tasted so much better. Fortunately it's possible to have these benefits today, and at less cost. The method is simple. Buy a hand- or motor-driven home grain and flour mill. While there are many varieties on the market, here are two that are typical of what you can obtain in a store or by mail.

The hand-operated Corona corn and grain mill is manufactured by Landers, Frary and Clark in New Britain, Conn. If you live on the West Coast, you can order one (Model No. 1C) for about $12 from El Molino Mills, 3060 W. Valley Boulevard, Alhambra, Calif.

There is a motor-driven flour mill called the All-Grain flour mill manufactured by the All-Grain Company, P.O. 115, Tremonton, Utah 84337. There are two models available. The smaller, Model A-33, will produce 8 to 10 pounds of bread flour per hour and costs around $160.

If you are fortunate, you may be able to locate a secondhand grinder for a considerable saving, but any investment will soon more than pay for itself in greater health.

How and Where to Find Natural Foods

The foods that nature has provided for use give us all the nutritional benefits we need. Unfortunately, for the convenience of packaged and processed foods we are giving up many of the valuable nutrients. Worse yet, other substances which are often worthless and harmful have been added in their place, primarily with the idea of keeping the foods from spoiling. Thus we are losing on two accounts.

It's really quite simple to avoid being poisoned or cheated, though. Just buy foods in as close to their natural state as you can. Here are some examples of these basic foods:

Apple cider—unsweetened, no preservatives
Baking yeast—cakes or dried
Buckwheat—whole grain, hulled
Buttermilk—from raw milk source
Cheeses—natural, unprocessed
Corn grits—freshly cracked, unfumigated
Cottage cheese—made from raw fresh whole milk
Eggs—fresh, fertilized
Flours—freshly ground, preferably stone ground

Fruit juices—unsweetened, unstrained, freshly squeezed

Fruits—dried, sun-dried, unsulphured

Herbs—preferably fresh

Honey—raw, unfiltered, 100 percent pure

Maple syrup—100 percent pure

Milk—fresh, raw, certified if possible

Milk powder—low heat, spray process

Nuts—fresh, raw, unsalted, unoiled

Oil—of vegetable origin, unhydrogenated, crude, fresh, cold-pressed

Peanut butter—from whole peanuts with skins, no additives

Rose hips—fruit of the rose

Rye—whole grain

Seeds—whole, untreated, not fumigated

Soy flour—freshly ground, unfumigated

Soybeans—organically grown

Sprouts—from whole untreated seeds, beans, or peas

Vegetables—fresh, unsprayed

Wheat germ—raw, fresh

Yogurt—made from Bulgarian yogurt culture

It's obvious that you can enjoy a hearty and nutritious diet from this large selection of foods. There's no need at all to buy "junk" foods when so much that is healthful and inexpensive is available.

To find sources for buying these natural foods, look in the Yellow Pages, both for your own city and for the largest one nearby. Look under listings such as groceries, vegetables, health foods, hay, feed and grain, fish markets. etc. Try the wholesalers, too. Sometimes you can buy in quantity, as with a neighborhood co-op arrangement where a group gets together, buys in large amounts, and splits up the cost along with the bulk purchases. This way each individually is able to realize a considerable saving.

In summary, there are many sources for finding natural foods and purchasing them economically. Drive into the country and look for roadside stands. Many offer natural, home or farm grown produce that is cheaper and far fresher than anything you can buy in the city markets.*

How to Cut Your Food Bills 20 Percent Instantly!

This heading sounds as if we're promising miracles. Well, we are. We can tell you in one four-word sentence how to spend 20 percent less on food and here it is: CUT OUT ALL WASTE.

According to studies of the habits of the American public, almost 20 percent of all food purchased for the home is thrown away. How can you prevent this? There are several steps.

*For organic, natural food sources, send for a copy of *Guide to Organic Food Shopping and Organic Living*, Rodale Press, Emmaus, Pa., $1.

1. *Buy only what you will really eat*

Supermarkets are designed to get you to spend more than you intended to spend. There are several ways to counter this fiendish assault on your food budget:

A. Take a shopping list and stick to it, using iron will and a pair of blinders.

B. Take only enough money to buy the basics you planned to buy.

C. Have someone shop for you.

D. Shop by phone—many markets have this service now.

E. Never shop when you're hungry—you will find yourself buying high-priced gourmet foods and delicacies.

2. *Cook only enough for one meal*

Many foods are not palatable when reheated and so are wasted. Then, too, there is always the temptation to eat up the balance of a dish, if you have prepared too much. This is the road to obesity and wastefulness. Cook adequate amounts, but only just enough.

3. *If you do have leftovers, use them up in these ways:*

Cooked meats, poultry, fish in—
Casseroles
Creamed foods
Curries
Hash
Patties
Pot pies
Salads
Sandwiches

Cooked potatoes in—
Fried or creamed potatoes
Meat or potato patties
Meat pie topping
Potatoes in cheese sauce
Salads
Soups, stews, or chowders

Cooked vegetables in—
Casseroles
Creamed dishes
Meat, poultry, or fish pies
Salads
Sauces
Scalloped vegetables
Soups
Souffles
Omelets

Bread in—
Bread pudding
Croutons
Dry crumbs

Fondues
French toast
Meat loaf
Stuffings
Cooked wheat, oats, corn, or rice in—
Fried cereal
Meat loaf or patties
Souffles
Puddings
Muffins
Vegetable cooking liquids in—
Gravies
Sauces
Soups
Stews
Cooked or canned fruits in—
Fruit cups
Fruit sauces
Quick breads
Salads
Upside-down cake
Yeast breads
Fruit cooking liquids or syrups in—
Fruit cups
Fruit sauces
Fruit drinks
Puddings

There is a French method of using everything up. It's the centuries-old *pot au feu* . . . a kettle of soup that simmers on the back of most country people's stoves. This ever-new dish contains bits of everything that might have gone to waste. Naturally, it changes its character and flavor somewhat each day . . . but is that bad? Try this in your quest for good eating for less money.

Eat Less, But Better—Stay Slender and Healthy on Better Foods

One easy way to save money on foods is simply to eat less. An Italian found this out many centuries ago and his story is worth retelling. Luigi Cornaro, a Venetian, came from a wealthy family and wasted his early years on riotous living, drunkenness, and gluttony so that by the time he was forty, degenerative diseases had reached such a state that physicians despaired of saving his life.

Given up to die, Cornaro retired to a small country estate and took stock of himself. He was an intelligent man, well-educated for his times, and capable of profound reasoning. He came to the conclusion that the human body was designed to function most efficiently and well on the minimum amount of food that would maintain normal weight and strength. Overeating was not simply a waste of food but a definite strain and burden upon the body organs. He decided to experiment upon himself and found that, in his case, an intake of about fourteen ounces of solid food daily with a pint of wine best satisfied his needs. His food was the plainest and simplest kind—a coarse whole grain bread, a little meat—usually fowl—and a green salad. Caloric values were unknown five hundred years ago and so Cornaro concerned himself only with quantity. He found that in his own case the balance between enough and too much was so delicate due to damaged organs, that the addition of only two ounces more than he required would produce a severe digestive disturbance. This was perhaps fortunate, for it strengthened an already formidable resolution and Cornaro was able to stick to his diet so faithfully that he regained his health, became a noted architect and one of the leading citizens of the powerful Venetian republic, fathered a large family, and lived comfortably to the ripe old age of 102.

Cornaro wrote of his experiences and advised others to follow his example. He prescribed no diets, but suggested that each person experiment with the needs of his own body to discover the kinds and minimum amount of food which would maintain health, weight and vigor. He recognized that this would vary with the individual and the kind of exercise and work performed.

But, although Cornaro's advice has been widely read and his writings translated into many languages and published many times over, it is rare that anyone can be found with the courage, resolution and willpower to adhere to them. One notable exception was John D. Rockefeller, Sr., who recovered his health and lived to the age of ninety-six through careful attention to a minimum diet. In his case, as in Cornaro's, it must be pointed out that severe digestive

troubles practically forced the limitation of diet. With most of us, food and the pleasures of eating are so important that we can seldom summon the willpower to practice such Spartan restraint. It is, however, a valuable goal, for the nearer we can approximate this end, the greater will be our reward in improved health and a comfortable long life.

How to Eat Well on As Little as Two Dollars a Week   During a recent trip to Mexico, I discovered an intriguing fact about the price of food in that country. The government establishes a maximum price for staples—cornmeal, beans, rice and macaroni. Thus, even though a family might be extremely poor, they can always count on being able to buy at least some basic foods for the family for a few pesos (a peso is 8 cents).

Actually, this situation also exists in the United States. Seldom has the price of basic foodstuffs gone out of sight. Take a look at some current prices of staple items, selected just as this book went to press:

Potatoes	5¢ per lb.
Cabbage	8¢ per lb.
Cornmeal	20¢ per lb.
Flour	10¢ per lb.
Whole grain wheat	6¢ per lb. (in quantity)
Rolled oats	5¢ per lb. (in quantity)
Spaghetti or macaroni	22¢ per lb.
Pinto beans	15¢ per lb.

As you can see, a dollar still goes a long way in buying many pounds of these items. To show how these basic foodstuffs can be used to supply a reasonably varied and an assuredly healthy diet, read the following excerpt from an interesting experiment performed several years ago. In this test a man was challenged to live on *one dollar's* worth of food for an entire *week*.

Here is my report, and I'm willing to seal it with blood, notarize it, and swear on a stack of Bibles if you insist.

PURCHASED SUPPLIES

3 pounds whole hard wheat from feed store	.12
1 pound soybeans from feed store	.05
2 pounds powdered skim milk from bakery	.20
1 pint blackstrap molasses from bakery	.10
1 package iodized salt from grocery	.05
1 yeast cake from grocery	.05
1 pound salt pork from market	.24
Total	.81

There are several varieties of soybeans; and I like the big white ones—the kind used to make bean sprouts.

Blackstrap molasses is the refinery residue and contains all the concentrated minerals and vitamins removed in processing for white sugar. Bakers use it for flavoring and sweetening.

Buying is important when there is need for economizing. At the time these purchases were made, the market for select hard wheat was $2.22 per hundred-weight; for soybeans, $2.43. These are the prices the growers get for their top quality. The feed store is entitled to a fair mark-up for handling. But a local health food store asked 35¢ a pound for whole wheat in a fancy package; 25¢ a pound for soybeans; 30¢ a pound for powdered skim milk; and 30¢ a pint for blackstrap molasses. They have a very limited market and must charge accordingly, but you don't have to buy at these sources.

Milk dryers were charging 5¢ a pound retail at their plants. I don't know what blackstrap was selling for at the refinery, but it is comparatively inexpensive; most of it goes into stock feed. The very dark molasses at the grocery is "blackstrap"—they just don't admit it. They priced it at 18¢ for twelve ounces.

Of course no one likes to sell in these small quantities and you wouldn't want to buy in dribbles either. Wastes too much time and temper. Better economy would be to buy fifty or even a hundred pounds of wheat, if you can keep it dry and clean; ten to twenty-five pounds of soybeans; a five-gallon tin of blackstrap and ten pounds of powdered milk, providing you can keep it in air-tight tins, or tight glass jars. It absorbs moisture from the air and turns rancid if exposed needlessly.

Tuesday

Breakfast consisted of a couple of slices of bread, toasted lightly and smeared with a little salt pork drippings, plus a cup of "coffee." I put a tablespoon of the blackstrap into a cup and pour boiling water over it to make coffee. Then I stir it up good and lighten it with a little milk. Tastes about like Postum, and now that I'm accustomed to it I prefer it to the tannic acid solution that used to give us heartburn and indigestion in the Navy.

For lunch, I warmed up the soybeans and polished them off with a glass of milk and a slice of bread. You'd like my bread . . . it is 100 percent whole wheat and no fooling; heavy, dark, with a rich nutty flavor. It's the kind of "swarzbrod" the poor peasants of Europe had to eat while the nobility ate cake. But you'll remember that the peasants lived long and heartily while the aristocrats lost their teeth and their heads at an early age.

For supper, I took half a cup of soy grits, which I make by grinding them coarsely through my coffee mill, a pinch of salt and some salt pork drippings for added flavoring, and boiled the mixture in the simmer-cooker to make a thick rich soup—very like old-fashioned split pea soup. A slice of bread, a cup of mint tea, and a dish of raspberries and milk filled me up.

Afterward I cooked up a batch of whole wheat cereal with bits of salt pork from which I had fried out most of the grease. When it was thick and done, I poured the mixture into a pan to cool and set overnight, to make a variation of scrapple.

Friday

Breakfast: whole wheat cereal and molasses coffee.

Lunch: two slices of bread made into a sandwich with a filling of chopped watercress and a glass of milk.

By bringing the prices this resourceful gentleman quotes up to date, we find that he could do the same thing today for about two dollars.

I think that the moral to this story is that you could—if you had to—live satisfactorily on a very small amount of food purchased for a very few dollars. The way to view this experiment is to imagine that you have twice as much money and spend the extra sum on little touches to brighten up the menu. And even these odd foods need not be expensive. For example, raisins purchased in large paper sacks cost about twenty cents a pound. Added to cereal while it is cooking or to bread makes a whole new taste adventure out of these plain foods. Another good example is the common peanut. Available for about forty-five cents a pound in the shell, they can be ground into fresh peanut butter (something else, we assure you), chopped and sprinkled into cereal, on pancakes, waffles, or toast, added to bread, biscuits, or muffins, or just eaten plain with anything.

Another fine low cost "extra" food is honey. It is one of those foods that cost much less than one would expect and is loaded with all kinds of good qualities. (We'll go into that in another chapter).

Now let's have a reprise of one of our dollar-a-week meals with raisins, peanuts, and honey available to brighten it up. Tuesday's breakfast was really rather spartan . . . a couple of slices of bread toasted and smeared with salt pork drippings plus a cup of "coffee." Suppose you cook some raisins in a small amount of water. Eat those as a starter. Then chop up some peanuts, spread them on one of the pieces of toast and smother with honey. Hell's fire—even the kids who demand sugar-coated flakes would go for this sweet treat.

Three wonderful low-cost menu brighteners are the so-called variety meats—heart, kidney, and liver. Always available at a fraction of the cost of beefsteak, let's see how these could be added to Tuesday's lunch. With those beans, a rasher of liver fried almost crisp would have been just great . . . heart or kidneys could have been added to the beans while cooking, giving them added flavor, body, and nutrition. Friday's lunch was just a watercress sandwich with a glass of milk—very austere, you'll agree, but necessary if you want to stay within that dollar a week budget. But let's add a small amount of ingenuity rather than money to that meal. Regardless of where you live, there are many foods that can be had for the gathering. For example, wild rose plants bear a smooth round fruit known as rose hips. These can be eaten raw, cooked into a syrup, or made into an excellent jam. Few areas in the world don't have some form of wild, edible berry. There are blueberries, wild blackberries, whortle, deer, bear, tangle, and dingleberries, not to mention excellent wild cherries and cranberries. All can be eaten plain or cooked into a number of delicious concoctions.

So Friday's lunch could also include a dessert of baked wild cranberries made as follows:

> Dissolve ½ cup of honey in ½ cup water. Add 1½ cups of wild cranberries. Then cover and cook in a slow oven until tender. Remove from heat while berries are still whole and bright red. Eaten warm or cold, it could make a watercress sandwich meal something special.

While you may not ever reduce your food expenditures to the level described here, it's always nice to know what the lower limits are. It should also make you appreciate the advantages of having such a generous budget as a dollar a day!

How to Bargain for Foods

Few things in this world are real bargains. We've all had the experience of buying something for price alone and later regretting it. However, it is possible to find real food bargains if you know where to look and how to go about it.

For example, if you live near a food market that is closed on Sunday, drop in and make the acquaintance of the manager some late Saturday evening just before closing. Tell him that you are a regular customer and that you are interested in helping him by buying items which are not up to selling standards but which are still edible and wholesome. For example, it's hard to sell an apple that has a worm hole or soft spot when there are perfect apples for the same price. There's nothing wrong with an apple of this type that a paring knife can't cure in about two seconds.

Your task is to buy foods of this type as cheaply as you can. Remember that your grocer usually doesn't waste this food—he takes it home and eats it himself. Therefore, he is not about to give it away, since it has value for him. However, when stocks are plentiful in this area, you can be sure that he is willing to sell it for very little. This is where your bargaining abilities can be put to good use. It's quite certain that a middle ground can be reached between you and the grocer as to a fair price for his produce that must be sold for cash on the barrelhead *now*. Once you have established this

BROWN TROUT

rapport, it will be simple for you to do almost all your fruit and vegetable shopping at the end of the week. If you should latch on to a whole box of soft peaches, make peach jam. If it's overripe tomatoes, stew them slightly then chuck them into your blender for instant sauce, which you can freeze or bottle. Perhaps you'll be acquiring a large quantity of oranges with dry skins . . . great for juice but hard to sell. Squeeze them and freeze the result.

Variations on the Theme

This same technique can be applied to many other types of stores—bakeries, meat markets, fish and seafoods shops. For example, many bakeries will not hold products over the weekend. This gives you an opportunity to stock your freezer with low-cost baked goods for perhaps half their regular retail price. Meat markets are coming under stricter control as far as selling older meat is concerned. Unless meat is actually spoiled, the darkening caused by too much exposure to light in the display case has nothing to do with its wholesomeness and nutritional value. You can eat much higher on the hog by taking advantage of the aversion of many to buying anything in the meat market that is not blood-red, fresh cut beef.

Fish and seafood shops are especially vulnerable to sharp bargainers. Fish is notoriously poor in keeping qualities. Thus, you can make an agreement with your local fish monger to take anything off his hands that is approaching unsalability. What can you do with a fish that will only last another day? Well, you can cut it up and freeze it, make it into a bouillabaisse and freeze that. Further, you can smoke it for almost indefinite life in your refrigerator. It's a lamentable fact that thousands of tons of perfectly good food are thrown away each day in America simply because we are a rich nation and care little for the losses that accrue from this wasteful practice. But you can take advantage of it by becoming a weekend warrior with regular attacks on the bargain counters.

How to Buy Wholesale

In a medium-sized American city there are two families occupying a huge old-fashioned house. The heads of the families, one a minister and the other an attorney, have learned to apply their natural intelligence and training to the problem of high food costs. Here's how they helped to chop their food budget to a minimum.

First of all they went to a local wholesale grocer, the kind that provides staple foods in modest amounts to small "mom and pop" grocery stores. The terms are usually cash on the proverbial barrelhead. The attorney and the minister told the wholesale grocer that they too would like to buy wholesale. Since they agreed to abide by the cash terms, the wholesaler was pleased to cooperate. What was the result? The team now buys hundred pound sacks of dried beans,

THE GREAT FOOD-BUYING CONSPIRACY

**PEOPLE'S OFFICE
BERKELEY, CALIFORNIA**

The food-buying co-ops take cooperation among members to make them work but savings are really something (20–50%). They function this way:

1. Neighborhood groups of five to eight living units get together and send representatives to a Thursday night central meeting. Every adult pays a non-refundable, one-time kitty fee of $2.00 or more as a cushion for fronting the money to buy things. At the meeting, orders are taken from the representatives of each group for fruit and vegetables.

At 6:00 AM Saturday morning, three or four people go down to the Farmer's Market in San Francisco and buy organically grown fruits and vegetables in boxes or crates and save lots of money.

Between 10:30 and 12:30 everyone comes and gets his stuff at a central location. The price per lb. is a bit marked up to cover waste—there's always left-over stuff since you have to over-buy a little (crates come in standard amounts). Mark-ups might be 1¢/lb. for items under 10¢/lb., 2¢ under 20¢/lb. 3¢ under 30¢/lb. etc.

You'll need:

1. large vehicles (two if over 30 living units are buying).
2. Two bookkeeper-cashiers and a table.
3. Space-two or three spaces in your parking lot.
4. Two or three scales ($1–$3 used at Value Village in Richmond or Oakland or at Flea Markets, baby scales are best).
5. CASH to pay the farmers—no checks accepted.
6. Paper bags and boxes so people can carry their stuff home.
7. One person to dispose of left-overs (see "Dry Goods' below).

2. Domestic and imported cheese at a 20% discount (on 20 lbs. or more) is available from the CheeseBoard on Vine near Walnut in Berkeley.

The order, composed of each group's orders combined is phoned in on TUESDAY MORNING (make sure and tell them you're a new group), and picked up at 8:00 PM Friday night. It is paid for then.

The cheese is cut up and weighed on Friday night, and put into packages for each group. It is distributed TO GROUP REPRESENTATIVES on Saturday morning with produce or dry goods (see below). Group reps pay the cashier for their group's order.

You'll need two-three people to handle cheese.

3. Once a month or so you may want to buy good, organic dry goods. The prices are well below even non-organically grown things bought in the supermarket. You may want to contact Bill O'Connell or Marcia Binder at FOR THE LOVE OF PEOPLE, on Telegraph in Oakland just this side of the new freeway overpass on the right as you head south. (No phone). They are a health food co-op and they get good things at low prices if you buy in large quantities (like 100 lbs. of flour, 30 lbs. of raisins, etc.

FOR THE LOVE OF PEOPLE needs our help in going and getting the stuff, as their truck can't hold too much. Contact other co-ops to find out when everybody's going, and a caravan of People's Co-ops can go together to the wholesalers.

Sometimes dry goods can be purchased in large quantities at very reasonable prices therefore:

1. Storage space is needed, preferably a kitchen or room with a sink. Maybe you could wheedle out a basement room from your landlord or manager (ask the latter to join, if he's a resident!) near where you distribute produce.

   You also need plastic-bag lined garbage cans and five gallon ice cream containers for storage, as well as ladies, scoops (cut out plastic bleach bottles are great!) and funnels. Also jars for honey, peanut butter and oil.

2. Lots of front money is needed—one way is to sell $5.00 or more worth of SCRIPT to members, enough to cover the cost completely each time you make a dry goods run. Members then pay in script for dry goods!

The same price mark-up system as for produce is advised. There is always waste.

Dry goods are distributed at the same time as produce.

Bookkeeping for dry goods is easy with script. Script in $1.00 amounts can be used, with purchases which come to under or over the even dollar being paid in script and change You'll need one or two cashiers, and one or two people to help weigh things out. (P.S. Script could be paper, coins, special stamped objects, you name it.)

GENERAL HINTS: In the case of produce and dry goods, everyone weighs his own and tallies his bill, with the cashier checking the addition. Equal participation and equal responsibility. It works if you're careful to be accurate. Cheese is another story. Cutting is tricky as cheese varies in density from one kind to another. Waste is more costly at 70-90¢/lb.

Produce buyers should try to get to know the farmers and should draw up the price list on the way back. A blackboard is handy for listing prices.

rice, and other basic staples, huge wheels of cheese and spices in bulk form. The big house that the two families occupy has an enormous storage room or pantry and this has begun to look like a wholesale grocery facility itself.

Cooperative buying of this type is extensively practiced in many fields and is one of the simplest and most effective ways of cutting costs. Even if you operate alone, find out where the wholesale food sources are in your town and attempt to make arrangements to buy there as often as possible.

How to Save on Food Bills by Preserving Your Own Foods

There are a number of practical ways to preserve foods. These include drying, smoking, freezing, and canning. The advantages of knowing some or all of these methods are obvious.

Let's assume that some fisherman friend has just presented you with a twenty-pound yellowtail or half a dozen four-pound barracuda. You cut off and eat what you can of the fresh fish and then debate what to do with the balance. Nothing tastes better than smoked fish, so knowing how to smoke one will pay off both financially, nutritionally, and in the gourmet department.

The same holds true for a windfall of fresh apricots. Perhaps you have made arrangements to pick them up in some farmer's orchard for a few cents a pound. Here a knowledge of drying, canning or freezing will make your winter more pleasant.

So consider learning how to save foods for future use with some or all of these methods.

Drying The easiest way to preserve anything from cuts of beef to apricots is to dry them. Beef, for example, is cut into long strips about one-half inch thick. The strips are then hung in a dry place that has plenty of sun and air circulation and is well-protected from insects. They will gradually dry to a hard, leathery texture, creating what is known as beef jerky.

The jerky may be kept almost indefinitely without refrigeration. It can be eaten as is or cut up and used in stew, soup, or other beef dishes. For a low budget it's hard to beat for economy and good taste. Keep in mind that all kinds of meat can be preserved in this manner, including venison, moose and bear.

The equipment needed for drying fruit can be very simple. In order to work rapidly after the fruit is picked it will help to get the equipment ready ahead of time. Be sure it is clean. You will need:

1. Sharp knife to pare and cut fruits (stainless steel prevents coloration)
2. Wooden board to make cutting easier

3. Pan, kettle, or pot in which to wash the fruit

4. Plenty of clean water

5. Trays or mats on which to spread the fruit to dry—trays should be thoroughly scrubbed and dried

6. For each tray or mat, a piece of clean, loosely woven cloth, two inches longer and two inches wider than the tray.

Then follow these step-by-step directions to dry the fruit:

1. Select the best quality of fruit, as the finished food can be no better than the fruit with which you start. Select fresh, ripe fruit. Gather it as early in the morning as possible. When fruit is right for eating it is right for drying. Fruits bruise easily so handle with care.

2. Place the fruit in the pan and pour clean water over it. Wash carefully, lift fruit from the water, empty the pan and repeat if necessary.

3. Peel or pit the fruit as needed.

4. Cut or slice the fruit into thin pieces, as needed. Thick slices dry slowly.

5. Spread fruit on clean dry trays or mats, one layer in thickness.

6. Cover with loosely woven clean cloth, mosquito netting, or wire screen to keep insects and dust from getting on the food. Fasten the cloth so it will not blow off.

7. Place the trays of fruit in the sun to dry. Raise one end of the tray if necessary so that all the fruit is in direct sunlight. In order to circulate air freely over and under the fruit, place the tray on blocks or stones. In order to keep them away from dust, animals and people, it is best to place the trays in a high location, such as on the roof.

8. Turn the fruit two or three times each day to speed drying.

9. Continue drying for several days until two-thirds dry.

10. Squeeze a handful of fruit to test for dryness. If there is no moisture left on your hand and the fruit springs apart when the hand is opened, the fruit is properly dried. Berries should rattle on the trays.

11. Put the fruit in a large container and cover it with a cloth or wire screen. Leave for eight to ten days, stirring the fruit two or three times daily.

12. Store the dried fruit in moisture-proof jars, pots, bags, or tin boxes with tight-fitting lids. Small containers are better than large because the food is less likely to become contaminated by mold or insects.

13. For containers with loosely fitting lids, dip a strip of cloth in melted paraffin and wrap, while it's warm, around the lid, overlapping it onto the jar.

14. If the food has been put in bags, place the small bags in a large container and seal it.

15. Store in a clean, dry, dark, and cool place. Check the foods often to see that they stay dry.

Smoking   There's nothing quite like a chunk of well-smoked fish for flavor and economy—the latter especially if you have smoked it yourself. Many people believe that smoking fish (and other vittles) is difficult. Nothing could be further from the truth. All it takes to smoke fish or meat is a source of smoke and some kind of container to retain the smoke.

Construct a wooden shelter to any convenient size from a small shed to one perhaps six feet square and eight or ten feet tall. The wood can be logs or poles and the siding anything convenient. Inside place crosspieces from which to hang the fish, meat, or hams to be smoked. Alternatively, you can add framed squares of ordinary one-inch mesh chicken wire on which to toss your smoked goodies-to-be. Next dig a shallow pit or line an area on the floor with cobblestones. Keep in mind that what you want to achieve is a cool smoke . . . thus your fire should be small and made from green hardwoods such as oak, hickory, and birch. Alder, willow and similar woods work fine but stay away from the soft, sappy woods such as pine and fir.

From here on it's just common sense and some experience. Place your meats and fish on the frames or hang them from the crosspieces. Build a small, smoky fire and then go about your business.

The smoking process should do its flavorful work in twenty-four to forty-eight hours. There are all kinds of fancy touches to be applied to the delightful avocation of smoking your own food. You can rub spices or garlic into the meat. If the food is somewhat dry at the start, rub on some butter, or a good quality cooking oil. A family I know resmokes all the ham they buy. It adds immeasurably to the flavor of store-bought ham or bacon.

Canning and Freezing   So much has been written by experts on this subject that we won't labor the point further. To find out how you can freeze and can surplus foods of all types, invest in these USDA booklets. Just send your order to U.S. Department of Agriculture, Washington, D.C. 20250.

For canning:

> *Home Canning of Fruits and Vegetables*
> Rev. 1967, 32 pages, illustrated
> Catalog No. A 1.77:8/5   15¢

> *Home Canning of Meat and Poultry*
> 1966, 24 pages, illustrated
> Catalog No. A 1.77:106   15¢

For freezing:

Home Freezing of Fruits and Vegetables
Rev. 1967, 48 pages, illustrated
Catalog No. A 1.77:10/5   20¢

Home Freezing of Meat and Fish
Rev. 1967, 24 pages, illustrated
Catalog No. A 1.77: 93/3   20¢

Home Freezing of Poultry
Rev. 1967, 24 pages, illustrated
Catalog No. A 1.77: 70/3   15¢

These booklets contain solid, no-nonsense information that can make you an expert in the field of home food preservation. What kind of money can you save? In many cases the food that you preserve will come to you free. Therefore the only expense will be for the materials and time involved in preserving the food. Bradford Angier describes in his book *How to Live in the Woods for $10 a Week* how people who live in the wilder parts of the U.S. and Canada are able to acquire enough meat to last all year from just one moose or elk. Preserving some by smoking and some by canning or freezing can give a rural family enough variety to make them the envy of city folks who are shelling out one to three dollars for one pound of beef (and full of chemicals at that!).

The Ten Commandments for Meat Buying

If a housewife will carry these with her when she is shopping and conform to the instructions, she will cut her meat budget by 25 to 35 percent, depending on how badly she has squandered her money previously. Her family will eat better and she will not feel so insecure at the meat counter.

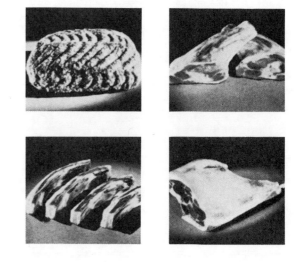

1. Read the weekly specials on the day they come out (usually Thursday), paying attention to the fine print. Look at the smaller ads as well as the big specials, and then decide where to spend the meat budget money.

2. Sit down and make a sensible shopping list, then stick to it at the market. Never include any prepared foods, such as luncheon meats, cooked chickens or ribs, prepared seafoods or stews, where you are buying 50 percent sauce in the expensive package.

3. Buy ground beef in the form of ground chuck and either watch the specials or patronize a market that sells consistently lean and flavorful ground meats.

4. Buy U.S. Choice only and watch out for so called "House" brands.

5. Demand trimmed meat, i.e., all the tails off steaks and no hidden chunks of fat in the roasts, or they go back.

6. Always try to buy boneless cuts during sales, remembering that one pound will serve at least three adults. These will be top sirloin steaks for charcoaling, rolled and tied boneless chuck roasts with little fat and no gristle. If any appreciable gristle appears during serving, show it to the butcher and yell.

7. Figure out the per portion cost of lean meat that you serve.

8. Do not buy standing rib roasts, wasteful short ribs, wedge bone sirloin steaks, stew meat at a dollar a pound, blade cut chuck roasts or cube steaks, "family" steaks, filet mignons, or fat briskets or flanks.

9. Never buy meat with yellow fat on it.

10. Buy various sized, airtight refrigerator containers to hold leftovers from meat cuts so that every three or four days you can serve a "no-cost" meal.

Forty-Nine Ways to Save on Food

1. Soak whole grain wheat overnight. In the morning grind it or place it in a blender. Add raisins, nuts, or other goodies. Eat hot or cold, with or without milk and honey. Inexpensive and nutritious.

2. Earn extra money to buy food by preserving wild blackberries in various sized jars with your own hand-printed label and selling them to tourists.

3. Mexican food is both tasty and cheap. Find the nearest Mexican food store . . . the kind where the Chicanos trade. There you'll find fresh tortillas for less than any market, chili peppers, chorizo, and other items that will make a frugal meal extra delicious.

4. Do the same thing with other foreign food markets, such as Italian and Chinese. They all cater to people with low budgets.

5. To stretch scrambled eggs, add a handful of cracker crumbs.

6. When strawberries are in season, find a roadside stand selling them by the flat at bargain prices, purchase one, and make fifteen or twenty jars of your own jam.

7. Swiss chard grows like crazy in any back yard, is better for you than spinach, and tastes better too.

8. Don't throw away the dandelions from your lawn; you can eat both root and leaf cooked or in a salad.

9. Is there a spaghetti factory near you? If so, go in and ask to buy their broken spaghetti in bulk. Many times they will send the "bends" of spaghetti very cheaply. Broken or bent, it will taste just as good when adorned with your favorite spaghetti sauce.

10. The author and his wife recently followed a tomato picking machine and ended up with enough ripe tomatoes to

make gallons of sauce. Much food is wasted during harvest . . . take advantage of this.

11. Bakers frequently sell, at low cost, loaves which do not conform to their standards. Too big, too small, broken slices, torn label, all point toward low-cost bread for you. Be sure it's real bread and not the common plastic foam in loaf shape.

12. Another tip: Did you know that many small bakeries will sell you unbaked dough? It's cheap and you can buy as much as you need. (Again, make sure that the bread has some food value).

13. For cheap fish loaf, use canned mackerel. If you add some good seasoning, it's hard to tell the difference.

14. Some people call it anise, others call it fennel and it grows wild all over the world. The stems can be eaten like celery or cooked with mushrooms, tomatoes, and olive oil.

15. You can grow your own fresh meat in a corner of your backyard. Rabbits are easy to care for and taste great fried or braised.

16. Here are three things to do with leftover bread (never throw it away):

Dip it in an egg-milk mixture for French toast.

Cube it, then sprinkle with melted butter and garlic salt for croutons.

Toss it in your blender for crumbs for meat loaf and other recipes.

17. One of the best investments you can make to save money on food is a big cauldron, the type that witches used for their magic brews. Use this big pot to boil up vast quantities of soups, stews, apple sauce, or chili beans. A great adjunct to the witches' pot is a five-gallon ceramic crock to store pickles or sauerkraut.

18. Speaking of sauerkraut, to make your own, simply shred the cabbage, sprinkle a little salt between layers, weight it down with a press of wood and a rock in a crock, and let it ferment.

19. If you live near the ocean or a lake or river, try setline fishing. A setline consists of a piece of line with as many hooks as you want to put on it, plus something to anchor it and a float. The latter can be just a piece of wood or an empty bottle. Bait the hooks and throw the whole thing in the water. Check periodically for fresh fish.

20. If you can locate a rotary meat slicer, you can make the toughest meats taste like T-bones. Just boil or roast meat, set the blade for the thinnest slice and go to work.

21. A great source of protein is MPF or Multi-Purpose Food. For further information on what it is and how to buy it, write Meals for Millions, P.O. 1666, Santa Monica, Calif. 90406.

22. Potatoes are cheap and give you a high return in

food value. For ideas on how to use them more often, send fifteen cents to the USDA, Washington, D.C. 20250, for their booklet of potato recipes.

23. For terrific onion rings, dip them in a batter of beaten egg, milk, and equal parts of cornmeal and flour and fry in your favorite oil. It's an inexpensive accompaniment to meat.

24. Eggplants in season are mighty inexpensive and highly nutritious. Try them stewed with onions, tomatoes, green peppers, mushrooms, and a pinch of Italian seasonings, or simply dip in egg batter and sauté.

25. For low budget scallops, buy shark steaks from fishermen. Cut out circular discs with a small biscuit cutter. Cook as usual and I defy anyone to tell them from real scallops.

26. World's cheapest soup: Add a handful of broken spaghetti and all the water you dare to leftover spaghetti sauce. Presto, spaghetti soup!

27. Keep an open mind; horsemeat can be used in lieu of beef in any recipe. It's only prejudice that keeps people from using this high-quality protein.

28. Liver, kidneys, and beef heart are far cheaper and really more nutritious than any of the so-called muscle meats. Consult your recipe books for some tasty ways to fix these inexpensive meats.

29. Somebody give you venison? Just grind it up with equal parts of rather fat hamburger. This is a great meat stretcher.

30. Do the same with bear, elk, moose, and other wild-tasting beasts.

31. Never forget, eggs have the highest quantity of high-quality protein per pound. Be sure they come from organically grown or "free-running" chickens though.

32. Buy a hundred-pound sack of organic brown rice. It only costs about twenty to thirty dollars by the sack. Then add it to everything you cook, from soups and meat loaves to puddings and muffins.

33. Real chicken is always a bargain and can be cooked in a hundred ways. Try slow-roasting one for five hours at 200°. It's the Spanish barbecue way and you'll never taste a more tender chicken.

34. Don't throw away that Halloween pumpkin. Steam it in your pressure cooker, puree it in your blender, and bake pumpkin cookies, pumpkin bread, pumpkin cake, pumpkin pie, and how about pumpkin ice cream? They're all yummy.

35. Know what rose hips are? They grow on any rose bush. Gather, clean, and use them in your favorite orange marmalade recipe.

36. Tough-meat tip: just braise it slowly and baste generously with cheap red wine.

37. Free tea: just gather mint from any wild damp place, dry it, and use it like tea leaves. Camomile blossoms make great tea also.

38. Cabbage rose leaves dried will give you still another no-cost tea.

39. Always use nonfat dried milk in any recipe calling for fresh milk. You'll save hundreds of dollars in your life-time—and be healthier.

40. Know what scrapple is? It's fried cornmeal or other cereal that was boiled and let harden. Slice it when cold, fry in butter or oleo, and serve with syrup or honey.

41. Did you know that soybeans can be cooked fresh or used in the form of flour, grits, milk powder, cheese, sprouts, sauce, milk, or pulp? These versatile beans yield a complete protein, comparable in quality to milk, eggs, and meat with-out the cholesterol. Best of all, you can buy twenty-five pounds of soybeans for what it would cost to buy three or four pounds of beef. They are available in many feed stores, or write to El Molino Mills, 3060 W. Valley Boulevard, Alhambra, Calif. 91803. El Molino Mills has a cookbook which includes soybean recipes . . . $1 postpaid. Other sources of information on how to use soybeans are the American Soybean Association, P.O. 158, Hudson, Iowa 50643, or the National Soybean Processors Association at 1225 Connecticut Avenue N.W., Washington, D.C. 20036.

42. Want to feel better fast? Give up all forms of refined sugar.

43. For a free copy of a great recipe on how to make your own mead with raisins, write Paradise Publishers, P.O. 88, West Point, Calif. 95255.

44. Next time you use a pumpkin, save the seeds, dry them, crack or crush and put them in water. The hulls will float and the kernel will stay at the bottom. Drain, dry the kernels a bit in the oven, and eat. Voila, a delicious nutmeat, chock-full of vitamins and minerals.

45. While you're at it, gather wild sunflower seeds and do the same.

46. For a great breakfast, boil whole wheat kernels in salted water for about twenty minutes or until tender, adding raisins or dates toward the end. Serve with milk and honey.

47. Cheap source of protein: Boil chicken necks and backs till tender, with rice, celery, and salt.

48. You can find wild black walnut trees all over and nobody seems to bother to pick the nuts. Take your family out for a picnic, gather a bushel or two (wear gloves, they stain your hands) and you've got a wonderful source of crunchy flavor to add to your baked goods.

49. For the ultimate in saving money on fruits and vegetables, how about growing your own. One packet of seeds will produce pounds.

Wild Apple

EDIBLE MATURE FRUIT

Fruiting branch

WHERE FOUND:
Tropics—Savanna.
Temperate—Evergreen scrub forest.
Temperate—Hardwood (seasonal) and mixed hardwood-coniferous forest.
Temperate—Coniferous forest.
Temperate—Mountainous area (undifferentiated highland).

The common apple known in cultivation came from Europe. Many kinds of wild apples, all relatives of the common apple, occur in the United States, especially the eastern part, and a few kinds occur in western United States. Wild apples are common throughout the temperate parts of Asia and also in Europe. Wild apples are found in open woodlands, and rarely can be found in densely forested regions. Most frequently, they occur on the edge of woods or in fields.

APPEARANCE. Most wild apples look sufficiently like their domesticated relatives to be easily recognized by the survivor, whether it be in Turkey or in China. The size of wild apple varieties is considerably smaller than cultivated kinds; the largest kinds usually do not exceed 2 to 3 inches in diameter, and most often less.

WHAT TO EAT. Wild apples may be prepared in the same manner for eating as cultivated kinds; that is, they may be eaten either fresh when ripe or cooked. If it becomes necessary to store up food for some time, the apples can be cut into thin slices and dried.

English Walnut

WALNUTS

EDIBLE WALNUT MEAT

HUSK

WHERE FOUND:
Temperate—Evergreen scrub forest.
Temperate—Hardwood (seasonal) and mixed hardwood-coniferous forest.
Temperate—Mountainous area (undifferentiated highland).

The English walnut in the wild state is found from southeastern Europe across Asia to China, and is abundant in the Himalayas. Several other species of walnut are found in China and Japan. The black walnut is common in the eastern United States.

APPEARANCE. Walnuts grow on very large trees, often reaching 60 feet in height. The divided leaves are characteristic of all kinds of walnut species. The walnut itself is enclosed by a thick outer husk which must be removed to reach the hard inner shell of the nut.

WHAT TO EAT. The nut KERNEL ripens in the autumn and may be broken out in the ordinary way by cracking the shell. Walnut meats are highly nutritious because of their protein and oil content.

NOTE: The husk of "green" black walnuts can be crushed and sprinkled into small, sluggish streams and pools to act as a fish stupefying agent.

Wild Onion

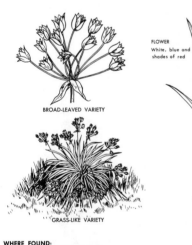

BROAD-LEAVED VARIETY

GRASS-LIKE VARIETY

FLOWER
White, blue and shades of red

Ground level

EDIBLE BULB
3-10" in ground
½-5" in diameter

WHERE FOUND:
Temperate—Evergreen scrub forest.
Temperate—Hardwood (seasonal) and mixed hardwood-coniferous forest.
Temperate—Prairie.
Temperate—Steppe.
Any climatic zone—Desert scrub and waste.
Temperate—Mountainous area (undifferentiated highland).

Wild relatives of the common onion occur widely throughout the North Temperate Zone. Many occur in North America in both moist and arid regions. In Europe and Asia, wild onions are very common over a wide range of habitats: moist areas, deserts, and mountain tops. They are especially common in Central Asia.

APPEARANCE. The onion plant grows from a bulb, which may be buried 3-10 inches below the ground. On most kinds of onions, the leaves are usually somewhat grasslike, although there is a whole group of wild onions with leaves that are several inches wide.

Onion flowers are white, blue, and shades of red. The bulbs of some kinds are very small—½ inch in diameter—whereas some of the larger kinds may be 5 inches in diameter.

WHAT TO EAT. The BULBS of all onions are edible. The foliage and bulbs of all onions emit a characteristic oniony odor and taste. This is a good test to distinguish them from other kinds of bulbous plants.

Wild onions are never poisonous.

Foods for Free

Much has been written on this in recent years. Experts like Bradford Angier and Euell Gibbons have produced a raft of fine books. Most are available in your local library and some are in paperback. In addition there are some inexpensive government texts on the subject. Include this batch in your no-cost food reference library.

Survival, USAF	$4.25	From U.S. Government Printing Office Washington, D.C. 20402
Survival, U.S. Army	$3.50	From U.S. Government Printing Office Washington, D.C. 20402

Take a look at what you'll find in the above books. With help of the pictures and the text, you'll find yourself gradually adding items to your diet that will not only be absolutely free, they'll be fresh, wholesome, and free of pesticides and chemical fertilizers.

6 Houses, Sixty-Five Dollars Each and Up

Housing takes the biggest bite out of a paycheck. The main reason for this is that someone is making one hell of a profit. Whether you buy a little green and yellow, ticky-tacky box or rent a paper-walled apartment, you will pay out much more than you need to stay out of the rain. More than 130 years ago, gentle but incisive and independent-minded Henry David Thoreau gave this matter some thought. He decided to prove that housing need not cost a small fortune. This is his own story about the home that he built for himself next to Walden Pond, not far from Concord, Massachusetts:

> Near the end of March, 1845, I borrowed an axe and went down to the woods by Walden Pond nearest to where I intended to build my house, and began to cut down some tall, arrowy white pines, still in their youth, for timber. I hewed the main timbers six inches square, most of the studs on two sides only, and the rafters and floor timbers on one side, leaving the rest of the bark on so that they were just as straight and much stronger than the sawed ones.
>
> By the middle of April, my house was framed and ready for the raising. I had already bought an old shanty for boards. I took down this dwelling . . . drawing the nails, and removed it to the pondside by small cartloads, spreading the boards on the grass there to bleach and warp back again in the sun. . . .

Similar in concept and structure to Thoreau's Walden house, this all-cedar cabin has survived more than one hundred winters in the rainy state of Washington. Incidentally, since this one is totally abandoned, it would be a great place for some short- or long-term hiding-out with little expense. (USDA)

At length I set up the frame with the help of some of my acquaintances. I began to occupy my house on the 4th of July, as soon as it was boarded and roofed for the boards were carefully featheredged and lapped so that it was perfectly impervious to rain . . . before boarding I laid the foundation of a chimney at one end, bringing two cartloads of stones up the hill from the pond.

I have thus a tight shingled and plastered house, ten feet wide by fifteen long and eight foot posts, with a garret and a closet, a large window on each side, two trap doors, one door at the end, and a brick fireplace opposite. The exact cost of my house was as follows:

Boards	$ 8.03½	mostly shanty boards
Refuse shingles for roof, sides	4.00	
Laths	1.25	
Two secondhand windows	2.43	
One thousand old brick	4.00	
Two casks of lime	2.40	That was high
Hair	0.31	More than I needed
Mantletree iron	3.90	
Nails	3.90	
Hinges and screws	0.14	
Latch	0.10	
Chalk	0.01	
Transportation	1.40	I carried a good part on my back
In all	$28.12½	

Recently I visited a small commune in the Western hemisphere (that's as close as the members want it identified) and found a young couple who had built a complete home for a

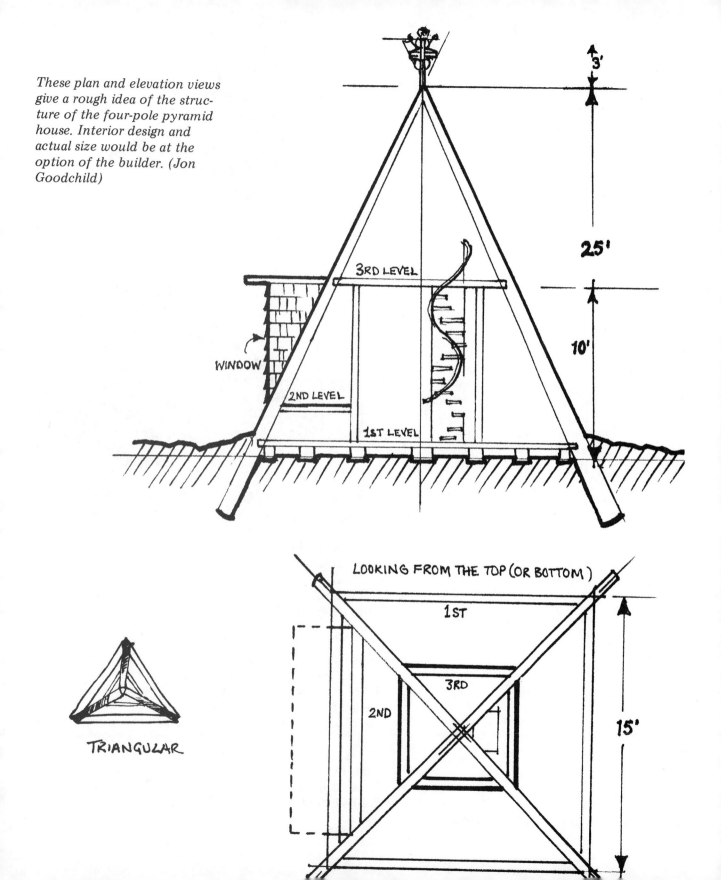

These plan and elevation views give a rough idea of the structure of the four-pole pyramid house. Interior design and actual size would be at the option of the builder. (Jon Goodchild)

3'

25'

3RD LEVEL

WINDOW

10'

2ND LEVEL

1ST LEVEL

TRIANGULAR

LOOKING FROM THE TOP (OR BOTTOM)

1ST

3RD

2ND

15'

Exterior views of the sixty-five dollar wilderness pyramid show shingling but virtually any materials could be used. For example, the optional extension employs glass panels. (Jon Goodchild)

total cash outlay of $65. Here's the way it looks and here are some general plans. Their bill of materials reads quite differently from Thoreau's since they used practically all native materials or obtained them for nothing.

Insulation	$50.00
Nails	10.00
Miscellaneous items	5.00

Here are some of the methods they used to keep the cost down:

1. They gathered fallen logs from the nearby forest and hauled them to a small sawmill. The sawmill operator agreed to cut the logs into rough planks for 50 percent of the finished output. Thus they obtained as many planks as they needed for only the cost of gathering and hauling them. Since the trip to the sawmill corresponded to their normal shopping trips, nothing was deducted for transportation expenses.

2. They were able to get permission to dismantle two small old houses and one rather large abandoned workshop. These structures yielded enough windows, doors, hardware, finished lumber, and miscellaneous items to complete their house.

3. The main components of the house, i.e., the twenty-foot long logs that comprised the basic "tipi"-like structure, were cut down on their property during routine land-clearing operations.

4. The only utility in the house is water piped from a nearby lake. They are content with Aladdin kerosene lamps, heat from their native stone fireplace, and a cast iron kitchen stove which someone gave them, and an outside Chic Sale. During the summer, bathing is done in the nearby lake and wintertime finds them heating a big cauldron over the fireplace for indoor showers at the hearth.

This kind of house could be comfortable even when world conditions deteriorated to an all-time low. They have sought and achieved virtually total self-sufficiency. They determined to find substitutes for the kerosene that they used in the Aladdin lamp and for the electricity that was now used to pump the water up from the lake. The lamp could be operated with melted fat or tallow rendered from farm animals and the water could be pumped up from the lake with a small windmill.

You may not want to sacrifice your favorite comforts to achieve this degree of independence. However, it makes sense to look ahead to the day when everything we have taken for granted may not be readily available. Think of the great sense of security you would have from knowing that no matter what happened to the outside world, you would be assured of a warm and reasonably comfortable place to live. A house like this in conjunction with a small piece of farmland would make you a veritable Robinson Crusoe, or, with a family, a Swiss Family Robinson.

Basic Housing Requirements

Now that you've seen with your own eyeballs actual proof that housing can be constructed inexpensively, we'll go into more detail. A good way to start the process of building is to write to the Superintendent of Documents, U.S. Government Printing Office, Washington, D.C. 20402, and ask for their 1972 price list. It's free. This leaflet lists hundreds of government publications relating to the construction and maintenance of homes. For example, it lists a publication on a solar-type farm cottage. It tells you how to obtain plans for cabins, A-frames, farm buildings, and simple shelters. Through the Government Printing Office you can obtain the addresses of facilities in your state that provide complete plans for cabins and homes costing as little as three dollars per plan.

In addition to basic planning information, the booklets listed cover such subjects as fireplaces and chimneys, built-in furniture, plumbing, roofing, sewage disposal, water supplies, and landscaping. All publications are extremely reasonable

and could be your best source of basic information on how to build your own home.

Another good idea is to go to your library and check the files for books on do-it-yourself home construction. About twenty years ago a book was published titled *Your Dream Home—How to Build It for Less Than $3500* (W. H. Wise and Co., N.Y., 1950). This book is typical of many written on the subject of home construction. You may be able to find a copy in your library or perhaps in a used bookstore.

If you want to build and own your own home far from city hassles, one typical solution is some form of cabin.

There is a tremendous amount of material available practically free on how to design and build your own country cabin. For example, write to the U.S. Government Printing Office, Washington, D.C. 20402, enclose a fat nickel and ask for Miscellaneous Publication No. 1074; you'll get back a sheet describing a picturesque two-bedroom cabin with a dormitory loft. An open-type ceiling gives a feeling of spaciousness to the kitchen and living area and cuts construction costs. The cabin is intended to be framed with poles, with a pole-supported deck; rough-sawn native materials, such as bark slabs, are proposed for the exterior.

This is a basic plan you should have, whether you build this model or not. After reviewing the general idea, you can buy the complete working drawings from the agricultural engineer at any state university. If there's a charge at all, it will be quite small (under five dollars for sure). To find out the location of your state university agricultural engineer's office, simply send your request to:

Agricultural Engineer
Federal Extension Service
USDA
Washington, D.C. 20250

He will forward it to the correct university.

The USDA has many other plans for rural buildings. They will send you a list on request.

One of the best books on constructing cabins is available from Lane Books, Menlo Park, California. It's called *Cabins and Vacation Houses* (a Sunset Book).* It has basic plans for very simple to super-elaborate rural cabins. One is the Tepee Cabin. It's only about 500 square feet on the main floor but has another 100 square feet for a sleeping balcony plus another 100 feet in a third floor storage attic. They figure the cost at between $4,000 and $5,000, including foundation, fireplace, plumbing, kitchen, and electricity. If you were to rough it for a while, they figure that the shell alone would cost about half this amount.

*Two dollars, plus ten cents for California residents. You might also write Lane and ask for their latest catalog.

pole-frame CABIN

Typical of the plans available from the USDA, a set of working drawings can be purchased for less than five dollars. (USDA)

24' x 24'

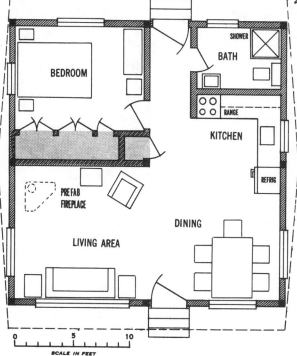

BEDROOM

SHOWER

BATH

RANGE

KITCHEN

REFRIG

PREFAB FIREPLACE

DINING

LIVING AREA

```
0        5        10
SCALE IN FEET
```

This one-bedroom structure, simply designed for comfort and economy, can be used as a vacation retreat or campsite. It features low-cost pole-frame construction, design simplicity, and flexibility of arrangement.

The use of poles permits rapid erection, minimum site preparation, and decreased foundation expenses, and they act as the wall framework to which other members are fastened. The life expectancy of a pole-frame structure, with the commercial preservative-treating processes in use today, can be as much as 75 years. The structure can be made very attractive both inside and out, depending on materials available, taste, and cost.

Maximum use is made of rough-sawn native lumber such as the board-and-batten siding. Several kinds of material are available for use as coverings.

Location and type of window treatment is flexible.

With a kitchen and bath suggested, the interior is efficiently arranged for pleasant living. A prefabricated fireplace could be installed if necessary.

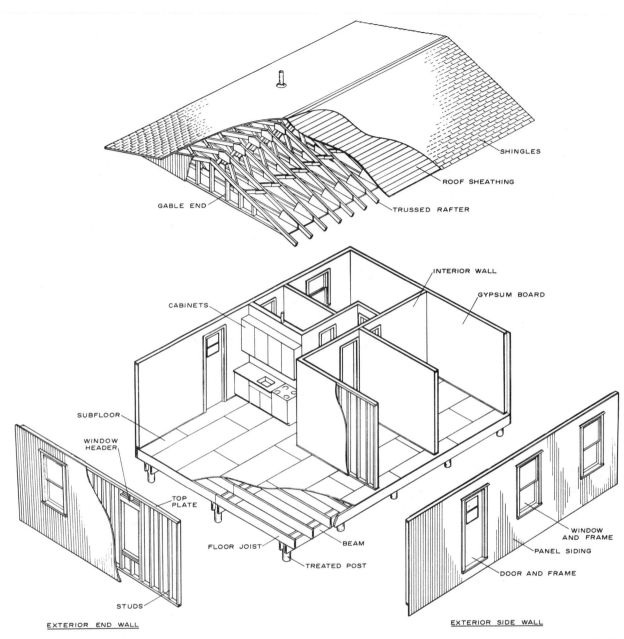

SHINGLES

ROOF SHEATHING

GABLE END

TRUSSED RAFTER

INTERIOR WALL

GYPSUM BOARD

CABINETS

SUBFLOOR

WINDOW HEADER

TOP PLATE

FLOOR JOIST

BEAM

TREATED POST

WINDOW AND FRAME

PANEL SIDING

DOOR AND FRAME

STUDS

EXTERIOR END WALL

EXTERIOR SIDE WALL

M 135 102

One of the best manuals on wood home construction is a government publication titled Low-cost Wood Home For Rural America. *(USDA)*

FIGURE 1.—Exploded view of wood-frame house.

Another design is the expandable "core." This core can be built in a couple of days and provides the absolute basics for cooking and sleeping. It's intended, of course, to be expanded as money and time permit. The cost of the core would be about $400.

Such a rudimentary, low-cost, easy-to-build initial dwelling is highly recommended for a survival-oriented, country-bound individual. It will give you the chance to try your hand at building without making too large an investment or too many construction mistakes. If the venture succeeds, then go on to further effort.

In another part of this comprehensive book on cabins there is a review of how a cabin can be built in four stages. A cabin lends itself to stage-by-stage development, since livability is possible at every stage. Also, rough construction (amateur hammer and saw work) is compatible with cabin appearance. Furthermore, lots of materials can be found right on site. The article suggests that a five-year building program can be practical and specifies the elements to be completed at each given stage.

Another good basic work on log and frame cabins is *The Wilderness Cabin* by Calvin Rustrum. This one is available through *The Mother Earth News*, P.O. Box 38, Madison, Ohio 44057, for $5.95 postpaid. They can also provide you with such useful books as,

Dome Cookbook (This one tells how to build a geodesic house from junked car tops)

Indian Tipi

How to Be Your Own Electrician and Plumber

Still another book, which is out of print but may be found in used book stores, is *How to Build Cabins, Lodges and Bungalows*. This one has heavy emphasis on log construction, which is hard work but has been eased by the use of chain saws and other power tools.

Try writing to *Popular Science* and see what they have available in the line of cabin construction booklets and books.

A gold mine of house plans, drawings of interiors, and building tips may be obtained from the following organizations for free.

American Plywood Association, 1119 "A" Street, Tacoma, Wash. 98401

California Redwood Association, 617 Montgomery Street, San Francisco, Calif. 94111

Simpson Lumber Co., 2000 Washington Building, Seattle, Wash. 98101

Western Wood Products Association, Yeon Building, Portland, Ore. 97204

Cooperative Farm Building Plan Exchange, U.S. Dept. of Agriculture, Beltsville, Md. 20705, or

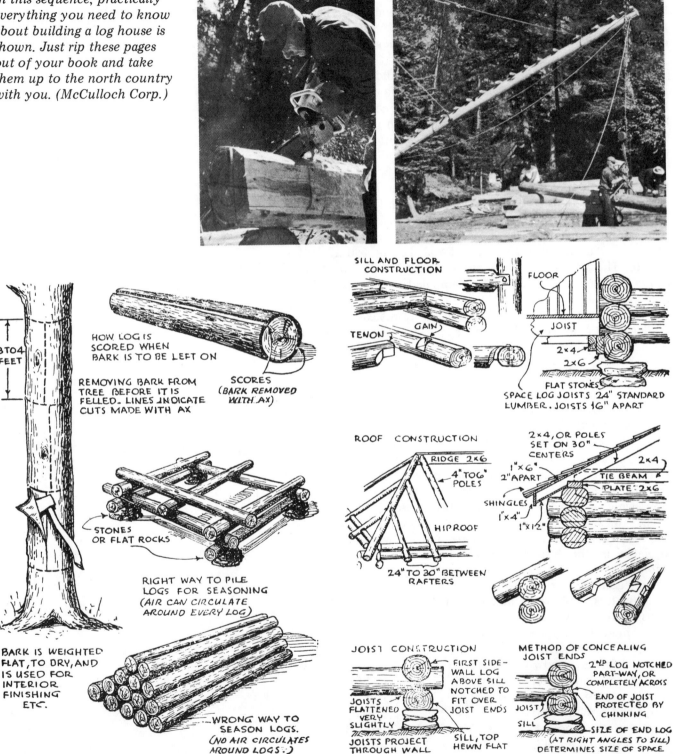

In this sequence, practically everything you need to know about building a log house is shown. Just rip these pages out of your book and take them up to the north country with you. (McCulloch Corp.)

3 TO 4 FEET

HOW LOG IS SCORED WHEN BARK IS TO BE LEFT ON

SCORES (BARK REMOVED WITH AX)

REMOVING BARK FROM TREE BEFORE IT IS FELLED. LINES INDICATE CUTS MADE WITH AX

STONES OR FLAT ROCKS

RIGHT WAY TO PILE LOGS FOR SEASONING (AIR CAN CIRCULATE AROUND EVERY LOG)

BARK IS WEIGHTED FLAT, TO DRY, AND IS USED FOR INTERIOR FINISHING ETC.

WRONG WAY TO SEASON LOGS. (NO AIR CIRCULATES AROUND LOGS.)

SILL AND FLOOR CONSTRUCTION

FLOOR

TENON

GAIN

JOIST

2×4
2×6

FLAT STONES

SPACE LOG JOISTS 24" STANDARD LUMBER. JOISTS 16" APART

ROOF CONSTRUCTION

RIDGE 2×6

4" TO 6" POLES

HIP ROOF

24" TO 30" BETWEEN RAFTERS

2×4, OR POLES SET ON 30" CENTERS

2×4

1"×6" 2" APART

TIE BEAM

PLATE 2×6

SHINGLES 1"×4"

1"×12"

JOIST CONSTRUCTION

FIRST SIDE-WALL LOG ABOVE SILL NOTCHED TO FIT OVER JOIST ENDS

JOISTS FLATTENED VERY SLIGHTLY

JOISTS PROJECT THROUGH WALL

SILL, TOP HEWN FLAT

METHOD OF CONCEALING JOIST ENDS

2ND LOG NOTCHED PART-WAY, OR COMPLETELY ACROSS

END OF JOIST PROTECTED BY CHINKING

JOIST

SILL

SIZE OF END LOG (AT RIGHT ANGLES TO SILL) DETERMINES SIZE OF SPACE

Manner of removing bark from tree before it is felled, the scoring of logs, and the right way of piling them to dry are shown above

In the illustrations above, directions are given for building a cabin floor, raising a roof, and constructing the joists

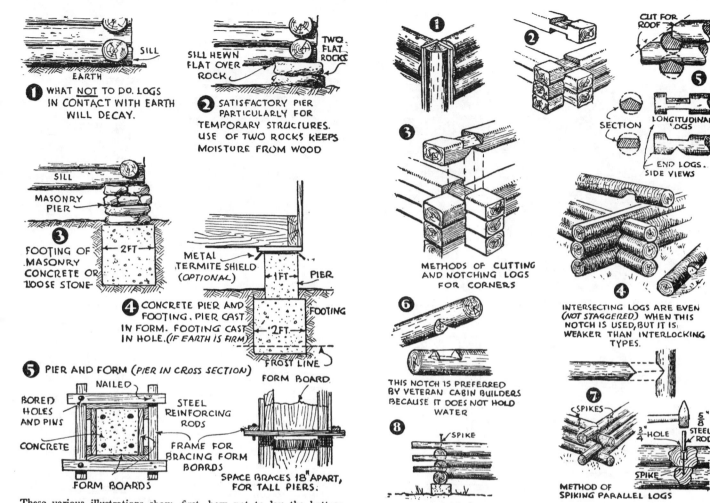

1 WHAT NOT TO DO. LOGS IN CONTACT WITH EARTH WILL DECAY.

SILL
EARTH

2 SATISFACTORY PIER PARTICULARLY FOR TEMPORARY STRUCTURES. USE OF TWO ROCKS KEEPS MOISTURE FROM WOOD

SILL HEWN FLAT OVER ROCK
TWO FLAT ROCKS

3 FOOTING OF MASONRY CONCRETE OR LOOSE STONE

SILL
MASONRY PIER
2FT

4 CONCRETE PIER AND FOOTING. PIER CAST IN FORM. FOOTING CAST IN HOLE. (IF EARTH IS FIRM)

METAL TERMITE SHIELD (OPTIONAL)
1FT
PIER
FOOTING
2FT
FROST LINE

5 PIER AND FORM (PIER IN CROSS SECTION)

NAILED
BORED HOLES AND PINS
CONCRETE
STEEL REINFORCING RODS
FRAME FOR BRACING FORM BOARDS
FORM BOARDS
FORM BOARD
SPACE BRACES 18" APART, FOR TALL PIERS.

These various illustrations show, first, how not to lay the bottom logs of your cabin, and then the proper methods that will insure long life to a cabin's foundation

1

2

CUT FOR ROOF

5

SECTION
LONGITUDINAL LOGS
END LOGS. SIDE VIEWS

3

METHODS OF CUTTING AND NOTCHING LOGS FOR CORNERS

4 INTERSECTING LOGS ARE EVEN (NOT STAGGERED) WHEN THIS NOTCH IS USED, BUT IT IS WEAKER THAN INTERLOCKING TYPES.

6 THIS NOTCH IS PREFERRED BY VETERAN CABIN BUILDERS BECAUSE IT DOES NOT HOLD WATER

8 SPIKE

7
SPIKES
3/4" HOLE
5/8" STEEL ROD
SPIKE
METHOD OF SPIKING PARALLEL LOGS

Here are a variety of corners from which to choose. No difficulty will be experienced in making any corner if these directions are followed

SILL CONSTRUCTION FOR LOG SIDING

2"×4" STUD

JOIST

FLOOR

LOG SIDING

2"×8"

FOUNDATION PIER OR WALL

OUTSIDE WALLS

2"×4"'S

INSIDE WALL

ONE FORM OF CORNER POST

FRAMING WINDOW OPENING (ALTERNATE METHOD)

DOUBLE STUDS (OPTIONAL FOR SMALL OPENINGS)

STUDS

2"×4"

1½" SPACE

2"×4"

WINDOW

HEADER

PLATE

TWO 2×4's ON EDGE

2×4's

SILL

THIS CONSTRUCTION PREVENTS BINDING OF WINDOW. UPPER 2×4 HEADER CAN BEND UNDER ROOF WEIGHT WITHOUT CAUSING WINDOW TO BEND.

LOG SIDING IS MADE WITH ROUNDED FACE LIKE WHOLE LOGS AND WITH SHIP LAP EDGE SO THAT EACH PIECE FITS SNUGLY INTO THE NEXT

These illustrations show the proper manner of building sills, walls, and windows when log siding is used in a cabin

WINDOW AND DOOR CONSTRUCTION CONTINUED:

RUSTIC WINDOW SHUTTER, MADE OF SAND-BLASTED WOOD, STAINED TO LOOK WEATHERED

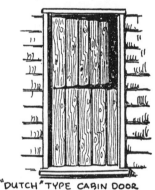

"DUTCH" TYPE CABIN DOOR MADE OF LOG SIDING.

FURNITURE:

BUNK

CORNER DETAIL OF TAKE-APART BUNK.

STOOL

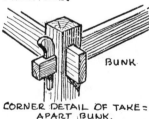

17½"-HIGH

12" TO 14" DIAMETER

1½-IN. POLES

DROP-TABLE CUPBOARD

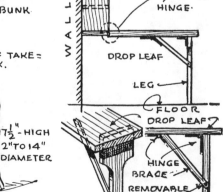

WALL

CABINET FOR DISHES ETC.

HINGE

DROP LEAF

LEG

FLOOR

DROP LEAF

HINGE

BRACE

REMOVABLE PIN

The manner of making window shutters, divided doors, and **rustic** furniture is clearly shown in these sketches

Extension Agricultural Engineer, Oregon State University, Corvallis, Ore. 97331

Write to Weyerhaeuser Corporation in Seattle, and they'll send you information on how to use their products. The U.S. Plywood Corporation of New York has published extensively detailed booklets on the use of plywood in home construction. Other sources of home-building information are the manufacturers of electrical equipment and plumbing supplies.

Available in increasing numbers are prefab dwellings. There are many advantages to prefab since all of the planning and design work is done for you. Some include packaged plumbing, wiring, windows, and doors. Prefabs range in size from the tiny "Bachelor's pad," 240 square feet, to relative giants such as the 1,500 square foot "Sequoia" model. These two are sold by K Products Corp., Box 489, Santa Rosa, Calif. 95402, and the Intermountain Company, Box 247, Auburn, Calif. 95603, respectively.

To decide whether a prefab fits your own country survival plan, send for the catalogs of various firms that manufacture them. Here is a list of prefab manufacturers scattered across the country.

ABC Package Homes, 2616 Springs Road, Vallejo, Calif. 94593

The Huntridge Corp., Box 18574, Kearns Station, Salt Lake City, Utah 84118

Nassau
21'8" x 23'

Cork
11' x 8'4"

Killarney
16'4" x 25'

Belfast
16'4" x 16'

Dublin
16'4" x 32'

Prefabs range in price from a few hundred dollars on up. Here is an assortment of prefabs by Lindal Cedar Homes. Notice that the Belfast unit can be easily expanded to become the Kilarney. (Lindal Cedar Homes)

Hurford Cedar Homes, Box 647, Burbank, Calif. 91503
Justus Solid Cedar Homes, 2116 Taylor Way, Tacoma, Wash. 98421
Lindal Cedar Homes, 9004 S. 19th Street, Tacoma, Wash. 98466
Pritchard Products Corp., 4625 Roanoke Parkway, Kansas City, Mo. 64112
Red-E-Cut Log Industries, 327-22nd Street, Oakland, Calif. 94612
Techbuilt, 127 Mt. Auburn Street, Cambridge, Mass. 02122

Building your own house could be the most rewarding thing you've ever done. Being able to create your own interior environment exactly as you want it is a gratifying experience, as anyone who's done it will tell you. Certainly there's lots of hard work, problems along the way, and often greater expense than you originally anticipated, but the end product is sure to delight you.

Many people have been convinced that house building is difficult and complicated. Actually, when reduced to its fundamental elements, it's very simple and within the capability of the average man or woman. Here's what you gain by building your own home:

1. Labor amounts to about 75 percent of the cost of a house. This means that if you build a $10,000 home yourself, it will cost you only about $2,500.

2. While you are building, you may decide that it would be nice to have a window in the shower, or a stairway and a trap door leading to the attic. It is no problem to suit yourself as you build.

3. You're absolutely sure of the quality of the house, since you will have selected and nailed down every last stick.

4. Building your own home satisfies the strong creative urge that we all have. When finished, the house will be not so much a house as an extension of your personality and life style.

If You Don't Want to Build You Can Always Bring Your Shelter With You

One of the best inventions for housing is the modern version of the gypsy wagon . . . the trailer. Recently the author and his wife purchased an eighteen-year-old, all aluminum Land Yacht. It was in poor condition inside, but the structure was basically sound. We spent $400 on paint, varnish, foam mattresses, linoleum, and carpet remnants, and now this venerable two-wheeler is the envy of all our friends. Twenty-five feet long with a separate bedroom, it's big enough for extended periods of living.

You can find fix-it-yourself trailer bargains all over the U.S. The best ones are those that are too big to use as travel

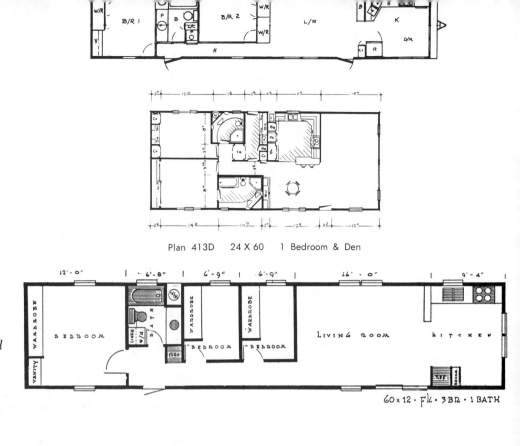

Plan 413D   24 X 60   1 Bedroom & Den

60 x 12 · FL · 3 BR · 1 BATH

These mobil-home plans reveal that all the conveniences of a conventional and far more expensive home may be obtained. The cost is often one-third, and you get the advantage of mobility.

trailers but too small to classify as a mobile home—from about twenty to thirty feet. The shorter ones can be expanded by adding a room, but if you buy one much longer than thirty feet you can run into towing problems.

Finding a secondhand trailer is easy. First check the classified ads. Then tour your community, looking into back yards and empty lots. Many times people leave a trailer unattended, thinking that no one will want it. If you approach the owner with a cash offer, you will probably get it for what you want to pay. Another good source of trailers are contractors, who often gut them and use them for field offices. When they are through with the project, they may want to sell the trailer.

Then there are the local insurance companies. They may handle the payoffs on fire- or collision-damaged trailers. They can tell you where the salvage is stored or to whom it was sold. In addition, they will be happy to put you on their list of bidders for trailers that are "totaled."

You might also try the older mobile home parks. The owners of these parks sometimes acquire trailers by death of the owner or default in rent and may want to dispose of the older models to make room for more modern mobile homes.

If you don't want to take the trouble to tow your own

The Sioux tipi is by far the most beautiful and practical tent ever invented by man. Its tall silhouette crowned with branching lodge poles are in harmony with nature. The Sioux consider it a temple as well as a home. The floor symbolized Mother Earth, and the cover represented the heavens. The lodge poles were trails leading to the Great Spirit. Truly the tipi was Big Medicine. (Courtesy Red Fox Tipi Co.)

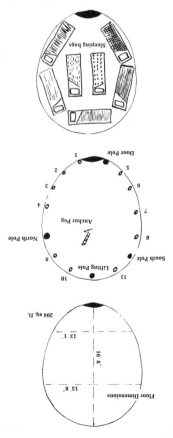

trailer to a country site, you can have this done by a professional trailer towing company. While their charges may seem excessive, keep in mind that a trailer hitch adequate to pull a large trailer costs upward of $200 and you must have a car or truck in good condition to pull it.

Throughout the United States there is much pressure against bringing in and living in trailers or mobile homes. These pressures are brought by building trades associations and local property owners who feel that trailers downgrade a residential area. However, if you find a piece of land far enough back in the boondocks, you probably won't be troubled. Furthermore many people have used a trailer house as the "core" of a larger house, which they built around it. You can view many examples of this if you travel down the coast of Baja California. Many trailer owners have completely surrounded their vacation trailers with quaint beach cabanas.

The advantages of bringing a trailer or mobile home to a rural site are many:

1. You'll have instant housing.
2. It will be paid for.
3. You can concentrate your efforts on making a living, growing vegetables, or otherwise doing your own thing.
4. If you decide that a place is too hot or too cold, sell or lease the property, hitch up your trailer and move on.
5. Trailers are really lots of fun. They give the owners the great sense of freedom and independence that the gypsies of Europe have enjoyed for centuries.

For further information on trailers and trailer living, I suggest that you write to the following publications:

Trail-R-News Magazine, 545 W. Elk, Glendale, Calif. 91204
Trailer Life, 10148 Riverside Drive, North Hollywood, Calif. 91602
Western Mobile Home News, P.O. Box 1131, Long Beach, Calif. 90801
Wheels Afield, 5959 Hollywood Boulevard, Los Angeles, Calif. 90028

(More on this in Chapter 11.)

Living Like the Indians

The American Indian enjoyed a way of life that you can re-create. Through centuries of development, he perfected a canvas shelter, the tipi. If you have never been in one, you'll be amazed at its feeling of solidity, warmth, and coziness. You can build one yourself from poles that can be found in any wooded area. Young pines, birches, or eucalyptus would make fine tipi uprights.

Waterproof canvas can be obtained from any supplier, directly or by mail. Just look under canvas specialties in the

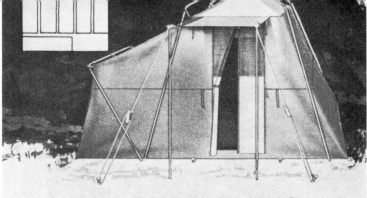
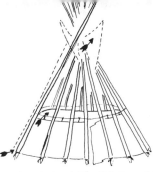

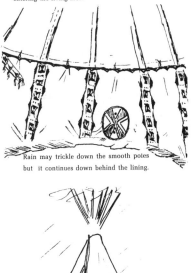

The Lining is an inside wall. Its lower edge rests upon the ground and may be overlapped with a ground tarp to seal out insects, water, and drafts. Air circulates upward between the cover and lining to ventilate the tepee. The lining prevents rain from entering the living area.

Rain may trickle down the smooth poles but it continues down behind the lining.

Smoke Flaps securely closed, and Anchor Rope tied to the Anchor Peg within, the tepee can withstand the heaviest downpours.

Smoke Flaps open wide and the cover propped up, the Red Fox Tepee becomes a giant umbrella during sweltering weather.

Yellow Pages. You can follow the plans as given in the tipi book mentioned above or just do your own thing. If you cook out of doors, you won't need the rather elaborate smoke-venting system required in Indian tipis. Another source of inexpensive fabric structures is your local war surplus dealer. They often have army tents at bargain prices. The Leonard Joseph Company, 1800 Stout Street, Denver, Col. 80202, has a beautiful complete stock of surplus army tents, ranging from huge ones to house twenty people down to small two-man units.

In many parts of the country, canvas shelters are placed on permanent wooden platforms. This is done so that the tent can be removed in case of extremely heavy snowfall or flood conditions. If you plan to live only part of the year in an area, this could be the answer to truly low-cost housing.

Geodesics

A great friend of the earth, R. Buckminster Fuller, invented a really amazing home built of triangular panels and called a geodesic dome. To get plans for this type of home, send five dollars to Sun Dome, *Popular Science*, 355 Lexington Avenue, New York 10017. The five bucks will get you plans for three dome sizes—sixteen and a half, twenty-five, and thirty feet. These plans are for a geodesic dome intended to be covered with polyethylene film. However, you could cover the basic framework with waterproof paper, plywood, aluminum, plexiglas or any other materials you wished. Also, you can write Pacific Domes, General Delivery, Bolinas, Calif. 94924, for *Domebook Two* ($4.20). It gives plans and details on all aspects of every type of dome shelter. Total costs run from $350 to $950.

Thousands of Fuller's domes have been built from greenhouse-sized ones to one 384 feet in diameter.

131

10x12-ft. high-rise tent

- 6-ft. wall height
- 8-ft. center height
- Zip door, windows
- 88x67-in. awning

$159
cash or
$8 mo.

Best family 10x14-ft. tent sleeps 10

- Aluminized reflective roof coating
- "Magic-loc" poles adjust tension
- Poly grommets won't rip, pull out
- "Arctic Seal" finish keeps tent dry

$189
cash or $10 mo.

[M] **Our best selling family tent**—120 sq. ft. of standup living area. Sleeps 8. Fast, pitching outside aluminum frame plus 3 canopy poles (ctr. adjusts). 2 scenic side-windows about 112x23 in. Rear window about 84x23 in. . . . all with inside zip curtains and nylon screens. Half drill, half nylon screen 68x36-in. center zip door . . . two 18-in. bottom zippers, storm flap. Aluminized roof, awning, blue side-walls 7.68-oz. drill. 6.73-oz. pearl gray floor. Metal stakes.
60B9691R—Ship. wt. 84 lbs. cash **159.00**

[N] **Finest family tent we've offered** . . . combines extra space with light, cheery interior and unusual pitching ease. Larger than tent (M), has two extra front windows with new vinyl inside zip see-through flap—lets light in, keeps out rain. Full 108x68-in. 3-pole canopy. 6-ft. walls, 8-ft. center. 140 sq. ft. living area. Rot-proof nylon stake ropes. Roof, awning, blue sidewalls 7.68-oz. drill. 6.73-oz. pearl gray floor.
60 B 9694 R—Ship. wt. 90 lbs. . . . . . No money down or cash **189.00**

10x12-ft. high-rise tent. Similar to (M)—120-sq. ft., 7 ft. center, 5½-ft. sidewalls. 3-bow, exterior aluminum frame. 2 side windows 15x108 in.; rear window 15x84 in., zip curtains. ½-screen/½-drill door has center, bottom zip. Yellow 7.68-oz. roof, green 6.73-oz. walls. 75x68-in. canopy, two poles.
60 B 9692 R—Ship. wt. 74 lbs. . . . . **129.00**   or WARDS **853**

Tucked away out of sight, one of these homes could provide you with close-to-nature living for zero rent or payments. (Montgomery Ward)

Caves

Throughout the world many people live very comfortable lives in rent-free and tax-free caves. Are we suggesting that you find a nice dry snug stone cave for yourself? You can bet your everloving life we are. In my travels throughout the American West I have discovered many fine caves, some of them formerly occupied by the earliest Americans, the native Indians. One cave was outstanding. It was located in the side of a sandstone bluff and overlooked an all-year stream and a beautiful view of the valley below.

There are thousands of natural caves in the U.S. Some are on public property which means you would have to do a bit of hide-and-seek squatting. Others, on private land, could be purchased for just the price of the raw land. One man in Topanga, California, bought a natural cave that contained a spring. He used it for years as a summer resort, but as he approached retirement, he added on a lean-to cabin and now has one of the warmest and most durable rural homes around.

Tree Houses

If caves give you claustrophobia, then what about building yourself a tree house? There are lots of advantages . . . the foundation and most of the framing is already in. You could live a dry, snug camouflaged existence, free of termites, tax collectors, and other parasites.

A pickup load of old lumber and a few armfuls of second-hand shingles constituted the total materials list for this open basement beauty. (William Kaysing)

Smials

One man in Fresno decided to avoid summer heat, winter cold, and nosy neighbors, so he built himself a house underground. If you're ever passing through Fresno, ask someone to tell you where it is and go see it. In the meantime, check these photos. If you've read Tolkien's *The Hobbit*, you'll recall that these creatures enjoyed living in seclusion beneath the earth. If absolute quiet and privacy appeal to you, then consider digging your own smial. This is not really such a far-out idea since it's done in many parts of the world routinely. There are many areas where the earth is easy to excavate or volcanic rocks are soft enough to permit the creation of a large and comfortable underground home. Homes such as these can be found in Turkey, Greece, and east of Lone Pine, California. Many others are built in such remote areas that they will be forever hidden from public view. (But then this was probably the intention of the owners.)

An outstanding feature of an underground home is that it can be built anywhere. It lends itself to construction on level ground as the man in Fresno did it. Alternatively, even the steepest hillside can be an advantageous site for a smial, which would then be created by the same process as a mine shaft. All you have to do is begin digging horizontally and go as far as you like. Bracing the roof to prevent cave-ins is a good idea, regardless of the soil or rock characteristics. If you are constructing your underground dwelling in a wooded area, you can use the native timber for supports.

Even such details as ventilation for a kitchen or fresh air can be accommodated by means of small tunnels using natural draft or a small air pump which could be operated manually, electrically, by water, or with wind power.

If you've ever spent a summer in Fresno, you'll understand why Baldesare Forestiere built his home underground. Incredibly, this smial to end all smials ranges beneath the earth for hundreds of feet, involving almost seven acres total area. (Forestiere Underground Gardens)

One thing is for sure about this type of home—the cost will be small and its durability great.

Rammed Earth and Adobe Homes

There is one building material that's available practically everywhere on earth ... and that is earth itself. There are two extremely practical methods of utilizing this material:

1. Making bricks out of clay or adobe
2. Making bricks with a ram

The adobe method is the simplest. All you need is a source of clay soil and a few scraps of wood. The wood is cut and nailed to form a bottomless box to whatever size you wish your bricks to be. A standard size for adobe bricks is twelve inches wide, eighteen inches long, and four inches deep. This size brick is easy to make and handle in building, and it produces a wall thick enough to provide both structural stability and extremely good insulation from both heat and cold.

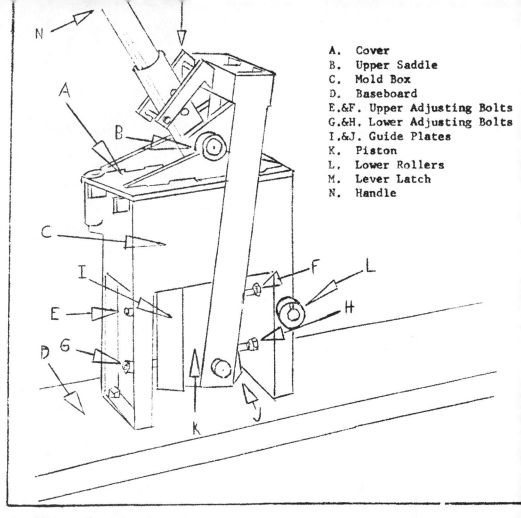

A. Cover
B. Upper Saddle
C. Mold Box
D. Baseboard
E.&F. Upper Adjusting Bolts
G.&H. Lower Adjusting Bolts
I.&J. Guide Plates
K. Piston
L. Lower Rollers
M. Lever Latch
N. Handle

To make the bricks, just add enough water to your adobe or clay soil so that it can be worked into a stiff mudlike consistency. (If you're getting clay or mud from a riverbank, it will probably be in a form that's ready to use.) To add strength to the bricks, you can mix in grass, hay, straw, manure, twigs, or other fibrous material. The mixed material is then shoveled into the wooden forms and packed down firmly to eliminate voids or air holes. If you have used clay that is stiff enough, you can remove the form immediately and reuse it for another brick. If your clay was a little on the drippy side, leave the form around it until it has dried sufficiently to remove the form.

The bricks are then dried in the sun until they are rock-hard. They can then be used to create whatever size or style house you desire. Often, the only wood in an adobe house is used for window and door frames or possibly a wooden floor. Of course, a pole and shingle roof is the simplest covering for an adobe house. However, you can create an all-adobe home like the Hopi Indians do by plastering the top with a fine clay and covering this with a lime or cement coating to waterproof it. Although not handsome,

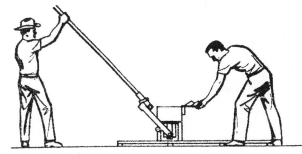

After you send for the Cinva *booklet, you may want to purchase a ram. However, a handy individual could construct his own from scrap steel. Another method of making blocks would be to use a simple mold and a hydraulic ram. The latter are available from many surplus outlets. (VITA)*

Tucked away in the nearly forgotten back country of America are tens of thousands of vacant houses and buildings. Often they can be occupied rent-free for the service of keeping them up. (William Kaysing)

many adobes have lasted centuries because they had shingled or metal roofs, which prevented the major enemy of an adobe home, rain, from melting the structure.

An improvement on adobe bricks is discussed in a booklet published by the VITA organization. This group, located at College Campus, Schenectady, N.Y. 12308, consists of a large number of volunteers who donate their time and knowledge to helping people throughout the world. One of their most useful publications concerns the CINVA Ram Press. This unit, which can be homemade or purchased, creates high-strength building blocks from dirt and other materials quickly and efficiently.

The bricks or blocks created by the press can be used in the same manner as adobe blocks. They can also be used to build walls, stables, cisterns, barns, and all sorts of other rural structures.

Extremely Far-Out Dwellings

If you need temporary or permanent shelter with a minimum of effort and expense, consider these houses. A simple pole structure built in an A-frame form can be covered with slabs of overlapping bark. In an area of young saplings, selected trees may be trimmed and bent to meet at a central point. The resulting curved-A-frame structure can then be covered with bark, canvas, plastic film, or other waterproof materials. This structure has the advantage of great durability and you don't even have to dig a foundation.

Advantage can be taken of extremely steep property to build long narrow dwellings at the foot of the slope using the bank as the rear wall. By erecting a pole structure extending out from the bank, a very cozy and inexpensive dwelling can be created.

Many years ago Frank Lloyd Wright designed a house that included a running stream. You can do the same thing by simply felling two large trees over a creek or stream and building your home directly on them. One important point—put all of your plumbing safely up the hillside to avoid

More than twenty-five houses and buildings comprise this true California ghost town. It is inhabited by squirrels and bluejays only. Great spot for a hardworking commune. Elect your own mayor and sheriff, and enjoy running the rednecks out of town for a change. (William Kaysing)

contaminating the water supply for other brothers downstream.

In many parts of the world there are enormous rocks which have created extremely durable shelters with no help from man. If you find one that looks solid enough to last during your intended stay, simply frame it in on the open side, lay down a rug or rush floor and you have instant housing.

If you can stand the noise, there are often large spaces behind waterfalls. Another no-cost dwelling can be adapted from abandoned mines and mine shafts. Here, however, it is important to proceed with great caution as these excavations often cave in at the most inopportune times . . . mainly when you are inside. However, with reasonable care and the judi-

FROM TRAILER

TO HOUSEBOAT

IN 5-10 MINUTES

cious strengthening of the ceilings, you can enjoy a no-cost home that may even yield some valuable minerals in your spare time.

Speaking of far-out housing, one man built himself a very snug dwelling inside of an abandoned water tank. Not only does he have privacy due to its raised platform position, he has a great view of the surrounding country. Water tanks, wood or metal, would make fine homes and many of them can be found totally abandoned throughout the country. Metal silos or circular corn bins with cone-shaped roofs can sometimes be purchased from farmers who no longer store these materials. They can often be found totally abandoned and be obtained for next to nothing.

To convert them into homes requires only the addition of suitable insulation, doors, windows, and floors to suit your taste.

Virtually every kind of square, round, cone- or pyramid-shaped structure could be adapted to rural shelter. This country has so many cast-off structures that there is no limit except your own imagination and creativity. We would appreciate hearing from readers who originate really unusual ideas or encounter homes that are far from the conventional.

Houseboats

Keep in mind that many of the water areas of America are free. For example, the 3,000 miles of waterways that comprise the San Joaquin-Sacramento River delta regions are

35' FIBERGLASS HOUSEBOAT

43' FIBERGLASS HOUSEBOAT

Probably the best way invented to live free of telephones and tax collectors, houseboats just have to be in the housing picture of the New America.

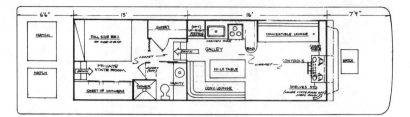

completely open to the public. While many people use these waterways for recreation, there is no way of estimating the number of people who live there cost-free, either ashore or afloat or in a combination of both.

Building a houseboat and launching it on the San Joaquin River would be an ideal way to escape both civilization and taxes. This idea could be extended to many water areas of the U.S.: lakes, lagoons, estuaries, rivers, and protected bays of the ocean. For example, one family built themselves a Ferro-cement sailboat and now spend their time sailing from one fair harbor to another. During the depression I encountered a group of people who had built fishing shacks on old rock barges and moored them in the backwater areas of Los Angeles Harbor.

All through the eastern United States there are extensive waterways which would permit a houseboat dweller to live and travel his entire life without ever covering the same stretch twice.

Windup

Before you begin your housing project, obtain copies of the following books, because they will help you create with minimum error.

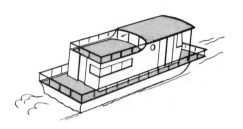

> *Culture Breakers, Alternatives and Other Numbers*, Ken Isaacs. Available from MSS Educational Publishing Co., 19 E. 48th Street, New York, N.Y. 10017. (Five dollars postpaid.) Among the many brilliant and innovative ideas that Ken presents is the fantastically inexpensive and efficient Microhouse. This is a perfect structure for an individual or group with very little money to spend.

> *Sanitation Manual for Isolated Regions*. Available from Environmental Health Center, Tunney's Pasture, Ottawa 3, Canada. (Free.) Housing may be considered only as good as the sanitation surrounding it. Thus, this book is a must for New America homebuilders. You'll find practical instructions on virtually every phase of sanitation from outdoor privvies to trash disposal. There are even plans for a sauna bath.

> *Village Technology Handbook*. Available from Department of State, Washington, D.C. 20523 (Write for cur-

rent price.) This thick, plainly written manual is packed with the type of down-to-earth information that peasants need to live healthfully. If you're going to make the rural scene, you'll need a copy.

The Owner-Built Home, Ken Kern. Available from the author, Sierra Route, Oakhurst, Calif. 93644. (Five dollars postpaid.) The entire book gives off good vibes and has drawings of some of the most original houses you've ever seen. Wait until you see the picture of the Spanish free-form house. One fascinating description concerns the use of discarded burlap bags filled with dry concrete mix, stacked in house form and then sprayed with water to set permanently. A similar idea is to dip sack material in wet cement and then use it as shingles.

Even though life in the New America may be somewhat arduous, the right clothing will see you through. (Levi)

7 The Functional Clothing Department

In Santa Barbara, California, there is a store in a nearly forgotten part of town that is used by charitable groups for rummage sales. Here, each weekend, people bring old wringer washing machines, books on how to sing really well, stuffed parrots and horned owls, 78 RPM records featuring some golden-throated tenor of the thirties and, especially, old clothes by the ton—so many old clothes that one merchant with a women's wear store has often complained that the rummage store is his biggest competitor. He's right. The word got around and more and more people found themselves picking up someone else's cast-offs for practically nothing.

The stigma of wearing old clothes has gone out with other formerly intimidating social stigmas. Today, it's an ecological good deed to use something up and wear it out. The people who make fabric and stitch it into fashions are not happy at all with the revolution in wearing apparel. After all, for many decades there was a campaign to get people to throw their wardrobes away every year and buy new ones . . . for no other reason than to be "in style." But style has proved to be an establishment trip. Today it's high style to dress your own way, make your own clothes, buy just what you need of high quality apparel (new or used), and then keep it in good repair for *years*! No matter how you dress, you're in style—YOUR OWN STYLE.

Here, then, are some ideas on useful, functional, good-looking clothes, from buying new clothes, to tanning leather,

Think of how relaxed you'll feel in your own version of the New America when you can wear loose, rugged outdoor clothing all the time.

to making your own. The information presented should be enough to get the author styled in a thick coat of midnight-black tar and fresh goose feathers, courtesy of the American Association of Wearing Apparel Manufacturers.

New Clothes

Here is a couple: The man wears a wash-and-wear dacron-cotton shirt that needs no ironing. His trousers are virtually indesctructible Levis. His T-shirt and shorts are of a top grade cotton. His socks are light wool with nylon reinforcement and he wears western-style boots of top-grain leather, fabricated by shoemakers who really wanted their product to last. His girl is wearing pants of a 100 percent textured polyester with a patterned shirt of dacron and cotton, both of which can be tossed in a washing machine and then hung up to drip-dry wrinkle-free, or even put in a cool dryer. Her brown leather sandals have PVC soles, which are almost impossible to wear out.

For the man the total cost was less than thirty dollars, for the woman, about forty-two. Both outfits should last a minimum of two years with just reasonable care. That means the cost per day is about four cents for the man and six cents for the girl. Compare this with what has to be spent to maintain an even halfway respectable wardrobe in the big city.

To get the most for your money when you buy new clothes, buy the best in terms of workmanship, material, and maintenance. The latter is important because your time is valuable and who wants to waste time ironing?

Here are some general pointers on buying new clothes.

First, learn the signs of good workmanship (how the garment is cut, sewn, and finished); then you will be better able to make selections that give longer wear. Look for generous seams, wide enough to allow for letting out and prevent fraying; garments cut with the grain of the goods; close and even machine stitching; hems and facings firmly attached; weak points reinforced; machine-made buttonholes firm and evenly stitched.

Be sure you know what fiber is used in the fabric. You need to know all you can about the material you are buying, regardless of whether it is in ready-to-wear or yard goods. Feel and appearance used to be the shopper's guide, but today you have to look for factual tags or labels. A label giving the fiber content is now required by the Textile Fiber Products Identification Act and the Wool Products Labeling Act. This is particularly helpful for telling you how to care for the garment, since the cost of upkeep is greater for clothes that have to be dry-cleaned, for example. If fabrics have a special finish requiring special handling (often indicated on the label), you should consider the extra time needed to care for the garment, when making your purchase.

Probably of major importance is the basic fit of the garment. Clothes that fit properly are more comfortable and will wear longer. You also avoid the time and expense of alterations.

Modern textile technology has liberated us in many ways. Imagine wearing itchy, woolen underwear next to your skin to stay warm. Older readers recall the hassles of ironing heavily wrinkled fabrics. Mothers over fifty know the trials of turning a frayed cotton collar. Today, you can wear quilted nylon with dacron filling . . . it's smooth, light and super-warm. If you like you can choose the new string-type underwear that keeps your body warm while it lets your perspiration evaporate. New, no-iron, wash-and-wear fabrics have

SPLIT-HOOD PARKA has outer shell made of 100% nylon. 16-oz. quilted lining. 34" split Dynel parka hood. Two storm pockets, and two flap pockets. Button-over fly front with heavy zipper. Knit wristlets. Navy blue color.

☐ **C190 Nylon Parka, S-M-L . $19.95**
        Extra large, size, 21.95

ARCTIC
PARKA

ARCTIC PARKA WAS DESIGNED by the Air Force for use in extremely cold areas. Ideal for the outdoorsman who wants the finest cold weather garment he can find. The sage green outer shell is made of 100% nylon. Inner shell also made of nylon, is international orange color. Insulated with 9 oz. Dacron.

HOOD IS TRIMMED WITH genuine wolf fur, and is lined with Dynel pile. Heavy duty front zipper with double protection button over flap. Raglan sleeves, warm knit wristlets. Elbows are double reinforced. Has four big roomy pile lined front pockets, with zippered cigarette and pencil pocket on the sleeve. Sizes S-M-L-XL.

☐ **C205 Arctic Parka, S-M-L $49.95**
        Extra Large Size 54.95

Dynel Pile Hood Lining

Genuine Wolf Fur on Hood

Knit Wool Inner Wristlets

Heavy Duty Concealed Zipper

Reinforced Double Elbows

Pile-lined "Hand Warmer" Pockets

Cold weather is a welcome variation when you have clothes like these. They're available by mail, in surplus stores and many used clothing outlets. (P & S Sales, Tulsa, Okla.)

made the old flat iron obsolete. How great it is (and you have to be over forty to appreciate this) to be able to wash a garment, hang it up, and when it's dry, just put it on.

By combining cotton with synthetic fabrics, extreme durability has been obtained. Everyone who owns a combination cotton-dacron shirt knows how true this is: they just don't wear out.

Actually, if you wear clothes suitable for what you're doing, there's not much effort involved in maintaining new clothes.

So if your budget allows it, buy a rural wardrobe from the great selection available in stores everywhere. If you live far out of town, buying by mail is lots of fun and often prices are lower. Besides the old standbys Sears and Wards, there are many mail order firms that will ship you new garments with complete guarantees of satisfaction. Here's a sampling of mail order clothing firms that emphasize garments for informal, outdoor wear.

Antarctic Products, P.O. 223, Nelson, New Zealand. Free catalog. In addition to cold-weather gear like parkas and sweaters, this firm sells sheepskins, raw wool, and yarn.

Herter's, Inc., Waseca, Minn. 56093. Big catalog for a dollar and it's a great investment, not only for clothes but for thousands of outdoor things. You can buy everything you need from Herter's, from socks and shoes to cold-weather outer garments. They have especially fine insulated underwear. One of their outstanding bargains is a three-quarter-length parka with zipper,

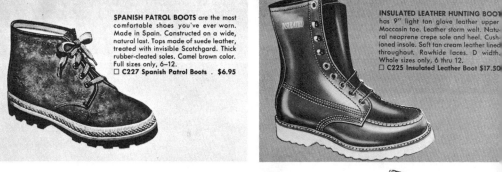

SPANISH PATROL BOOTS are the most comfortable shoes you've ever worn. Made in Spain. Constructed on a wide, natural last. Tops made of suede leather, treated with invisible Scotchgard. Thick rubber-cleated soles. Camel brown color. Full sizes only, 6–12.
☐ **C227 Spanish Patrol Boots** . **$6.95**

INSULATED LEATHER HUNTING BOOT has 9" light tan glove leather upper. Moccasin toe. Leather storm welt. Natural neoprene crepe sole and heel. Cushioned insole. Soft tan cream leather lined throughout. Rawhide laces. D width. Whole sizes only, 6 thru 12.
☐ **C225 Insulated Leather Boot** $17.50

Have you ever put on a pair of rugged shoes or boots and suddenly felt like some latter-day mountain man or western explorer? Half the fun of life in the new America will be well-clad feet. Point them in the direction of the woods and they'll take you there gladly. (P & S Sales, Tulsa, Okla.)

THERMAL KNIT cushion stretch socks give maximum warmth, real foot comfort. For use with shoes or boots. Red elasticized tops. Made of 85% cotton, 15% nylon. One size fits all.
☐ **C119 Stretch Socks** . . 85¢
4 pairs, $3.00

THERMAL KNIT WAFFLE stitch Stretch Socks have thousands of tiny air pockets that keep body heat in—cold air out. Gray color, red tops. Made of 40% wool, 30% rayon, 20% cotton, 10% nylon. Medium and Large sizes.
☐ **C220 Thermal Socks, $1.25**

NYLON INSULATED BOOTIE has a tan quilted nylon shell, bonded orlon insulated lining and ribbed anklet top. Maximum foot warmth without extra weight or bulk. Easily washable in lukewarm water. S—M—L—XL.
☐ **C135 Nylon Bootie** . **$2.00**

ARMY O.D. STRETCH SOCKS with cushioned soles are rejects from a government contract. Have slight imperfections, but none affect wearability. Tops are 50% wool, 50% cotton. Fits sizes 10½–11½.
☐ **C150 Socks** . . **2 pr. $1.25**

ELECTRIC WOOL SOCKS made of wool and powered two standard 6-volt batte carried in a belt case. V with snap-on connectors cor the current. (Batteries no cluded.) Sizes: 9 thru 13.
☐ **C124 Electric Socks** . $

ROLLER-CRUSHER. The woodsman's favorite. Can be shaped to suit your mood. Takes crushing, smashing, folding, and stomping in its stride. Tends to become very distinctive in shape after long wear. Colors: black, red, green. Sizes: 6-5/8 to 7⅜.
A701 . . . . ave. wt. 3 oz. . . . . . $ 3.00

BASQUE BERET. Made in traditional style of 100% wool felt. Leather head band. Colors: black or green. Sizes: 6⅝ to 7⅜.
A729 . . . . ave. wt. 4 oz. . . . . . $ 3.00

ORLON BALACLAVA. Looks good and gives maximum all-weather face protection. 100% Orlon double fabric knit. Colors: black, navy, red.
A710 . . . . . . wt. 3 oz. . . . . . . $ 2.25

It's often true that you become the person which your clothing image creates. For example, the man on the left will soon become a connoisseur of wild berries and nuts. The man in the middle is ready to join your partisan group, while the intelligent young lady on the right is raring to hitchhike all over northern Canada. (Ski Hut)

hood, and pockets in forest green vulcanized cloth for $4.69.

J. Barbour, Simonside, South Shields County, Durham, England. Free catalog. Their all-weather gear is great for boating, motorcycling or other wet and chilly activities.

Frostline Outdoor Equipment, P.O. 1378, Boulder, Col. 80302. Free catalog. Featuring sew-it-yourself sleeping bags, this firm also will provide complete do-it-yourself kits for clothing. Good source of supply for groovy fabrics and goose down.

Todd's, 5 S. Wabash, Chicago, Ill. 60603. Free catalog. Selection of outdoor shoes and boots.

White's Shoe Shop, West 430 Main, Spokane, Wash. 99201. Free catalog. Source of handmade shoes. Owners claim that they'll go along indefinitely if you keep them soled.

Golden State Surplus, 524 W. Main, Alhambra, Calif. 91801. Source of combat boots at low prices.

BLUE EYES MINE

THE LAST CHANCE MINE
PLACER COUNTY CALIF 1882

New America will just have to
come up with more super-
durable clothes. With fashion a
drag, and poor material and
workmanship unacceptable,
clothing manufacturers are
going to have to fall into line
behind the quality people.
(Levi)

Walter Dyer, 7 Bearskin Neck, Rockport, Mass. 01966. Long-lasting moccasins for silent tripping about in the forest.

Levis

Take a look at those two rugged gold-miners ... actually they're gone now, but if you poked around the mine you might find their trousers in wearable condition. A slight exaggeration perhaps, but you get the point. Levi-Strauss is a company that has (to my knowledge) never compromised on quality. I'm not just telling you this to get a free pair of Levis ... it's that when something is that good, everyone should know about it.

Tips to Remember When Buying New Clothes

1. Many medium-sized cities have women's apparel stores that liquidate overstocks at very low prices. Usually, the labels are removed but if you know what to look for in materials and workmanship, you can buy excellent garments at substantial discounts.

2. Many women love to wear textured polyester garments because they look fresh and bandboxlike all the time. No wrinkles even if you sit in the back of a pickup for a fifty-mile jaunt through the desert.

3. No one says you have to pay full retail price for your clothes ... If you're buying quite a batch, ask the store manager to give you a quantity discount. He won't let a big sale go by just to avoid giving you 10 or 15 percent or more off. Just remember, if you don't ask, you get no discount. If you do ask, you'll probably get it and save substantially.

4. When buying shoes, look for PVC (polyvinyl chloride) on soles and heels. This material will usually outlast the uppers. It can also be added to existing shoes.

5. When buying new clothes for your children, look for reinforced knees and elbows, or add them yourself.

6. Since children either outgrow or outwear shoes in short order, for all practical purposes outfitting them with sturdy and inexpensive tennis shoes is probably the best way to go. These have the added advantage of being machine washable.

Old Clothes

People in America throw away millions of dollars worth of usable clothes every year. Fortunately, a substantial percentage is recycled through the population.

Understanding why these clothes are thrown away, we can see why it's an excellent idea to *first* try obtaining old clothes before buying new ones. Here are some of the reasons why so much used clothing is available:

1. Young people grow out of their clothes and have no younger brothers or sisters to inherit them.

2. People die or are killed in accidents and their complete wardrobes often become surplus to the survivors.

This young lady is so proud of her new tennies that she gladly posed for this picture. (William Kaysing)

Fashioned from heavyweight satin, this classic gown is the pride and joy of its owner. Its deep crimson is a striking picture against any natural background. The cost—$1 at the local remnant store. (William Kaysing)

3. Styles change and, for the style-conscious, this can mean the "death" of their wardrobe.

4. Even if styles don't change, people simply become tired of certain clothes and must give them away to make room for new purchases. Most people have clothes that they wear over and over again. They often leave the greater percentage of their garments to grow dusty, unwanted and unloved, on the hangers. Eventually, they give them away.

5. Often when people move they don't want to carry their wardrobes with them and will give them to a charity.

6. Believe it or not, many new garments find their way into used clothing stores for the simple reason that they couldn't be sold as new. To capture some of the investment, the wholesalers will release quantities through any outlets available.

7. Many a purchaser's mistake ultimately finds its way to the used clothing centers when the buyer faces the fact that the garment he has purchased is simply unsuitable or does not fit properly.

8. Wealthy people and many people in the entertainment or fashion field have to completely refurbish their wardrobes each season to keep in style. Their barely worn cast-offs are sometimes sold in special shops.

It is clear from the above that the traditional concept of "old clothes" must be thrown out. Today, it is ecologically sound as well as economically strategic to buy used clothing, because it is often hardly used at all.

Where to Find Good Used Clothing Everyone is familiar with such charitable organizations as the Salvation Army, Goodwill, St. Joseph's, and hundreds of other "lend-a-hand" organizations. Stores owned by these groups nearly always have plentiful supplies of clothing, ranging from baby booties to fur hats suitable for the upper reaches of the Yukon. Not quite as prominent are smaller secondhand stores selling a variety of merchandise and often with clothes on a rack in the back. While these outlets may not have the practically giveaway prices of the charitable organizations, they are still far more reasonable than a garment store selling new merchandise. A half brother to the two major types of outlets is the periodic rummage sale. These are usually conducted by an organization known as the Junior Women's Assistance League. They feature the cast-off clothing of the sponsoring group, as well as those clothes collected at random throughout the community. If you arrive early, you will often find new or nearly new clothing selling for two or three cents on the dollar. Perfectly good coats go for fifty cents to two dollars at many of these rummage sales. In my small, High Sierra town a rummage sale is held each Friday. There is always a rack of blouses in a rainbow of colors, a kaleidoscope of styles, in sizes to fit midgets to mammoths, and none of them costs over five cents!

Another source of good used clothing, particularly for men, is the surplus store. While they often offer phony military items made in Japan, it's not difficult to pick out the high-grade, used military clothing. Boots, wool hats, fur-lined gloves ... all intended for rigorous military use ... are offered for perhaps ten cents on the original dollar cost to the hapless gummint.

Head shops, little stores tucked away in the backwaters of college towns, and other freaky, far-out establishments often carry a line of secondhand clothes. Just ask whenever you are in one.

Cleaners often have uncalled-for clothing which you can buy for the proverbial song, and shoemakers will sell you shoes that have been gathering dust for months.

An excellent source of new-used clothes is your local dressmaker. She will occasionally custom-make something that the customer refuses. She can only dispose of it at the best price possible. Theatrical costumers often have funky garments that they will sell cheaply for any one of many reasons—no further call, damage, etc.

What You Can Do with Good Secondhand Clothing   Besides wearing them as is by merely taking up a hem or sewing on a button, you can make old clothes both the inspiration and the basis for a completely individual wardrobe. For example, fringes and beadwork can be added to old jackets to give them a contemporary look. Fur coats can be remodeled into western-style vests with the fur inside or out as you prefer. Much fine, imported woolen material goes into men's suits and these can be taken apart and remade into jackets, skirts, or sexy hot pants.

Shoes, gloves, hats, scarves can all be remodeled, repaired, dyed, and rejuvenated to become newer than any clothes you'll find in a retail establishment. And they will reflect your own imagination and skill.

We'll talk more about making things in the next section ... suffice it to say here that secondhand clothing can provide you with a way of looking and feeling your best at totally rock-bottom prices.

Here are a few tips from experts:

1. Always get to a rummage sale before it opens, or at least early. That way you'll have the best selection.

2. If a garment is really inexpensive but you're debating whether to buy it, buy it anyway. You can give it to a friend as a present even if you can't wear it. Besides, many places will take it back on trade.

3. As with new clothes, learn to bargain, especially if you buy an armful.

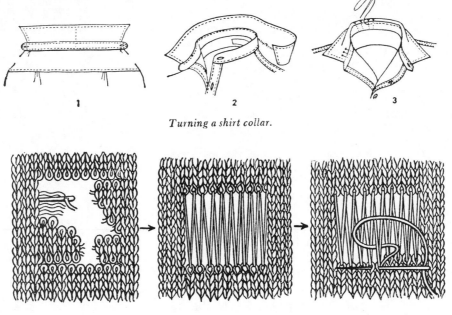

Turning a shirt collar.

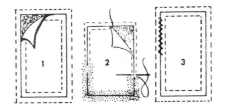

Mending sweaters.

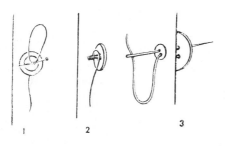

Darned-in patch.

Darning a sock

Replacing buttons.

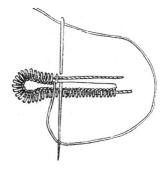

Worn buttonholes.

Here's a guide to a few of the things you can do to bring good clothes back to wearable condition. It's not only easy, but it's fun, and even men would enjoy it if they tried it. (USDA)

4. Don't hesitate to acquire a pair of old shoes that just need soles and heels. If they fit right and are comfortable to walk in, you can sole them yourself with a kit available in dime stores, or you can stick on a chunk of used automobile tire with super-strong epoxy cement.

5. Trade your old clothes for other old clothes.

Making Your Own

Eskimos tan animal skins and sew them into durable clothes. (They often sew them right on themselves to stay until the garment falls apart.) In the South Pacific, natives create handmade cloth from natural bark and fibers, then adorn themselves in colorful sarongs. In the mysterious streets of Marrakech, equally mysterious Arab types skulk along swathed in yards of cool, heat-reflecting Egyptian cotton. No buttons or zippers to bother them. In many parts of rural America—the still frontierlike hills of Virginia and the tranquil, half-hidden Ozarks—people still make their own cloth and sew their own clothes.

If you have the time and the inclination, you can sew your own handsome and individualistic raiment from a tremendously diversified selection of fabrics and material.

What's Available The textile mills of America spew out billions of yards of fabrics in every conceivable pattern, color, and basic material. To create your own wardrobe you can select from cotton, linen, wool, and a fabulous array of the new synthetics. You can choose from polyesters, acetates, dacrons, nylons, and even the old standby, rayon. Many of the new fabrics have characteristics far superior to traditional materials.

In addition to fabrics, you have a choice of dozens of different leathers and furs, as well as items like hand-woven blankets, canvas, and, of course, material salvaged from used clothing and other previously sewn fabric items such as sails, parachutes, and tents.

By combining new and old materials, you can come up with some unique new approaches to being well-clothed. For example, ordinary aluminum foil sewn to the inside of a windbreaker jacket will preserve 90 percent of your body heat. Because of its lightness and cheapness, aluminum foil can also be used for other sewing projects, such as sleeping bags and tents. Another inexpensive way to keep warm without spending money is to shred newspaper and quilt it between pieces of inexpensive fabric.

Many materials can be combined to take advantage of the best characteristics of each. Putting leather elbows on jackets is an old trick, but have you mothers out there ever thought of adding top-grain horsehide to the knees of your children's blue jeans?

Sewing Equipment The traditional needle and thread can be used to make your own garments. However, if you have

Here's something else you can do with scrap pieces of fur. (William Kaysing)

Try sewing on just a touch of adornment—a few beads, a little colored edging, leather, semi-precious stones, or even colorful seeds. You'll be surprised how a little creativity can transform conventional clothes into garments you'll be happy to wear. (William Kaysing)

This girl makes most of her own clothing. It's an expensive year if she spends more than $25 on material and thread. Her machine? It's an old treadle-type Singer that works magic with fabric. (William Kaysing)

153

the bread, it's best to invest in a sewing machine. If you'd like to conserve on America's power supply, look around in secondhand stores for the old treadle-type Singers. Millions of them were made and since they are practically indestructible, there are plenty of them still around. You can buy them for a twenty dollar bill or less . . . often much less. Electric machines aren't too much more expensive than the treadle types. They begin at about $60 for a new, straight-stitch model. In between these two extremes is the possibility of having your treadle machine electrified; the total cost would be less than $25 to take all of the work out of machine sewing.

Once you have a machine, fabric and thread, plus accessories like buttons, zippers, beads, lace, and perhaps freaky, far-out adornments like seeds, polished pebbles, and bits of fur or feathers, you are ready to go. Because there are many fine publications on *how* to sew, we won't include that information in this chapter. Here are some of the many books available:

> *The Illustrated Hassle-Free Make Your Own Clothes Book*, Sharon Rosenberg, Joan Wiener, 1971, $7.95 postpaid from Straight Arrow, World Publishing Co., 110 E. 59th Street, New York 10002

> *Coats & Clark's Sewing Book*, 1967, $3.95 postpaid from Golden Press, Inc., 850 Third Avenue, New York 10022

> *Successful Sewing: A Modern Guide*, 1969, $8.75 postpaid from Taplinger Publishing Co., Inc., 29 E. Tenth Street, New York 10003

> *Sincere's Sewing Machine Service Book*, William Ewers, 1968-70, $9.95 postpaid from Sincere Press, Box 10422, Phoenix, Ariz. 85018.

Keep in mind, as you learn to sew your own, that an easy way to start is by remodeling existing clothes—changing the length of a skirt, or adding some new fur trim to an old, plain-looking jacket. Another good way to learn sewing is to take a garment apart with a razor blade, examine the separate pieces, and then sew it back together again. This will give you some experience before you work on newly cut-out fabric.

The subject of making your own clothes is so vast that to encompass it within the covers of this book would be impossible. Thus, we are presenting a compendium of tips and ideas to trigger your own imagination. These were compiled from people who have had years of experience in sewing for themselves and others:

Spending a lot of money for clothes was a part of the mythical American dream. Today you can enjoy comfortable, long-wearing clothing and be happy as this early nineteenth-century wheat farmer.

1. Once you find a basic pattern that you like, simply modify it according to your own tastes and preferences. For example, a basic shift pattern can be made short, long, sleeved or sleeveless, decorative or plain, depending on your budget, mood, or climatic requirements.

2. We mentioned taking apart a garment to study how it was made. You can do this with a garment that's worn out that you wish to remake in another material.

3. Sewing clothes is like painting a house: the material costs are a very small percentage of the total cost. Therefore, always buy the best fabrics you can afford. These coupled with good workmanship will give you garments that will last for years.

4. Small scraps from your sewing projects can be made into bean bags and rag dolls for your children or pot holders for your own kitchen.

5. Many communities have adult education courses in sewing (check YMCA-YWCA) that not only teach you the art but let you use their equipment. The cost is usually very small, a dollar or two per semester.

6. If you and your friends are about the same size, you can save time by cutting out two, three or more patterns at

one time. They can be in different materials if you wish—the scissors won't know the difference. A variation on this is to cut out several garments at one time, sew one for yourself and sell the others on consignment in a head shop.

7. Making your own garments allows you to be creative in a productive way and express your real personality through what you wear. In addition, the pride of owning a homemade, handmade garment has to be felt to be appreciated.

8. A good source of clothes designs are old history books. Check out what pirates wore, or eighteenth-century farmers. For the best designs in leather, get a book on the Lewis and Clark expedition. Alternatively, you can get ideas from old period movies. Randolph Scott or John Wayne playing a Daniel Boone role would give you enough ideas to keep your leather-working equipment going for months.

9. If you'd like to start one step earlier, you can weave your own. Many looms are on the market. Here's a couple of loom and weaving material sources:

Newcomb 45-inch 4-harness, $185, from Newcomb Loom Co., Davenport, Iowa 52808

Lorellyn 14-inch 2-harness table model, $35; 20-inch 4-harness floor model, $65.50; 30-inch 4-harness floor model, $85.50, f.o.b. Chicago Park, Calif. Crating charges run from $2.50 to $3.50. Free brochure. Write Lorellyn Weavers, Box 56, Chicago Park, Calif. 95712.

10. Dig animal skins? Get this booklet:

Home Tanning Guide, Harding's Books, 2878 E. Main, Columbus, Ohio, 43209, or

Whole Earth Catalog, 558 Santa Cruz Avenue, Menlo Park, Calif. 94025

11. Here are some free booklets that relate directly to making your own clothes.

Sewing Magic for Teenagers, Greist Manufacturing Co., 501 Blake Street, New Haven, Conn. 06515

For the following write USDA, Washington, D.C. 20250:

Simplified clothing construction, 1967 G 59
Removing stains from fabrics, 1968. G 62
How to prevent and remove mildew, 1968. G 68
Making household fabrics flame resistant, 1967. L 454

Protecting woolens against clothes moths and carpet beetles, 1966. G 113
Buying your home sewing machine, 1960. G 38
Clothing repairs, 1965. G 107
How to tailor a woman's suit, 1968. G 20

In summary, making your own clothes can be one of the most rewarding activities of your life in the New America. You can take advantage of all the old pioneering know-how and combine it with new materials, techniques, and equipment to produce clothing that will make you look and feel good. These feelings will be mirrored by everyone you encounter, who will enjoy seeing a person not only becomingly dressed, but happy to be expressing his own personality in what he wears.

We could make some allusions to Eve and the Garden of Eden here, but what we're really trying to say is "Dress to please yourself and you'll probably please everybody." (William Kaysing)

8 Low Cost Transportation: The Motorcycle

The engine in this giant piece of Detroit iron has a displacement of seven liters (7,000 cubic centimeters).

Many lightweight motorcycles of this type have engines only one-hundredth as large. The nonpolluting factors are commensurately favorable.

If you were on a boat far from land, and it slammed into a huge log and began to sink, what would you do?

1. Abandon ship without delay.

2. Present arguments to the other passengers about the benefits of steel hulls.

3. Plug the leak as best you could and begin bailing.

If you picked three, then you're with me. We can draw a parallel between the sinking boat and the state of our mutual air supply. If something isn't done mighty soon in America about the consumption of gasoline in cars, you won't need to worry about your future, or anyone else's for that matter.

1. America loves wheels. We weren't sold the car, we bought the car. It's a terrific way to go from point A to point B in comfort, privacy, and (outside of Manhattan) at a good clip.

2. The average wage earner uses his car to go to work.

3. An immediate replacement of solo transportation by mass transportation is outside the realm of possibility.

So it looks like we're stuck for a time, although, as everyone who's seen a big city from the air knows, it may not be long before we all die of asphyxiation. But this problem has a built-in solution. Simply *reduce* the amount of gasoline burned each day but allow everyone to keep a set of wheels . . . in this instance two wheels. In three sentences, here's an interim solution to the air pollution problem in America.

1. Put a dollar-per-gallon tax on gasoline, the proceeds to go toward developing a non-gas-using vehicle.

2. This will encourage many people to trade their monsters in on V-dubs, Pintos, and the like. It will also stimulate lots of interest in motorcycles that get a hundred miles per gallon.

3. Create some special privileges for small-car and cycle users; things like no-charge parking lots, special lanes on major highways, and a bonus at the end of the year.

The result will be:

Better air for everyone

Lower cost per mile for you

The thrills of a sporting way to go anywhere

But suddenly a voice cries weakly from the intensive care ward . . . "Okay, Bill, it may work, but motorcycles are *dangerous.*"

Hoo ha . . . that's what everyone says except the people who really know how to ride them safely. And how do they learn? Simple, they just read the following material and then carefully put it into practice.

Selecting the Best Machine for You (On the Road)

If you live in an area where motorcycles are ridden (which is everywhere today except certain inner regions of the Gobi Desert) then you've probably seen the following sights.

Two large people aboard one small motorcycle are wobbling down the street with the rear tire bulging, the front wheel barely touching the surface, and the engine gasping under the overload. The rider's control over the machine is marginal and all components, from brakes to frame, are overstressed.

In contrast, there is the small boy (just licensed) aboard a 1,000 cc twin. When he stops, his feet barely touch the ground, and if the machine did fall over on him, it would take another small boy to lift it off his slightly flatter leg.

Many new riders seldom take the time or effort to determine just what motorcycle will be suitable for them. The two most important considerations in choosing a cycle should be intended use and safety. If you select the machine that best fits your needs, safety will be a cost-free and most welcome bonus feature. Note that cost is not mentioned as a significant factor . . . because if you are injured as a result of mechanical failure, you won't really enjoy any "savings."

Just as a tack hammer would be unsuitable for driving spikes, a 5 hp lightweight would be both unsafe and inappropriate for long-distance touring by a fair-sized couple. But, as sledge hammers make awkward tools for tacks, a 600-pound street bike with radio, heater, and fox tails would be most unwieldy for following a six-inch trail down the cliffs of the Grand Canyon.

Manufacturers have responded with both speed and resourcefulness in supplying the increasing demand for specialized machines. Today, most motorcycles are designed for a specific purpose, although many become dual- or triple-purpose bikes with factory or rider modification. There are swift street machines, sturdy trail bikes, ingenious combination street and trail motorcycles, jet-age racers in as many categories as there are races, plus a goodly number of miscellaneous varieties.

What Kind of Riding Will You Do?   Do you intend to ride the street or off the road? How far are you going on each surface and how often? Do you anticipate you'll carry a passenger, baggage, parcels? Are you planning to travel a lot in cold weather or at night? Is the machine mainly for fun, or will you rely on it for steady, day-in and day-out transportation? Race bug bit you yet? In the old days you had to make up your own—today you can choose from a really hot set of haulers. Is hill-climbing your cup of tea? Then you're in luck—there are a few big singles and a couple of twins that should go right up any slope as soon as they are uncrated.

After you've decided what type of riding you'll be doing most of the time, carefully examine the motorcycles that suit each category.

Street Machines   In this category there is a make and a model to suit everyone. There are some to suit youngsters in high school, and some for granddads who years back first threw a leg over a Henderson or Crocker. Women who think young can easily find a gentle, soft-spoken step-through model. Inveterate vagabonds desiring a monster machine capable of carrying a tent, sleeping bag, and 150 pounds of corned beef and cabbage up the Alcan Highway have a fine group of heavyweights from which to choose.

Lightweights—Under 100 cc   These low-cost, sharp-looking motorcycles are by far the most popular motorized units of two-wheeled transportation sold in the world today. This group is popular for many reasons, including the fact that they are:

1. Truly light—under 160 pounds soaking wet

2. Inexpensive to buy—about one-sixth of what a new car would cost

3. Inexpensive to operate—important if you happen to live where gasoline is much loot per liter

4. Safe to operate—with relatively low speeds, good braking capability, and simplicity of controls

Lightweight machines have been around for many decades, beginning with the early versions that were merely motorized bicycles. Today's lightweight incorporates all of the latest discoveries in metallurgy, electronics, chemistry, and mechanical engineering. A great many advances in electrical devices have permitted such time, dignity, and leg-saving equipment as electric starters. This fact alone has allowed

MT-50R Trailhopper

Anyone can ride it. 3 hp. engine. 3 speed automatic. Full suspension, hand-brakes. Adjustable seat, handlebars. CCI automatic lube.

F-50R Cutlass

"Step-through" frame. 3 speed automatic. 50cc reed-valve engine. 45 mph. CCI automatic lube. Nearly 200 mile per gallon economy.

TS-50R Gaucho

The only 50 built like a real motorcycle. 5 speeds. Enduro-styling. 60 mph. CCI automatic lube. Rotary-valve engine.

TS-90R Honcho

The "king" of the lightweight enduros! 65 mph. Alum. rotary-valve engine. 5 speeds. Tube frame. CCI automatic lube.

TC-90R Blazer

Ride it on street or trail. 8 spd. dual-range trans. Tube frame. CCI automatic lube. Dual passenger seat. Alum. rotary-valve engine.

TC-120R Cat

Ride it on street or trail. Dual-range trans. – changes with a kick. CCI automatic lube. Chrome luggage carrier.

T-125R Stinger

125 cc's of quickness. 70 mph. Parallel twin carbs & pipes. Tach & Speedo. Competition styling. CCI automatic lube. 5 speeds.

TS-125R Duster

The 125 enduro machine. 13 hp/7000 rpm. Bead stoppers. Primary kick. 5-way adjustable rear shocks. CCI automatic lube. 5 speeds.

TS-185R Sierra

Outperforms anything in its class. 17.5 hp. 5-way adj. rear shocks. 3-way adjustable front forks. 5 speeds. CCI automatic lube.

TS-250R Savage

Built like the world champion moto-cross Suzuki. 23 hp @ 6500 rpm. Alum. engine. PEI ignition. CCI automatic lube. 5-way adjustable rear shocks. 5 speeds. Single leading shoe front brakes.

T-250R Hustler

The fastest 250cc street bike made! 15.1 quarter. 100 mph. 6 speeds. CCI automatic lube. 6 port power. Double leading shoe front brakes.

T-350R Rebel

Outrides any 350 made. 13.8 quarter. 40 hp. 6 speeds. CCI automatic lube. 6 port power. Double leading shoe front brakes.

TM-400R Cyclone

Complete moto-cross competition racer. 40 hp. Alum. alloy rims. Competition muffler. 5 speeds. Single leading shoe front brakes. CCI automatic lube. PEI ignition.

T-500R Titan

Championship performance. 13.2 quarter. 47 hp. 5 speeds. CCI automatic lube. Deep cushion dual saddle. Double leading shoe front brakes.

Even if you can't find exactly what you want from this array, there are hundreds of other makes, models, and types available. (Suzuki Corp.)

Many lightweight machines are as much at home off the road as they are on. (Suzuki Corp.)

many women to ride motorcycles, who previously would never dream of kicking one over in front of the local pharmacy.

The under-100cc lightweights come in several styles . . . some are step-through like a motor scooter, while others have the conventional "toss a leg over the tank." The former are great for ladies and businessmen interested in keeping the grey flannels spotless. The latter type should suit almost anyone who appreciates a little dash and flair in his transportation. The ultra-small lightweights are fine for the occasional shopping trip, as a sort of spare car in case of an emergency, or for a short trip to school.

Where high-speed roads and freeways are used, put a few more burners in the fireroom. Here's why. If you are traveling in the mainstream of heavy traffic and encounter a sudden rise or hill, a few degrees of slope can steal all the power from a small engine and cause you to slow down—a most dangerous condition and one which could cause someone to climb your rear fender inadvertently. The newest family of modest displacement machines has put a lot more zip into the ultra-lightweight class, but to get more power for utility and safety, consider the larger weights.

Plus 125cc Machines   Actually, you don't need to travel very far up the cubic centimeter ladder to get lots of speed. With recent developments in engine design, it is not at all unusual to find engines producing two or more horsepower per cubic inch! This means that a machine with as little as 125ccs can produce a substantial 15 hp and road speeds above 65 miles per hour. The fact that you have power does not mean you must use it. However, as all riders have discovered, it certainly comes in handy if you're jostling with 300-horsepower automobiles. In fact, many freeways now require minimum horsepower to protect riders from being run over by traffic.

Approaching the 250 Machine There are motorcycles in several displacement increments from 125 to 250 cubic centimeters. As they grow larger they usually begin to physically resemble their bigger brothers. Furthermore, they come mighty close in performance . . . sometimes even surpassing them. A 250 cc machine developing about 28 hp and weighing in at 240 pounds gross has a hp-to-weight ratio of one hp for every 9.2 pounds of bike weight. A larger machine, say a 500cc single, might develop only 9 more hp but add 110 pounds of motorcycle poundage due to a larger frame, shocks, wheels, etc. For comparison, this machine would then have a hp-to-weight ratio of one hp for every ten pounds of weight. It would actually be slightly inferior in this important category with all other factors (such as rider weight) remaining equal. Many 250 cc machines have "cleaned the plows" of larger bikes in races. When buying a 200 or 250 cc lightweight, the rider should be aware that he is not buying a little "round-town putt-putt" but possibly a lightning-fast accelerator with a top-speed potential in the high eighties or nineties. From a safety standpoint, a lightweight rider should and must treat his mount with the respect due a powerful machine that forgives few errors in judgment. For this roundabout reason, it may be more to the novice's advantage to buy a larger machine which usually creates the respect due any piece of powerful machinery. This is particularly true if the larger machine is more suited to his transportation needs.

Neat design, careful workmanship, reliability, and long life are characteristics of this 175 cc European import. (American Jawa Corp.)

Two-Strokes or Four? Whether to buy a machine that delivers one power stroke per revolution (two-stroke) or one power stroke every two revolutions (four-stroke), is a problem confronting the first-time motorcycle buyer. First let's establish that both types have been developed to a high degree of perfection and reliability. Both have advantages inherent in their design (two-strokes have no valves—four-strokes idle like contented cats) and a few disadvantages. So be sure to give both engine types a thorough trial and evaluation ... then buy the one that sounds happiest to your own ears.

Heavyweights Here we enter the subject of big bikes. This includes all engines over 250 cc, and the road-eating monsters above 1,000 cubic centimeters (larger than engines in many small sports cars).

Big motorcycles with tremendous power are, in my estimation, the most exciting invention of the era ... far exceeding such prosaic discoveries as the automatic washing machine and atomic power. To anyone who has ever ridden a four-cylinder motorcycle of any make or vintage, no explanation of the previous statement is necessary. To anyone who hasn't had this privilege, no description is possible. If you like thrills by the bushelful, then by all means get a "big bore." If you like to travel far afield with camping gear and a companion on the pillion seat, then a big "lunger" or smooth twin should be your choice.

Starting at about the 300 to 350 cc level, we find a number of fine motorcycles with every modern feature. If you are the average rider who uses his machine for travel to and from work with a lunch box and an occasional pillion passenger, this size could be appropriate for you. The horsepower-to-weight ratio is usually about the same as that of some of the smaller machines, but there are advantages; the usual over-300 cc machines appear comfortably dressed with windshield, well-filled saddlebags, turn indicators, and even a first-aid kit, toolbox, and fire extinguisher. As we proceed upward in displacement, we find some truly handsome machines. There are many motorcycles in the 500, 650, and 750 cc category. Motorcycles of this class are in widespread use throughout the world for many business and pleasure purposes. Then, as we emerge on the high plateau of 1,000 cc and up, we are truly at the point of fun and sport defying description. Everyone who rides a motorcycle, regardless of year, make, or model, should take at least one careful and thoughtful ride on a 1,000 cc machine. It is an education that will broaden his horizons immediately and lastingly.

Try out the machines that seem most appropriate in size, engine displacement, and accessory equipment until you find the one that seems best suited to your needs. All dealers will allow a trial ride of one of their demonstrators. This is

If you haven't enjoyed a jaunt into the country astride a beautifully balanced, smooth-running machine like this, you've missed out on a lot of living. (BMW)

one of the best ways to become familiar with the models, since the majority of all demonstrators are brand new and in top condition mechanically.

Once you've found the machine that best suits your individual needs for safety and utility, then consider the economics. Initial cost, gas mileage, upkeep, repair costs, tires, insurance, and miscellaneous expenses should be your final consideration.

Motorcycle Controls

John Warmshoe, a motorcycle rider with about nine months' experience, is sitting astride his mount at a busy intersection. The red light has stared him to a complete stop. He is idly revving his engine up and down. Suddenly, against the light his powerful twin leaps into the intersection directly into the path of a loaded gravel truck. An examination of the flattened machine reveals that John's instant departure from the cycle world was totally unnecessary. A little preventive maintenance would have helped, but most important, an understanding of motorcycle controls would have eliminated the accident completely.

Many millions of people are being introduced to the sport of motorcycling each year. As soon as one person on a block buys a bike, everyone else wants to try it out. "Here's the clutch and here's the throttle . . . turn it like so, pull on this and away you go . . . here, I'll start it for you." This is all the instruction a novice gets. Wobbling a bit at the start, he goes flying down the street and is up to 40 or 50 miles per hour before he remembers that no one told him where the brake pedal is located. Many riders have been injured or killed just because they didn't take the pains to find out how to stop it before they got started. Even after they learn the rudimentary mechanical operation of the cycle, they proceed to blast down streets and highways, off the road and into the hills, without considering all of the special problems characteristic of motorcycling in general. When you buy a motorcycle, the seller or dealer will usually take the time to point out the basic operation. Sometimes you get a manual of instructions. But the really fine points . . . the kick stand left down on takeoff, the fatigued clutch cable . . . are usually left to the rider to find out for himself—often at the price of a spill, an injury, or worse.

The accident described above was simply a case of mechanical failure coupled with ignorance of motorcycle controls. Several decades back most American motorcycles were equipped with a clutch actuated by a foot-operated, spring-loaded rocker, built to stay either in the engaged or disengaged position. Many riders removed this safety feature and thus invented what came to be known as the suicide clutch. This type of clutch engaged automatically whenever the rider's foot was removed from the pedal, intentionally or not! If the rider was at an intersection with the transmission in gear and accidentally lost his balance, his foot would be inadvertently removed from the clutch and the machine would move forward against his will. Such a large number or riders were injured or killed by this type of accident that the clutch was given its proper descriptive adjective.

Most modern motorcycles have the clutch lever on the left handlebar, thus removing the hazard of using the foot as both a balancing device and the clutch lever actuator. However, the modern clutch employs a braided wire cable connecting the actuating lever with the clutch mechanism below. How long does this wire last and why is it important? Let's go back to actual cycle operation. Most experienced riders will downshift through all the gears as they approach a stop. This saves brakes and maintains their gear ratios in perfect match with road speed. As they approach their stopping point, they shift into neutral. Why? . . . simply because when the machine is in neutral it cannot go anywhere—clutch in or out. What has this got to do with the clutch cable? Well, when the late John W. was at the intersection he had the clutch lever depressed, the transmission was in low gear, and he was amusing himself by running the motor up and down the scales, racer fashion. His life now depended on the clutch cable which was badly frayed and in need of replacement. At the instant when the cable broke, the engine was wound to propel the cycle into the intersection against the light. The moral of this example is threefold.

1. Learn all you can about any mechanical device before operating it.

2. Always shift into neutral when your cycle is stopped and the engine is running.

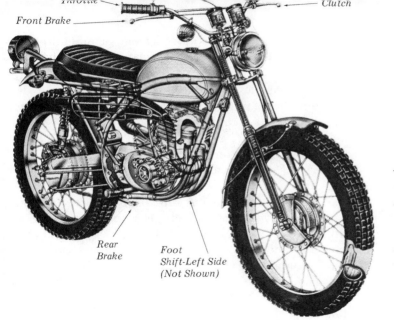

Front Brake

Rear Brake

Foot Shift-Left Side (Not Shown)

Much literature is available free from motorcycle companies. It will help you familiarize yourself with a particular machine's operating characteristics before you venture out on your first ride. (For names of companies, buy a copy of Cycle World *magazine. It's the best there is, and lists practically all motorcycle manufacturers in every issue.) (Yamaha)*

3. Treat your cycle like an airplane and keep it in topnotch condition with preventive maintenance.

Basic Elements

Assuming that the machine is in top mechanical condition, the first thing to learn before you start it is how to stop it. Mount the machine and operate the hand and foot controls. The foot pedal varies from left to right but the hand brake control is usually on the right side. This fact can be a lifesaver when you have temporarily forgotten just where-in-the-hell the foot pedal is located. Work these controls until you are thoroughly familiar with their feel and location. Paddle the bike ahead a few feet and test them out. See if the brake comes on slow and easy, grabs, or even acts like a brake at all! Once under way, practice smooth, steady braking using both front and rear binders. This accomplishes two important objectives; it equalizes the wear on the brakes and allows quicker, smoother stops. In an emergency, using both brakes can be the difference between hitting some immovable object or merely advancing your pulse rate. Practice braking under nontraffic conditions. You will soon discover that too much front brake can throw the machine out of control . . . particularly when going down steep hills or under rough surface conditions. Also, too much rear brake will cause the machine to "lie down"—a situation which might be desirable in some desperate circumstances—but which is to be avoided on busy highways. Air travel has an enviable safety record, partly because of the continuing policy of constant control checks. Before an airplane takes off, the pilot operates his control surfaces. During flight he will switch magnetos to see if the spare is functioning. Do the same with your motorcycle. Before leaving, try out the brakes, and occasionally while running, touch lightly to see if all necessary parts are still with you. This is particularly important after you have worked on your machine. I can vouch for the fact that there is no feeling of helplessness quite like the sensation of depressing the brake pedal and having it go all the way down to the street. All you have to do to duplicate this feeling is leave off the wing nut that secures the brake rod to the actuating arm following a reinstallation of the rear wheel.

There is an old rule about braking that holds true for both two- and four-wheel drivers. If you have had to apply the brakes hard more than once in the past year, you are driving too fast for safety; mend your ways now. This is especially true for bike riders since they are their own radiator ornaments and will bear the brunt of any fast frontal contacts. To summarize—an experienced rider seldom uses his brakes at all. He merely downshifts and allows engine compression to slow the cycle. He tries to avoid situations where hard braking is necessary.

Starters Eventually all motorcycles will probably come equipped with electric starters. However, since a great majority still have starter levers, a word about their proper use and control. First of all kick the lever through once or twice with ignition and gas off to check compression. Some of the larger bikes (and a few of the smaller) have enough compression to launch the novice over the bars, or at least respond with a swift and painful kick in the shin. This usually occurs when the piston doesn't quite make it over top dead center and the engine fires backward, thus kicking the starter lever violently back in the direction from which it came. Some of the larger machines have a compression release which can take the hurt out of starting. About twenty-four years of motorcycle starting have indicated to me that there is really no general rule to apply to the problems of cycle engine starting; each machine seems to have a temperament and personality of its own. In time, its owner becomes familiar with his machine's idiosyncrasies in gas and spark setting. Although thousands of cyclists who have kicked their bikes millions of times without results will disagree, it is reasonable to assume that a bike engine will start if it has the right combination of spark, gas, compression, and timing. The important thing is to keep your machine in good mechanical order so that it will start with a starter.

The Throttle Check Check out the cycle throttle carefully before you take a bike for a spin. Does it have a long or short travel? This is important since it determines just how fast the machine will accelerate. Many modern cycles have more horsepower than the average rider can use. "Fishtailing" or "breaking loose" can cause the novice rider to lose control. More common but also a hazard is the tendency of the novice to grab a handful of throttle and roar away from an intersection, only to have to stand on the brake to keep from piling into the glut of cars waiting at the next stoplight. This misuse of the throttle is hard on the bike, the public image of motorcycling, and eventually the rider's health and welfare.

When you have started the engine, rev it up and down a few times to get the feel of the power available. Then apply just enough power to get the machine underway and up to speed through the gears. The throttle on a motorcycle is fairly trouble-free but does have one tendency which bears mention ... sticking in the open position. This attribute, along with bad brakes and snapping clutch cables, has probably accounted for the many loss-of-control accidents. It can be caused by a number of different troubles, but the major ones are kinked or frayed throttle cable wires and dirt between the slide and the carburetor. Again, preventive maintenance will cure these ills before they happen, but always be prepared to have the throttle stick at any position. Gear your mind to this event and it will not catch you unprepared. If and when the throttle sticks, pull in the clutch lever and begin braking. The motor (relieved of its load) will begin to scream, so reach up and hit the kill button or ignition switch. When you have the machine safely stopped, make a thorough examination of all parts of the throttle linkage. If necessary, hitch a ride to town and get new parts.

Clutches: Engaging and Releasing Motorcycle clutches are highly variable. Some engage at the beginning of lever release and others at the end. A good plan is to start the motor and gently release the clutch against a low gear to find the engagement point. Next determine whether it is a "gentleman's" or a racing-type clutch. The former is smooth, can be easily depressed and engages slowly; the racing clutch is designed to come all at once and has stiff springs. A fast-acting clutch of this type coupled with 40 or 50 horsepower can loop a cycle or even leave the rider behind as it takes off. The experienced rider releases the clutch lever smoothly and steadily while applying power with the throttle. The result is smooth takeoff appealing both to the mechanical health of the motorcycle and to the viewing public. If you like the fast takeoff get an American Motorcycle Association license to race and take up dragging or flat track. Both are sure to satisfy anyone's urge for riding the rear wheel.

Gear Shifting The gear shift is a foot pedal on almost all modern motorcycles. However, it varies in position and mode of operation. For example, most English makes have the pedal on the right side and follow an "up for low and down for second, third and fourth" pattern. The Triumph and 1971 BSA models have a right-hand lever but then reverse the pattern to down for low and the balance of the gears are changed by toeing upwards. Most German machines use this pattern but with the lever on the left side. The Japanese have followed this lead, although they have one new design which allows a change in the up and down pattern. What if you're driving a new machine after years on one with the gear lever on the opposite side? You are tearing down a long hill and a herd of mountain goats comes out from behind a granite outcropping. What do you do? You automatically stomp down on what used to be the brake, only now it's the gear shift lever and presto . . . you are in a higher gear sailing through the goats.

Ask any racer who rides one type of machine on the street and another on the track, and he will probably tell you that there are times when he must stop and think about where the gear lever is located and which shift pattern it has. If you are a street rider, it is extremely important that your responses to all emergencies be automatic. There is virtually no time to think about which foot you are going to use when someone stops a Greyhound in front of you. That is why it is best to stay with one shift pattern . . . especially if you ride both street and the track. Don't forget to leave the transmission in neutral until you are ready to travel on.

While not itself a control, the side stand used to support a bike at rest needs some controlling. The bicycle type which consists of a U-shaped piece of metal is not much of a problem, since it will just bounce around on the street if it gets away from its holder. The side stand, however, can be a killer. Another example: while taking off on a mountain road one sunny afternoon, I neglected to put up the side stand on my 21-inch Velocette. While banking into the first left turn, the stand touched the pavement and before kicking up automatically, which they are supposed to do, it lifted the bike off the street and caused an instantaneous loss of control. The bike recovered itself with no help from the appalled operator, but a good lesson had been learned. Make it your habit to check that the stand is up and also assure yourself that the spring or other holding device is in good condition.

Steering Control   Often neglected in the roster of cycle controls is the steering damper control located directly over the steering head assembly on most machines. Turning it clockwise will increase the resistance of the forks and wheel to turn in either direction. The purpose of this stiffening action is to allow the cycle to track straighter and with less effort by the rider when traversing a rough surface. It may be left free or nearly free when the machine is used on smooth surfaces. Use this control with great care. A steering assembly that is too tight can cause poor control on any surface. Work up to its use gradually.

Absorbing Shocks   Approach adjustable shock absorbers in the same manner. . .by trying the various settings to determine which will give both the best ride with easiest control on varying surfaces. Shocks that are too stiff will give a jolting ride and cause you to feel that you are riding an upended bed frame. Shocks set too mushy will cause the bike to continue bouncing after passing a bump. This could be the cause of speed wobbles or other loss of control. Experiment with shock settings on different road surfaces until you get the feeling that the machine is holding the road as well as it can.

A bike is more like an airplane than a car. Almost anyone can hop in a four-wheeler and drive it down the highway. But like an airplane, a motorcycle can bank, fly (for short distances) and loop, and will unexpectedly resent neglect of precise control. Treat your cycle accordingly. Thoroughly understand each and every control of every machine that you ride even if you are only going for a short spin. A motorcycle will always respond consistently. . .it will give you excellent performance in return for excellent and intelligent control.

The Open Road

Analyses of motorcycle accidents have shown that many mishaps involve only one vehicle—the motorcycle itself.

The general rule about driving defensively holds true even when there is no other wheeled traffic around. The motorcycle rider must be prepared to defend himself from a variety of hazards. . .some of them peculiar to the motor-cycle. For example, the condition of the road surface is extremely important. Here are some of the hazards that may exist on *any* road.

1. Holes in the road surface
2. Concrete channels used to drain water at intersections
3. Railroad and streetcar tracks
4. Various foreign objects—bottles, cans, lumber, bricks, wire
5. Objects which suddenly fall off other vehicles—hubcaps, wheels, mufflers, tailpipes
6. Animate objects—cats, dogs, birds
7. Oil, water, mud, ice, wet leaves, sand, gravel, and other lubricating substances
8. Parked vehicles, low branches, wire stretched across a road, and other miscellaneous hazards

Not all holes and crevices in the road will cause the rider to lose control. This is a function of the speed and skill of the rider, type of cycle, tire tread pattern, size and shape of the pavement defect, and other variables of infinite variety. Almost everyone has had the humiliating experience of spilling while going about two miles per hour. A bike has little stability at low speeds. Once I was riding double down a steep mountain road on a '39 Harley "45." The road made a sudden turn, revealing a large curved section of asphalt washed out by recent rains. A fast slowdown did no good—

The inherent stability of a motorcycle forgives many errors of judgment and control. Also, once you've perceived this fact, you can relax and enjoy "flying" a bit. (William Kaysing)

the curved section caught the front wheel at exactly the right angle and turned the wheel sharply to the right and into the mountainside. My passenger and I suffered only a few cuts and bruises, but it could have been more serious if the curvature had been directed to the other side of the road where an unfenced 100-foot cliff was waiting. Motorcycle riders, new and old, should never assume that the road surface will be perfect indefinitely. A rider must be constantly alert and watch the road surface carefully as far ahead as his speed warrants. Not all defects will be seen, since some are subsurface, but many reveal themselves by broken pieces of asphalt or concrete at the edges or by water seepage. In most cases, a turn to the right or left. . .and the hazard is avoided. However, what if the hazard is large—say a foot deep and clear across the road? If a complete stop is not possible, then simply "riding" it out without applying brakes is advisable.

Anyone who has ridden or spectated at a cross country race event such as a hare and hound or enduro knows that a motorcycle, at speed, is a fine double gyroscope and is extremely difficult to upset. Your machine may buck like a bronc and fly through the air, but the odds are in your favor that it will come down pointed dead ahead. If you have any race experience you can do a "wheelie"—simply apply power, slide back on the seat, and pull up on the front bars just as your front wheel touches the edge. If the hazard is more in the nature of a wall or a truck, you can "lay it down," which simply means applying the brakes so hard (rear one first and hardest) that the rear of the cycle falls in the direction in which it's leaning. Any motorcycle-riding police officer can explain or demonstrate this to you since they are all trained to apply this last-chance measure.

The custom of installing a concrete sluiceway at the intersections of asphalt-paved streets comprises a special hazard to motorcyclists. These wheel-catchers are just about the same width as the average motorcycle tire, so that the tire falls in and is held securely while the bike proceeds to lose all stability. These crevices are death traps and should be outlawed. What can you do about them? Short of filling them with cement some dark night, you should do the same as you would if you encountered a streetcar or railroad track. Cross them at right angles or as nearly so as possible. In wet weather be doubly careful.

Roadway Debris

How about objects in the roadway—cans, bottles, and other debris? Well, the larger ones you can avoid without trouble; the smaller pieces of glass are hard to see and, unless you see them in time, unavoidable. (It would be a fine idea if all motorcyclists did what motorcycle officers always do—stop and clear the road of foreign objects.) If you have run over a

The best place to learn how to ride a motorcycle is far, far away from vehicular traffic. (Suzuki)

sharp object, stop at the earliest opportunity and examine the tread carefully. The same precaution should apply if you run over a sharp-edged object, like a brick. Here, if damage is suspected, take off the wheel and tire, then examine your tube for rim cuts.

Long pieces of wire can be hazardous if they are caught up by the spoked wheels or by your chain. They are spun up on the axles or around sprockets almost instantaneously and can cause extremely rapid braking effects. (Even at the moderate speed of 30 mph, the average motorcycle wheel is turning seven times per second!) Since wire can produce the same effect as locking the brakes, look sharp. Nails are another almost-impossible-to-see hazard, and you are bound to pick up a few from time to time, so your best defense is regular inspection. Make it a habit every time you take a trip to examine your tires while the machine is still on the stand. Turn the wheels slowly and look carefully. Remove any glass or metal with a pair of needlenose pliers. Squeeze the tire to see if it has gone soft.

Pushing and Towing

When two people are pushing a cycle to get it started, neither one of them is paying much attention to the traffic. Towing is even worse and should be shunned by anyone seeking to live long enough to teach his grandchildren how to ride. In the first place, the person doing the towing (whether by cycle or by car) cannot devote full attention to both front and rear activities. Thus he is likely to neglect one or the other, with the usual disastrous consequences. The man on the cycle being towed is in an even worse predicament. He is trying to do too many things at once. He is trying to ride a motorcycle which is being propelled in an unnatural way . . . usually by a rope tied around the steering damper knob or on one side of the handlebars. In addition, he is busy choking, clutching, shifting, throttling, and praying the ugly beast will spit some fire. It is easy to go out of control under these circumstances—the rider may spill and be dragged by the fallen bike. Also, if the engine starts suddenly, the rider may not be able to shut it off soon enough. Find out what is wrong with your motorcycle engine and fix it. Then start it with the starter lever or button that the manufacturer provided for this purpose.

Falling Objects

More dangerous than stationary objects in the road are the chunks of junk that fall off our four-wheeled adversaries occasionally. This can happen with astounding speed and without warning. Once on the freeway a large hubcap whirled off an approaching car and spun through the air like the blade of a giant chrome meat slicer, just missing several cars and yours truly. Assuredly there is little defense against this type of accident. However, if you see anything dangling from a car ahead or in the approaching lane, stop and take cover or, if possible, pass the car and indicate in some way to the driver that he is about to lose some parts. Keep an eye on trucks loaded with loose boxes or cars bearing mattresses held down with twine. These objects would be no great problem for an auto driver but to a motorcyclist could cause a big hurt.

Animated Objects

Our four-legged friends also come under the unpredictable category. Cats are forever running races to see if they can make it across the street in front of a speeding vehicle. If you can't swerve to miss dear puss, then just hold the bars firmly and plow through.

Dogs, especially large ones, present a more formidable problem. Many dogs have a thing going about bikes. It is said that high frequency sound emissions from cycle engines annoy dogs to the point where they attack the source. Whatever the reason, it can be dangerous when a large dog comes out of concealment to startle and/or bite a passing motorcyclist. The best solution is to twist the throttle and simply outdistance the yapping brute, rather than kicking at the dog. It is too easy to become engrossed in fending off a canine attack and then run into a real obstacle. Keenan Wynn, in his autobiography, tells of such an accident. "On Sunset Boulevard a dog ran out alongside of me barking. I glanced down at him and pushed out a leg to keep him away.

In front of me a car suddenly swung out in a U-turn, unnoticed by me. I slammed headfirst against a door handle. That was all I remembered. . . ."

Wynn, a staunch apostle of motorcycling, nearly died from his injuries.

Some hounds have been in training for years and chase cyclists with real skill and accuracy. This type leads his victim like an AA gunner and matches his speed before closing in for the bite. The trick here is to shut off when you see Bowser on the horizon lining you up in his sights. Then just as he comes alongside, pour on the coal; it shakes all but the most highly skilled. Turning directly toward a dog as he runs alongside will frequently startle him back to the curb. This is not recommended, since some dogs will panic and run under your front wheel. Some barkers and biters are kamikaze types and simply dive in without thought of injury. The best defense here is to place your feet on the bars and bore through.

Paper route carriers and other cyclists who must approach houses daily frequently use a large water pistol full of diluted ammonia to discourage local bowsers. As a very last resort, you can stop and try to make friends with the frisky little critters. But remember—if it is a case of hitting an animal or swerving into the oncoming traffic or a parked vehicle, hit the animal.

Road Surface

Probably the greatest single cause of motorcycle spills is a slippery road surface. It doesn't have to be very slippery either, since only a few square inches of tread are in contact with the road at any given instant. And when you are braking, a slippery surface can easily "lay it down" for you without your help. There are few men in the world who can sense the instant when adhesion is about to be lost between the tire and the road. These lucky individuals are the world's fastest car and motorcycle drivers. For the average motorcycle rider, it would be best to stay well within the limits of adhesion . . . far enough within so that any additional friction-decreasing elements will not cause a spill. There are many of these elements but the primary ones are water, oil, mud, ice, sand, gravel, wet leaves, chemicals, small branches, and stones. A cycle rider must be constantly on his guard for the presence of any of these "lubricants" on the road.

I had traveled a winding road in Topanga Canyon, California, for many years without incident until one chilly morning the front wheel touched a patch of ice on a banked curve . . . crash-bang against another damn mountain! On another occasion while winding up a steep road into the Simi Hills, a banked curve taken at too steep an angle resulted in a bad spill which bent up both bike and rider. Why? Well, when you are accustomed to a certain degree of bank at a certain road temperature, maintaining this same bank after the sun has heated the center oil slick will produce a swift crash. Again, a rider, no matter what his experience or skill, must constantly observe and evaluate the road surface for any indications of a substance or condition which will reduce needed adhesion.

Another important factor to be considered is the condition of the tires and tire pressure. It is a false economy to ride on motorcycle tires that have lost their tread, particularly the sides of the front tire, since the sides provide all adhesion in turning. The rear should not be smooth either, since you need "bite" for braking and accelerating out of turns. Pressure is extremely important since only a few pounds difference can vary the amount of tread in contact with the road surface. Keep tires inflated to the pressure specified by the manufacturer for the weight of the rider(s) and load. Both too high and too low pressure are equally bad. I was once carrying a passenger with the tire pressure too low (following a session of hill climbing). Upon my accelerating out of a turn, the tire rotated on the rim pulling out the tube stem. The tire went flat at 45 mph, throwing the machine into a nearly disastrous spill . . . my passenger was just missed by an oncoming car and I stopped sliding a few feet short of a large and solid sycamore.

The moral: buy an accurate tire gauge and check your own tires often, taking into account loading and temperature.

Miscellaneous Hazards

There are a good number of rarer catastrophes worth mentioning, since most of them have happened to either me or my fellow riders at one time or another and could easily happen again. Here are some examples:

1. When riding down fire roads, watch for chains or cables stretched across them. A fellow rider caught one of these cables with his midsection at about 35 per, nearly ending his riding career.

2. If anyone is sitting in the driver's seat of a parked car, watch for that door to fly open just at the wrong time.

3. The painted divider strip down the center of any road is just about as slippery as a pig dipped in chicken fat. Stay off it.

4. When riding through a forest, watch for low branches or, in windy weather, the falling kind.

5. Some roads have a sawed expansion joint cut in the center. Stay clear. A good friend of mine had his bike thrown into a speed wobble (violent oscillation of the front wheel) which ended when the machine went end over and nearly ended the rider.

6. Birds sometimes miscalculate your approach and take off directly in your path. If the bird is large enough the rider could be stunned. I've had a small bird bounce off my helmet and fall dead.

7. Don't ride at high speed down unfamiliar roads and don't travel fast at night on any road, familiar or not. All of the daytime hazards are there, but you can't see them. One of the cycle-riding fraternity is no longer with us because he rode too fast at night and failed to see the dim lights marking a large street excavation.

8. It is safe enough to ride on wet pavement, but always wait 15 minutes after the start of a rainstorm to let the road film wash away from the pavement.

In closing—remember, use constant attention, ride defensively, expect the unexpected, wear a helmet, and you will have a long and happy life aboard the most fun-filled vehicles ever invented.

9 Free Schools

When casting about for solutions to the desperately serious problems of the world, almost all of us form the same conclusion: what the world needs is education for its people. With education, family sizes could be controlled. With education, the hostility and suspicions of one nation toward another could be allayed. With education, better food and more of it could be produced. The real obstacle is simply communicating knowledge. Many people find themselves in the same predicament as the British fighter pilot who bailed out of his plane in a remote area. He landed on a bed of purslane, a nutritious wild vegetable, but starved to death because he simply didn't know that this was a good food. So what we are concerned with mainly in this chapter is not the knowledge itself, which exists in such plentiful supply, but the methods of imparting it.

We're going to take a look at free schools, learning by encounter, the apprenticeship method, and the exciting, highly efficient technique of learning at a distance.

Free Schools

The trouble with school is that it interrupts your education.

A YOUNG L.A. BLACK

Back in the Forties, high school boys began adding an extra exhaust pipe to Ford V8's. It wasn't long before Detroit caught on and twin pipes became standard.

Establishment people are keeping a sharp if rheumy eye on the rise of free universities. This is evidenced by such creations as the new Empire State College. This "college without a campus" is supported by a million-dollar grant from large establishment foundations. As cited in a recent *Saturday Review* article:

> The central idea of Empire State College is to create an academic program that will free the student of the restraints of residence on a single campus and make available to him the resources of the entire university system.
>
> A combination of home study, off-campus work-study experiences, educational films, cassettes, correspondence courses, and periods of study elsewhere in America or abroad will enlarge enormously the options open to each student. While some may elect to do half or two-thirds of their work in residence at one or more of the State University's institutions, others will spend most of their time studying off-campus. Time limits, too, will be freer. A college degree may be attained in two, three, four, or eight years, depending on the individual student's specific circumstances and individual capacity for academic work.

So the fastest way to overall educational reform is to do your own thing and then let the existing order update their reactionary, nineteenth-century institutions. A totally with-it group in that town of seething academic ferment—Berkeley—has done exactly this.

With headquarters at 2200 Parker Street, Berkeley, Calif. 94704, FUB (Free U. Berkeley) is unquestionably a model for the educational system in the New America. Impossible to describe in mere words, see for yourself the relevance, the humor, the overall good vibes that are produced when people create their own free school.

If there's no equivalent of FUB in your neighborhood, and you don't dig leaving your environment, then how about starting your own school? To gather reference material, write to some or all of these organizations:

Bay Area Radical Teachers' Organizing Collective, 1445 Stockton Street, San Francisco, Calif. 94133. "With others who share our needs and our understanding, we hope to change the schools and the society. Our primary objective as BARTOC is to take part in the development of a new socialist movement that will make those changes." They publish a periodical, *No More Teachers' Dirty Looks*; $2 for four issues.

*It's possible that we could sell
FUB this book as the text for*
Making It in the Country *(I
think Mike Hunter's going to
try).*

BIOENERGETICS

Bio-energetics is a science of psychiatry: How to make people feel better. It uses analysis, but its analytic tool cannot be learned from school or book, for it derives from nature, from one's own knowledge of the nature of being human.

A human is an energy system, apart from and, at the same time a part of the total energy system of the universe.

When spring comes, all life is loving; so, when sun shines on grassy fields, we, as sisters & brothers move toward each other with loving confidence. When it is stormy & wet, the whole bio-sphere contracts, the sky into million gallon water pools, the animal draws in its reaching, wanting-to-know energy-sensory system. People with cancer or muscular rheumatism have "pulling pains" (contracture of the neuro-bio system), and psychics say that during thunderstorms powers do not function.

Wilhelm Reich, by discovering the true function of the orgastic convulsion, discovered the primary energetic link between living and non-living nature. Prana, qi, orgone, time, bio-plasmic, fire-of-fire, odyle, and X are a few names which have been given to this vital energy which governs the total creative process of nature. This vital life-energy is the energy governing gravitation, light functions, primal therapy, psychokinesis, acupuncture, E.S.P., yoga, zen, karate, alchemy, mesmeric healing, telepathy, levitation, occultism, orgone and bio-energetic therapy, etc., etc., etc.: It is the primary force in nature -- the energy of growth, per se.

It is hard to feel attached to all creation growing up on a stage in this sick, robotized, atomic particle, ego-plastic society as we have, though to Tibetan farmers under the stars in a vast field of moonlight, it makes perfect sense that the force which moves eyes also moves planets: A small child knows this immediately, he knows his breath to be the breath of all life.

Life is breath, so therapy is centered on developing natural breathing. Whoever breathes naturally will never get cancer. Humans are much more sick than animals primarily because they breathe poorly.

Bio-energetic therapy-education is so r-evolutionary because it is the first which works primarily with biological expression, secondarily with psychological expression. Work is directed at releasing muscular, psychological, and emotional blocks so that the energy of life streams freely, and with that, one becomes able to love, feel, and be cosmically aware. The feet contact the earth, the breath the air, and the eyes the sun and sky, so we work especially at freeing the expressive movements in these energetic poles of the body. Emotion = energetic movement. Other therapies ask the student to talk, usually we ask him not to.

We'll learn to "read minds", to say "no", to sense pain, and pleasure, & to be more human. Laughter, & the knowledge that we are all Buddhas will come to us. Christ: What is man's greatest secret? One: His pain--because it, too, is his uglyness.

When I read about this course, I wanted to stop writing this book, drive over to Berkeley, and enroll. It looks as though they have a new approach on the Einsteinian unified field theory (see paragraph 4).

Have you ever seen a curriculum description as beautiful as this?

185

the PRIMAL TRIP

A group of people to discuss & relive acid trips with the aid of gestalt, psychodrama, etc. I would like everyone to be leader & tripper in this group. Maybe we can get closer.
Steve

Couples Consciousness

Couples Consciousness -- Many people are living in heterosexual pair relationships. We would like to explore the implications and possibilities of a pair relationship - roles - male & female and transcending them, problems peculiar to a one-one relationship. Would like to get someone from male & female lib.

Marge & Charlie
First meeting June 5

non-attachment workshop

We will attempt to deal with **attachments**, compulsions, self-defeating behavior, etc. by actually trying out alternative modes of behavior and seeing what happens. At weekly meetings members will report to the group on their experiences and compare notes. The group will (hopefully) **provide** moral support and advice.
Paul Klerman
Time & Place TBA

RADICAL PSYCHIATRY

Once again Radical Psychiatry. Briefly, this course deals with what is wrong with Psychiatry as practiced today; how medicine has usurped its practice away from those who would practice it as legitimately as M.D.'s and more competently. How the medical concepts of mental illness and diagnostic categories and the use of drugs in the public practice of Psychiatry are used to maintain the oppression of the people. It will be shown how individual psycho-therapy is a device that maintains troubled (oppressed) people alienated from each other and mystified about their oppression and its source. The Psychiatric hocus-pocus of diagnostic tests and "insight" therapies will be exposed. It will be shown that Psychiatry is a political activity and that Psychiatry's so-called "neutral" stance squarely supports the pig establishment. The proper practice of a people's psychiatry based on the experience at the Berkeley Rap Center, of which we were recently expelled, will be taught. It will be shown that while alienation = oppression + mystification, liberation = awareness + contact. The oppression of children, women and other human beings will be shown to be at the core of Psychiatric disturbance. Paranoia is heightened awareness. Drug abuse is taught to children by their alcoholic, nicotinic, aspirinic elders. Depression is the result of loss of contact with other humans.

This one speaks for itself.

Psychiatric difficulties are the result of oppression and most Psychiatrists operate as enforcers of oppression. Schizophrenia is saner than "normality" in this mad world. "Frigidity" and "impotence" are the result of the oppression of women and their guerilla warfare against male sexual imperialism. Power to the people!

The course will cover the ideas of Laing, Berne, Szasz, Marx, Fanon, Marcuse, Reich, Malcolm X - with readings from The Radical, The rapist, It Ain't Me Babe, The Berkeley Tribe and numerous papers written by various radical psychiatrists. The course will be taught by Claude Steiner and other radical psychiatrists. This course will be offered with opportunities to become trained at the new Rap (Radical Psychiatry) Center. Serious individuals who are interested in becoming part of the center will be trained as leaders of problem solving groups for women or mixed. Orientation meetings will be held every Tuesday and Thursday from 5 - 7 P.M. Radical Psychiatry also has a volunteer program at Contra Costa Co. Hospital, a winter's group, several training groups for group leaders and is providing problem solving psychiatric groups for about 100 persons.

Sun. 8 pm (continuous with last time)
(Rap Groups) Tues. & Thurs. 5 pm

ART

1. Pen & ink drawing
    learn different techniques
    composition & balance
    color & ink

2. Mosaics
    using a lot of imagination
    experiencing different textures
    composition
    color

3. Mobiles
    using imagination with different materials
    form & design
Cathleen Imp
Tuesday 6 pm
June 8

SILK SCREENING

Setting up your own shop.
Knife cut stencils and
photographic stencils.
Ed Burns
Monday 10:00 pm
June 14

BRINGING YOUNG 3rd WORLD PEOPLE TOGETHER in the COUNTRY

A workshop in organizing a project for bringing young third world people together in the country. Many skills & much work necessary to get this thing going. Everyone with any interest come to the first meeting. Working farm, stepping place for the wilderness & school.

Max Garcia   Monday June 7 8 p.m.

On the ROAD

Drawing from each others experience, the class will discuss how to make it on the road, and where to go. The class will also be used as a meeting ground for traveling companions. The course organizer expects to go around the country in his school bus - camper with some class members.

David Thurs. 4:00
First Meeting June 17

floating commune

Freaks interested in sharing, buying, renting a schooner, houseboat or 40 foot cabin cruiser. Or want 5 to 10 people with bread to buy in on a large boat. Freaks with serious interest in & knowledge of boating.

Robert   Check at FUB office.

BERKELEY ATOMIC ENERGY COMMISSION

WHERE ⌐⌐ is OUR middle NAME

An alternative cultural center and hang out. We will plan a theatre for the outrageous arts & look for a suitable place for it to live.

Bob Touby
First Meeting 9 a.m. Sunday
June 14

The first three courses listed here would give you a masters degree in Nomadics.

Big Rock Candy Mountain, Portola Institute, 1115 Merrill Street, Menlo Park, Calif. 94025, is a catalog of resources for education—both school and self-education. It is published six times a year; subscriptions are $8.

Education Center, 57 Hayes Street, Cambridge, Mass. 02139, is an organization of reform-oriented teachers and education students which creates alternative educational environments, produces films, and sponsors conferences on alternative education.

Education Exploration Center, 3104 16th Avenue South, Minneapolis, Minn. 55403, is an information source for the Twin Cities area.

Gemini Institute, Consultants for Experimental Educational Programs, 8160 Sycamore Road, Indianapolis, Ind. 46240, was formed to support and promote experimental education in the Midwest. They are primarily concerned with curriculum design and development, as well as aiding in the adoption of alternatives by extant public and private schools.

Learning Center, c/o Exploring Family School, Box 1442, El Cajon, Calif. 92021, is a regional clearinghouse for information about Southern California community schools, public school teacher organizing projects and the establishment of new schools.

New Directions Community School, 445 10th Street, Richmond, Calif. 94801, publishes the New Skools Manual about how they started their school and how others can do the same. Minimum donation $1.

New Schools Exchange Newsletter, 301 E. Canon Perdido, Santa Barbara, Calif. 93101, is a central resource and clearinghouse for people involved in experimental education. The twice monthly newsletter is $10 per year. A directory of experimental schools is available free to subscribers.

New Schools Movement, 402 15th Avenue East, Seattle, Wash. 98102, is a group of teachers, parents, and others dedicated to supporting humanistic schools, developing additional models, providing a forum for new ideas, and sponsoring conferences, lectures, and films.

Outside the Net, P.O. Box 184, Lansing, Mich. 48901, is edited for those who seek a radical and humane alternative to America's educational system. It will serve as a link to the underground press to spread information about change in education. Send $.50 for a sample copy.

Summerhill Collective, 137A W. 14th Street, New York, N.Y. 10011, is a collective of five adults, serving as ex-cons, to free the millions of kids imprisoned in schools. They publish a bulletin ($3 a year), sponsor a teacher-training program, generate consciousness-raising groups on kids' liberation, and are a clearinghouse for information on Summerhill-type schools.

Summerhill Society of California, 1778 S. Holt Avenue, Los Angeles, Calif. 90035, puts out a monthly bulletin, has a list of schools that claim to follow the Summerhill approach, conducts workshops, and has the film "Summerhill" available for screenings.

New York Summerhill Society, 339 Lafayette Street, New York, N.Y. 10012, is essentially a duplicate of the above.

Teacher Drop Out Center, Box 521, Amherst, Mass. 01002, is set up to help alternative schools find teachers and to help teachers find alternative schools. The Center has a list of over 1,100 free community schools, with descriptions. These are broken down by state and constantly updated. They also send lists of job openings every three to four weeks. This service is $17 a year.

Washington Area Free School Clearinghouse, 1009 19th Street East, Suite 401, Toronto, Ontario, Canada, is a central resource of information for people interested in alternatives in education, free schools, or public school reform in the Washington area. They publish a newsletter and have a continuing directory. They're interested in articles, information, or inquiries and appreciate any donations.

One of the most famous of these, *Big Rock Candy Mountain*, contains a vast amount of information relevant not only to new schools but to new methods of learning. Pertinent to the former is this "quick hard summary of how to open a free school and keep it open."

People: If ten people will contract (written) to work to support one or two of their number to run a school, if necessary, you can open a school.

Money: Good books fanatically kept. Planned purchasing with ferocious control of buying and nothing retail. About $2,500 for day school and $4,000 for boarding. ETS in Princeton will sell you a weighting for scholarships or you can make your own simple one. Everyone should pay something. Get one semester up front—banks will loan readily to parents, but not to you. The nicest people will deadbeat, poor mouth, lie, cheat, and otherwise do you in. Conservatives pay their bills much more faithfully than liberals and forget about so-called radicals. Be warned. Don't go for or even want Federal or State money. It's not worth it. (Repeat 9 billion times.)

Records: Print an honest transcript form that says you are an ungraded school and what follows are teacher rankings of grade and class equivalents. Give them names and credit hours on the usual 16 high school hours. Give a class rank equivalent. It is a waste of time to try to convert admission offices and you owe your brats an honest attempt at a prediction. Use STANDARD TESTS and give HONEST scores. Academic tests are a gas in a free school, a game. Don't cheat at soccer, why cheat at tests? If the kid can't play, you know he's in trouble. Keep complete health records, make sure you have a waiver for hospital and doctor care on each kid from his mama and daddy. Keep an ongoing log of every sick complaint and every vitamin pill, etc.

Food: Make up a two or three week cycle of meals. Stick to it. Calculate from the cycle what you need and buy cheaper wholesale. If you change (you own plan not reverse) also change the plan. Expect to lose and buy two or three sets of tableware and dishes every year.

Work: Teachers at a free school are mostly about cleaning, sorting clothes, carrying garbage and all that stuff most Ami's hire niggers to do. America moves on invisible black grease and when you give it up, and give up the coercions that keep juniors in line, ecch! Slime-o and bubonic plague unless you rotate the schlock work and don't hesitate to separate yourselves from people who won't do dirty work. World is full of incompetents and lazies.

Curriculum: You've got to make a formal one for the State, urp. Otherwise tons of books, magazines, newsprint, things. Hard areas. Reference room, serious art, library, labs run like SS training camp. Books are treasures, not things to be left in rain. The same is true for microscopes, etc. As long as kids are free to have acres of soft areas and lolligag, what harm? They may learn that expensive equipment is liberating if kept operating, but tyrannical if schlocked up. And you may have the exceptional free school that produces some grads with competence to help save Mama Earth with green technology instead of more editors and other paper and tree users.

Officials: Write every conceivable agency and invite their inspection, supervision, admonition, guidance, etc. Be as open as your heart. Cooperate them to death. Of course, as soon as possible, set aside legal fund for inevitable clashes when they want you to crucify babies on 5,000-year-old idiocies. But don't fight the health department, nor the fire department—they are really on your side, if dumb at times. Question is, is defecating on the grass a more important freedom than having happy self-regulating kids? Of course you get along with these parasites better if you wear straight uniform, but those struggles are up to you. Me. I'd rather the kids be free for their childish games and I have more time for goodies than have long hair, etc.

Finally: Opening and keeping open a free school has much more to do with being tough, anal, compulsive, cantankerous and agile than with love. The real genius at Summerhill is Mrs. Neill who sees to the kitchen, housekeeping, bills and billing. I cannot too strongly tell you how all those nice folks you take in for nothing will be the first to run screaming to the fuzz about how vile you are—meantime owing you for the medicine, food and clothes you bought their brat. Them facts ain't nice, but there aren't too many free schools around and I made about six of them. There is an illustion created by Summerhill Society, New Schools Exchange and others that the woods are just full of free schools. What the woods are really full of is dreamers—and some bastards who want the publicity but make the kids play whatever their hanger happens to be. I know one "free" school that makes the babes pray over their food—out loud. Man. Jesus said not to do that!

I keep getting plaintive letters (many dittoed) asking for reading lists, histories, thoughts and other bull.

The way to open a free school is to open it.

The way to run a free school is to hand those parts which are kid stuff (learning) to the kids and ferociously plan and organize those things which are daddy/mommy stuff (food, shelter, tools, special care) without getting too tight about the separation.

The way to keep a free school open is to be compulsively sure you want it open, hardnosed about business, and WORK. America's most lamented four letter word.

This is all ex cathedra from George von Hilsheimer himself.

Some other samples from *Big Rock*.

Everything we learn is only real to the degree that it contributes to what we are. Direct knowledge of ourselves, the reality of the world we live in, and the facilitation of our inner growth and change are the ultimate goals of education. For the most part, self-knowledge has been limited to mysticism, psychoanalysis, and various beyond-the-fringe activities, and education has been limited to a culturally determined range of ideas and techniques. We have been estranged from the knowledge of ourselves; it is no wonder that we are left empty by the present educational process both in and out of school.

The BIG ROCK CANDY MOUNTAIN seeks to aid in the acquisition of this knowledge; not by molding the learner into a pre-established pattern, but by providing resources to help him quench his thirst; not by teaching meaningless stockpiling leading to a dissatisfied life, but by encouraging growth in the present leading toward a joyous old age; not by changing people, but by awakening a desire to change. This is our motivation for doing this catalog. [Portola Institute, 1115 Merrill Street, Menlo Park, Calif. 94025]

The Voice of the Children

The Voice is a collection of poems by a group of black and Puerto Rican kids. It's not precocious or unusual writing, but a lot of it hits home. The book came into being because, as June Jordan says, "our children have no voice—that we listen to. We force, we blank them into the bugle/bell regulated lineup of the Army/school and we insist on silence." If the children's liberation movement ever gets it together, these will be the leaders—kids who already know the language of oppression. Power to the children.

P.F.

I'm No Animal
What this that came
through the
mail?
A letter!!! Yes!!! A letter
the school sends
note to my
house like
crazy
They sends notes to
my mother
like tickets
to a animal

> *show*
> *Just because I act up*
> *a bit that not*
> *a ticket to*
> *my performance*
> *I'M NO ANIMAL*
> *I'M NO ANIMAL*
> *I'M NO ANIMAL*

CARLTON MINOR, AGE 15

The City

THE CITY IS FULL OF PEOPLE
PUSHING AND RUSHING FOR THE CHECK
THE CITY IS KIDS PLAYING IN THE
PARK, AND TELLING THEIR MOTHERS THE
HELL WITH THEM. IT'S FULL OF
HATE AND WAR, WITH PEOPLE
NEVER KNOWING WHO TO TURN TO
FOR HELP. IT'S A PRISON
WITH PEOPLE FIGHTING FOR
FREEDOM BLACK WHITE
THE CITY'S FULL OF THEM

JUANITA BRYANT, BROOKLYN, N.Y.

Sun, God of living
Live above us. We sometimes
Say something like a prayer.

JUSTIN NEZ, BRIGHAM CITY, UTAH

To show you that it can be done despite monumental opposition and with the disadvantage of being nonwhite, here's a precedent-setting publication from DQU. Members of these minority races (Indians and Chicanos) put together a proposed university program and then proceeded to obtain their own facility in Davis, California. This facility is the former 640-acre U.S. Army Communication Station. Power to the people!

To implement new free schools, there is available a wealth of new educational media ... learning aids such as filmstrips, kinescopes, phonodiscs, phonotapes, programmed instruction materials, slides, transparencies, and videotapes. A catalog listing these new media is available from the American Library Association (50 E. Huron Street, Chicago, Ill. 60611). Write them for the current cost. This catalog will save you a lot of time by providing directions toward all kinds of educational material, many of them free to schools. Here are examples of the latter:

Educators Guide to Free Guidance Materials, Saterstrom & Steph, Educators Progress Service, Randolph, Wis.

Indians, Chicanos Get Their University

INTRODUCTION

In the United States today there are approximately 7 to 8 million persons of predominately Native American descent, of whom about 1 million are "Indians" descended from tribes native to the United States area and balance are "Mexican-Americans" or Chicanos descended from tribes native to regions south of the present international boundary or from tribes native to the Southwest (Arizona).

The Indian and Chicano peoples possess a great deal in common, aside from their common racial origin. First, they both possess cultural traditions of wh t might be called a "folk" nature. Second, they both possess cultures and values quite different from the dominant society. Third, they both have little desire to "assimilate" and instead seek to retain their unique identities, languages, etc. Fourth, they both suffer from an extreme degree of neglect and discrimination, being literally at the bottom of all indexes relative to education, employment, income, life expectancy, etc. Fifth, they both have been denied higher educational opportunities and, in shar; contrast to the Black community, do not possess their own universities and do not receive federal support in any way comparable to that received by Black colleges and universities.

For these and other reasons large numbers of Chicanos and Indians have considered the wisdom of initiating higher education programs designed to meet the needs of their people. This proposal for the Deganawidah-Quetzalcoatl University is a direct outgrowth of that concern.

For more information about this startling, exciting and totally heartwarming development, write to D Q U, Route 1, P.O. 2170, Davis, Calif. 95616.

2. To provide special training for future tribal and community leaders, including courses in Indian law, tribal law, Indian culture, Chicano heritage, welfare rights, etc. This training could be intensive short-duration courses and could be offered in tribal or local areas.

3. To train students in Native American and Chicano arts at an advanced level. This training could be both on-campus and in the community.

4. To train social workers and government personnel especially for work with Indian and Chicano communities, both in regular course work and in special summer programs.

5. To attempt to foster American Indian and Chicano Studies by having strong programs in history, anthropology, religion and folklore.

It is very important that Indian and Chicano students be trained as historians, sociologists, folklorists,

6. Native American Cooperative and Small Business Maagement
7. Native American Water Resource Mangement
8. Fish and Game Management for Reservations
9. Forestry and Mineral Resource Management for Reservations
10. Native American Food Science

Native American Education
1. Fundamentals of Native American Education
2 2. History of Native American Education
3. Current Demonstration Projects in Native American Education
4. Teaching Native American Children: Pre-School and Kindergarten
5. Teaching Native American Children Elementary Level
6. Teaching Native American Children: Secondary Level
7. Native American Curriculum Development Workshop
8. Vocational Education for Native Americans

Literature
1. Chicano Literature of the Southwest
2. Chicano Poetry
3. Chicano Creative Writing
4. Mexican Literature in Transition
5. Mexican Literature in Translation
6. Chicano Prose: Creative Writing
7. Prehispanic Literature
8. Mexican American Literature
9. Literature of Modern Mexico
10. Chicano Composition
11. Chicano Linguistics (pocho, manito, Tex-Mex)
12. Oral and Written Communication for the Spanish speaking

History
1. History of the Chicanos
2. History of the Chicano Labor Movement

53956, 1966, $6.50. Contains listings of free and free-loan educational and informational guidance films, filmstrips, tapes, phonorecords, study guides, handbooks, charts, posters, brochures, and books. Includes details such as title, distributor, date, running time, speed, silent or sound, color, availability of scripts, limitations of distribution, etc.

Educators Guide to Free Social Studies Material, Suttles & Hartley, Educators Progress Service, Randolph, Wis. 53956, $8.50. Contains listings as above.

There's probably a free university near you that offers a relevant education. When you write for a catalog, enclose a small donation as most of these New America universities operate on a peanut budget.

Alternative University—69 W. 14th St., New York, N.Y. 10011 (catalog on request)
Baltimore Free U—c/o Harry, 233 E. 25th St., Baltimore, Maryland 21218
Berkeley Free U—1703 Grove St., Berkeley, California 94709
Bowling Green Free U—c/o Student Council, University of Bowling Green, Bowling Green, Ohio 43402
Colorado State Free U—Box 12—Fraisen, Colorado State College, Greeley, Colorado 80631
Detroit Area Free U—Student Union, 4001 W. McNichols Rd., University of Detroit, Detroit, Michigan 48221
Detroit Area Free U—343 University Center, Wayne State University, Detroit, Mich.
Georgetown Free U—Loyola Bldg., Rm. 28, Georgetown University, Washington, D.C. 20007
Golden Gate Free U—2120 Market St., Rm. 206, San Francisco, California 94114
Heliotrope—2201 Filbert, San Francisco, California 94118
Illinois Free U—298A Illini Union, University of Illinois, Champaign, Illinois 61820
Kansas Free U—107 W. 7th St., Lawrence, Kansas 66044
Knox College Free U—Galesburg, Illinois, 60401
Madison Free U—c/o P. Carroll, 1205 Shorewood Blvd., Madison, Wisconsin 53705
Metropolitan State Free U—Associated Students, 1345 Banrock St., Denver, Colorado 80204
Michigan State Free U—Associated Students, Student Service Bldg., Michigan State College, East Lansing, Michigan 48823
Minnesota Free U—1817 S. 3rd St., Minneapolis, Minnesota 55404

Monterey Peninsula Free U—2120 Etna Place, Monterey, California

New Free U—Box ALL 303, Santa Barbara, California 93107

Northwest Free U—Box 1255, Bellingham, Washington 98225

Ohio-Wesleyan Free U—Box 47—Welsh Hall, Ohio Wesleyan University, Delevan, Ohio 43015

Pittsburgh Free U—4401 Fifth Ave., Pittsburgh, Pennsylvania 15213

Rutgers Free U—Rutgers College, Student Center, 1 Lincoln Ave., Newark, N.J. 07102

St. Louis Free U—c/o Student Congress, 3rd floor BMC, St. Louis University, St. Louis, Missouri 63103

San Luis Obispo Free U—Box 1305, San Luis Obispo, California 94301

Santa Cruz Free U—604 River St., Santa Cruz, California 95060

Seattle Free U—4144½ University Way NE, Seattle, Washington 98105

Southern Illinois Free U—Carbondale, Illinois 62901

Valley Free U—2045 N. Wishon Ave., Fresno, California 93704

Washington Area Free U—5519 Prospect Place, Chevy Chase, Maryland 20015 and 1854 Park Rd. NW, Washington, D.C. 20010

Wayne-Locke Free U—Student Congress, University of Texas, Arlington, Texas 76010

Real strides have already been made by the students of the New America. There's only one regret—those of us who sat through a mindless four years to get a piece of paper feel both heartbroken and cheated. But there's a consolation . . . our children won't be.

Learning by Encounter

Schoolroom education is an indirect process in most instances. The teacher tries to communicate knowledge through his or her own experiences. One parachute jump will teach you more about parachute jumping than all the books, audio-visual aids, and professors of aeronautics could do in a lifetime.

Encounter life directly by hitchhiking. There are thousands of miles of wilderness trails in the U.S., all of them free for the using. Imagine the knowledge to be gained in the following categories if you walked from Mexico to Canada on the 2,000-mile Pacific Trail . . .

Botany
Animal life
Entomology
Home economics: Foods that are best for physical exertion

Meteorology: The science and beauty of cloud formations

Geology: Firsthand inspection of granite, quartz and perhaps (from the rivers) a little gold

Sex: Especially if you take a companion of the opposite

History: Many relics abound along wilderness trails . . . mines, old cabins, and ghost towns

Environmental studies: From high mountains you can usually see air pollution clearly . . . its extent and boundaries

Encountering the world first-hand can be far more educational than sitting in a schoolroom.

The Short-Term Job Approach   A dentist once told me that he had made up his mind to become a dentist long before he was aware of the disadvantages of dentistry as a profession. Unfortunately, he was committed, locked in by financial constraints, and could not extricate himself (or so he thought). However, the point is clear: a young person should not have to commit himself to a life's work before he has an opportunity to check it out firsthand. Therefore, there's another form of education that is not only fun, it's profitable: getting jobs exactly like, or close to, what you may want to do and keeping them for only a short time—then repeating the process as many times as you wish.

A bandit was killed in southern Thailand in a battle that broke out when bandits disguised as policemen attacked a group of policemen disguised as bandits.

SAN FRANCISCO CHRONICLE

Freaked-Out Encounter Techniques

Some years ago, a book titled *Black Like Me* told the story of a white man who had his skin darkened and then proceeded to observe firsthand how it was to be black in the South. (Devastating, in case you're interested.) But let's pursue this fascinating "learning by disguise." Let's pretend to be blind. Wouldn't you learn for yourself how people treat the blind? Wouldn't you feel their sympathetic horror, their attempts to communicate through your blindness by speaking louder? Of course, the experiment would have to take place in an area where you weren't known, but this would make it all the more authentic. Take a look at some other suggestions on how to learn by encounter by actually being another kind of person.

Police Officer   Uniforms can be rented from costume supply stores for a few dollars a week. If you need a badge, you can order one from any police supply house by mail (try Sa-So, Inc., 1185 108th Street, Grand Prairie, Tex. 75050) or can buy them in many gun stores. Next you can buy or rent a gun to complete the ensemble. Now just walk down any street and see what happens. Go up to someone in a car and watch their reactions to a simple question.

Take a tour of a black neighborhood, go on campus . . . your own if you're still doing the college thing. No need to take all the fun out of it by telling you what could and will happen. We'll let you use your own imagination and then, if you can stand it, see for yourself in person!

Hippy If you haven't already, let your hair grow long or wear a wig, buy some clothes, the oldest you can find, from the Salvation Army, put on sandals and a string of beads. Now you can see what life is like from the opposite end of the social spectrum. Repeat the same tour that you made as a policeman. We are as we dress. Clothes make the man . . . and uniforms most of all. (Isn't a hippy outfit really a uniform?)

Man of God You can become a genuine, bona fide, ordained minister of the Church of Universal Life, an accredited church based in Modesto, California. For your diploma and registration card, just write to them at 601 Third Street,

(a)

(b)

(c)

(a) *These are sold in many gun stores and through the mail.*
(b) *Hurry up and get one before they're declared illegal.*
(c) *With the cap, shield, and badge, a bus driver's uniform becomes quite formidable.*

Universal Life Church, Inc.

HEADQUARTERS: 601 THIRD STREET, MODESTO, CALIFORNIA 95351 • (209) 537-0553

Credentials
OF MINISTER

This is to certify that the bearer hereof __WILLIAM CHARLES KAYSING__

of ___CALIFORNIA___ State or Province of ___Calaveras County___

has been ordained by Universal Life Church, Inc. this day ___June___

19 _69_,

Board Members

Dr. Lowell B. Coate
Rev. Susetta Lykins
A. D. deBettencourt
Lida G. Hensley, *Secretary*

SEAL — Universal Life Church INCORPORATED MODESTO, CALIFORNIA

President — Kirby J. Hensley, D.D.

This document made the author a bonafide minister. It qualified me to legally perform marriages, hold services, and any other ministerial duties that I chose. Since receiving it in mid-1969, I have conducted the services at two funerals. It is strongly recommended that you send away for this credential. Even if you never use it for religious purposes, you can escape traffic tickets and get half-fare on airlines.

Modesto, Calif. 95351. Tell them that you want to become a minister. That's all there is to it . . . there's no charge unless you want to donate.

Anyway, whether you go through these changes or not is immaterial because anyone can become a minister by merely wearing a dark suit, well-shined shoes, and a reversed collar.

If you want to be super-authentic, then rent a ministerial outfit from your friendly theatrical costumer . . . the same one that loaned you the cop outfit. Now you are in for some surprises . . . different for everyone who tries it. You can pull off this sociological experiment in your own community. Let your friends in on the gag but keep it quiet otherwise. Tell old girlfriends that their refusal to make love caused you to renounce the straight world. Tell your old Hell's Angel type buddies that you saw the light . . . and then deliver a forty-five-minute nonstop sermon.

Be sure to carry a Bible. Even if you don't know Luke from John, you'll awe the natives.

Incidentally, if you want to assume a really heavy masquerade, have a friendly seamstress create a monk's outfit. Complete with a heavy cross (useful for defense if needed); it will create an effect . . . especially with old ladies and young kids. You'll be positively amazed at the reaction of people when you engage in the most ordinary activities . . . like riding a motor scooter, going into the neighborhood bar for a beer, or even just climbing a tree.

Don't forget that this costume allowed many a bad guy to walk around unscathed in the Dark Ages. (Remember Friar Tuck . . . he was really one of Robin's most valued lieutenants . . . especially with the cross staff.) It can be used today to ensure that whatever you and your people are up to comes off.

Girls can have fun with this rig too, since the face can be concealed. Alternatively, females can dress up as nuns.

The Angels From Hell   In the last few paragraphs we've been leading up to a really wild deception. This is the one where you stop bathing, get a pair of black Levis, and roll around in the mud for a day or so. Then acquire an old mangy pair of cycle boots, a dirty T-shirt, a fright wig, and to crown it off, a leather jacket with the Hell's Angels insignia on it. No detail should be neglected, including your H.D. chopper.

Whether you know how to ride or not is immaterial. You can push the chopper to wherever you intend to make your appearance. Of course if you don't have the bread to buy or rent a big hog, just forget it. Your appearance alone will stop most activity.

Now visualize yourself in this rig walking up to:
1. The Registrars Office at your local university
2. The local police station
3. The principal of your old grammar school
4. One of your unmarried aunts
5. An old girlfriend

Be Your Own Nigger   Did you know that a handful of green walnuts will start you off on a trip from which you may not return? Here's how it works. Take the green walnut hulls and grind them up in a blender or meat grinder . . . or else just cut them up in little pieces and boil them in plain water for half an hour or so. The precipitate will be a beautiful dark brown liquid which you then rub on your face. Burns a little, doesn't it? That's the tannic acid going to work on your outer skin. Soon you will be as brown as you want to be. Now if your hair doesn't look particularly representative of the black people, just wear a hat or perhaps some native headgear that you'd see in Africa. The rest of your costume can be your choice.

The first place to try this disguise is the local bar and grill. See if you get instant service or whether, in an empty restaurant, you are told there's no room. Next stop, a bus trip so you can see where you get to sit. Then try this if you feel brave. Get hold of this replica Thompson submachine-gun. Walk down the street in front of your local police station, or if you are feeling really on top of it, in some redneck neighborhood. And be sure to report back if you survive the experience . . . we'll include your remarks in our revision.

There is a fine book on this subject of disguises, published by the U.S. Government itself. It's called *Evasion and Escape* and contains all kinds of valuable information on how to make uniforms, fake credentials, passes, and such. After all, if the gummint approves of this in print, it's just *got* to be a groovy way to go. Send $3.50 to the Superintendent of Documents, U.S. Government Printing Office, Washington, D.C. 20402.

Each one, teach one.

POPULAR AFRICAN SAYING

The Apprentice and the Journeyman

Many centuries ago young people would learn their skills, not from teachers, but from the experts . . . the journeymen of each trade. Here's how it worked. If the child showed a talent or proclivity, he was sent to live with the craftsman in the field. Then, for room and board and little else, he labored each day with the master. For example, a craftsman in silver would apprentice two or three youngsters. At first they would do little but watch. Then they could be given the simple tasks of polishing or working the bellows. Later, as their familiarity with the skill increased, they would begin heating and cooling precious metals, drawing designs, etching, hammering, engraving—all of these procedures in graduated steps. Naturally, many of the inherently talented young boys were experts before they were grown.

This process of learning has all but disappeared, since it does not, for many reasons, fit in with the modern industrial world where most work is routine and automatic and the worker is really only a machine that has not been invented yet. In a few areas, the building trades for example, apprentices are still employed to train replacement workers. But what an opportunity this system can be for anyone who seeks to learn useful skills outside of the regular educational channels. Let's look at some possibilities.

The Apprentice Writer Although few colleges and universities will ever let you know this fact, there are thousands of ways to make a living as a writer, many allowing complete independence. The usual routine in school is to have someone who has never made a name for himself as a writer criticize class work. Much of the time he turns off the novice writer by making comments based on knowledge that he gained ten, twenty, or even forty years ago. Sometimes he is openly hostile to a student who has great ability. Occasionally, the teacher is simply sadistic, enjoying the squirms of embarrassment as he rips a novice's works to hapless shreds.

2 Glass-Blower

1 Cooper

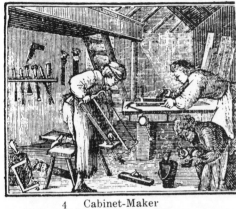

4 Cabinet-Maker

3 Coach-Maker

6 Builder

5 Brick-Maker

7 Paper-Maker

7 Potter

Many of these eighteenth-century trades have a twentieth-century equivalent and all lend themselves to the apprenticeship method of learning.

Wouldn't it be much better for you, as a writer-to-be, to find an established writer and take lessons? These could be either by mail or in person, as the circumstances allowed. In the latter case, the professional could assign work to the apprentice much as the silversmith let his young students scratch out new designs on scrap metal. What a great, productive, and profitable relationship this could be . . . the student doing much of the research, writing the rough notes and outlines, while the professional performed the final polishing. Then, as the apprentice gained experience and confidence, he could take over major writing assignments, leaving the master craftsman to explore, to read, to enter into areas of learning where formerly he might not have had the time.

Alternatively, the young writer could work in a newspaper office . . . first as copy boy, rewrite man, or headline writer, later graduating to reporter and feature writer. However, this routine would lack the great advantages of a close personal relationship.

An Apprentice at Living Itself   Just making a living is not too difficult . . . but living a life that has meaning and fulfillment can be for many people. Thus, there is the possibility of apprenticing yourself to an older person if you are young and a younger person if you are old. Either way the apprentice would gain new insights based on the experiences of his mentor.

High above the city of Santa Barbara lives a remarkable man . . . Vernon Johnson. His life makes fiction seem stale and contrived. As a young man he already understood the importance of living life to its fullest. During WWII, while trying to land a disabled B-17, he crashed in an Italian street. Vernon was blown out of the pilot's seat, losing a leg in the process and nearly losing his life from severe burns. After two years of convalescence, he returned to his home in Santa Barbara and pursued a successful career in real estate. Then, when Nikita Khrushchev visited the town, he saw Vernon in the railway station and asked to meet him. They struck up a friendship that was to continue for years.

As Soviet/U.S. relationships deteriorated in the early Sixties, Vernon bought a bus and began a two-year tour of the entire globe.

While in Russia, he visited Khrushchev in the Kremlin. Their friendly discussions, in the opinion of many, made it easier for Nikita to be as conciliatory as he was during the Cuban crisis. Some of Vernon's friends go so far as to say that he literally saved the world . . . and perhaps he did. In any event, Khrushchev gave Vernon carte blanche in Russia and a free trip with his bus via the Trans-Siberian railroad clear across Russia.

Vernon Johnson is a man who has learned not only how to live, but how to transmit his enthusiasm for a productive, worthwhile life to those about him. His home, known as the Castle, is a meeting place for hundreds of young people. Although there has been no attempt at formal teaching, there is no doubt that many people have been inclined toward a more meaningful life by contact with Vernon, his wife Ann, and their children. Can you see becoming an apprentice to such a man . . . listening to his musings, his reprise of errors, his doubts. This was the method that Socrates and many other great teachers after him used with students. It may be one of the truly successful methods of teaching in the future. We recommend a try.

Some Other Thoughts on Apprenticeship as a Way to Knowledge Here is a list of occupations that could lend themselves to apprenticeship methods:

Actors and actresses
Airplane pilots
Appliance servicemen
Archeologists
Architects
Biologists
Bookbinders
Carpet layers
Chefs
Dairy farmers
Dentists
Dietitions
Doctors
Dressmakers
Druggists
Editors, film, TV
Electric arc welders
Electricians, maintenance
Engineers, mining
Fashion illustrators
Hairdressers
Hotel Managers
Interior decorators
Jewelers
Laboratory technicians, dental
Land surveyors
Lathe operators
Legal secretaries
Librarians
Machinists
Masons, stone, brick, cement
Musicians
Optometrists
Painters
PBX operators
Platemakers, printing

Plumbers
Portrait photographers
Poultry farmers
Radio service technicians
Realtors
Recording technicians
Reporters
Securities salesmen
Seismologists
Sewing machine operators
Silk screen operators

How You Could Get Started   After you have selected a way to go, sit down and write letters to people who have already achieved success in the skill, profession, or way of life that interests you. Tell them about yourself . . . your goals, desires, special talents, and skills. Offer to help them as much as you are able, in exchange for their services without charge. There is little doubt that a certain percentage of those you query will express an interest in the arrangement. The final decision will come, of course, after a person-to-person meeting, or after the details of an apprenticeship by mail are worked out.

The important thing here is to continue the search . . . to keep trying, even if your early attempts are not successful. As these journeymen-apprentice relationships become more common, the path will be easier for those who follow.

Correspondence Courses

Approximately two decades ago I was appalled to learn that I lacked just six units for a degree. Smog and traffic were getting bad around the University of Southern California even then, so I looked for an out. By chance I found that the University of Indiana gave correspondence courses which would be accepted by another university for full credit. So I petitioned the Dean of Men at USC to take the six units from the University of Indiana. The petition was granted and within two weeks the first lessons for an English History course and advanced German Literature arrived in my mail box.

Wonder of all great wonders . . . no dirty looks from professors, no necessity to dress up, and best of all, no need to drive fifteen miles to an urban campus. Instead, I sat in my own living room reading Frau Sorge and learning all about the Palatinate. My unseen instructors in Bloomington were patient, friendly, and dedicated. I learned more from these two correspondence courses than I had from most of my in-class studies. An added bonus was that I could progress as rapidly as I wished. Therefore, in less than six weeks I completed both courses, took a final exam under a monitor at USC and received fat A's on both charges.

After this happy educational interlude, I began wondering why I had not heard of correspondence courses sooner. Certainly correspondence education could and should be a great advantage for many people.

Some further considerations which speak well for mail order learning:

1. It is far less costly since the "university" can be in one's own tipi or VW camper. Also, it is far more efficient in that one professor can accommodate more students and use teaching assistants for all of the routine chores.

2. Instead of being concerned about whether there will be five students or five hundred, with the accompanying physical structure problems, correspondence courses can be expanded or contracted by simply increasing or decreasing the teaching staff.

3. Despite the distance between student and teacher, a highly personal rapport can be established. Since communication is in writing, a lot of excess oral verbiage is eliminated.

4. As mentioned, one of the greatest benefits is the option of the student to proceed as fast or as slowly as he wishes. What a boon this is when for reasons of accident, illness or economic stress a student must drop a class because he cannot be there. With lessons arriving by mail, he would have to be in a coma to avoid his assignments.

There are many other spin-off benefits to learning by mail and these you will have the pleasure of discovering for yourself when you take your first correspondence course.

A good way to get started is to send for a copy of *A Guide to Independent Study.* This booklet is available for fifty cents from the National University Extension Association, Suite 360, One DuPont Circle, Washington, D.C. 20036. The Association is the major national information clearinghouse for a great number of public and private institutions offering extension (correspondence) education. You will find virtually every subject offered by "in-residence" colleges in this overall guide, from that dullest of subjects, Accounting, to the great field of Writing.

The booklet also lists high school, junior high, and elementary courses given by the Home Study Institute. Here are some sample subjects:

Aeronautics
Bible
Black Studies
Composition
Journalism
Literature
Public Speaking
Remedial Reading
Reform in the U.S.
Health
Chinese Civilization

AGRICULTURE

Agronomy
Animal Nutrition
Beef Cattle
Beekeeping

Buildings
Cooperatives
Crop Production
Dairying
Economics (Ag.)
Entomology
Extension Service
Farm Accounts
Farm Law
Feeds and Feeding
Fertilizers
Financing
Forage and Field Crops
Forestry
Fruit
Gardening
Horses
Horticulture
Insect Control
Land Utilization
Landscape Planning
Livestock
Management, Range or Farm
Marketing Farm Products
Meat Handling
Plant Propagation
Plant Sciences Introduction
Poultry
Sheep
Soils
Special Problems
Swine
Turf Grass Culture
Vegetables
Vocational Education (Principles)
Weed Control   47.
Wildlife Management

For less than four dollars you can learn all about any of these subjects. This has got to be the greatest bargain in education going today. (Penn State Correspondence School)

Contents

The Penn State Correspondence School catalog shows a diversity of offerings. Note in the reproduction of one of the catalog pages, course No. 159 . . . Self-Improvement. Who wouldn't want to improve oneself for a total cost of $2.25 plus postage?

making the best use of time and money; to help homemakers, their husbands, and children develop good food habits; and to look to reliable sources for accurate nutrition information. *6 Lessons, 7 Study Points, Cost $2.65. Reviewed 1970 by Louise W. Hamilton.*

158. FINANCIAL DECISIONS FOR YOUNG FAMILIES. This course is designed to stimulate engaged and recently married couples to think about what they want to achieve with their money now and in the future. It presents the pros and cons to consider in making decisions that most young families face for the first time. Included are discussions on wives employed outside the home; using credit; providing life and health insurance for the family; buying a home; buying major household equipment; and buying a car. In addition, guidelines for developing and using a spending plan are included. *9 Lessons, 8 Study Points, Cost $3.85. Written 1966 by Mrs. Magdalene Foster.*

159. SELF-IMPROVEMENT—A COMMON SENSE APPROACH. Each individual has his philosophy of life. This course is directly concerned with the "intangibles"—a philosophy for life and living and concrete suggestions on improving one's self. Thought-provoking evaluation of the individual initiates the course. Consideration is given to the meaning of a "full life" and common sense tips on enriching life by knowledge and experience. *5 Lessons, 5 Study Points, Cost $2.25. Reviewed 1970 by Mrs. Alene M. Mintz.*

170. RETIREMENT—A PERSONAL EXPERIENCE. Discusses you as an individual in retirement. Its aims are to guide you in preparing yourself for a happy retirement. Topics included are retirement — relationships with others; characteristics of older people; you as grandparents; and where you will live. *6 Lessons, 6 Study Points, Cost $2.65 Written 1969 by specialists.*

171. PLANNING YOUR OWN RETIREMENT. When you made your first contribution to Social Security, you started a retirement fund. The earlier one makes a plan, the less it usually costs. Written for all ages, the course is designed to answer your questions about "how" one plans early for retirement. The lessons discuss financial security; governmental services; wills; you in the community; ideas to make your home a safer place as you grow older; clothes for the aging figure; and keeping healthy. *8 Lessons, 8 Study Points, Cost $3.45. Written 1968 by specialists.*

Homemaking
Norwegian
Portuguese
Swedish
Music
Religion
Science
Conservation
Forestry
Wildlife
Arc Welding
Woodwork
Home Mechanics
Home Wiring
Plumbing

Many of the colleges listed have specialties. For example, Pennsylvania State (3 Shields Building, University Park, Pa. 16802) has an extensive array of correspondence courses in agriculture. The average cost is about $3.50 per course. Pennsy has a relaxed, down-loose way about them that you'll enjoy ... at least we've found this true of their correspondence courses.

Here's a complete list of colleges that are members of the independent study division of the extension association:

University of Alabama
University, Ala. 35486

Auburn University
Auburn, Ala. 36830

University of Alaska
College, Alaska 99701

University of Arizona
Tucson, Ariz. 85721

University of Arkansas
Fayetteville, Ark. 72701

University of California
Berkeley, Calif. 94720

University of Colorado
Boulder, Col. 80302

Home Study Institute
Tacoma Park, Wash., D.C. 20012

University of Florida
706 Seagle Building
Gainesville, Fla. 32601

University of Georgia
Center for Continuing Education
Athens, Ga. 30601

Adult Education Building
University of Idaho
Moscow, Idaho 83843

University of Illinois
Champaign, Ill. 61820

Correspondence Study Division
Loyola University
8320 N. Michigan Ave.
Chicago, Ill. 60611

Correspondence Study Division
Roosevelt University
430 S. Michigan Ave.
Chicago, Ill. 60605

Ball State University
Muncie, Ind. 47306

Correspondence Study
Indiana University
Bloomington, Ind. 47401

Division of Extended Services
Indiana State University
Terre Haute, Ind. 47809

Instructional Services
University of Iowa
Iowa City, Iowa 52240

Director of Field Services
University of Northern Iowa
Cedar Falls, Iowa 50613

Independent Study
University of Kansas
Lawrence, Kans. 66044

University Extension
University of Kentucky
Lexington, Ky. 40506

Correspondence Study
169 Pleasant Hall
Louisiana University
Baton Rouge, La. 70803

Correspondence Study
Massachusetts Dept. of Education
182 Tremont Street
Boston, Mass. 02111

Correspondence Study
University of Michigan
412 Maynard Street
Ann Arbor, Mich. 48104

Off-Campus Education
Central Michigan University
Mount Pleasant, Mich. 48858

Field Services
Eastern Michigan University
Ypsilanti, Mich. 48197

Field Courses
Northern Michigan University
Marquette, Mich. 49855

Division of Continuing Education
Western Michigan University
Kalamazoo, Mich. 49001

The Evening College
Michigan State University
East Lansing, Mich. 48823

Independent Study
250 Nicholson Hall
University of Minnesota
Minneapolis, Minn. 55455

Correspondence Instruction
University of Mississippi
University, Miss. 38677

Dept. of Correspondence
University of Southern Mississippi
Southern Station, Box 56
Hattiesburg, Miss. 39401

Correspondence Study
Mississippi State University
Box 5247
State College, Miss. 39762

Independent Study
University of Missouri
Columbia, Mo. 65201

University Extension Division
University of Nebraska
Lincoln, Neb. 68508

Correspondence
University of Nevada
Reno, Nev. 89507

Continuing Education
University of New Mexico
Albuquerque, N.M. 87106

Continuing Education
State University of New York
30 Russell Road
Albany, N.Y. 12206

College of General Studies
State University of New York
1400 Washington Avenue
Albany, N.Y. 12203

Correspondence Instruction
University Extension Division
University of North Carolina
Chapel Hill, N.C. 27514

Correspondence Instruction
North Carolina State University
Raleigh, N.C. 27607

Continuing Education
University of North Dakota
Grand Forks, N.D. 58201

Division of Supervised Study
State University Station
Fargo, N.D. 58102

Independent Study
Ohio University
Athens, Ohio 45701

Independent Study
University of Oklahoma
1700 Asp Avenue
Norman, Okla. 73069

Correspondence Study
Oklahoma State University
Stillwater, Okla. 74074

Independent Study
Oregon State System of Higher Education
1724 Moss Street
Eugene, Ore. 97403

Correspondence Study
Pennsylvania State University
3 Shields Building
University Park, Pa. 16802

College of General Studies
University of South Carolina
Columbia, S.C. 29208

Independent Study
University of South Dakota
Vermillion, S.D. 57069

Division of Continuing Education
University of Tennessee
Knoxville, Tenn. 37916

Correspondence Study
University of Texas at Austin
Austin, Tex. 78712

Correspondence Division
Southern Methodist University
Dallas, Tex. 75222

Division of Continuing Education
Texas Tech University
Lubbock, Tex. 79409

Correspondence Study
University of Utah
Salt Lake City, Utah 84110

Independent Study
Utah State University
Logan, Utah 84321

Chairman, Home Study
Brigham Young University
Provo, Utah 84601

Home Study Dept.
University of Virginia
Charlottesville, Va. 22903

Independent Study
University of Washington
Seattle, Wash. 98105

General Extension Service
Washington State University
Pullman, Wash. 99163

Continuing Education
Central Washington State College
Ellensburg, Wash. 98926

Extension Services
Western Washington State College
Bellingham, Wash. 98225

Independent Study
227 Extension Building
University of Wisconsin
Madison, Wis. 53706

Correspondence Study
University of Wyoming
Laramie, Wyo. 82070

Probing Around for Other Mail Order Learning If you happen to drift off to Canada from the New America, all is not lost. Many Canadian universities offer correspondence courses. The University of Saskatchewan has a catalog which they will mail you free. Just write them at Saskatoon, Saskatchewan, Canada.

Everyone's heard of the famous ICS . . . they are in virtually every men's magazine published. So rather than be redundant about this mail order organization, we'll tell you

Our Methods Make
Learning a Pleasure!

SOME OF THE SUBJECTS YOU WILL LEARN ABOUT

Antique locks and keys • History of craft
How to identify key blanks • Metals used
Principal parts of cylinder keys • Groovings
accurate visual comparisons • Using a key blank
catalog • Applying pre-cutting coating • Line-up and
parallelism • How to clamp and set • Key
gage use • Key filing • Cut progressions
• Finding depths • Final shaping • Deburring
finishing • How to identify keys without
grooves • How to use substitutes
when exact numbers are not availab
stands and commercial key racks
mask • Pivotted lever tumble
• Correcting throat cut • R
hidden tumblers • Rim and
tumbler cylinders • Function
Basic principles of all key machi
• Speed factors • Cutter rotation
Supporting irregular shape keyways in key machine vises • Setting double sided keys without losing alignment •
stops • Narrow vs. wide angle cutters • Purpose of the retractable shoulder guide • Key machine care and mainte
of running speeds for most modern key machines • How to determine the correct speed for the cutter of your ma
and adjusting • "Third generation" test method • How to read special key micrometer • Resetting guide when m
Vise travel and taper • Automatic key duplicating machines • Multipurpose machines • Turret type machines • M
• Changing the combination of pin tumbler cylinders • Rearranging lower pins to fit new key • Two standard
Altering follower to fit odd shape plugs • Filing keys to fit new combination • Use of existing keys of different c
precut key • Servicing the shell • Making all locks operate from one key • Checking cylinder diameter, threads, le
master keying • Principle of master key operation • Use of 3rd set of pins • Making a master key • The Law and L
of public security • Regulations affecting the locksmith business • Law concerning duplication of restricted key:
• How they operate • Raising the discs to clear the seat • Variance in disc sizes • How position of slot affects d
plug • Fitting a key to disc tumbler locks • Changing the combination • Reading disc tumblers • Marking key for p
• Observing rub marks • Making keys by number • Use of code book • Where to find code numbers on locks •
Checking code sheet to discover "equivalents" • Sidebar cylinders • Comparison between sidebar, pin tumbler an
diagrams of cylinder operation • Exploded view of sidebar cylinders • Removable and fixed sidebar cylinders • Use
• Trunk and glove compartment • Comparative list of GM blank manufacturers • Setting up a sidebar cylinder • 3 n
tion of key • Use of depth gauge • How to read a guide chart • Method of installing tumblers, springs, spring
cylinders • GM • Ford • Chrysler • American • Removal of cylinders • Fitting keys to glove box to open lock
method • Foreign automobile lock and key supplement • Auto latches • How to remove and repla
replaced • Method for replacement of broken remote control spring • Proper lubrication • Lock
and wrench • Electric Vibrator picks • Gun picks • Disc tumbler lock picking • tryout keys
remove the plug in order to fit a key • Where to drill • Replacing lug • Flush and Mortise
keys • How to mount a suitcase lock • Making cutouts • Riveting filing keys to fit
control key • Cylinder cross section • Core assembly explode Making the change key • Filing
and control key • Removing core from cylinder • Use of special turning wrench • Schlage wafe
old and new style locks • Difference between #10 and #20 models Identifying series wafers • Combination wa
alike • Schlage keys by number • Master keying • Servicing other keys in the knob locks • Fitting keys
of rim night latch • How to alter a rim night latch to fit doors opening in inside or outside • De
lock security devices • Installation of rim night latches • Dummy cylinders • Mortise
• How to install • How thumb turn locks and operates functions
anti-friction dog • School locks • Hospital locks • Hotel locks • Prope
and left handed locks • Fitting keys by impression • How to manipulate key to gain impressions • Sighting impr
file • Tapping method • Pullout method • Measurements to obtain correct spacing • Extruded pin tumble
the pins and springs • Removing the plug • How to remove the shackle and locking bolt • Fitting the key • Variation
• Locks using retainers instead of individual caps • How to remove retainers • 2 piece padlocks • How to measu
Extracting a broken key • Types of extractors • Duplicating a broken key • Duplicating worn keys • Cleaning loc
excessively oiled • Emergency opening procedures • Forcible entry • Fabricating necessary tools • Drilling cylin
to use the Jimmy neatly • Opening window locks • Opening automobiles • Other methods of opening locked d
Making your own car opening tools • What to charge for your locksmithing work • Combination safe locks • Key Cl
combinations • "Snap-in" type tumblers • Picking up the next number • Testing your combination • Other types
business • Selecting a location • Statistics on average U.S. lock and key shops • Average prices charged • Becc
concessions • Choosing a name • Shop layout • How to get business • Advertising • Publicity • Salesmanship
and banking • Keeping records • etc., etc., etc.

A six-cent postcard mailed to Locksmithing Institute, Little Falls, N.J. 07424, will produce a fascinating brochure on how you too can open doors without having the key.

about some of the more obscure sources of postal perspicacity.

A publisher, Ken Books, 1368 9th Avenue, San Francisco, Calif. 94122, will send you a catalog of books pertaining to civil service positions.

As it says in the ad, "Locksmithing offers freedom from financial worries, security in your own business, respect and trust in your community." What they are selling is a complete course in locksmithing. (In the event you can't make a living at locksmithing, then you could probably become one of the best second-story men in the business.) For information, write to Locksmithing Institute, Little Falls, New Jersey 07424.

Want to find out what makes sex offenders do the things they do? Interested in con games, rackets, and the slang words used by criminals? For just forty dollars you too can become a criminal investigator! Just write to National Law Enforcement Academy, 1100 N.E. 125th Street, North Miami, Fla. 33161. They have a great course on drug addiction that will tell you all about the soft and hard stuff, myths about addiction, plus rehabilitation if you succumb to the weed half-way through. Other courses offered are traffic patrol and control, and how you can be a member of the fast-growing private security forces.

For a complete inventory of accredited private correspondence schools, write to National Home Study Council, 1601 18th Street N.W., Washington, D.C. 20009, and ask for their free directory of home study schools.

"See My Purse, I'm a Poor Poor Man" If you can only rassle up a dollar, it will still buy a complete correspondence course on poultry. For just a little more money ($2.95) you can become an expert on the human foot. There are many other courses offered in subjects like gunsmithing, railroad signaling, and practipedics (whatever that is), and they are all available in good used condition from an unusual company called, appropriately, Used Correspondence Courses. Just write them in Pisgah, Ala. 35765, and they'll send you a free catalog. Another organization with secondhand correspondence courses is Smith Instruction Exchange, 124 Marlborough Road, Salem, Mass. 01970.

In summary, just buy a roll of stamps, sharpen up your pencils, and start mailing. Think of how much fun it will be to master sophomore humanities while stretched out in your garden hammock.

10 Nomad

No need to write down histories. From now on our history is the flesh of our children.

Villages and settlements all over the mountain west from New Mexico to Alaska, with travelers carrying news between them on foot and by canoe, sometimes using the roads but never needing them, free exchange of energy and materials and ideas, take what you need and leave the rest, one nation invisible, no taxation, no representation, no rights, no wrongs, no future, no past, one tribe, one flesh nowever. Nameless human network gently heels planetskin cancer by eating malignant cells and nourishing healthy ones. Scavenger heaps clear up trash heaps. The force of growing grass breaks concrete from underneath.

It is all done one step at a time. Don't follow me—I'm gone. Your dream self will show you the way. When it forgets to pay the insurance premium, let the policy expire. When it loses your keys, unlock your doors. When it makes your mouth tell someone the truth, look him in the eye. Let your waking life run on dream time. Every day is a step of the way. Don't look back. Take your time. Start now.

JOHN WILCOCK*

*John is the editor of *Other Scenes*, a fine movement publication that deserves support and readership—P.O. Box 8, Village Station, New York, N.Y.

(Life Support Tech.)

Because of the beautiful thought expressed in the above paragraphs, this may well be the most important chapter in the book. Historically, large numbers of people drifted away from urban centers as they sensed the end approaching. Today there is a small trickle of individuals returning to the country or wilderness. Tomorrow this trickle could be a flood. Whether you believe that the presently rigid (but swaying) structure of the American corporate state will last or not, it could be to your advantage to gain some experience in the nomad life.

In an issue of a movement paper devoted to libertarian thought, there are some strong arguments for nomad life either on an individual, group, or family basis. As they point out:

FREEDOM: Live out-of-sight, out-of-mind of those who extort and enslave. Work, trade, eat, dress, learn, or love as you want. Live your own life. Do it now.

SAFETY: Preserve yourself and your loved ones from the city firestorms, plague, famine, slave labor roundup. Gain experience and have a head start toward your emergency retreat.

MOBILITY: Live free now yet remain untied; be able to take advantage of emerging opportunities anywhere in the world.

ECONOMY: Cut shelter expenses by one-half or more; pay no apartment rent; pay no property taxes. Reduce commuting time and expense.

CONSERVATISM: Maintain easy access to jobs and shops while liberating your home life. Become free in steps; minimize burning of bridges behind you.

RECREATION: Explore and forage on mountains, seashores, deserts, and forests. Migrate with the seasons for comfort and change of scenery. Enjoy fresh air, clear skies, and wide-open spaces.

LUXURY: Reap the fruits of industrial technology in the freedom and splendor of the wilderness. Enjoy the best of the old while building the new.

PROFIT: Exchange services, goods, information, or affection in freedom with those who share your values.

ADVENTURE: Help pioneer a new community concept, a liberated, evolving lifestyle.

RATIONALITY: Live as you believe. Eliminate contradictions between what you say and what you do. Offer your children a consistent and inspiring physical/cultural environment in which to grow.

DEVELOPMENT: Gain experience applicable to future free living, be it as a continent, raging nomad, an oceanic freedomite, or a new country pioneer. Learn about liberty by being free.

It's a great convenience for the establishment if you stay in one place. First of all you're probably paying high rent or making payments on a giant thirty-year mortgage. Supporting a big house or apartment requires that you have a car, a job, lots of furniture, a couple of insurance policies . . . as Zorba would say, "the full catastrophe." Staying put makes it easy to find you if they want you for any reason. Even the post office doesn't have to spend any time or money forwarding your mail. In short, you become one of those nice, neat statistics that the census bureau loves—a person with visible means of support and a commendable (in their eyes) record of conspicuous consumption.

However, staying in one place can get to be a drag. Are there alternatives? You bet! Lots of them . . . many more than you've probably ever realized. One of the greatest is to become a nomad. A nomad is a wanderer, a man, woman, child, or family with no permanent address. Gypsies are the most famous nomads. Next in line would be the Bedouins, who wander the arid reaches of the Sahara. In the United States there are large groups of nomads known as fruit pickers, who follow the crops. One variety of nomad is called a pilgrim—a person with no permanent home but one who has a specific goal. For example, history records both individual and group treks to places of religious significance. The people in Chaucer's "Canterbury Tales" are a good example. So are the Crusaders, and the Mohammedans who want to visit Mecca at least once in their lives.

Nomading—it has become so popular that there is even a magazine by that name (write to John Wilcock at P.O. Box 8, Village Station, New York, N.Y. 10014). Most people think of nomads in their modern form, traveling about in sleek trailers.

However, there are many other ways to become a happy wanderer without the expense, vulnerability, and contribution to pollution that motor vehicles involve. These include hiking, hitchhiking (the car is going in your direction anyway), bicycles, motorcycles, horses, sheep wagons, rafts, and houseboats. But because the motor vehicle is currently the most popular and feasible, we'll discuss it first.

The Nomad on Wheels

There are about as many variations on this theme as there are motor vehicles. Probably the simplest form and one of the most popular is the VW camper or bus converted to full-time living. If you purchase it already equipped there is no problem. However, if you want to build a nomadic vehicle's interior to your own specifications, here are some guidelines.

Water. Even more important than food is an adequate supply of potable water. This can be as simple as a clean, one-, two-, or five-gallon container from which

Old America had nomads, and very successful ones at that, long before the corporate state made such a mess out of things. (Nevada Office of Information.)

There's no groovier feeling than the one you'll have when you find yourself completely on your own.

Sanitation has always been and will be a problem but this little jewel can save your day. (Wards)

you pour your supply as you need it. A more elaborate system involves letting the water flow by gravity to a faucet or pumping it there manually or electrically. If you have a flowing water supply, then you must make some provision for eliminating the used water. Again, this can be as simple as a container which you empty periodically by the side of the road, a drain which is simply a hose leading to some external point, or much more elaborately, a holding tank which allows you to travel about without visibly discarding anything. Actually, there is no law yet that says you cannot discharge ordinary water on a public street. However, if it is contaminated in any way (soapsuds or dirt) you can get arrested. That's why if you're going to travel much through cities, don't take the chance of getting busted by letting anything other than practically pure water drain from your vehicle. Keep in mind that there is much repression and control coming down on those who defy and anger the establishment by living the gay gypsy life.

Once you have sufficient water to drink and wash your hands and face, you must consider the elimination of excrement. This gets very heavy because of stringent sanitation laws governing the deposit of anything as odoriferous as waste products. There are a variety of ways to cope with this daily problem, ranging from an ordinary ten-quart bucket to this little plastic beauty which is good for two or three dozen flushes.

Once you have overcome the problem of an adequate water supply and can get rid of it safely without messing up our mutual environment, you have about 90 percent of the nomad problem solved.

Cooking Facilities. Unless you're stuck on cold food, you'll want to have some provisions for cooking simple meals. This can consist of the old, reliable, and well-proven primus stove, which has been used on boats for many decades. Some require kerosene; others use alcohol.

One admonition: inside a motor vehicle be very careful with anything that emits a flame. Gasoline fumes from your own tank could turn your tour into something that goes straight up. That's why many nomads do all of their cooking outdoors like this. The Volkswagen people consider the fire hazard so important that their official camper has a folding shelf so that a portable stove will be used *outside* of the vehicle itself.

Sleep Tight. You may want to forego the preceding homelike comforts, but there's little doubt that you would enjoy the coziness and security of sleeping inside of your own nomadmobile. Provisions for sleeping are the simplest and easiest of all of the comforts you may be seeking. All you really need is a mattress, waterbed, or some other soft object between you and the hard floor. One of the least expensive beds is a piece of four-inch-thick polyurethane foam that can be cut to fit your vehicle exactly. If you don't want to sleep directly on the floor, a raised platform can add a touch of elegance plus the advantage of having convenient storage space beneath. A more complicated arrangement, but one with great advantages, is the bed that makes up into a dinette (usually called a dinette which makes up into a bed).

Meals never taste quite as good as when they're prepared on small-scale equipment like this.

The mini-refrigerator works on 12 volts DC, 110 AC, and bottled gas.

This World War II heavy-duty carryall was purchased in 1946 at a veteran's sale and used by the author for several years as his away-from home. (William Kaysing)

Hammocks are a unique and practical solution to sleeping accommodations in a small vehicle. These can be either the type bought in a sporting goods store or discount house, or the metal type that swings down from the side of the vehicle with the outer edges suspended by chains. This type of bunkbed permits you the full use of the camper interior during the day, since mattress, blankets, and pillow all swing up with the bunk. These bunks can often be purchased from a surplus store, since they are used on naval vessels. Even an army cot can be hinged in this style.

Storage. Storage in a nomad vehicle presents no unusual problems. The book *Storage Ideas for Your Home*, published by Sunset (Lane Publishing Co., Menlo Park, Calif.), is an excellent reference. The only thing you have to do is scale down the size of the storage containers to fit your vehicle.

Equipment. There is an extremely wide variety of tools available to enable you to eat and sleep in comfort. The problem is not a lack of equipment from which to choose, it is an excess. Most families who flee the cities in their store-bought pickup campers are so loaded down with Sony TV's, hi-fi stereo units, motorized, electrified, and gasified barbecues, portable washing and sewing machines, high-speed ice cream makers, portable refrigerators and freezers, plus gasoline-powered generators to run everything, that they don't really have any time to commune with nature. They are much too busy acting as stationary engineers for the complex equipment which ensures urban comforts amid wilderness surroundings. As Thoreau pointed out, most manufactures are superfluous to having a really good time.

Here is a modest inventory of items that require no power and little maintenance but can increase your enjoyment of the wandering gypsy life.

Operating Manual for Your Nomadic Home. Recently the city of San Francisco passed an ordinance which prohibits anyone from living in a vehicle parked on the city streets. This effectively cuts off the possibility of a short-term visit to an urban area . . . or does it? One of the first principles of a successful nomad is to be as inconspicuous as possible. The era of the gaudily painted, highly flamboyant "hippy wagon" is definitely over. This era of establishment anxieties about people's freedom ensures that you will have little peace or privacy if you insist on advertising the fact that you are having a great, groovy time galavanting all over the geography. Instead, a vehicle should be maintained in the establishment image. For example, if you have converted an old bread truck, either leave the words "Fresh

NEW ISSUE ARMY MESS TRAYS are made of heavy plastic. Tan colored, new condition. More durable than metal, they keep their shape and won't dent. Designed for man-sized meals, they have five compartments and are excellent for camp or picnic use. They nest for easy storage and save on dish washing since all food is on one tray. Size: 13¾"Wx10¾"x1".
☐ **S834 Plastic Mess Trays** **$2.95**

5-PIECE MESS KIT, made of aluminum, is a must for camp chefs. Consists of five pieces—a frying pan with folding handle, a plate, boiler, boiler lid and drinking cup. Constructed of heavy gauge aluminum, the set will give lots of service. The five pieces nest together compactly when not in use. Nested size, 7¼" diameter x 3" high.
☐ **S704 5-Pc. Mess Kit** **$2.00**

OUTDOOR DISHES FOR FOUR are provided by this 12-piece cook set. Perfect for camping or picnics. The pieces nest into each other to form a compact package 9" in diameter x 6¼" high. Set consists of four plates and four cups made of heavy-duty plastic, 1 frying pan, 2 kettles with handles and one coffee pot made of heavy gauge aluminum.
☐ **S756 12-Pc. Cook Set** **$7.50**

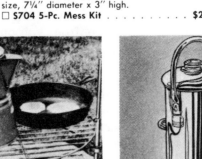

FRENCH ARMY SURPLUS 3-Piece Mess Kit can be used for cooking as well as serving. When nested together, the kit is 6" high x 6" long x 3" wide. Made of heavy gauge aluminum, kit consists of three containers: a 6" deep stewing pan with bail handle; a 2" deep frying pan with folding handle; and a 1½" deep sauce pan. Campers are sure to like this one.
☐ **S7088 French 3-Pc. Mess Kit** . . . **$2.50**

SWING-AWAY CAMPER'S GRILL safeguards against burned foods, scorched fingers. Swings away from fire when you prepare foods, serve, etc. 18" round grill easily adjustable up or down. Made of heavy duty chromed steel. Dismantles into two sections for storage. Wt., 5 lbs.
☐ **S7111 Swing-Away Grill** . . **$6.95**

PALCO 14-CUP COFFEE PERCOLATOR makes and keeps 8 to 14 cups of perfectly brewed coffee ready at your campsite. Made of stainless steel with unique water diffuser. "Swing-lock" stainless steel handle and hand grip. Can't break or burn. Non-drip spout.
☐ **S831 14-Cup Percolator** . . **$25.95**

OUR SALT 'N PEPPER PACK is the ideal container for carrying your seasonings on picnics and camping trips. It's a fool-proof plastic salt and pepper shaker that screws together when not in use; no tops to cover, yet cannot mix. Screw out the plastic bottoms to fill. Keeps out moisture, nothing to corrode, will float if dropped in the water.
☐ **S855 Salt 'n Pepper Pack** . . . . . **$1.**

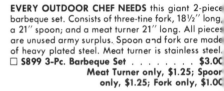

KNIFE, FORK AND SPOON SET was designed for outdoor living. Made of heavy gauge stainless steel, it's light, compact and easy to carry—but it will perform heavy duty service for you at chow time! As an added feature, the three pieces clip together when not in use so they won't get lost or separated. Each set comes with a plastic carrying case.
☐ **S762 Knife, Fork, Spoon Set** **$1.00**

ARMY MESS KIT consists of an oval frying pan and a two-compartment metal plate. Made of heavy gauge aluminum. Used very good condition.
☐ **S705 Army Mess Kit** **$1.25**
ARMY KNIFE, FORK AND SPOON fits inside the Army mess kit.
☐ **S760 Army Knife, Fork, Spoon** **$1.00**

EVERY OUTDOOR CHEF NEEDS this giant 2-piece barbeque set. Consists of three-tine fork, 18½" long, a 21" spoon; and a meat turner 21" long. All pieces are unused army surplus. Spoon and fork are made of heavy plated steel. Meat turner is stainless steel.
☐ **S899 3-Pc. Barbeque Set** **$3.00**
Meat Turner only, $1.25; Spoon only, $1.25; Fork only, $1.00

For less than a twenty-dollar bill you can equip yourself for virtually permanent outdoor living. (P & S Sales, Tulsa, Okla.)

Bread—Daily Delivery" on the side or paint on a new sign to identify your vehicle as performing some useful service for industry or commerce. There is no law that says you can't paint "Acme Furniture," "Feinstein's Fish," or "Radioactive Materials—Stay Away" on the side of your vehicle. In fact, you might go so far as to paint trademark names like Sears, Wards, Penney's, or United Parcel on your truck or van. There is one possible danger in using a well-known name . . . some official of the company might spot your truck parked near the old swimming hole with you and your clan having just too much fun cavorting in the cool water. He'll either confront you on the spot or have the company minions make a quick check on who's having the good time.

Along with the straight-looking nomadic vehicle, it's a good idea to dress the part. For a few dollars you can buy a set of khakis and a cap. If you want to extend the image, have a name like Stan or Ollie embroidered above the left breast pocket. For an even greater commitment, have the same name as your truck sign embroidered on the back of your shirt. Then, no matter where you drive or what you do, you'll get a friendly wave from local constables and other people whose lives are bound by time schedules. We are still operating under the Puritan concept of "work is noble." Thus, anyone not working is thought to be ignoble. But no one minds if the working man occasionally stops by the side of the road to have a picnic or even a dip in the local river. The real problems arise if you go about looking like you're having a positively permanent bash.

To embellish your image as a part of the establishment, maintain your nomad vehicle in top condition. This means that all lights and turn indicators function perfectly, your license plates and other required symbols of conformity are in good order, all paper work such as registration slips and inspection certificates are up to date and totally kosher. In addition, your vehicle should be sparkling clean inside and out, otherwise suspicion that you aren't what you pretend to be could be generated. To maintain a mailing address for your paper work, rent a post office box in a town where friends live. The cost is small and your friends can receive and forward your mail.

Here are some additional tips that will permit you the maximum fun in America with the fewest hassles:

1. Obey all traffic laws scrupulously.

2. Carry a complete set of maps of any area where you operate so that you do not have to ask questions of nosy service station attendants and especially local authorities.

3. When you park at night in an urban or suburban area, pick a location where your truck will look completely

natural. As one of the canny Greeks once said, the best place to hide a pebble is among pebbles. Therefore, a truck marked "Feinstein's Fish," dripping a little water, would look completely at home in front of Solomon's Market. Alternately, Johnson's Furniture Delivery could be parked on any business or residential street without attracting the least attention.

When you are in the country, the problem is a little more difficult. Here the presence of a strange truck parked down some rural lane could cause the instant suspicion of a cruising sheriff. If you are going to park in the boondocks, hide your truck. Park it in a thicket or down some almost forgotten logging road. Even with these precautions, it is possible that you will be awakened in the middle of the night by some heavy rapping on the side of the truck. The proper response is to say in a sleepy voice, "I was on my way to (name of next town) and I got sleepy, so I pulled off the road to rest awhile, officer." This will usually do it, although some uptight law enforcement personnel may ask you to move. If this is the case, put on your uniform and move the truck without any argument whatsoever. Invariably this will satisfy even the most irritable country constable. If he does demand to see your credentials, you'll be glad that you had everything in the proper order. Of course you will take great pains not to reveal the true nature of your truck. Even if you are found out, you may be able to talk your way out of it by treating the whole thing as a big joke. Some officers won't see the humor in this and you could be hauled off to jail. In this event, refer to the chapter on legal procedures useful in the New America.

4. Keeping your nomadic home supplied with good water is really a problem. City water and much of what you find in the country is heavily contaminated with strange chemicals and, besides tasting bad, could make you sick. Thus, it's a good idea to keep your eyes open in the country for running springs. Many of these can be found in mountainous areas, complete with handy pipes that make it easy to fill your storage containers. Because a change of water will often upset your system, try to keep as much of one kind of water on hand as you can.

5. Carrying an adequate supply of spare parts plus the tools to install them makes good sense. This is particularly true if your vehicle is an odd brand or very old. An extensive supply of expendable items like fan belts, water pumps, grease seals, distributor caps, spark plugs, points, and condensers should be carried. A good source of these is the J.C. Whitney Co., 1900 S. State, Chicago, Ill. 60616. Send for their free catalog and keep it handy. Another good source of usable parts is the eyesore of America—the rural junkyard.

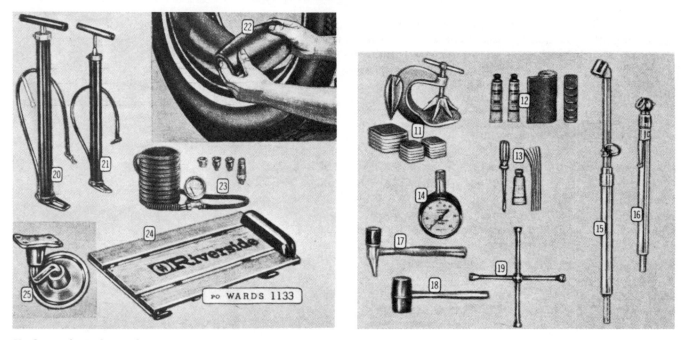

To be truly independent, you should have the know-how, the equipment, and the parts to keep yourself rolling. Here are some items that will free you from dependence on garages. (Wards)

Here, all you'll have to do is find a comparable make and model and buy whatever you need to keep your vehicle running.

6. Crossing borders can be a problem. Here again you can see the importance of having all your papers in good order. Operating as a disguised truck can be a great advantage, since border patrolmen normally do not impede the transit of commercial goods. However, if a patrolman sees that the interior of your vehicle is equipped for permanent living, you may have some problems. Simply telling the truth about your situation is possibly the best way of handling this problem. If they won't let you across the border in one place, try another. If you can't get across the border at all, it's likely that the country is so uptight anyway that you shouldn't be there. Once you do get across, you can change the appearance of your truck to conform to your new environment. For example, you can paint out "Feinstein's Fish" and crudely letter "Fresh Tortillas" when you are in Mexico. In Canada a well-executed drawing of a maple leaf plus the legend "Saskatchewan Sarsaparilla Suppliers" will even get you through hippy-conscious Vancouver, B.C.

In summary, life as a nomad in a power vehicle can be both fun and games if you are properly prepared. But without intelligent forethought, it is likely you'll be hassled from Pillar, Missouri, to Post, Minnesota. Close attention to detail is the secret of living loose in America.

Variations on the Theme

Death is still a taboo subject in America. You can take advantage of this by simply buying an old hearse, restoring it

*Once you get this big establish-
ment rig towed to a fresh-air
spot like this, sell the car to a
passing WASP and live happily
forever after in the trailer.
(Terry Trailer Co.)*

to its original appearance, and then proceeding to live in it. It
helps if you dress in black. At the opposite end of the
spectrum (or maybe it's really a close parallel), obtain a
secondhand camper, borrow someone's unwanted children,
get a loud sport shirt, and go about America as a member of
the silent majority on vacation. It helps if you throw your
empty beer cans out of the window while traveling and do a
lot of yelling at the kids. The police won't suspect a thing.

Trailers Descendents of the old gypsy wagons, modern
trailers provide all the comforts of a permanent home no
matter how far you roam. If you include the recently developed double-wide, essentially prefab structures called mobile
homes, the range in trailers is astounding. The smallest can be
towed behind a VW, while the largest require special equipment to move them. For life in the New America, consider all
types and sizes.

The low-profile trailer that can be towed by practically
any size vehicle is a most convenient way to have a home
away from home. The typical arrangement is a roomy double
bed with a few small storage compartments coupled with a
complete kitchen in the back. Naturally, you stand outside to
cook but this can be an advantage since you get to enjoy
fresh air and scenery while the stew is bubbling. The cost of
these Lilliputian two-wheeled homes ranges from a few hundred dollars up ... but not too far up. Light as a utility
trailer, you'll hardly know that it's on the back of your car.

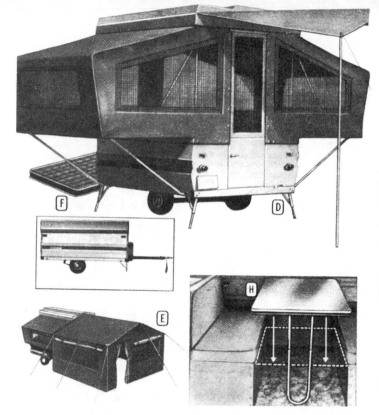

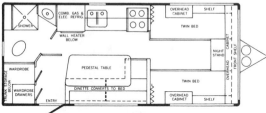

16 STANDARD

▪ FRONT GAUCHO, "L" SHAPE DINETTE, SIDE KITCHEN, FRONT STUDIO BUNK — SIX SLEEPER ▪ Tire Size: 775 x 15 — Load Range "B" ▪ Approx. Gross Wt: 2100 Lbs. ▪ Approx. Hitch Wt: 350 Lbs. ▪ Approx. Height: 8'9" ▪ Approx. Length: 16'6" ▪ Butane Light ▪ Stainless Steel Sink ▪ 110 Volt and 12 Volt Lights ▪ 3 Burner Range With Oven ▪ Large Wardrobe (Optional 12 Volt Recirculating Toilet Available) ▪ 20 Gallon Water Tank ▪ 75# Ice Box

21 TRAVEL PAK®

FRONT TWIN BEDS, "L" SHAPE DINETTE, SIDE KITCHEN, REAR BATH, FRONT OVERHEAD CABINET, TANDEM AXLE ▪ Tire Size: 775 x 15 — Load Range "B" ▪ Approx. Gross Wt: 3250 Lbs. ▪ Approx. Hitch Wt: 260 Lbs. ▪ Approx. Height: 8'9" ▪ Approx. Length: 21'1" ▪ Large Combination Butane/Electric Refrigerator ▪ 4 Burner Range With Window Door Oven and Stainless Steel Range Cover ▪ 15,000 BTU Wall Heater W/Unitrol ▪ 6 Gallon Water Heater ▪ Double Stainless Steel Sink ▪ 12 Volt Fluorescent Light ▪ Wide Track Axle and Wheel Skirts

Also, because they are low, reduced gas mileage due to wind resistance is practically eliminated.

Halfway between this mini trailer and a full-sized one are the accordian-like tent trailers. The smallest have only sleeping and storage facilities. If you want cooking and/or sanitation equipment, you'll need to supply heavy bread ... over a thousand dollars for some of the newer and posher ones.

The next order of magnitude is the stand-up-inside trailer that ranges in length from about twelve to twenty feet. These come in an array of styles. Curiously, the very smallest have all the essentials, cooking, sleeping and even sanitation facilities in the same scale as their larger counterparts; the biggest difference between a twelve-footer and a twenty-footer is in storage. Thus, if you resist the temptation to haul a lot of just plain "stuff" with you, you'll find that your basic comfort level is the same.

In 1962, I decided to tour the America West since, at the time, it appeared as though it might become highly radioactive at any moment. After examining a large number of possible rolling homes, we all agreed on a 16½-foot Fireball with an overhead bunk for our two daughters. This trailer had a flush toilet with a holding tank (a must for the fair sex while on the road), but no shower. For a shower you would have to carry water with you (at eight pounds per gallon), heat it, use it, and then find some acceptable way of

It's surprising how little room one needs to enjoy life after you've dumped the eight to five routine.
For maximum economy (initial cost and towing expenses), tent trailers can't be beat. (Terry Trailer Co. and Montgomery Ward)

The car cost $200, the boat was home-made, and the trailer had an overall cost for one year of less than $200. All units performed beautifully on this family-type exploration of the West. (William Kaysing)

getting rid of it. The problem is formidable for a small trailer. If you allow a modest ten gallons of water per person for a family of four for showers then you must load, store, heat, and eliminate 40 gallons or 320 pounds of the drippy element. Frankly, it's just too much of a hassle and expense. It's much better to use the space and dollar expense of showering for some other essential like food, clothing or, say, musical instruments. You can almost always camp by a river, lake, or stream or a public trailer park and use either the natural facilities or a regular shower installation. If nothing is available, then a sponge bath with a pot heated on the stove can suffice. Even after almost a year of living without a built-in shower bath, we all agreed that external showering and bathing was the most practical solution to the personal cleanliness problem. But for the relatively fastidious, a portable shower could be improvised with some canvas, a bucket, and an extra pair of hands to help.

Another trailer item that can be eliminated easily is the icebox or refrigerator. Early in our tour we found that buying ice for our box was much more costly than the savings in food being preserved. This was brought home forcefully one evening when I rassled in twenty-five pounds of ice that cost seventy-five cents and found that it was only going to chill a quart of milk and a small bowl of leftover chili beans. From then on, the icebox became our paperback book locker and we simply made do without refrigeration. It's actually easier than it sounds. Here are the principle points:

1. Cook only as much as you will eat for any given meal.

2. Buy your cold stuff fresh and use it promptly.

3. If you find you must keep milk or butter overnight, wrap it up in a moistened towel and put it under the trailer or in any other cool spot. (A nearby stream makes a great free "frig.")

4. Whenever you get a penchant for something really cold, buy a small bag of ice cubes and really live it up. Then you'll be able to go without it for quite a spell. What happens is that you begin to treat ice and cold things as a special treat. The money you save by not having to refill your butane tanks or generate electricity for refrigeration will make you even more independent . . . and that's the game we're playing. Relevant to this subject is a booklet which tells how to cook thirty-six great dishes using only sixteen non-perishable staples. Write to the McIlhenny Co., Avery Lisland, La. 70513, for the booklet *Space-Saving and Time-Saving Cooking for Men on the Move.*

You'll find the two basic items found in all trailers that produce the most in terms of creature convenience are the butane or bottled gas stove and the water tap and sink. With these amenities, you can cook dishes like Irish stew and bean soup and clean up afterward. Most small trailers have an oven beneath the stove burners, but it's recommended that you go easy on its use since it requires lots of your precious gas supply. If you do use the oven, make the most of it. Load it with loaves of homemade bread dough and cookies, and fill all the corners with potatoes that you can eat hot or slice for panfries later.

To enjoy hot food and the luxury of flowing water requires adequate supplies of bottled gas and water. The former is usually known as liquid petroleum gas, or LPG for short. It is also referred to as butane. Stored in a strong steel bottle or tank at the hitch point of your trailer, it can be refilled at many service stations. The cost is under fifty cents per gallon, although many suppliers charge a minimum, because of the cost of labor in hooking it up to a supply tank. We found that a five-gallon tankful lasted over a month, even though we cooked three meals a day for four persons. Naturally, we were careful in its use and always used low heat for cooking and heating wash water. Remember, too, our trailer did not use the gas for any other purpose ... no water heater, no gas refrigerator, no lights or heating unit.

Many trailers have two five-gallon tanks connected in such a way that when one becomes empty, you can switch over to the other. Then by filling the empty tank at the next supplier, you'll never run out of gas. Even if you go the spartan way with just one tank, you don't need to run out if you keep a check on the tank. Here's how to do it: Boil a small amount of water and let it run over the side of the tank. Now run your hand up and down the tank. You'll be able to feel the level of the gas indicated by a lower temperature. When the tank level gets below one-fifth of its capacity, it's time for a refill.

Equally important is your water supply, which can be gravity flow or pumped. The former is simpler, since all it requires is a tank elevated above your sink; the only disadvantage is that the weight of the water has a tendency to make small trailers more top-heavy. Tanks below the faucet level require a pump. One system of pumping employs air pressure—the water tank is filled almost full, then air is pumped into the tank through a conventional air valve from a compressor or hand pump. I found the compressor rather unsatisfactory ... when the pressure was high, the water came roaring out of the faucet seething with air bubbles; then, after a short period of conventional pressure and flow, there came a long period of trickling which ended in no water at all. A hand pump would be my choice next time ... a little work, to be sure, but at least you wouldn't be caught with soapy hands and no water to rinse them.

The other method commonly used is the electric pump

Butane or propane gas bottles now come in several sizes, tailored to suit your needs.

... either 110 volts AC or 12 volts DC. Both currents work great *if you have them*. However, if you intend to make it up the Alcan Highway, it would be best to have an alternate (hand or gravity) system.

There are many fine books on the subject of living comfortably and happily in a trailer. So before you start, buy one and read it carefully. What you won't find in any book on trailering is advice on how to avoid hassles, so we'll refer you back to the Operations Manual for living in a converted truck . . . the rules apply equally well to trailer living.

Before we leave the subject, here's an important point to remember about trailers. Once they are towed to a desirable location, you can plant vines around them and in a few months, you'll have a camouflaged home that will keep you secure from both bill collectors and IRS men.

The Sheep Wagon

A number of years ago a man from Minnesota decided to pack up and head West. Since he was a farmer and had little money, the most logical way for him to travel was in a large farm wagon. He tossed his children and all of the family belongings into it, covered it in the fashion of pioneer covered wagons, hitched up his horses and headed out of town. While his progress was slow, he and his family were able to enjoy the natural wonders en route at a leisurely and relaxed pace. Furthermore, the horses grazed most of their food along the roads he traveled. Since he was a farmer, he was welcomed by other farmers and ranchers along the way. Thus, he had little trouble in finding suitable overnight camping places.

There is much open country on the North American continent where this mode of travel would be suitable. Naturally, you would shy away from busy freeways, but there are many almost abandoned back roads that lend themselves to this super-casual way of living the nomad life. The very pastoral appearance and nature of your venture would ensure a minimum of hassles by the Man.

A rig like this could travel untroubled throughout the American West for decades. With its peaceful flock of sheep nearby, it is the symbol of solitude and tranquility. Thus, it could assure freedom from hassles for its owners.

It takes a little while to build up a flock like this, but the wagon can be built in a few days by any handy man. Write John Shuttleworth, P.O. 38, Madison, Ohio, and ask him to send you the issue of Mother Earth News *in which the plans for a sheepwagon appeared. (Utah Chamber of Commerce)*

In a minor variation, one could build a traditional sheep wagon and even have a few head of the woolly creatures trotting along behind for authenticity. A gypsylike conveyance such as this would be totally accepted on millions of acres of rangeland in Utah, Nevada, Idaho, Oregon, and similar states.

The Saddle Tramp

A common sight throughout the West until well after the turn of the century was the picturesque cowboy with all of his belongings aboard his faithful horse. These men traveled the vast reaches of the American West, working when necessary but often finding living so easy that work was unnecessary. Even though the day of the six-gun and unfenced rangeland is over, the life of a nomadic saddle tramp is still an opportunity for one person or a group to escape the horrors of urban life and to enjoy the pleasures of living close to nature at minimum expense.

A good horse can cost as little as $150. Saddles start at

The Old West isn't dead. On the contrary it's waiting for you to make it a part of your New America. (USDA)

under $100. Beyond these expenses you only need the usual "live-outdoors" equipment, such as sleeping bags, cooking equipment, and perhaps a trusty 44-40 Winchester. I visualize a small group of outdoor lovers ... men, women, or a compatible mixture of both ... making their way along some of the historical trails of America. They could follow the route of Lewis and Clark from the Midwest up into Oregon and Washington. Freedom from use of conventional roads would permit a group of saddle tramps to go cross-country through the vast wilderness reaches of central and northern Idaho. Then there's Canada ... ! Just think of it—for a few hundred dollars you could live the life of one of A.B. Guthrie's mountain men, or enjoy the delights of a Kit Carson lifestyle. Caring for faithful old Paint is much simpler than you think. Most open land has natural grass that will provide the basic diet. This, plus a handful or two of oats or other grains and a supply of fresh water, will keep your mount in trim condition. There are many books on the subject of horse care. One of the best is *Horses: Their Selection, Care and Handling*, M.C. Self, $5.95, from *Whole Earth Catalog*, 558 Santa Cruz, Menlo Park, Calif. 94025.

The Iron Mount

Closely related to the saddle bum on a four-legged animal is the modern motorcycle gypsy. With sleeping bags lashed to the luggage rack, these easy riders can be seen on virtually every highway and byway in North America, and in many

The bond between a man and his reliable motorcycle can become as close as that which earlier writers had with their four-legged friends. (William Kaysing)

countries overseas. With the advent of reliable, low-cost motorcycles, this mode of wandering and exploring has become tremendously popular.

The requirements are little more expensive than vagabonding by horse. A good secondhand motorcycle of about fifteen-cubic-inch displacement (250 cc.) or greater can be had for $300 and up. Even new machines suitable for long-distance travel will cost less than four figures. A more elaborate discussion of makes and models is in the chapter on transportation. Here we are concerned mainly with the use of a motorcycle as a nomadic vehicle.

About the only qualification for your two-wheeled magic carpet is that it be large enough to carry you, your luggage, and a passenger if you plan to take one. Obviously, it would be better to be somewhat overpowered than underpowered. The extra horses will be useful in going around slower vehicles without spending too much time in the suicide lane. Also, to continually labor a small engine will cause it to heat up and wear out much more quickly. That's why we recommend that no smaller than a fifteen-cubic-inch machine be considered for long-distance travel. Even then, a heavy load could overstress the mill. A better choice for long-distance touring with a heavy load would be a machine of 30 cubic inches or more.

Among the accessories that will make life aboard your bike more comfortable are the following:

1. A windshield of generous proportions will shield you from dust, hot blasts of desert wind, large bugs, and rocks thrown by cars ahead. It's also much warmer in cold weather behind a wind screen.

2. A good helmet and goggles or face shield will do much more than keep your valuable head and eyes safe. They provide a cranial cocoon that prevents you from being buffeted by strong gusts and the usually high level of noise from the engine and rush of air as you travel.

3. A good luggage rack plus Fiberglass, leather, or fabric saddlebags will provide a secure storage facility for your belongings. The sleeping bag can be securely fastened with bongee cords to the luggage rack while the saddlebags can hold your food, cooking equipment, personal articles, and old copies of *Cycle World*. (Don't forget to toss in a copy of *Intelligent Motorcycling*, available from Parkhurst Publishers, 1499 Monrovia Avenue, Newport Beach, Calif. 92660.)

Motorcyclists all know the feeling of total freedom provided by a motorcycle, camping equipment, enough money for food and fuel and sufficient time to explore the still beautiful parts of North America at a leisurely pace. You'll know this feeling too when you swing a leg over your own well-equipped mount. With the off-the-road capabilities designed into many modern motorcycles (good suspension, all-terrain tires, large gas tank) you will have almost the freedom of your horseman counterpart. In many parts of the world, you can simply turn off a conventional road and literally head for the hills. There you'll find the freedom that you once dreamed about. Imagine shutting off the ignition of your trusty Triumph by the banks of a beautiful, wide river. Lean the machine against a nearby tree, spread out your bedroll, build a fire and then take your telescopic fishing pole and catch fresh trout for dinner. Idyllic? You can bet your last overhead valve it is. Those who have tried it have had great trouble in going back to a conventional 9-to-5 life. Those that do, work only long enough to re-liberate themselves via the two-wheeled route.

A large segment of the population has received its "knowledge" of motorcyclists from the Hell's Angels-type picture. No matter how carefully you dress or how immaculate your BSA is maintained, you'll still be considered an "H A" by a lot of people. Your only defense is simply to stay out of sight and range of these deluded individuals. To avoid having the rednecks come to "visit you" at your campground, do what a friend of mine has always done . . . he makes his way so far back in the forest and conceals himself so well that no marauder has ever found him.

The Bicycle for One, Two, or More
All of the pleasures of roaming the world aboard a motorcycle can be yours without the expense and noise by simply

For less than $100 new, and much less used, you can tour the New America without polluting one cubic centimeter of air.

doing your thing on a bike. Today the modern ten-speed, *derailleur* bicycles are so easy to pedal that it's almost like continuously coasting downhill to ride one. Even an expensive one won't cost you much over $100 new, and you can find lots of good used ones for half that.

Bicycle tours have long been popular in Europe and this enthusiasm is being rapidly transmitted to America. A common sight today along the byways of the U.S. is the bike rider with a small pack on his back and a lightweight sleeping bag tied behind the seat.

There are many advantages to touring by bicycle:

1. Initial cost and upkeep are both extremely low.

2. You do not have to feed or fuel a bicycle.

3. Bicycle riders are seldom troubled by the establishment or its power arm.

4. You can travel for months, even years, with your only expense being the food you buy and an occasional tire for your bike.

A group of bicycle-riding nomads could tour the entire North American continent without even having an initial grubstake. The trip could be funded by occasional jobs in the towns through which they pass (see Chapter 3, on making a living). What better way to enjoy the wonderful scenery that abounds away from large cities than from the saddle of a quiet and virtually cost-free bicycle. Another great advantage is that bicycling will keep you healthy.

Shank's Mare

If you eliminate all means of transportation, you can enjoy what vagabonds have enjoyed since man first inhabited the earth. On your own two strong legs you can journey from the Pacific to the Atlantic, from the deserts of Mexico to the snow-crested peaks of Canada. Let's face it . . . a man can go where nothing else can go. Furthermore, the cost of being a hiking nomad is the least of all. You need buy no feed nor fuel nor parts when you are afoot.

The basic requirements for a leisurely and rewarding walking tour of America can consist of as little as comfortable shoes, a couple of blankets, and an aluminum mess kit. These articles, along with a knife, spoon, and some matches, or flint and steel, will make you a totally independent knight of the road. Many books have been written on the subject of the joys of hiking and here are the titles of some of the best:

The Complete Walker by Colin Fletcher, $8.18 postpaid from Alfred A. Knopf, Inc., 33 W. 60th Street, New York, N.Y. 10023.

The Sierra Club Wilderness Handbook, David Brower, Editor, $.95 postpaid from Whole Earth Catalog, 558 Santa Cruz Avenue, Menlo Park, Calif. 94025.

From them you'll learn everything you need to know about touring on two feet. Imagine ambling along the banks of the upper Fraser River. Around each bend lies a new vista of water, trees, rocks, and often a shy deer or elk. As the day draws to a close, you begin to select a comfortable campsite. A sandy beach with a backdrop of aspens, plenty of dry driftwood and a few round stones for a primitive fireplace, can provide the setting for an evening of great tranquillity and happiness. Just the simple act of building a crackling fire, boiling some brown rice and fresh wild vegetables can be a totally rewarding experience. Then later, you can settle back in your fur-lined sleeping bag and observe the stars.

Wigwam on the Water

Not too long ago a man who had been one of the cogs in the great grinding gears of the Establishment had a mild heart attack. His doctor suggested that he simply forget what he was doing and change his way of life. Because the man didn't have much money, he substituted some ingenuity. He had been working in the San Francisco Bay area and was familiar with the Delta country near the confluence of the great Sacramento and San Joaquin Rivers. This is a vast region of broad river channels, winding canals, and back bayous overgrown with junglelike growth. The area had always appealed to our escapee from the rat race, so he began thinking of living there. Rather than rent a house in one of the small communities like Rio Vista and Isleton, he flashed on a great plan: he would build or buy a houseboat and live on the waterways that extend for thousands of miles throughout the Delta country. He ended up by doing both, by buying an unfinished houseboat and proceeding to complete it according to his own needs and tastes.

The houseboat consists of a wooden scow as the main flotation. Built above this is a very small house which resembles one of the smaller trailers. In it are a large bed, a small stove, a gravity flow water tank, and plenty of storage space for his fishing tackle, a .22 rifle and a 20-gauge shotgun. A bright coat of green paint and some colorful pennants cut out of scrap cloth give his floating home a gala appearance. It is propelled by a small, secondhand outboard motor that pushes it along at about three miles an hour.

"There is no need to go any faster," he says, "I'm really not going anywhere." So the ex-harried businessman now lives in the serenity and quiet beauty of a region mostly untroubled by "civilization." He has his choice of many picturesque anchorages. Some, like the Meadows, resemble the most lush Amazonian jungle. The water is overhung with tangled vines and trees that are usually festooned with bright junglelike blossoms. Fish of many kinds abound and the banks of the rivers and canals are alive with small animals, many of them edible. Although he doesn't publicize the fact,

Not all of the rivers of America are badly polluted. This young lady enjoys a daily dip in this flower-festooned, crystal-clear swimming hole. (William Kaysing)

our man often makes a meal of fresh vegetables gathered from the extensive fields planted by commercial growers adjacent to the waterways.

Of course this man is not the only aquatic gypsy in this region. Actually, there may be thousands of men and women who already have found a refuge from progress in these tranquil byways.

The cost of becoming a river nomad can be as little or as much as you wish. A dozen fifty-gallon drums, well-painted, sealed, and held in a strong wooden framework will provide a floating platform for your houseboat. Once this movable foundation has been built, you can let your imagination run absolutely free. Pitch a tipi on this platform and live like a floating Indian. Or build a simple dwelling with lots of windows and doors plus a sundeck and observation platform on the roof.

Houseboats can be built and used in many parts of the U.S. There are large lakes, quiet ocean bays, and the oxbows and bayous of large rivers from which to choose. Some advantages of living on the water:

1. No rent to pay, although you might get ripped off for some bureaucratic licensing fees.

2. The freedom to move whenever and wherever you wish. This can be done with a big sail when the wind is right or a very small motor since you won't be in any hurry; or you can simply drift with river current or tides.

3. The availability of fish or other aquatic goodies. And waterway land areas provide homes for many kinds of game birds and animals.

4. No water problems for drinking, cooking, or other purposes. In some areas you may have to boil the water before drinking it, but this is no great problem.

5. Friendship . . . most of the people that you meet will be people just like yourselves. Thus you can establish easy-

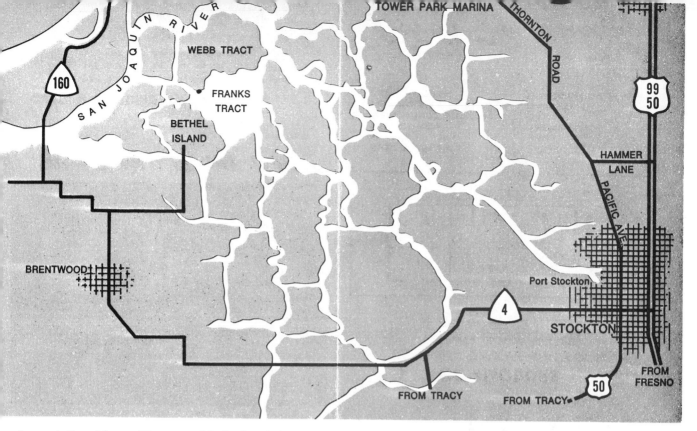

Map labels:
- TOWER PARK MARINA
- THORNTON ROAD
- WEBB TRACT
- SAN JOAQUIN RIVER
- 160
- 99 50
- FRANKS TRACT
- BETHEL ISLAND
- HAMMER LANE
- PACIFIC AVE
- BRENTWOOD
- Port Stockton
- 4
- STOCKTON
- FROM TRACY
- FROM TRACY
- 50
- FROM FRESNO

going relationships with many kindred spirits. (I see swimming parties, fish fries, and just general good-time get-togethers among the river people. Conversely, if you enjoy seclusion and a hermitlike existence, you can slip away unseen at any time.)

6. Freedom from the irritations of civilization, telephones, meter readers, and political fund solicitors.

7. A closeness to nature at its best . . . an ever-changing vista of water, land, and sky; sunsets and sunrises on the water are especially striking.

As our land becomes more crowded, more people will turn to the water. Fortunately there's lots of it in America so that you have a wide choice of water-based wandering.

Variations on Water

If you don't want to extend yourself financially, there are other ways you can enjoy life on the water. As the rat said in *Wind in the Willows*, "There's nothing that's so much fun as just messing around with boats."

Your wandering watercraft can range from a good-sized sailboat or cruser down to a simple raft composed of lots of inner tubes, stout lines, and canvas. With these various floating devices, you can cruise almost indefinitely. This is especially true if what you use is highly portable . . . such as a two-, four-, six- or eight-man raft. These can be deflated for land transport and then reinflated when you find another river to explore.

The natives who live in the Delta country between Stockton and San Francisco don't take too kindly to people bringing in things like draft notices and subpoenas. But the welcome for a brother can be most warm. (There are 3,000 miles of waterways represented by this map.)

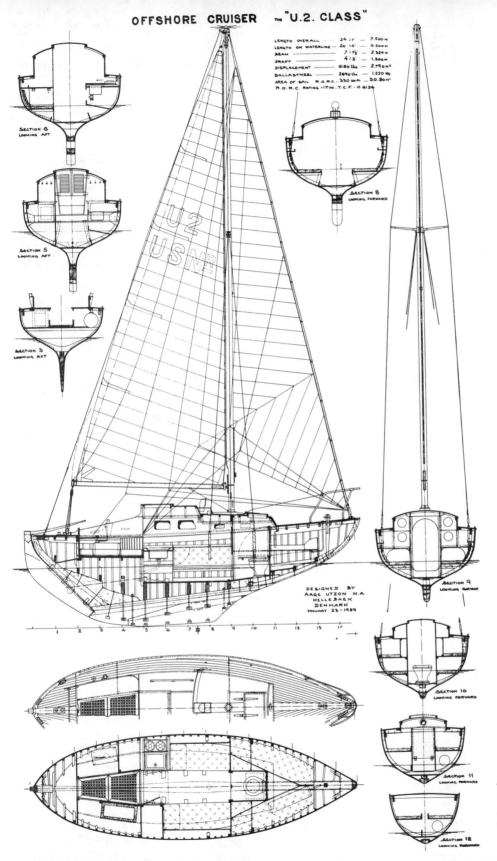

OFFSHORE CRUISER ᴛʜᴇ "U.2. CLASS"

LENGTH OVERALL	24′3″	7.300 M
LENGTH ON WATERLINE	20′4″	6.200 M
BEAM	7′7½″	2.324 M
DRAFT	4′3″	1.300 M
DISPLACEMENT	6150 lbs	2.790 M³
BALLAST KEEL	2690 lbs	1.220 Kg
AREA OF SAIL R.O.R.C.	330 sq.ft.	30.80 M²
R.O.R.C. RATING · 17.00 · T.C.F. · 0.6124		

SECTION 6
LOOKING AFT

SECTION 5
LOOKING AFT

SECTION 3
LOOKING AFT

SECTION 8
LOOKING FORWARD

SECTION 9
LOOKING FORWARD

SECTION 10
LOOKING FORWARD

SECTION 11
LOOKING FORWARD

SECTION 12
LOOKING FORWARD

DESIGNED BY
AAGE UTZON N.A.
HELLEBAEK
DENMARK
JANUARY 23 - 1959

A trim vessel like this can provide a floating home for four congenial people or one of those trim two-children families.

Most men who have followed the sea—and I should say women too—have received a broad, generalized education in life and people and a knowledge of the extremely tenuous hold we have this side of the briny deep.

Imagine spending a year or two floating down the Bow River in Canada or the mighty Snake in Idaho. Advantages of life floating down a great river are too numerous to list . . . you'll just have to take a look at these pictures and then try it yourself.

Reprise

Everyone should have his *wanderjahr* . . . a period when he casts off responsibilities and duties and simply lets himself move about freely. There are so many ways to do this—most of them quite inexpensive—that there is no reason why even a couple with children cannot rent, lease, or sell their house, take whatever savings they have accumulated, and visit the scenic wonders and fascinating backroads of this huge country while they're still young enough to enjoy it. No one should have to wait until he is too old to enjoy a brisk swim in an icy river or a vigorous hike to a nearby pine-studded peak.

One thing is certain: you'll never regret the time, effort, or money that you invest in a nomadic life in the New America.

Like a scene from the opening of The Planet of the Apes, *this weird, wonderful lunar-landscape adjacent to the Colorado River is yours for the price of a small boat and the spirit of adventure. (USDA)*

While some of the rivers in Idaho have been ruined by pulp mills and "progress," there are so many miles of them, you'll still find as much white water as you care to ride. (Idaho Chamber of Commerce)

If all else fails as far as transportation is concerned, "Keep on trucking." (Idaho Chamber of Commerce)

11 Amerikan Law and How to Avoid It Plus Some Encouragement in Case You Don't Make It

We have the papers we need to arrest him. You know his movements, we know the law.

J.C. SUPERSTAR

Here Are a Selection of Reasons . . .
Why you should be wary in the New Amerika:
New Senate Bills:
SB 5, Whetmore: Makes it a crime to maliciously disrupt normal operations, specifically on a college campus.
SB 20, Harmer: Provides for the dismissal of state employees who disrupt campus activites.
SB 28, Harmer: Provides for expulsion of students for disruption of campus activities.
SB 32, Walsh: Defines pornography and prohibits exhibitions of such in dramatic productions at any state college.
SB 34, Walsh: Increases the penalties for inciting a riot on a campus.
SB 51, Whetmore: Amends Mulford Act by increasing penalties for refusing to leave campus if ordered to do so.
SB 56, Harmer: Permits the president of a college to declare a state of emergency and restrict access to his campus.
From a Movement Paper . . .
It is worth describing this equipment somewhat specifically because I think it is significant and not generally known. This is from a list of appropriations approved by the Common Council in the bond issue:

700 12-gauge shotguns
100 Stoner machine guns
1,000 M-1 carbines
25 gas guns
25 .30-.06-caliber rifles
with 4-X scopes
1,200 gas masks
5,000 chemical mace dispensers
1,500 flak vests
9,000 sets of fatigue clothing
500,000 rounds of various kinds of ammunition (of which the largest single appropriation is for 150,000 rounds of .223-caliber ammunition for the Stoner machine gun)
8 armored personnel carriers
4 mobile support vans with radio equipment
2 prisoner buses

Freedom? Press?

A book company once called Panther Press is now called Paladin Press. Within the past year they have had a "change of heart" about selling books (see illustration) on such subjects as explosives, unconventional warfare, and demolition. If any reader can provide the reason for this change of heart, we'll be happy *happy* to present it in the revised version of this book.

To get these books, have a letterhead printed as follows: Corn County Sheriff's Department and your PO Box. Is this legal to do? Hell, we don't know.

PALADIN PRESS

Box 1307

Boulder, Colorado 80302

Special Forces Operational Techniques	$7.50
Combat Training of the Individual Soldier & Patrolling	$4.00
Counter-Guerilla Operations	$3.50
Napoleon's Maxims of War	$3.00
Combat Intelligence	$3.50
Guide to Germ Warfare	$3.50
Guide to Chemical and Gas Warfare	$5.00
The AK-47 Assault Rifle	$3.50
The FN/FAL Automatic Rifles	$3.00
The UZI: Submachine Gun	$3.00
The Krag Rifle and Carbine	$1.50
The Browning Automatic Rifle	$1.00
Rifle Musket, Model 1863	$2.00
1873 "Trapdoor" Springfield, M1873 Colt & S&W Schofield	$1.50
Firearm Silencers	$4.00
Fundamentals of Small Arms	$3.50

WARNING! RESTRICTED: All books on explosives and demolitions, including but not limited to: Unconventional Warfare Devices and Techniques, Special Forces Demolitions Techniques, Explosives and Demolitions, British Textbook of Explosives, Demolition Materials, Military Explosives, and German Explosive Ordnance sold only to law enforcement agencies, government agencies, firemen or military personnel. Use your official letterhead to order.

I am going to turn back to my seat with the realization that everything I have learned throughout my life has come to nought, that there is no meaning in this court, that there is no law in this court, and these men are going to jail by virtue of a legal lynching.

BILL KUNSTLER, AT THE CONCLUSION
OF THE CHICAGO SEVEN TRIAL

Throughout the world there are tens of thousands of people imprisoned, a great majority of them victims of unjust laws wielded by the power system. Remember that law is an aspect of control by the Establishment. As Ken Kloke states, "Its primary purpose is the quelling of violence and the orderly processing of claims of competing capitalists."

Most of us have come to realize that in the New America there are two distinct kinds of law . . . one for the rich and one for the poor. If you are in the latter class, you would be wise to avoid all contact with the law since it is unlikely that justice will be done.

Staying Out of Trouble

To avoid conflict with the law and its minions, you have several choices. First, you simply do nothing wrong. Second, if you do something wrong, avoid being caught. Third, stay out of sight whether you break the law or not.

It is often difficult for people who oppose the Establishment directly or indirectly to avoid conflict with the law. For example, if you are a member of the SDS, the Weathermen, the Black Panthers, or even part of such a benign group as the Draft Resisters, it is possible that you will be sought out and arrested on a trumped-up charge. The average citizen in America breaks three or four laws daily; these may be minor traffic infractions, doing something "indecent and unnatural" in one's own bedroom, or possibly some larcenous activity during the course of regular business hours. But whatever the nature of these crimes, the great majority are passed over by law-enforcement people because *they do not directly threaten the power structure.* But if anyone is involved in an effort to rip off the power structure itself, they will be sought out by the law, arrested, charged, and convicted for some other offense. A quick way to eliminate a threat to those in power is to plant evidence (drugs, firearms, etc.) on the person or property of the threatener. The more people involved in any given project, the more likely it is to be exposed.

The obvious conclusion is that whatever you propose to do in the New America, do it as a loner. And after the deed is done, restrain yourself from taking an ego trip to tell everyone how noble you are. With two hundred million people in America, it is difficult for any agency, regardless of its budget, to capture just one silent man or woman.

If you have ever flown over the United States, you are

aware that vast regions are uninhabited. There are millions of acres of both private and public land where one or two people, or even a small group, could live untroubled for an unlimited time.

There are many historical precedents for this method of avoiding the law. The Essenes avoided the short swords of Roman legionnaires by hiding out in the caves surrounding the Dead Sea. Later, Robin Hood and his Merry Men made a joyful sanctuary of Sherwood Forest. (The legend is really based on fact.) In the decades preceding the Civil War many runaway slaves fled into the hills, bayous, and delta country, and their descendents live there untroubled to this day.

To enjoy life in the New America requires freedom from interference with your own individual pursuit of happiness. Thus, whatever you plan to do, remember that Big Brother is never very far away. The secret is to hang loose and play it cool, far from the clutches of the legal grinding system until 1985 rolls around.

In the event that this advice and counsel fails to accomplish its intended purpose, i.e., to keep you free, here is a reference guide for "what to do" and "where to go" if the Man gets you.

Pocket Lawyer of Legal First Aid

1. If you are stopped and/or arrested by the police, you may remain silent; you do not have to answer any question about alleged crimes, you should provide your name and address only if requested (although it is not absolutely clear that you must do so). At all times remember the Fifth Amendment.

2. If a police officer is not in uniform, ask him to show his identification. He has no authority over you unless he properly identifies himself. Beware of persons posing as police officers. Always get his badge number and his name.

3. Police have no right to search your car or your home unless they have a search warrant, probable cause, or your consent. They may conduct no exploratory search, that is, one for evidence of crime generally or for evidence of a crime unconnnected with the one you are being questioned about. (Thus, a stop for an auto violation does not give the right to search the auto.) You are not required to consent to a search; therefore, you should not consent and should state clearly and unequivocally that you do not consent, in front of witnesses if possible. If you do not consent, the police will have the burden in court of showing probable cause. Arrest may be corrected later.

4. You may not resist arrest forcibly or by going limp, even if you are innocent. To do so is a separate crime of which you can be convicted even if you are acquitted of the original charge. Do not resist under any circumstances.

5. If you are stopped and/or arrested, the police may search you by patting you on the outside of your clothing. You can be stripped of your personal possessions. Do not carry anything that includes the name of your employer or friends.

6. Do not engage in "friendly" conversation with officers on the way to or at the station. Once you are arrested, there is little likelihood that anything you say will get you released.

7. As soon as you have been booked, you have the right to complete at least two phone calls—one to a relative, friend, or attorney, the other to a bondsman. If you are black, call the local Black Panther Party office and the Party will post bail if possible.

8. You must be allowed to hire and see an attorney immediately.

9. You do not have to give any statement to the police, nor do you have to sign any statement you might give them, and therefore you should not sign anything. Take the Fifth and Fourteenth Amendments, because you cannot be forced to testify against yourself.

10. You must be allowed to post bail in most cases, but you must be able to pay the bail bondsman fee. If you cannot pay the fee, you may ask the judge to release you from custody without bail or to lower your bail, but he does not have to do so.

11. The police must bring you into court or release you within forty-eight hours after your arrest (unless the time ends on a weekend or a holiday, and then they must bring you before a judge the first day court is in session). [In areas like New York, this often is not done due to overcrowded court schedules.]

12. If you do not have the money to hire an attorney, immediately ask the police to get you an attorney without charge.

13. If you have the money to hire a private attorney, but do not know of one, call the National Lawyers' Guild (or the Bar Association of your county) and ask them to furnish you with the name of an attorney who practices criminal law.

FROM *THE BLACK PANTHER*

Here is a list of Lawyers' Guild contacts:

Cambridge: 595 Mass. Avenue, 02122 (617-661-8898)
Detroit: 5705 N. Woodward Street, 48202
Los Angeles: c/o ACLU, 323 W. Fifth Street, 90013 (213-626-5156)
New York: 1 Hudson Street, 10013 (212-227-0385)
San Francisco: 197 Steiner Street, 94117 (415-863-5193)

Outside of these areas there are no offices but people to contact in the following cities are:

Flint, Mich.: Carl Bekofske, Attorney, 510 W. Court, 48502 (313-234-6623)
Philadelphia: A. Harry Levitan, Attorney, 1612 Market, 19103 (215-563-8825)
Washington, D.C.: S. David Levy, Attorney, 2812 Pennsylvania Avenue, N.W., 20020 (202-965-1144)

ACLU The American Civil Liberties Union has the task (and it's a tough one these days) of preserving and hopefully strengthening the freedoms and rights that were guaranteed to all citizens under the U.S. Bill of Rights. As they say,

... we believe that no one should have the privilege of deciding who is deserving of the rights ... these rights belong to all—WITHOUT EXCEPTION.

Here is a list of ACLU offices. And remember, if you have any spare bread, send it along to the main office at 323 W. 5th Street, Los Angeles, Calif. 90013.

Alabama: Box 1972, University 35486
California: ACLU of Northern California, 593 Market Street, San Francisco 94105 (415-433-2750)
Colorado: 1711 Pennsylvania Street, Denver 80203 (303-825-5176)
Georgia: 5 Forsyth Street N.W., Atlanta 30303 (404-523-2721)
Illinois: 6 S. Clark, Chicago 60603 (312-236-5564)
Michigan: 234 State Street, Detroit 48226 (313-961-4662)
Montana: 2707 Glenwood Land, Billings 59102 (406-657-2328)
New Mexico: 131 La Vega S.W., Albuquerque 87150 (505-877-5286)
New York: 156 Fifth Avenue, New York 10010 (212-WA9-6076)
North Dakota: Ward County (Minot), Box 1000, Minot 58701 (702-838-0381)
Ohio: Suite 200, 203 E. Broad Street, Columbus 43215
Washington, D.C.: (NCACLU) 1424 16th Street N.W., Suite 501, Washington, D.C. 20036 (202-483-3830)
West Virginia: 1228 Seventh Street, Huntington 25701
Wisconsin: 1840 N. Farwell Avenue, Room 303, Milwaukee 53202 (414-272-4032)

To obtain a complete list of all the ACLU chapters, write: American Civil Liberties Union, 323 Fifth Street, Los Angeles, Calif. 90013, or call 213-MA6-5156.

The LSCRRC The Law Students Civil Rights Research Council at 156 Fifth Avenue, N.Y. 10010, can aid you. They have a record of working with law students around the country.

The No-Knock Law Just so you won't run around in your cell screaming that you didn't know about it (recall that ignorance is no excuse), here is a late rundown on how police officers can come into your home without an "Avon calling" preannouncement. There is a law now on the books, popularly called the "No-Knock Law," that permits law enforcement personnel to enter your home at any time of the day or night without knocking and without your permission. All they need is reason to believe that you might be inside busily destroying evidence that could convict you of a crime.

The following is from a book titled *Police Guide to Search and Seizure, Interrogation, and Confession* by A. Specter and Marvin Katz. This selection describes a case involving a man named Ker, who took his narcotics conviction to the Supreme Court.

May the Police Seize Evidence Without a Search Warrant Incident to a Lawful Arrest? *Generally yes.** The Supreme Court has approved a reasonable search for narcotics in the defendant's apartment, for example, after his arrest there on probable cause. The probable cause for the arrest in that case consisted of

1. Police observing the defendant go through the motions of seeming to buy from a known narcotics supplier, although the police did not actually see the narcotics exchange hands;

2. Information from a previously reliable informer that the defendant was buying narcotics from the known supplier and using the apartment where the search was made to sell narcotics.

May the Police Enter the Defendant's Home With a Passkey Without Warning to Make the Arrest and Search? Yes, if necessary to avoid the destruction of the evidence. In Ker's case, the Court accepted the view that the narcotics seller, if forewarned, might well destroy the evidence. After the police observed his apparent "buy" from the known supplier, the defendant made a U-turn and eluded the police secretly following him. The police, when they reached his apartment, could reasonably believe he might be expecting them. If the evidence, such as narcotics, could be easily destroyed, the police had the right to enter with a passkey and *without warning.**

> The law perverted! And the police powers of the state perverted along with it! The law, I say, not only turned from its proper purpose but made to follow an entirely

contrary purpose. The law became a weapon of every kind of greed. Instead of checking crime, the law is itself guilty of evils it is supposed to punish!!

Sound contemporary? This was written more than 100 years ago ... prior to the French revolution of 1848. The author was Frederick Bastiat, a French economist, statesman, and author. Here is his definition of law:

What Is Law?
What, then, is law? It is the collective organization of the individual right to lawful defense.

Each of us has a natural right—from God—to defend his person, his liberty, and his property. These are the three basic requirements of life, and the preservation of any one of them is completely dependent upon the preservation of the other two. For what are our faculties but the extension of our individuality? And what is property but an extension of our faculties?

If every person has the right to defend—even by force—his person, his liberty, and his property, then it follows that a group of men have the right to organize and support a common force to protect these rights constantly. Thus the principle of collective right—its reason for existing, its lawfulness—is based on individual right. And the common force that protects this collective right cannot logically have any other purpose or any other mission than that for which it acts as a substitute. Thus, since an individual cannot lawfully use any force against the person, liberty, or property of another individual, then the common force—for the same reason—cannot lawfully be used to destroy the person, liberty, or property of individuals or groups.

Such a perversion of force would be, in both cases, contrary to our premise. Force has been given to us to defend our own individual rights. Who will dare to say that force has been given to us to destroy the equal rights of our brothers? Since no individual acting separately can lawfully use force to destroy the rights of others, does it not logically follow that the same principle also applies to the common force that is nothing more than the organized combination of the individual forces?

If this is true, then nothing can be more evident than this: The law is the organization of the natural right of lawful defense. It is the substitution of a common force for individual forces. And this common force is to do only what the individual forces have a natural and lawful right to do: to protect persons, liberties, and properties; to maintain the right of each, and to cause "justice" to reign over us all.

The Desire to Rule Over Others

My attitude toward all other persons is well illustrated by this story from a celebrated traveler: He arrived one day in the midst of a tribe of savages, where a child had just been born. A crowd of soothsayers, magicians, and quacks—armed with rings, hooks, and cords—surrounded it. One said: "This child will never smell the perfume of a peace-pipe unless I stretch his nostrils." Another said: "He will never be able to hear unless I draw his ear-lobes down to his shoulders." A third said: "He will never be able to see the sunshine unless I slant his eyes." Another said: "He will never stand upright unless I bend his legs." A fifth said: "He will never learn to think unless I flatten his skull."

"Stop," cried the traveler. "What God does is well done. Do not claim to know more than He. God has given organs to this frail creature; let them develop and grow strong by exercise, use, experience, and liberty."

Let Us Now Try Liberty

God has given to men all that is necessary for them to accomplish their destinies. He has provided a social form as well as a human form. And these social organs of persons are so constituted that they will develop themselves harmoniously in the clean air of liberty. Away, then, with quacks and organizers! Away with their rings, chains, hooks, and pincers! Away with their artificial systems! Away with the whims of governmental administrators, their socialized projects, their centralization, their tariffs, their government schools, their state religions, their free credit, their bank monopolies, their regulations, their restrictions, their equalization by taxation, and their pious moralizations!

And now that the legislators and do-gooders have so futilely inflicted so many systems upon society, may they reject all systems, and try liberty; for liberty is an acknowledgement of faith in God and His works.

Here is a bibliography of more or less straight books on the subject. After all, the more you know, the more real power you have.

Your Laws, Frank Kelly, G.P. Putnam's Sons, N.Y.
A Guide to California Law, Harry Koch, Ken-Books, San Francisco.
The Law, Frederic Bastiat, Foundation for Economic Education, Irvington-on-Hudson, N.Y.
Your Inalienable Rights, Philip B. Yeager, John R. Stark
So You're Going to Court, Robert W. Smedley, Fountainhood Publishers, Inc., N.Y.
A Wilderness Bill of Rights, William O. Douglas, Little, Brown & Co., Boston.

The Anatomy of Liberty, William O. Douglas, Simon & Schuster, Inc., N.Y.
Up Against the Law, The Legal Rights of People Under 21, Jean Strouse, New American Library, Inc. N.Y.

Here's a description of a new book called *Confrontations, Riots, Urban Warfare* by Raymond M. Momboisse.* Might as well find out what they're saying about us . . .

Peaceful demonstrations have led to nuisance demonstrations and civil disobedience, which in turn led to scattered violence and eventually rioting. Now violence is organized and frighteningly destructive. Guns and bombs are used. Personal terror, assassination and extortion are becoming accepted tools of the dissatisfied. Militant organizations are training and arming for insurrection! This manual spells out the tactics to meet the challenge of student rebellion, race riots, Watts and Detroit type civil disorders, and the new urban guerrilla warfare.

These are the chapters:

The Challenge
Crowds—Mobs
Demonstrations—Civil Disobedience—Riots
Preventive Measures
Crowd Control
Demonstration Control
Civil Disobedience Control
Strikes
Riot Control—General
Riot Tactics—General
Control of Organized and Guerrilla Riots
Counter-Insurgency Operations

Other books on the same subject from the same publisher are:

Riot Protection Checklist for Business and Store Planning for Riot Survival
Riot and Civil Emergency Guide for City and County Officials
Rumors
Control of Student Disorders (Second Edition)

OKAY, THAT'S THE END OF THE LEGAL DATA SECTION . . .
Now, if all fails; if you are actually incarcerated in some dismal bastille, do not give up hope. First of all, it is not only

*From Paladin Press.

no stigma to be imprisoned, in many cases you are a hero to the movement.

You can do what's known as hard time . . . stewing in your own bitter juices, feeling sorry for yourself . . . or you can serve your time productively: reading, writing, helping others less serene. So here's our contribution if you can get the book in with you. It's a montage of both movement and straight literature. Some of it is from Mitchell Goodman's great book, *The Movement Toward a New America* (which, not incidentally, inspired the title of this book). The balance is from many sources . . . yellowed old books of proverbs, hardbacks of the Twenties, paperbacks of the Seventies, letters. . . . We hope that it serves its purpose of making down time in the New America productive up time later.

I have talked a great deal of myself but I even forgot to name Sacco. Sacco too is a worker from his boyhood, a skilled worker lover of work, with a good job and pay, a good and lovely wife, two beautiful children and a neat little home at the verge of a wood, near a brook. Sacco is a heart, a faith, a character, a man; lover of nature and of mankind. A man who gave all, who sacrifice all to the cause of Liberty and to his love for mankind; money, rest, mundane ambitions, his own wife, his children, himself and his own life. Sacco has never dreamt to steal, never to assassinate. He and I have never brought a morsel of bread to our mouths, from our childhood to today—which has not been gained by the sweat of our brows. Never. Oh, yes, I may be more witful, as some have put it, I am a better babbler than he is, but many, many times in hearing his heartful voice ringing a faith sublime, in considering his supreme sacrifice, remembering his heroism I felt small, small at the presence of his greatness and found myself compelled to fight back from my throat to not weep before him—this man called thief and assassin and doomed. But Sacco's name will live in the hearts of the people and in their gratitude when Katzmann's and your bones will be dispersed by time, when your name, his name, your laws, institutions, and your false god are but a dim remembering of a cursed past in which man was wolf to man. . . .

If it had not been for these thing I might have live out my life talking at street corners to scorning men. I might have die, unmarked, unknown, a failure. Now we are not a failure. This is our career and our triumph. Never in our full life could we hope to do such work for tolerance, for joostice, for man's understanding of man as now we do by accident. Our words—our lives—our pains—nothing! The taking of our lives—lives of a good shoemaker and a poor fish-peddler—all! That last moment belongs to us—that agony is our triumph.

BARTOLOMEO VANZETTI, LAST SPEECH TO THE COURT

A revolution is a force against which no power, divine or human, can prevail, and whose nature it is to grow by the very resistance it encounters ... the more you repress it, the more you increase its rebound and render its action irresistible, so that it is precisely the same for the triumph of an idea whether it is persecuted, harassed, beaten down from the start, or whether it grows and develops unobstructed. Like the Nemesis of the ancients, whom neither prayers nor threats could move, the revolution advances, with sombre and predestined tread, over the flowers strewn by its friends, through the blood of its defenders, over the bodies of its enemies.

PROUDHON

Economic domination carries with it as well the threat of cultural subjugation—not a threat, but a positive virtue, from the point of view of the colonial administrator or, often, the American political scientist delighted with the opportunity to preside over the "modernization" of some helpless society. An example, extreme perhaps, is the statement of an American diplomat in Laos:

"For this country, it is necessary, in order to achieve any progress, to level everything. It is necessary to reduce the inhabitants to zero, to disencumber them of their traditional culture which blocks everything."

At another level, the same phenomenon can be observed in Latin America. Claude Julien comments:

"The revolt of Latin American students is not directed only against dictatorial regimes that are corrupt and inefficient—nor only against the exploitation by the foreigner of the economic and human resources of their country—but also against the cultural colonization that touches them at the deepest level of their being. And this is perhaps why their revolt is more virulent than that of the worker or peasant organizations that experience primarily economic colonization."

FROM *KNOWLEDGE AND POWER* BY NOAM CHOMSKY

Socialist literature has never been rich in books. It is written for workers, for whom one penny is money, and its main force lies in its small pamphlets and its newspapers.

KROPOTKIN WRITING IN ABOUT THE 1860'S

So there's a very interesting and a very key connection between insurrection and acts carried out by oneself, a private, personal civil war. We define a civil war as when a society splits down the middle and you have two opposing sides. Does that have to be the definition? Can 5,000 people launch a civil war? Can 4,000, 3,000, two or one? Or one-half of 1,000? Or half of that? Can one person? Can one person engage in civil war? I'm not a lawyer. I'm definitely not a judge, but I would say that one person acting alone could in fact be engaged in a civil war against an oppressive system.

ELDRIDGE CLEAVER

We live in confusion verging on chaos, in the midst of a process of change we barely understand. Only the young (and those who grow with them) begin to understand: they are native to a world in which there is no predictable future, in which governments offer control and terror in place of the "pursuit of happiness." A world in which war criminals are called leaders. They lie, day after day. Masses of men driven by greed and fear swallow the lies of those leaders and hate themselves for it, and turn on one another, seeking the "enemy" on whom they can vent their rage. There is no sense of shared interest, of shared belief. There is no center. The country falls apart. Men who prepare to commit the crimes of nuclear and germ war try to impose "law and order." They fail. The law is suspect and disorder is built into the system. The courts are revealed as agents of control, not justice. Capitalism shows itself as engaged in never-ending social and economic warfare. Profit is a form of theft. War profit is a form of murder. Land, air, water and peoples' minds are polluted for profit. Police take the law into their own hands, using terror to crush out spirit that offends their own mechanical lives. They will fail, here as in Vietnam.

MITCHELL GOODMAN

Our movement is not very strong today. It is not united, it is not well organized. It is very confused and makes a lot of mistakes, but there is the beginning of an awakening in this country which has been going on for at least fifteen years, and it is an awakening that will not be denied. Tactics will change, people will err, people will die in the streets and die in prison, but I do not believe that this movement can be denied because whoever falsely applied the American ideal was from the beginning when it excluded black people, and Indians and people without property, nonetheless there was a dream of justice and equality and freedom, and brotherhood, and I think that that dream is much closer to fulfillment today than it has been at any time in the history of this country.

DAVID DELLINGER

1. KNOW WHO YOU ARE: If you know who you are, you'll know what to do.
2. WHAT IS THE BEST ROAD TO SURVIVAL: What are your best tools for communicating with groups (movement, sound, words).
3. WHAT ARE THE BEST WAYS OF CONNECTING WITH THE COMMUNITY: Find the simple way which won't turn people off. Begin where they're at.

EVERGREEN, OCTOBER, 1968

Somewhere like a flea on the hide of this great groaning continent a group called the Anonymous Artists of America are hanging out, cooking rice, raising kids and making music. They'll play anywhere, garages, warehouses, jails and weddings, and having never allowed their gig to get bigger than the group, they have that backroad courage that seems more than phonomenon.

Dear anonymous artists, I know who you are. Where, however, is always another question.

KEN KESEY

HOW TO TAKE CARE OF YOURSELF WHEN IT HAPPENS

Tribe . . . An organism, one flesh breathing joy as the stars breathe destiny down on us, get going, join hands, see to business, thousands of sons will see to it when you fall, you will grow a thousand times in the bellies of your sisters . . .

When it happens heavy—the pig will shut off all utilities (water, gas, electricity). Stores may be closed for weeks. So . . .

STORE: food (per person)
20 lbs. brown rice and whole wheat flour
10 lbs. corn or oat meal and beans (high-protein like soy, kidney)
5 lbs. salt (sea salt is best)
2 quarts of oil
dried nuts and fruits, canned tuna
(don't forget the dog and other necessities like soap)

STORE: water—in 5-gallon jugs
   fill bathtub at first news of trouble
      always keep tub clean
STORE: fire—matches
   Coleman and/or hibachi stove and lots of fuel
STORE: first-aid supplies
   drugs to be used with the greatest discretion: speed,
   downers, painkillers, antibiotics, vitamins
STORE: power—flashlight and radio batteries
LEARN: first aid and healing and not to freak at
   blood . . .
   your neighborhood: how to get out of your house the
   back way, neighbors you can count on for help and
   shelter
CONSTRUCT: a one-man hiding place in your house
BE PREPARED: to split—have your tickets, your bread,
   extra ID to use your piece—learn to aim at the penny
   arcade: "but remember, the guns will not win this
   one" at tribal gatherings—wear clothing you can move
   in. Carry motorcycle helmets (they save heads), no
   glasses or contact lenses . . . wear a wet bandana for a
   gas mask

". . . Even the poorest of us will have to give up something to be free . . ."
   ". . . Meditate, pray, make love, be prepared to die at
any time . . . get started, someone will finish . . ."

How to Wake Up Your Brother: The First Step

Tell him: that he's dreaming if he thinks he isn't oppressed
   that he's dreaming if he thinks he can get away
   that he's with the enemy if he's "just minding my own
. . ."
Posters: people read the walls
   use pages of our newspapers, circulars, your own art-work,
   don't use staples . . .
   put up your stuff with the idea in mind that the pig wants
   to tear it down . . .
   use glue (wallpaper kind or just flour and water)
Write your own: you won't know if you can 'til you try . . .
   all our people have newspapers . . . see if they'll print your
   stuff. Or have it mimeographed and just pass it out.
                    POWER TO THE PEOPLE
                      VIVA LA RAZA!
   "It's better to die on your feet than to live on your knees"

Self-Defense

**Self-Defense With Hands and Feet and Knees and Elbows,
The Body** Many people are beginning to realize that they
are not capable of preventing a physical assault on their
person. Women, exposed to continual verbal abuse and quite

often to rape, attempted rape, and physical molestation, are one group of people who are actively learning some form of self-defense. Another group of people interested in self-defense are those, both male and female, who have had their heads beaten by the police.

There are a lot of pseudo-experts in the various arts of self-defense and there are hundreds of publications that teach you the "amazing super-mean killing techniques." I would suggest that you avoid this type of instruction. I have seen people who learned this way to fight, and they usually get torn up. People who have learned this way of self-defense usually have a false confidence. This can lead to his/her trying to defend himself in situations where it would be best to escape. In this situation they will end up getting hurt.

When you enter into the world of self-defense you should first of all find an instructor who is qualified. This is true in any one of the martial arts (karate, judo, kendo, akido, kempo, etc.). An instructor of quality—one way to judge is what belt he/she has—will not only teach you the moves and techniques but also how to judge a situation: how to tell what kind of experience the aggressor has at a glance, to tell if he is a threat or a paper tiger, to tell how to use your physical surroundings to your advantage, to see what avenues of escape are available, and if the aggressor has any physical handicaps that can be used to your advantage. This type of knowledge is not only dependent upon the instructor but on your experience.

One choice you may have to make is whether it is more important to learn self-defense in a hurry or whether you have the time to work under a really good instructor. Many times an instructor will not teach anything about combat situations until a solid basis has been learned. This basis is usually how to walk, how to punch, how to kick, forms (called katas in karate) and something about the ideology of that particular form. In either case you will probably be able to learn enough to defend yourself.

Another positive and not-to-be-thought-of-last result of studying any martial art is the knowledge-of-self gained. Most people while studying self-defense become aware of the functions of their body. To realize that the design of your body is more suitable to certain movements than others is a surprisingly new discovery. In the study of martial arts, a person learns to think clearly even though the rate of movement is fast—many times faster than you can see. If a person studies and learns a form of the martial arts he/she has achieved a great amount of discipline.

Conclusion

We have had to conclude:

that the American Dream was a myth;

that the economic reality of America is, perhaps, better described as a nightmare;

that the heralded "high living standard" was obtainable for only a small proportion of the citizens, while the greatest number of its people on the barest necessities;

that with the passage of time, and as the social growth multiplied productivity, the great majority of the people received a lesser and lesser proportion of what they produced;

that the economic production is no longer carried on to satisfy human needs and desires, but only to perpetuate the commercial machinery of capitalism;

that medicine has become butchery; schools have become prisons; agriculture destroys food; stores sell taxes and debt; and that with the profit motive on the principle incentive to human productivity, people have become like machines, driven by aspirations they can never reach.

Now human considerations are superfluous to the system; human life has become surplus and a liability. The spectre of death hangs over us all: death by bombing and burning; death by a slow and fast starvation; death by poisoning; death by suicide; and the living death of alienation.

The average citizen seems totally entrapped. On the one hand he pins his sanity to the shattered remnants of his aspirations; on the other, he is brutally assaulted by a host of social mechanisms designed to repress any suspicion he may have that he holds a losing hand in a crooked game.

The idea that the citizen is *really* entrapped is to us just as much an illusion as the American Dream was. The sense and the idea of entrapment are both social mechanisms designed to produce inertia in the face of a reality that demands action for social change.

In the broadest sense we suggest a restructuring of the economic relationships in the society to eliminate all production for profit. The principle is certainly not new, we know, and there are many sources for political mobilization for those people who subscribe to this principle.

We feel the need to stress the importance of concluding, perhaps in the narrow sense of social responsibility, that a person must move into the arena of social change *where he or she is at*, at his or her level of social consciousness, though his or her objectives may be, and surely must eventually be, a total structual change in the whole society.

> *Betrayal of the American Dream*
> *The Economic Facts of American Life* ($2.00)
> by Student Research Facility
> 1132 The Alameda
> Berkeley, Calif. 94707
> Authors of this report—Martin Brown,
> Joe Woodward, Cy Schoenfield

Courage consists not in hazarding without fear, but in being resolutely minded in a just cause.

Privilege

As a white working class American citizen I would like to list for the enlightenment of the bourgeois reactionary upper middle class student Weatherman faction some of the "privileges" that imperialism grants me:

The privilege of busting my ass 40 hours a week; the privilege of paying $50 a week in taxes to enable my government to kill Vietnamese; the privilege of producing goods I cannot afford to consume; the privilege of being systematically robbed by my union; the privilege of working for 48 years so that I can retire for those three glorious years from 65 (social security date) to age 68 (my life expectancy date); the privilege of having upper middle class students discount me as a revolutionary force because my moral fiber has been weakened by these privileges.

ERVIN F. McCORMICK, PETALUMA, CALIF.

We came, therefore (and with many Western thinkers before us) to suspect that civilization may be overvalued.

From *Earth House Hold* by Gary Snyder, NEW DIRECTIONS

The endless confusions and obscenities which make up America will not be transformed in a week, a month, or by a stroke of fortune. They will be changed by people who struggle to rise from the status of consumers and functionaries to that of human beings, by men and women seeking to become the center, rather than the play-things and objects of events.

JEFF LUSTIG

The DRV—democratic republican/revolution of or in Vermont—is a community of about 13 people on a 100-acre farm in the green hills of Vermont. The community began in the summer of 1968 and is now experiencing its first Vermont winter. Consequently, anything I can say about the way the community operates and what it stands for must be judged as tentative. We are just learning what it means to be a community. And we are first discovering how to live close to the land and in harmony with the natural world that surrounds us.

The land holds a special magic that we had all forgotten. The American Indians knew about it, and so do a few very old and wise Vermont farmers. The pioneers experienced the magic but were too caught up in Western values to properly appreciate it. Now it is up to the people of the New Age to rediscover the land and learn what it has to offer and teach. We do not consider

ourselves Rousseauean dreamers or Jeffersonian agrar-
ianists harking back to the simple virtues of the past. We
are very much children of the 21st century, with our
chain saw and tractor—and stereo system blasting forth
the Beatles, Bach, and Ornette Coleman appreciative of
our times.

But our technology does run amok. It functions as an
end unto itself, with nothing whatever to do with the
rhythms, harmonies, and cycles of life. The sun rises,
the sun sets. But the machines clatter on. The Old Age is
governed by artificial values that are technology oriented, profit serving, and power seeking. The cities
teach violence and destruction; the country teaches time
and space and life and creation.

The DRV gives us the time to learn about the land
and about ourselves. We have to reevaluate our technology, sift out what is destructive and useless, and harness
what is left to the delicate working order of our natural
environment. To create a New Age we must learn to live
at peace with ourselves and to be at home with our land.

MARTY JEZER

Law is one aspect of control by the major wielder of
force and coercion. Its primary purposes are the quelling
of violence and civil strife, and the orderly processing of
claims and competing capitalists for more money
through rules drawn by capitalists in accordance with
custom. Almost every aspect of the law has to do with
money or money claims. Most of the Constitution does
not concern the freedoms of Americans. Those sections
were only amended on by mass action. Most of it
concerns business, structure and finances of government. Similarly, most of the law is of, by and for the
wealthy, who, at every stage of the proceedings, are
afforded more than the poor. Furthermore the law has
always been structured in favor of the power elite. It is a
condition for the existence of a ruling class, and upon
the existence of class society. All are relationships of
power, for the purpose of maintaining property relationships and increasing advantage to some by decreasing it
for them.

Law is an aspect of the exertion of power by one
class against another. Law is the rationalization of force,
coercion, and murder, and the primary means by which
obedience is exacted. A judicial system arises and flour-
ishes when, where, and to the extent that class interests
cannot be reconciled. Thus, the judicial system is not
only an attempt on the part of the ruling class to
provide a forum for the resolution of class disputes. It is
an attempt to control the outcome of those disputes by

making sure that those with greater wealth stand the better chance of winning, and by making itself party, law-maker, prosecuter, judge, jury, and hangman.

KEN CLOKE

Vocations for Social Change is a decentralized clearing house for persons struggling with one basic question: How can people earn a living in America in 1969 and ensure that their social impact is going to affect basic humanistic change in our social, political, and economic institutions. Nobody has any "real answers" to this question, but many ideas are being developed out of people's experiences. VSC helps make these ideas available to the general public so that each person's individual search can be enriched.

The newsletter serves as the main gathering point for ideas with which we have come in contact. Not only do we include descriptions of job openings with groups working for social change from a wide variety of viewpoints, but also proposals for new projects that need help in getting started; new ideas that can be developed and adapted in one or many locations; descriptions of places where you can learn more about social action in an educational setting, articles on topics relating to working for social change on a full-time basis, and resource groups and people to contact. What all of the people behind these various ideas have in common is a genuine concern for causing basic change in American institutions.

Informing you of available opportunities for involvement in social change is only part of our goal. We also hope that the information that we have gathered will stimulate you to think about what new roles need to be created and to consider the possibility of actually finding a new role for yourself. Many more dedicated people are needed if we are to see significant change in our lifetimes.

VSC, CANYON, CALIF. 94516

Local VSC Counseling
The main goal of VSC is to encourage people to think about ways they can become involved in working for social change on a full-time basis. We realize that the publication can hardly give you a fair picture of what it is really like to become involved in the projects described. Person to person contact with those who have had experience in areas similar to the VSC listings could well be a partial solution to this communication gap.

So, a few of our friends (we're looking for more) have found experienced social change workers of all kinds in their communities who are willing to share their experiences with people like you. If you are interested in experimental education, for example, you might contact one of the persons we've listed below who may in turn know of someone in their area who has actually taught in a liberated school setting and is available to talk with you about what it was like.

If you live in one of the cities below, or are traveling through, get in touch with our contact. Likewise, if you would be able to provide this kind of service to people in your community, let us know.

California, San Francisco: Bill Anderson, American Friends Service Committee, 2160 Lake Street, 94121 (415-752-7766)

Humboldt County: Doug Glasser, Bell Hill Road, Eureka, 95501 (707-443-6428)

Santa Barbara: Harvey Haber, 2840 Hidden Valley Lane, 93105 (805-969-0898)

Wyoming, Laramie: Dick Putney, U.C.M., 1215 Grand Ave., 82070 (307-742-3791)

Colorado, Denver: Nell Sale and Steve Johnson, 1566 High St., #3, 80218 (303-399-6769)

Wisconsin, Madison: Patricia McFarland, 211 Landon St., 53715 (608-257-2350)

Ohio, Yellow Springs: Marj Leslie, 128 W. Davis St., 45387 (513-767-1965)

Illinois, Chicago: Noel Barker, 5301 Cornell St., 60637 (312-324-2327)

Pennsylvania, Philadelphia: Judith Chomsky, Resistance, 2006 Walnut St., 19103 (215-561-8080)

New Hampshire, Portsmouth: Buzz Theberge, 215 Circuit Rd., 03801

New York, N.Y.C.: Marti Roberge, Emmaus House, 241 E. 116 St., 10029 (212-348-5622)

Bronx: Gerald Friedberg, Bensalem College, Fordham University, 302 Broadway, 10007 (212-298-7614)

Rochester: Elaine Greene, 32 Sanford St., 14650 (716-771-6753)

In the hum of the market there is money, but under the cherry tree there is rest.

The real battle is taking place in the chambers, behind closed doors. Here all the deciding is done and the rest is some type of stage production. I am being tried in an armed camp. I am over-guarded and the people are being intimidated. Come see, Bill, really! It's all a sham, they all are following orders that flow from the top down. Dig! Come and check the—out. Later on, Albert.

LETTER FROM PRISON, 1971

Life is a web, time is a shuttle, and man is a weaver. The principle of action is a thread in the web of life. Of that web, two things are true, that which enters therein will reappear and nothing will reappear which was not put therein.

J. NEWMAN

Up, sluggard, and waste not life; in the grave will be sleeping enough.

The greatest wealth is contentment with a little.

One More Round

James J. Corbett was once asked what was the one great thing about fighting or boxing, and Life in general for all of us. His reply is a classic. "Fight One More Round." When your arms are so tired that you can hardly lift your hands to come on guard and everyone seems to be against you, "Fight One More Round." When your nose is bleeding and your eyes are black and you are so weary that you wish your opponent would crack you on the jaw and put you to sleep, "Fight One More Round." Remember that the man or woman who "Fights One More Round" is never whipped.

ANONYMOUS

The world was simple . . . whether it was 1947 A.D. or B.C. suddenly became of no significance. We lived and we felt with alert intensity. We realized that life had been full for men before the technical age also, indeed fuller and richer in many ways than the life of modern man. Time and evolution somehow ceased to exist; all that was real and all that mattered were the same today as they had always been, and would always be. We were swallowed up in the absolute common measure of history, endless unbroken darkness under a swarm of stars.

THOR HEYERDAHL WRITING OF THE FEELINGS
OF THE KON TIKI CREW

Living directly on the sea where one had to take what she gave for better or worse, I stood alone with nature. Perhaps this is man's natural condition, one begetting a constant feeling of exhilaration and strength.

WILLIAM WILLIS, LONE SEA VOYAGER

What is great in man is that he is a bridge and not a goal.

NIETZSCHE

The cost of a thing is the amount of life which has to be exchanged for it, immediately or in the long run. When the essentials are assured, there is an alternative to struggling for luxuries . . . that is to savor life itself.

BRADFORD ANGIER

Discontents do not arise from our desires oftener than from our needs.

It is beautiful to see an injured and disappointed man, protective and kindly.

There is a scene in Spartacus when the gladiators finally break out of their prison. They push down a tall fence, seize the swords of the terrified guards and then proceed to hack their way to freedom. When I saw this scene I could hardly contain my emotions. Why, those weren't slave gladiators on that screen . . . those were the people who have been brainwashed, suppressed and put down by those who have always ridden roughshod over the people. The day is arriving soon when these former slaves will break out of their prisons, physically and spiritually. Then, as in Spartacus, the jailers had best flee. In fact, they had better start now.

DON COLE

A healthy body is my ambition, conscience is my guide, love is my law, truth is my goal, perfection is my desire, peace is my comfort, nature is my companion, beauty is my joy forever, work is my blessing, experience is my teacher, difficulty is my stimulant, mistakes are my lessons, neighbor is my brother, pain is my warning, wisdom is my forte, understanding is my aim, patience is my power, bounty is my inclination, future time is my promise. With the foregoing treasures I am adequately equipped to aid others.

ANONYMOUS

To be nobody-but-yourself in a world which is doing its best, night and day, to make you everybody else—means to fight the hardest battle which any human beings can fight, and never stop fighting.

E.E. CUMMINGS

Yesterday—ashes; tomorrow—wood; today—fire.

INDIAN SAYING

You've got to know when to stop going in little bits and save yourself up and make a big jump.

DALE EVANS

If you want to try a new way you've got to build something.

W.E.C.

The high cost of living in the urban areas, nevertheless reduces the workers' real income. Money incomes in the rural areas are lower than those in the city, but the cost of living is equally lower compared with urban living. The full development of cottage industry in the rural areas, can provide additional forms of incomes on the part of rural families, which could reduce the influx of population to cities in quest for employment. This ultimately would minimize social problems in urban centers.

CE CO CO EDITORS, KEN KERN

The Long Song
It saddens me that we all have never been able to make our times of functioning together really sing a long song, though maybe we are singing a long song that is more subtle that I can grasp—sometimes. I suspect this, but most often I think that the subtle song thought is a bunch of shit and we're really all raving and lost in different parts of the woods. Who knows? I continue to have an enduring desire for a lot of money to enable the realization of my dreams. In any event the denouement of our movie or movies will occur and etc. I hope eventually to live in the nice smelling pine trees in a house I've built and have a nice garden and animals and have clean streams and rivers and lakes and the hills and forests and congenial friends nearby and etc. But maybe we'll all live in a plastic 21st century or maybe we'll all die.

RON BEVIRT, GARDNER, COLORADO

Learn as if you were to live forever; live as if you were to die tomorrow.

Think of three things: whence you came, where you are going, and to whom you must account.

The Yukon's canoe routes are long and remote. With the reduction of commercial river traffic—most of this now going over the highways—the rivers are once more deserted. Waters in the Yukon average about 50 degrees even during a hot summer; lakes may not be ice-free until the middle of June and freezing temperatures and snow can be expected by the first of September. The rivers are large, supply points are few and far between. A canoe cruise should, therefore, include at least two, preferably three craft. Early September sees grizzlies feeding on salmon in the shallows so that the Department of Travel suggests that a rifle be carried during this period, to be used only in an emergency.

BILL RIVIERE

Meantime, the countryside, as oriented and fashioned by plane, by highway, and by electric information-gathering, tends to become once more the nomadic trackless area that preceded the wheel.

MARSHALL McLUHAN

Poets and artists live on frontiers. They have no feed back, only feed forward. They have no identities. They are probes.

ANONYMOUS, from the Movement Press

"Wiretapping" quoth the raven, "is a threat to identity. Why not beat 'em to the wire? Get rid of your identity now."

ANONYMOUS, from the Movement Press

Travel is the best education. The best way to meet people while traveling is to hitch. If you decide to leave school, jam a few paperbacks in your pockets, pack a bag and hit the road. It's nearly free. You'll learn about people and places.

ANONYMOUS, from the Movement Press

Now with old age and at the upper end, Nature restores freedom of choice and permits, once again, that rightful irresponsibility to enquire and explore regardless of consequences. Being relieved of the armor of authority and the enforcement instruments of command, those in second maturity are once more at liberty to enquire rather than to order, and to question rather than reply.

GERALD HEARD

The fairest life ever lived on earth was that of a poor man, and with all its beauty it moved within the limits of narrow resources.

ANONYMOUS

I have come more and more strongly to believe that the ultimate moral goal, even the moral necessity, of the American people must be to become the Aborigines of the American land. An aborigine, my dictionary says, is "an indigenous habitant . . . as contrasted with an invading or colonizing people." An an indigenous person is one "living naturally in a particular region or environment." In general, aborigines are preservers of their land, whereas invaders or colonizers are the exploiters and destroyers of theirs. White Americans have for the most part remained the invaders and colonizers of the American continent; their relationship to the land has remained economic, exploitive, superficial, destructive. American history is to fearful extent the history of a group of mercenary nomads. exhausting the land as they have moved over it. But we have a great deal to learn from all truly indigenous peoples. The agriculture practices of primitives and peasants ought to be particularly instructive to us, for these people have farmed the land with a sense of profound unity with it; their ways, formed slowly over generations out of an intricate knowledge of the land and its needs, have tended to preserve it.

F.H. KING

Cities aren't places any more. They're scenes, projected on screens, then bulldozed away, neighborhood by neighborhood, like cancelled TV shows. People who are tired of scenes are leaving, or wanting to anyway, longing for a place, torn between the joy of getting out of town, and a vague despair that maybe there ain't no such thing as place after all, that maybe all there is to do is ride around in outfitted buses, floating along the bloodless traffic arteries of the world.

GURNEY NORMAN

When you buy land in a place and start living there, you become a citizen of the county and state. Don't be surprised if other citizens are interested in you. Wouldn't you be?

STUART BRAND

Many mills in Northern Calif. being closed down in areas that have been logged out. Mill buildings made of redwood, heavy timbers, corrugated tin can be gotten for the effort of dismantling and hauling away. We built two small houses that way with a little help from our friends. Glass for windows from wrecked VW buses.

BEST WISHES,
STEVE JORDON
THE SEA RANCH, CALIF.

12 The Compendium

A compendium is a summary that gives much information in little space. That's what we propose to present in this chapter. Several of the subjects could easily become full-length books and still not begin to present all of the vital facts.

The items vary in length from a single line to many pages. Thus, you can fill up an idle moment waiting for the water to boil, or stretch out in your hammock between the walnut trees and learn about newspapering.

There is no plan, with the exception that we put the one we think is most important first. So here's the contents so that you can't say you weren't warned.

Power to the People
Possibly the most important single item in this book is the article on counties by Ted Radke. It is preceded by an equally fine editorial by John Lewallen. If you don't read anything else in this book, read these.

They were originally published in the August 1971 issue of *Clear Creek*, (617 Mission, San Francisco, 94105). Most people who have read *Clear Creek* agree that it is the most heads-up publication in the "save-our-environment" field.

Our thanks to John, Ted, and Pennfield Jensen, Editors of *Clear Creek*.

Editorial
Editing a wide-open environmental magazine is like being in an Asiatic war. One squats in a media vortex, inundated by all the fear, rage, and creativity verging on madness which spins in from modern America. The belea-

guered editor spades out a foxhole, letting his stories hiss overhead into oblivion, occasionally snapping back as one impacts his helmet.

Sometimes a concept comes down with the explosive authority of a 122 mm rocket. Such an idea is the focus on local American government, particularly county government, presented in this chapter.

The county idea comes during a period of doubt and disarray in the environmental movement. We recently attended an Environmental Priorities Conference, a meeting of environmental group leaders from throughout America. Environmentalists from Washington spoke of lobbying for passage of piecemeal laws to deal with a global crisis; laws which they generally agreed the present administration would not enforce. Local ecology action groups appeared to be locked in suspended animation, stomping cans and buying books as their biosphere continued to be ravaged. The eyes of the mass media, which drilled in the brazen ecologists of 1970, have turned elsewhere; and the most brutal corporate exploiters of our planet have swiped the environmental perspective, perverting it into a promotional tool.

There was an air of self-congratulatory optimism at the conference, shadowed by vague realization of the grim truth: the environmental movement has been castrated and sanitized, and its genuine exponents have been separated from the mainstream of American society and positioned as threats to every major interest group in this country. In this circumstance, a turn toward home, toward simple truth, has the potential to revitalize the environmental movement throughout America. While we have been mesmerized by the televised shadow play of national politics, our local governments—through their powers to zone, to tax, to set health standards, to enforce laws—have been dictating the destruction of our immediate environments. These governments are close to us, are inexpensive to influence, and are relatively easy to capture through the election process.

This is the dream: gradually, throughout America, people begin breaking out of their terrifying isolation and talking to their neighbors. The topic is their shared environment, and who controls it. Peoples' coalitions form, first to lobby their cities and counties about specific issues of common interest, then to run candidates for local offices.

In the process, ecology activists test and adapt their social concepts, expanding them to deal with the real problems of people struggling to live in a cruelly demanding society. Eventually, first at local levels, then in the states and the nation, a government emerges which represents a balanced human society in a balanced, and beautiful, natural environment.

To realize this dream, we need only to settle down and

begin working where we live. All it demands is clear-headed energy. The powers are close at hand, ready to be grasped. We are now living in the environments we deserve; and we shall continue to live in a world which is a reflection of ourselves and our society.

The revolution in America occurred when the technological evolution of our culture seduced us into allowing narrow commercial interests to seize control of our local institutions, and therefore of our personal environments. The counterrevolution, as described by this chapter would be a reassertion of community control over community resources.

JOHN LEWALLEN, FEATURES EDITOR
CLEAR CREEK

Selections from COUNTIES: LOCAL GOVERNMENT
AND THE AMERICAN ENVIRONMENT
A MANIFESTO FOR CITIZEN COUNTERREVOLUTION
First published in *Clear Creek* by Ted Radke

I know that the great tragedies of history often fascinate men with approaching horror. Paralyzed, they cannot make up their minds to do anything but wait. So they wait, and one day the Gorgon devours them. But I should like to convince you that the spell can be broken, that there is only an illusion of impotence, that strength of heart, intelligence and courage are enough to stop fate and sometimes reverse it. One has merely to will this, not blindly, but with a firm and reasoned will.

ALBERT CAMUS

In December 1970, 950 delegates from 142 Indiana church, civic, fraternal, labor and ethnic organizations founded the Calumet Community Congress. The common condition: they were all out of the club. The issues: racism, taxes, employment, education, social services, environmental abuse. The solution: take effective power at the local government level, so that these issues could be dealt with directly and immediately. It became apparent that this heavily industrialized town in the Gary, Indiana, area was politically controlled by a relatively small group of economically and politically powerful self-seekers. It was obvious that if change was to come, it would have to come from those whose needs—whatever they were—were not being met.

Similar moves are, will be, or should be underway in every part of the country. We've been wrong too long. The experience of the last ten years indicates that the only truly effective national strategy for solving our problems is establishing a community of interests among people and groups on the local government level, then organizing—not against the government—but to *become* the government! When such a coalition takes local power, it is likely to be able to control offices in the state legislature, and perhaps a congressman or two. It is also possible to take over the local party machinery in your area—which gives you a voice in national and state party affairs.

Also, from a base of institutional power you are in a much stronger position to affect the course of state and national policy—you are beyond the point of secular prayer. Similarly, again from a position of institutional power, you can work effectively with other groups or governments outside your immediate area on matters of mutual concern. The possibilities are limitless. This is the only way you can change state and national policy and *make it stick*—by getting people together in local areas, transforming the local government units, which then become a base for carrying the transformation to other local, regional, state and national government bodies.

Underselling the Fear Merchants   Rather than the old approach of going to the national or state government and getting clobbered—or, at most achieving a watered-down, selectively-enforced policy—the idea is to create spheres of influence, bases which generate others in a steady process which culminates in the transformation of the state and national government. Such a strategy, once undertaken, is irresistible in the long run. And it requires no large budgets, no national leaders, or organization (although these can help facilitate things). All that it requires is you getting it underway. To work, of course, it must be undertaken in more than a few places. But it will work if tried!

For too long now, we have permitted people to play minorities, workers, environmentalists, poor people, old people, and middle class homeowners against each other. When one group asks for something, they are told they can't have it because of the needs of the others. In recent months it has become a knee-jerk reaction for developers, industrialists and their politicians to attempt to create antagonism and fear between minorities and workers who need social services and income, environmentalists concerned with growth and environmental degradation, and middle class homeowners concerned with taxes. By such juggling, these fear merchants hope to keep people divided and mutually hostile in order to maintain their positions.

This is an extremely dangerous situation and under no circumstances can we afford to permit such tactics to be successful. The interests of these groups are not mutually exclusive and, in fact, are mutually supportive. This is clear at the local government level. All of these groups are being taken. It only remains for them, either individually or as a collective, to sit down and figure out how. In the meantime, it is everyone's job to see that empathetic understanding, care, and effort are exerted in order to prevent or correct dangerous suspicions and animosities.

Creeping Ecology: Bringing It All Back Home   A very good operating model to develop is that "virtually nothing can happen in a county without that county's permission." It is time to go from the hand-wringing Chicken Little stage of environmental action to seeking ways to implement the principles of ecology into public debate and public policy.

The first problem one encounters when he decides "to do something" is deciding what to do. The world-wide environmental crisis, if left at that level of definition, is simply a cause for despair rather than a guide for action. Ecology includes everything.

It is the first job of an organizer to transform the plight or bad scene into circumscribed problems and issues which can be dealt with because they are limited and point to immediate solutions. It is only when an amorphous plight is broken down into its component parts (limited problems and issues) that sustained action becomes possible.

Another perspective that guides us is the notion that the only way to change Washington or the state government is to get together with your neighbors and begin changing things in your community and county. It is the "democratic" rather than the "liberal" theory of social change.

It has been that people were directed to appeal to higher authority to correct injustice. For all their pugnacity, the basic tactic was petitioning the "king" or mass secular prayer —"please do something." People would mobilize, have a demonstration, get a few laws passed, and then go home in the belief that something had been done. But what the king giveth, the king can taketh away—particularly if you are no longer on hand to do anything about it. All the programs, regulations and laws in the world won't help unless they are administered properly.

The difference between having a law or policy passed and having it effectively implemented is the difference between prayerfulness and power. Or, as Thomas Jefferson once put it, "The execution of the law is more important than the making of them." In a very basic way, "administration is policy."

The only places where significant lasting gains were made, particularly in poverty and civil rights, were when *people organized and took institutional power at local government levels.*

A great part of control over our air, land, water, and human patterns is in the hands of county governments.

Why Counties?   They have the power . . . to move mountains; to change the courses of rivers; to destroy marshes and cement creeks; to turn rivers into sewers and air into lung-disease-producing garbage dumps; to permit exposure to practically every imaginable environmental health hazard; to rob from the poor to give to the rich; to ignore illegal slums; to sanction and yet punish poverty; to create earthquake and flood hazards; to force people into private polluters (cars) rather than public transportation or smog-free transportation; to turn agricultural land and natural areas into subdivisions, parking lots, sprawl and instant blight; to turn grasslands into deserts and hills into eroding ruts and slides; to block or subvert regional and state environmental planning and controls; to purchase ecologically irresponsible products, thus sanctioning such products; to misuse rather than reuse garbage as a resource. The point is that since they have the power to do these things—they also have the power to prevent and correct them.

Standards for environmental quality can be established and enforced immediately—on the city and county level. And what's more, the levers are already there. For while the power to do bad has been extensively used, those same powers can be used to do good—it only requires that you begin taking a look at the potential of your county, city, or special district, define the problems of your area, and then begin raising the issues.

County Powers Counties and cities are not necessarily subordinate to the state. Functions of a county include election administration, principal responsibility for health programs and regulations; law enforcement; administration of justice; upkeep of roads; administration of relief and welfare programs; maintenance of vital statistics and property records. Other key functions include administration of federal and state programs (public works, welfare, economic development, poverty programs, farm subsidies, etc.) within the county and, perhaps more important, almost unlimited planning and taxing powers. (Cities, however, usually have a limit on tax rate.)

Elective offices in counties usually include the board of supervisors, sheriff, district attorney, coroner, assessor, tax collector, treasurer, auditor, county clerk, recorder, public administrator, superintendent of public schools, and judges of the superior, municipal and justice courts. In addition, the board of supervisors appoints a long list of people to policy-making positions on commissions, special districts and regional districts and boards.

The board of supervisors is the chief legislative and administrative organ of the county, and has comparable power to a city's mayor and councilmen combined. It adopts the budget (which decides who gets what); sets the county tax rate (which decides who pays) on general property; enacts special taxes such as the 1% sales tax; and often sits as a board of equalization, to hear complaints against the property valuations set by the county assessor. The supervisors also have final authority over all planning, land use and zoning decisions.

In addition, boards of supervisors and city councils have the power to enact civil ordinances. These have been used recently in some areas to ban non-returnable containers, detergents containing phosphates, and to halt noise pollution. Much more could be done.

Boards also hire and fire county civil service personnel; approve all purchases made by the county; and market bonds floated by the county and by school districts. In election years the board serves as elections commission. Other ex-officio roles of the supervisors are to act as board of directors for county smog control, flood control, and road districts; or to serve on regional boards and commissions dealing with air and water pollution, regional government, transportation, etc.

Environmental Control Local governments have almost exclusive control over land use. If you have ghettoes, blight, suburban sprawl, water and air pollution, a lack of open space or recreation areas, factories lining waterfronts, strip mining, etc., "it is because your city wants it that way." To use land for any purpose requires county or city permission in the form of a zoning ordinance and building permits.

The almost unlimited power to grant, deny and revoke these permissions makes local government a place where we can get at the root causes of environmental and social problems, rather than treating the symptoms.

Upon receiving a request to rezone a piece of land, the planning commission and the board of supervisors—who again have final authority—can and should insure the community's welfare by placing environmental taxing and employment stipulations that must be met if the request is granted and development is to take place. In the form of ordinances, these conditions would be enforceable; and the county could revoke the permit if the conditions were not met, or if the owner violated any state law in connection with his development and use of the property.

Another possibility is the use of the method of eminent domain, by which local governments can take over areas being used irresponsibly so that they can be used or developed in the best interests of the community.

Planning and zoning are also the chief mechanisms for preserving natural areas, open space, and agricultural areas from speculation and irresponsible development.

For obvious reasons, planning commissions are of special interest to those who profit from development and pollution. And what's more, the commissioners themselves may not have any idea of just how extensive their powers are—or if they do, they may have good reasons for not acknowledging them.

In granting a zoning permit the commission must make sure that "... the granting of the permit will not be materially detrimental to the public interest, safety, health and welfare or injurious to other property in the territory in which said property is situated." In other words, the planning commission and the board of supervisors, who appoint the commissioners and have final review over all their decisions, can do just about anything they want in pursuit of the public welfare. Too often, however, these land-use levers are the captives of people pursuing private profit at the expense of the public welfare. The community's pollution and social problems are someone's profit.

Health Counties and cities are given broad discretionary legislative and policing powers in order to protect the health of the people within their jurisdiction. These powers offer another method for securing a future. "Counties can control anything that is a potential hazard to the community." Anything from pesticides, to sanitation, waste disposal, unwholesome food, dangerous products, air and water pollution, etc. All that is required is support in the form of ordinances and manpower, and imagination and firm direction from the policy-making body of the county—the board of supervisors.

Budget Cities, counties, and special districts are super-consumers—they spend vast sums of money. This spending power could and should be used to support ecologically sound manufacturing practices; and punish by boycott, ecologically irresponsible ones. Paper recycling, smog-free transportation, returnable containers, organic gardening methods, bio-degradable products, are but a few of the areas where an ecologically conscious and responsible local government can use its dollar votes to secure manufacturing practices more in tune with ecological realities.

In matters of environmental health and ecologically conscious purchasing, local governments can also launch campaigns to educate their constituencies in these important areas. This in addition to all the program budget decisions affect the quality of life.

Law and Order

> The execution of laws is more important than the making of them.
>
> THOMAS JEFFERSON

The way in which the sheriff's department and the district attorney's office spend their time and resources is, like taxing, planning, and health, a political decision. Again, local governments are given a wide range of general policing powers and an equally wide range of discretion in implementing them.

Both the D.A. and the sheriff could spend more time and energy in enforcing existing regulations, ordinances, and laws that have environmental implications. In many areas grand juries and the D.A.'s should also be investigating conflicts of interest that have dramatic environmental implications.

The D.A. in particular should have the responsibility of determining the legal authority the local government has in environmental matters, and testing that authority in courts when the limits of that authority are in doubt.

The D.A. should also involve himself in cooperation with planning commissions, health department, pollution control, and many other areas; if he is truly the people's lawyer, he can do no less.

Investigate your area, its particular problems and the particular institutional and political setup that can be used to solve them.

Find the Strings and Their Manipulators   The first job is to find out what the limits of your local government unit are. Get copies of charters and ordinances that are the bases for their authority. Additional information can be gleaned from general texts on state and local governments in your particular state. Other good sources of information include teachers with special interests in these areas, civic groups, and the local government itself. As likely as not you will find that the office holders don't know what powers they do have, particularly in environmental action.

This is not to say that they won't give you a long list of reasons why they can't do anything. But remember, your most powerful tool is your power and ability to define the situation. A good rule of thumb is that the powers of local government to enhance and protect the environment, and protect and provide for the health and welfare of the people, are much greater than is generally acknowledged.

The next task is to find out who is running things and why. This information may come from a copy of the county master plan, which shows regularly what those running things want to happen in terms of industrial development, population growth, urban slurb, agriculture, recreation and open space. Other key sources are health departments, taxpayer associations, labor unions, planning departments, and perhaps the most important, chambers of commerce and development associations. This information is usually very easy to obtain and free—just go in and ask. Many of these agencies, because they are tax supported, are required by law to give it to you. When they feel threatened, however, there are all sorts of ways they can hide things. So be thorough.

As you begin to piece things together, patterns begin to emerge. You will find that in local government, as in nature, everything is connected to everything else. Our problems are more a result of misplanning to promote special interests, than of no planning. And what's more, because local government has been generally ignored by people over the years, most of what you discover will be shocking news to all but a small group of insiders.

Planning Alternative Futures As a beginning, we need a clear picture of what is going on and how the issues are interrelated. We have passed the point where we can permit massive transformations of the environment, at an ever-increasing tempo, on the basis of promises, guesses, and simple-minded boosterism.

Groups could join together for an in-depth study of their city or county. These studies must be conducted by private consultants—independent of any interested private or public bodies. In addition, the worldwide resource picture, on which existing industries, agriculture and institutions are dependent, should also be clarified and related directly to the local situation.

We also need to know what plans various industries, including agri-business, have which will afffect employment and consequently social benefits.

When reliable information on all these matters is obtained, the people of your region should be presented with alternative futures—futures that, based on fact, they can have for themselves, their children and their children's children. These combination vision-plan-programs should then be presented to the people, who could then decide which of the alternative futures they want. When the decision is made, implementation should begin. The future belongs to all of us—so it is for all of us to decide.

Studying and then acting within your city or county will produce new and more sensible master plans, and zoning, planning, health and tax policies that will insure all of us a healthy and productive future in a pleasant and balanced environment. This is the way to come to grips with whether or not we can have a long and quality future for everyone.

Cheap, Legal Counterrevolution It all begins and ends with you. Your power is your imagination, responsibility, flexibility, and perserverance. You define the issues. You decide what to do. You, therefore, always have the initiative.

The industrialists, developers, and backward politicians must be on guard everywhere, at all times. You on the other hand can strike anywhere. They get drained and become weaker, while each action you undertake should make you stronger—regardless of whether you win or not. For your goal is to instill in the public mind a recognition of the ecological consciousness, and the interrelationships the issues have and how they affect people. In other words your goal is to educate people so they can begin to see things as you do—and begin acting on that new consciousness.

We have no time limit. Our concern is to secure a future, to transform practices and consciousness which are life-threatening to those which are life-sustaining. It will likely take us the rest of our lives.

A small number of people can begin laying the ground-work—doing the research, contacting groups, defining issues and informing the people. You should also appear before your city council and/or your board of supervisors with protest and proposals. Use their campaign forums to publicly raise issues that should be dealt with by asking probing, well-considered questions. This only takes one person and can begin to change the entire context of local politics.

You can't lose. If they go with you, good—if they go against you then you have given them an opportunity to act positively and through their failure to do so you begin to create a history of governmental inaction and irresponsibility that will be invaluable as to what needs to be done.

As far as politicians are concerned, don't join them, induce them to join you. Formulate your positions carefully, state them clearly, and if you are effective, and the people begin to see things your way, the politicians will come to you. If they don't, either you haven't been doing your job or they are flirting with political suicide. Keep them informed and encourage positive action, but don't compromise essentials for short term gains. If you begin to play political games, you risk losing sight of what you are playing for. And instead of becoming like you, you may become like too many of them—men who too easily sacrifice what's right and what should be, for what it is.

National organizations can be a tremendous facilitator at local government activities. Churches, minority organizations, labor organizations, national environmental groups, professional associations and political groups like Common Cause could add an entirely new dimension to their activities by carrying on internal education within their local units. As presently constituted, many of these groups and professional associations focus their attentions almost solely at national and state levels. Members pay their dues and the national office is supposed to take care of business. With very little effort, local members and units of these organizations are supposed to be pursuing at the local level the same goals and programs which the national organization are supposed to be pursuing at the state and national levels. These two directions complement each other considerably and, particularly at the local level, a little can go a long way. At present there are simply too many good, concerned people standing around wringing their hands anxiously. This is a tremendous waste that new directions from national organizations could begin to eliminate. With the cooperation between the various groups at the national level, we can really get things going.

True Morning   Unless you have credibility, you can accomplish nothing. It is, therefore, of the utmost importance to be as accurate and careful as possible—given your limits of time and resources. Never sacrifice truth for expediency—for while you may win battles, you will eventually lose the war. Remember, reason and honesty work better than fear in bringing about real improvements in the human condition.

In describing what he felt was the only possible way to really change anything, Leo Tolstoy urged "... that all enlightened and honest people should try to be as good as they can, and not even good in all respects, but only one; namely, in observing one of the most elementary virtues—to be honest, and not to lie, but to act and speak so that your motives should be intelligible to an affectionate seven-year-old boy; to act so that your boy should not say, 'But why, papa, did you say so-and-so and now you do and say something quite different?' This method seems very weak and yet I am convinced that it is this method and this method only, that has moved humanity since the race began. Only because there were straight men, truthful and courageous, who made no concessions that infringed their dignity as men, have all those beneficent revolutions been accomplished of which mankind now has the advantage ..."

On Nomading

The only psychological problem I have so far identified is one not unique to nomadic living but encountered, I suspect, by almost every opt-out, regardless of life-style: most of his life has been structured by other people and events; he has been told what to do and when to do it. Now, suddenly, he is largely free of all this. His life is all his to structure as he will. And this is a responsibility which overwhelms many people. I think this partly explains those who are loudly critical of the society around them—but firmly rooted, and who if propositioned will have no end of objections to ANY here-and-now self-liberation approach. Do they subconsciously sense their psychological dependency on some of the things they say they hate, and dread the thought of full responsibility for their own lives—no one else to blame for their shortcomings?

Perhaps "xenophobic rejection" of nomadic life stems not from its strangeness but from its accessibility: almost anyone CAN become substantially free this way—easily, inexpensively, through their own effort, any time they choose. It's an onus upon the exclusively armchair philosophers to "put up or shut up," and since they are not about to do either, they angrily reject any consideration of it. On the other hand, they will happily speculate about a Free America (or world) of the next millennium because it is safely distant—puts upon them no self-responsibility to act.

FROM *PRE-FORM*

The Whole Earth Catalog

Here is the way they put it:

The *Whole Earth Catalog* functions as an evaluation and access device. With it, the user should know better what is worth getting and where and how to do the getting.

An item is listed in the catalog if it is deemed:

1. Useful as a tool
2. Relevant to independent education
3. High quality or low cost
4. Easily available by mail

Catalog listing are continually revised according to experience and suggestions of catalog users and staff.

That says most of what is factual about W E C. But what it doesn't say is that the catalog has become the wish book of the movement people. You'll note in reading through it that much of the data and equipment are country-side oriented. Thus, we strongly urge that everyone who reads this book also acquire as many of the catalogs as they can afford. Write to Whole Earth Store, 558 Santa Cruz Avenue, Menlo Park, Calif. 94025.

Mother Earth News

This paperback-magazine from P.O. 38, Madison, Ohio 44057, is essentially a prose expansion of the *Whole Earth Catalog* concept. Published bimonthly, it is regularly loaded with well-written, highly detailed articles about how to build a cabin, raise chickens, and a hundred other essential bits of information about making it in the boondocks. When you write, tell Big John Shuttleworth that fellow executive-escaper W.C. sent you.

Have you ever thought of becoming a guerrilla minister?

Nasha Institute of Survival

This organization was founded for the purpose of collecting and spreading information on survival. It is supported mainly by donations and the sale of books related to this subject. They'll welcome your ideas and suggestions. You can join the Institute by writing them at P.O. 5286, Station A, Toronto 1, Ontario, Canada.

Better World News

As far as we know, this full-size newspaper is the only ecologically oriented country living publication being sold on the streets of a major west coast city. Started in early 1970 by me and my wife, it now has subscribers in every state (well, at least one in Montana) and several foreign countries. Plans are to expand its circulation to other metropolitan areas. *Better World News* contains up-to-date information on living off the land, country-type occupations, low-cost housing and how to build it yourself, non-polluting transportation methods, organic food and how to grow it or find it . . . in short, alternatives to city living to obtain the benefits of the vast regions in America that are still beautiful and natural. For a free sample copy write BWN, Paradise Publishers, P.O. Box 88, West Point, Calif. 95255.

You Spell Me and I'll Spell You

In early America, there were many tough jobs to perform; cutting timber, plowing, loading hay bales onto wagons. Teams of men learned to "spell" or replace one another to prevent fatigue or boredom. The same procedure can be used today . . . an era when shuffling endless pieces of paper can be as tiring as picking cotton or liftin' bales.

There are infinite variations on this theme. For example, two couples could alternate working and vacationing. While couple A is touring British Columbia in the community camper, couple B is regrettably tending machinery or shuffling papers in some corporate rattrap. However, while they are doing it, they can look forward to a groovy vacation lasting anywhere from three months to a year. This system can even be operated by two people—one works while the other plays. Whatever the numbers involved, its a truly great way to spend at least half your life in some worthwhile place.

The Movement Press

Everyone has heard of *Rolling Stone*, the *Freep*, and the *East Village Other*. But have you ever heard of *Protean Radish*, *North Carolina Anvil*, or *Eye of the Beast*? If not, then what you've been looking for is this list . . . names and addresses of the movement press. Send for some sample copies today.

Akwesasne Notes, Rooseselton, N.Y. 13683, $.50/issue
Albion's Voice, P.O. Box 9033, Savannah, Ga. 31401, $4/yr.
Alestle, c/o Paul Gorden, 7404 Tower Lake, Apt. 1D, Edwardsville, Ill. 62025
Alliance Magazine, Box 229, Athens, Ohio 45701
Alltogether, 44208 Montgomery, Palm Desert, Calif. 92260, $10/yr.
All You Can Get, R.P.O. 4949, New Brunswick, N.J. 08903, $3/yr.
Aquarian Herald, Box 83, Virginia Beach, Va. 23458
Atlantis, 204 Oxford, Dayton, Ohio 45407
Better World News, P.O. Box 88, West Point, Calif. 95255
Both Sides Now, 10370 St. Augustine Rd., Jacksonville, Fla. 32217, $2/12 issues
Broadside/Free Press, Box 65, Cambridge, Mass. 02139, $4.50/yr.

Burning River News, 12027 Euclid Ave., Cleveland, Ohio 4112, $5/yr.

Chinook, 1452 Pennsylvania St., Denver, Col. 80203, $6/50 issues

The Clam Community Liberation, Box 13101, St. Petersburg, Fla. 33733

Collective, 614 Clark St., Evanston, Ill. 60201

Come Out, Box 92, Village Station, New York, N.Y. 10014, $6.50/12 issues

Come Together, P.O. Box 163, Encino, Calif. 91316

Country Senses, Box 465, Woodbury, Conn. 06798, $5/yr.

Creem, 3729 Cass Ave., Detroit, Mich. 48201, $5/24 issues

Crossroads, Hill School, Pottstown, Pa. 19464

Daily Planet, Suite 2—3514 S. Dixie Hwy., Coconut Grove, Fla. 33133, $5/yr.

Dallas News (Corp), P.O. Box 7013, Dallas, Tex. 75209, $4/24 issues

Dallas Notes, Box 7140, Dallas, Texas 75209, $5/yr.

The D.C. Gazette, 109 8th N.E., Washington, D.C. 20002, $5/yr.

Different Drummer, Box 2638, Little Rock, Ark. 72203, $2/14 issues

Distant Drummer, 402 South St., Philadelphia, Pa. 19147, $7/yr.

Door to Liberation, Box 2022, San Diego, Calif. 92112, $4/26 issues

Dwarff, Box 26, Village Station, New York, N.Y. 10014

East Village Other, 20 E. 12 St., New York, N.Y. 10003, $6/yr.

Edge City, 116 Standary St., Syracuse, N.Y. 13201, $3/yr.

El Grito Del Norte, Box 466, Fairview Station, Espanola, N.M. 87532, $4/yr.

Everywoman, 6516 W. 83 St., Los Angeles, Calif. 90045, $2.50/10 issues

Eye of the Beast, Box 9218, Tampa, Fla. 33604

Fair Witness, P.O. Box 7165, Oakland Station, Pittsburgh, Pa. 15213

Feraferia, Box 691, Altadena, Calif. 91001, $4/13 issues

Fifth Estate, 1107 W. Warren, Detroit, Mich. 48201, $3.75/yr.

Filmmakers Newsletter, 80 Wooster St., New York, N.Y. 10012

Fox Valley Kaleidoscope, Box 252, Oshkosh, Wisc. 54901

Freedom News, Box 1087, Richmond, Calif. 94801, $2.50/12 issues

Free Spaghetti Dinner, Box 984, Santa Cruz, Calif. 95060, $4/yr.

Free You, 117 University Ave., Palo Alto, Calif. 94301, $6/yr.

Fusion, 909 Beacon St., Boston, Mass, 02215, $5/yr.

Gest, Box 1079, Northland Center, Southfield, Mich. 48075, $2/yr.

Great Speckled Bird, Box 54495, Atlanta, Ga. 30308, $6/yr.

Greenfeel, James Madison Law Institute, 4 Patchin Place, New York, N.Y. 10010

Guardian, 32 W. 22 St., New York, N.Y. 10010

Haight-Ashbury Tribune, 1778 Haight St., San Francisco, Calif. 94117, $10/yr.

Harry, 233 East 25th St., Baltimore, Md., 21218, $4/yr.

High Gauge, Box 4491, University, Ala. 36486, $5/yr.

The Hips Voice, P.O. Box 5132, Santa Fe, N.M. 87501, $5/24 issues

Home News Co., P.O. Box 5263, Grand Central Station, New York, N.Y. 10017

Hundred Flowers, Box 7152, Minneapolis, Minn. 55407, $9/yr.

Indianapolis Free Press, Box 225, Indianapolis, Ind. 48206, $5/26 issues

Inquisition, Box 3882, Charlotte, N.C. 28783, $2/6 issues

It Ain't Me, Babe, c/o W.L. Office, Box 6323, Albany, Calif. 94706, $6/yr.

Kaleidoscope, Box 5457, Milwaukee, Wisc. 58211, $5/26 issues

Kudzu, Box 22502, Jackson, Miss. 39706, $4/yr.

Las Vegas Free Press, Box 14908, Las Vegas, Nev. 89114, $7/yr.

Left Face, Box 1595, Anniston, Ala. 36064

Liberated Guardian, 14 Cooper Square, New York, N.Y. 10003, $10/yr.

Liberation News Service, 159 Claremount Ave., New York, N.Y. 10027, $15/month

Liberator, Box 1147, Morgantown, W. Va. 26505

Long Beach Free Press, 1255 E. 10, Long Beach, Calif. 90813, $6/yr.

The Long Island Free Press, P.O. Box 162, Westbury, N.Y. 11590, $6/2 yrs.

Los Angeles Free Press, 7813 Beverly Blvd., Los Angeles, Calif. 90036, $6/yr.

Madison Kaleidoscope, Box 881, Madison, Wisc. 53701, $5/yr.

Marijuana Review, California Institute of Arts, 7500 Glenoaks Blvd., Burbank, Calif. 91504

Memphis Root, Box 4747, Memphis, Tenn. 38104, $3.50/yr.

Metro, 906 W. Forest, Detroit, Mich. 48202, $4/yr.

Modern Utopian, P.O. Drawer A, Diamond Hts. Station, San Francisco, Calif. 94131, $4/yr.

Mother Earth News, Box 38, Madison, Ohio 44057, $5/yr.

News from Nowhere, Box 501, Dekalb, Ill. 60115, $5/yr.

New Prairie Primer, Box 726, Cedar Falls, Iowa 50613, $4/20 issues

★*New Times*, Box J, Temple, Ariz. 85281, $10/52 issues

New York Herald Tribune, 110 St. Marks Place, New York, N.Y. 10009, $5/lifetime

Nola Express, Box 2342, New Orleans, La. 70116, $3/yr.

North Carolina Anvil, Box 1148, Durham, N.C. 27702, $7.50/yr.

Northwest Passage, Box 105, Fairhaven Station, Bellingham, Wash. 98225, $5/yr.

Notes from Underground, P.O. Box 15081, San Francisco, Calif. 94115

Old Mole, 2 Brookline St., Cambridge, Mass. 02193, $5/20 issues

Oracle of San Francisco, 1764 Haight St., San Francisco, Calif. 94117

Other Scenes, Box 8, Village Station, New York, N.Y. 10014, $6/yr.

Other Voice, c/o Why Not Inc., Box 3157, Shreveport, La. 71103, $5/yr.

Our Town (Collective), Box 611, Eau Claire, Wisc. 54701

Palante Ylp, 1678 Madison Ave., New York, N.Y. 10029

Paper Workshop, 6 Helena Ave., Larchmont, N.Y. 10538, $4/yr.

Peoples Dreadnaught, Box 1071, Beloit, Wisc. 53511

Philadelphia Free Press, Box 1986, Philadelphia, Pa. 19105

Protean Radish, Box 202, Chapel Hill, N.C. 27514, $8/yr.

Protos, 1110 N. Edgemont St., Los Angeles, Calif. 90020, $3/yr.

Provincial Press, Madale Print Shop, Box 1276, Spokane, Wash. 99210, $5/yr.

Purple Berries, 449 W. Seventh Ave., Columbus, Ohio 43201

Quicksilver Times, 1736 R St. N.W., Washington, D.C. 20009, $8/yr.

Rag, 2330 Guadalupe, Austin, Texas 78705, $7.50/yr.

Rat, 241 E. 14 St., New York, N.Y. 10009, $6/yr.

Rearguard, P.O. Box 8115, Mobile, Ala. 36608, $4/yr.

Rebirth, Box 729, Phoenix, Ariz. 85001

Rising Up Angry, Box 3746, Merchandise Mart, Chicago, Ill. 60654, $5/yr.

Rolling Stone, 625 3rd St., San Francisco, Calif. 94107

Roosevelt Torch, 430 S. Michigan Ave., Chicago, Ill. 60605

San Diego Street Journal, Box 1332, San Diego, Calif. 92112

Second City, c/o The Guild, 2136 N. Halsted, Chicago, Ill. 60614, $5/26 issues

Second Coming, Box 491, Ypsilanti, Mich. 48197

Seed, 950 W. Wrightwood, Chicago, Ill. 60614, $6/yr.

Space City, 1217 Wichita, Houston, Tex. 77004

Spectator, c/o S. Indiana Media Corp., Box 1216, Bloomington, Ind. 47401

The S.S. Pentangle, Box 4429, New Orleans, La. 70118, $4/20 issues

St. Louis Outlaw, Box 9501, Cabanne Station, St. Louis, Mo. 63161

Sundance, 1520 Hill, Ann Arbor, Mich. 48104, $3.50/yr.

Susquehanna Bugler, 700 Market St., Williamsport, Pa. 17701, $.25/issue

Tasty Comix, Box 21101, Washington, D.C. 20009

The Times Now, Box 676, Coconut Grove, Fla. 33133

Tucson Free Press, Box 3403, College Station, Tucson, Ariz. 85716

Uproar, 44 Wimbleton Lane, Great Neck, N.Y. 11023

View from the Bottom, 532 State St., New Haven, Conn. 06510, $5/20 issues

Vortex, 706 Mass St., Lawrence, Kansas 66044, $5/24 issues

Walrus, Box 2307, Station A, Champaign, Ill. 61820

Water Tunnel, Box 136, State College, Pa. 16801, $3/yr.

Williamette Bridge, 6 S.W. 6th, Portland, Ore. 97209, $5/26 issues

Winn, 339 Lafayette St., New York, N.Y. 10012, $5/yr.

Worker's Power, 14131 Woodward Ave., Highland Park, Mich. 48203, $3.50/yr.

How to Start and Operate Your Own Newspaper

Thanks to the Underground Press Syndicate, Box 26, Village Station, New York, N.Y. 10014, we bring you complete instructions on how to do your own editorial thing. This could have made a chapter of its own, complete with pictures, and perhaps it will be in a revision of this book. If this doesn't answer all of your questions, write to Father William, P.O. 88, West Point, Calif. 95255, and he'll straighten you out on any unclear points. Father W. has had two or three decades in graphics and writing, and publishes his own movement paper.

Rolling the Ball   If you are going to start a paper, start it where the community needs one, not as a substitute for organizing that community . . . that is if you have a community you can call your own. If you don't—make one. A newspaper is a significant step in the right direction.

A newspaper is a tool—theirs, for keeping people under control. But we use that tool also. For change.

Most towns are one-paper towns, and all sorts of people feel the need for a paper not tied to the local establishment. While they may not desire a radical paper, many are willing to back one if it gets the news out. Most of these people are in opposition to the establishment—small property owners, small businessmen, academics, some of the churches, the hip community, the left liberals, and the radicals. A radical paper, reporting suppressed or overlooked local news, muck-raking the local establishment, and analyzing both news and establishment, serves these people's needs, shows them their common interests, organizes, radicalizes.

More likely than not, there are radical journalists already in your community. Possibly they write for a local college paper or you may find them active in politically oriented or consciousness-raising groups. It may be that some of them already put out a mimeographed newsletter in your area. By letting them know you are starting a paper you might be able to bring together a nucleus of people that can get things rolling and keep them that way.

Your basic staff needs will be in reporting, writing, and editing; layout and production; your advertising, distribution, and business. And even though you will probably find that certain people will naturally gravitate to specific areas in the operation, many papers have found that by rotating the position of editor with each issue, they provide an effective and refreshing change for the staff.

You needn't come out weekly. Biweekly publication gives you time to learn as you go along.

Costs   With a little bit of luck, you can put out a bi-weekly, 8-page, 4,000 copy tabloid for under $500 a month. That is not too much to ask from a community that needs a newspaper.

Your income will be from street sales, subscriptions, and sales from stores and stands, advertising and community underwriting. Don't expect advertising to pay the costs of printing, the yardstick generally used to measure newspaper success in straight journalism. Try going to the people who you think want and need a paper and ask them for money. Self-sufficiency should be an ultimate goal, and the point at which you become self-sufficient should be computed to keep you within reasonable bounds.

Expect your tabloid costs to begin with $100 for the press run and first thousand, $10-$25 per thousand thereafter for an 8-page issue. Headlines and photo work can cost $40 for an 8-page issue. You're going to need a place to work and keep the business of the paper straight, therefore an office is going to be necessary. Scout the town for an old cheap one. It's highly likely that you will find one for around $75 to $100 a month or even less. If you prepare your own copy for printing, you will probably want to use an IBM or comparable quality typewriter. An IBM Executive rents for around $25 a month, and sells reconditioned at about $400. Needless to say, foresight can save you a fortune: All jobs should be planned right from the beginning. This can be done best by talking to your printer and listening to his advice. It's not sensible to prepare a rush job and find out that it does not fit the available press, where by simply rearranging your material you could use a smaller press and save on the overall costs. For example: should your finished material be 6 X 9 inches (a size often used by letterpress) by simply rearranging your copy to 5½ X 8½ inches your copy will fall into standard offset press size and save you a considerable amount of money. Very few plants operate presses of all sizes so here is another reason why you should talk it over with your printer before attempting to lay out your paper.

Getting Copy   A good way to begin developing regular writers is to get someone primarily involved in the action to report it: someone going to the demonstration or involved in the fight for low-cost housing, or trying to organize his school.

As for collecting material which will be of interest to your paper, one of the most effective ways is for each member of the staff or collective to submit whatever he or she thinks is newsworthy or of community interest. Next the entire group gets together, discusses each piece, and decides whether or not it merits printing. This will make your paper well rounded, with a wide range of interesting material.

Community   If there are community-type operations in your area, such as a free clinic, drug aid, youth hostel, food or clothing co-op, community switchboard, etc., ensure each is given generous coverage and support. You might even consider giving some of these organizations a regular column. Keeping your community informed of what's going on is the whole idea, remember?

Another regular community feature in many underground papers is a list or directory of important phone numbers. An example of this might be:

Fire Department
Ambulance
Drug Aid
Community Switchboard
Food Co-op
FM Radio Station
Free Clinic

Health Food Store

Underground Paper

... and so on as far as your imagination will carry you.

One thing should be said about readership: think about who you are writing to. There's nothing more boring than reading an article that rants to the faithful; even the faithful get bored. Liberals reading radical muckraking need radical analysis along with it, not the mere accusation of evil. Radicals also need the analysis, too often having seen what is right or wrong without having understood why.

Photo Offset   Photo offset or lithography is quite a bit more sophisticated and expensive than mimeographing. Copy (typed matter, line drawings, or screened photos) is pasted up on a backing sheet. Plates can be made from a photo negative of, or directly from, the copy. The image areas on the plate are greasy and will repel water; non-image areas will hold water and, when wet, repel ink. After the plate is mounted on the press and dampened, only the image areas will pick up the ink. The image from the plate is transferred or offset onto a rubber roller and then transferred to the paper. Almost anything a newspaper would normally include can be reproduced by the offset process. Virtually any size can be printed by offset machines. General page sizes for our purposes are, in inches:

8½ X 11	... letter or digest size
8½ X 14	... legal size
11 X 17	... double letter or catalog
17 X 22	... tabloid size

Commercial prices for offset work up to 11 X 17 inches run as follows: a metal plate photographically made *with* photos (halftones) averages about $8.00. Without photos, a photographic plate should cost no more than $5.00. An electrostatically made plate costs much less—usually only $2.50. Electrostatic plates can do the same as photo plates but the quality is not as good and they will usually not last as long (perhaps only 10,000 copies).

If you are doing a tabloid you'll probably deal with only one printer who'll do everything. An all-inclusive average price for a 17 X 22 or 18 X 24 inch paper, four pages on newsprint can be from $60 to $100 for the first 2,000 copies. Additional copies will cost much less.

The most favorable conditions for printing offset are, of course, if you have a friend who has access to a press and plate-making facilities. If such ideal circumstances are not available, you must go out into the cold, nasty world to find others.

If there is a large underground press or movement printing shop near you, by all means investigate. If not, you'll have to go into the commercial market. There are many types of commercial establishments. Prices will vary greatly. We suggest you tear out the Yellow Pages section on printers and call on each one in your neighborhood asking for information and prices. When you go to printing places do not be afraid to suggest reduced rates, at cost, or free printing in exchange for a plug in your paper. In large cities, commercial printing plants will offer printing to fellow printers-publishers at drastically reduced rates. These deals are advertised in local printing trade papers. Add the word "company" to your paper's name and you automatically become a publisher. Wearing a suit and tie and having some calling cards for your presentation wouldn't be a bad touch.

Printing Production To start a newspaper in these days of the photo offset revolution all you need is a typewriter and someone who knows how to use it.

There are three types of typewriter ribbons: cotton, silk, and carbon. The cotton one you're undoubtedly familiar with. The silk, because it's thinner, produces a sharp, clear image. The carbon ribbon is actually a long strip of plastic film with a coating of carbon pigment. Carbon ribbons produce a clearer, sharper image than the other two, but they can only be used once. Ribbons come on thousands of different types of spools and cartridges, so be sure to buy the right one for your machine. Also, when you throw away old ribbons, it might be a good idea to save the spool—just in case.

About the machines themselves . . . Manual typewriters are fine for general copy preparation. Most manuals do not cut stencils very well. If none other is available, you must type with firm, steady strokes giving "closed" letters, such as *m* and *w*, more pressure. Electrics are generally better than manual typewriters. Probably the ideal typewriter to get hold of is the IBM Selectric. This typewriter has no keys (the things that strike the paper). The letter molds are on a sphere roughly the size of a golf ball. When you strike a key, a mechanism will rotate the sphere until the correct letter is in position. Then it will strike the paper. The carriage is stationary while the sphere and ribbon unit move across the page. The type sphere is interchangeable, giving you an enormous variety of different type styles to play with.

Layouts When you have decided on format, all else follows naturally (you hope). The size of the final product and the method of reproduction are major considerations. Generally a newspaper gives layout priority to articles and written work, and fits in the artwork, ads, etc., wherever and however they go best. If you are being the least bit conventional, you will first decide whether your copy will be presented in columns or the entire width of the page. Unless your page is unusually long and narrow you might consider using columns. Long lines of type will most likely discourage reading. The ideal column width is one-half to two lower case alphabets long. We've found that about 3½ inches is a good column width for typewritten copy. You might want to make a "dummy sheet" the size of your paper and experiment a little to see how many columns of what width and length you can accommodate. Be sure to take margin space into consideration. When you have done this, you can do your artwork, headlines, advertisements, etc. to fit the columns or the graphics of the page.

If you're into preliminary typing, we can give you two good arguments for doing it—but still suggest that it is really a waste of time in the end. The first thing is it will tell you if everything is going to fit, and if it's not, it gives you something to work with so you can decide what's going to have to be deleted. Secondly it gives you a good excuse to go ahead and justify your copy.

The lithographer can reproduce, within certain technical limits, anything the camera's eye can see. By simply pasting up your copy exactly as you want it finished, he can then photograph it, have the plate made, and run it off his press. Your original paste-up can be reproduced or enlarged by the photographer to the desired size. Your preliminary concern here is how to get your copy set up and ready to be photographed with the greatest accuracy and the cheapest cost to you.

As a preliminary to your paste-up, it might be a good idea to prepare a rough draft or working plan of what you intend to paste up. This rough draft will help you to visualize how the finished paste-up will look, and will guide you in fitting the pieces together. Your rough draft should be done on a sheet of paper the size of your finished job. Should your projected job be of more than one page, such as a folder, the layout should be done in pairs so that the open, two-page spread may be seen as a single unit.

First, the "tools" you will find essential and time-saving, and their uses:

1. CARDBOARDS on which to paste your copy. These must be white and fairly stiff. Mounting or illustration boards, purchased at any art supply stores, are best, but a 3 or 4 ply white bristol board will usually do as well. For certain types of work such as house organs or school publications, the printer may have boards already ruled up to give to his customers.

2. RUBBER CEMENT with which to do your pasting. DO NOT USE A SUBSTITUTE. Make sure that this is rubber cement for paper and not a rubber cement sold for household repairs. *Do not* use library paste, mucilage or glue as these substances tend to crinkle, stretch or soil the paper.

3. A NON-REPRO BLUE PENCIL: Lines drawn with a pencil of this color will not photograph if drawn lightly. Consequently they do not have to be erased from the fin-

ished paste-up. You use this pencil to draw in your margins, plans, and to call attention to errors. A warning—should you press too hard, this pencil *will* indeed reproduce, and cause headaches for you and your printer, so be delicate.

4. A TRIANGLE and/or T-square to align your copy. It is always best to see that all parts of your paste-up are *really* straight after they are pasted down. Do not trust your eyes, use the square!

5. AN EYEBROW TWEEZER: This little implement will help you handle the many small pieces of copy. Try to get one with flat ends.

6. OPAQUE WHITE PAINT or LIQUID TYPEWRITER CORRECTION FLUID: This stuff comes in small jars or bottles, there are lots of different brand names, and they are all good. You simply brush some of this white paint over the copy that is messed up and go back and type over it. This stuff is also good for cleaning up your finished layout.

7. SHARP SINGLE EDGE BLADES, SMALL SCIS-SORS, STEEL EDGE RULER, INDIA INK, AND AN EXAC-TO KNIFE. You'll find these out for yourself.

Whenever you prepare copy for offset work, the finished product will include all the dirty fingerprints, smudges, peanut butter and jelly stains, and cat prints you allow your paste-up to retain. Our suggestion is that any material which has the potential of being offset copy should be treated with a little respect. Buying a buck's worth of plastic report covers wouldn't be a bad idea.

Apart from textual copy, typewritten or typeset, you'll need headlines of some sort. If you have plenty of money you can buy a headline machine, a small photographic unit which rolls to different typefaces. On this the headline is set letter by letter via a photographic negative, then printed on glossy paper and cut out to be pasted into place. A much cheaper and slightly more laborious method is to buy pages of Letraset at about $2 a sheet which carry line after line of individual letters of different sizes. The Letraset page is placed carefully over the appropriate spot on the page and the letters rubbed off into place like a dry transfer.

You may find that you can operate quite well without headlines at all; so called "psychedelic" papers hand draw nearly all their titles and, in a pinch, you can always use somebody else's headlines, i.e. cut them out from news-papers, magazines, mailing pieces, posters, etc. It doen't even matter much if the headlines aren't particularly relevant—if they're eye-catching enough readers certainly won't ignore the stories below them.

When you do artwork for your paper, there are several points to consider. For the best results use a drawing or drafting pen with dense black ink on repro paper. For ruling lines or making circles, etc., drafting tools will be very helpful. Use white fluid for corrections.

In your graphics, to achieve a constant texture on solid areas, you should use art screens. These are plastic adhesive sheets with dots, lines, and other textures of various sizes and densities printed on them. To apply them, lay them over the desired area; burnish down area you want to stick with a smooth pen cap; cut and remove the excess with the Exacto knife we talked about. Screens can be bought at drafting and stationary stores for about one dollar for a legal size sheet.

You might want to break up the monotony of page after page of black type on white paper. There is an excellent way to bring about a refreshing change: *Reversal.*

You have often seen white letters printed on a solid black background. This may be done very simply when the offset method of printing is used. Your printing shop, through camera work, can reverse black copy printed on white paper into white copy on a black background. It's as simple as noting on the particular layout that you want the thing reversed. The printer will do the rest.

There is a particularly interesting effect, called Moiré, that can be obtained with two or more art screens. What causes the pattern is the interference of the two separate systems of lines on the sheets. With a little imagination stunning photos, and graphics too, can be produced.

With all your components and parts ready to be pasted down, your job now is to assemble these parts onto the illustration or bristol board. Here is where all your latent artistic talents should be given free rein.

With your non-repro blue pencil, draw the box on the cardboard which will show you the outside limits of your copy. This box should not include the margins, but rather just the confines of your printed matter. This is called the "image area" by printers and artists. Stay within this area. If you should paste up copy outside this space, you might create certain mechanical difficulties for your printer or cause the printer to reduce your copy to fit the designated space. If you are undecided as to what should constitute your image area, or if the overall paste-up calls for a reproduction, your printer will help in establishing these dimensions.

Your pasting should be as neat as possible. Don't rush. Be accurate. Remember that what you are pasting down will be reproduced exactly as you leave it. A line of type or column of copy pasted up at an angle will remain so, it cannot be corrected by the printer in the process of reproduction without extra cost. Use your rough layout as a guide to placing your various pieces of copy.

Smear a goodly amount of rubber cement on the back of the copy. Use some scrap paper on which to lay the copy upside down while you apply the rubber cement. Should you want the paper to adhere solidly, with permanence, apply the rubber cement to both the copy and the part of the board to which it will be pasted. Maneuver the copy into position. If the pieces of copy are quite small, use the tweezers to hold the copy while you apply the cement and place into position. If, for any reason, you must remove or move copy that is already pasted down, pour some rubber cement thinner or a little lighter fluid onto and under the copy. This will dilute the rubber cement, so that it can be easily removed. Incidentally, should your rubber cement thicken, some of this thinner or lighter fluid will thin out the rubber cement to a usable consistency.

Just tacking down the edges is really not enough. Use a sufficient amount of rubber cement to cover your copy completely. This will insure that the copy adheres sufficiently and won't curl at the ends or accidentally turn up at the corners. Loosely pasted copy will fall off and, in repeated handlings, get lost.

If you are using a typewriter for your copy, and you make a mistake in typing, do not try to erase or strike over. Just retype the word or line at the side of the copy or on a separate sheet of paper; cut out the word or line carefully and paste it over the correction. Make sure, however, that the correction has adhered *solidly*. Use your razor blade to help push the copy around to the desired position while the rubber cement is still in a liquid state and to slice away unwanted parts of the paper. Align your pieces of copy with a T-square and/or triangle. Make sure that it is square to the boxed lines of your image area. Again, do not trust your eye; be safe, use the tools at hand to make certain that the lines pasted down are *really* squared away.

Do not trim too close to your typed matter or art work. Allow about one-eighth of an inch of white paper beyond the typed matter. After you have pasted your copy down, smooth it with a clean sheet of scrap paper.

When your paste-up is completed, you should clean away all marks, smudges, rubber cement smears, and other markings which are not to appear on the finished product. Any excess rubber cement showing around the edges of the copy may be removed by rubbing it away very carefully with a clean finger, or a small ball of dried rubber cement. Use the white correction paint to eradicate other marks. Do not try to erase them. The cleaner your finished paste-up, the better your finished job will be. After you have cleaned your paste-up, give it its last check and admiring glance, protect it with a sheet of paper that will cover the entire board. This will help avoid damage in handling and carrying. You are now ready for the camera.

Distributing This is your biggest problem. In your own town try the most sympathetic bookstores—the ones that already carry underground papers. Sales through turned-on stores, head shops, the peace center and perhaps a few odd places like a mod dress store have to be developed. Until you can guarantee regular publication it's doubtful you will be able to find a distributor to place your paper on the news-stands. And, frankly, even when you do you can expect to be cheated; most distributors seem to be old-fashioned and puritanical in outlook, sloppily inefficient and as dishonest as they can get away with.

So, initially, plan to do your own distribution. Take the paper around to any place you can persuade to display it, on a consignment basis (i.e., you're paid for the copies they sell and they return the rest). In the early stages it's important, too, to spread as many free papers around as you possibly can; very few people will buy a new publication until they've seen a sample copy. Any public event where large numbers of people gather is excellent for free distribution (don't ask if you can hand out your papers because most people will refuse permission). Try poetry readings, political meetings, art gallery openings, lightshows, and other freak-outs—any-where there's a captive audience. Discotheques aren't very good because nobody wants to read there and it's too hard to even see a pile of papers much less pick one up. Compile a mailing list of everybody interesting or important you can think of: columnists on local papers, librarians, politicians, other small papers, and big ones, artists and galleries, head shops, boutique owners, coffee house proprietors, anybody who sees and talks to lots of people. If they like the free copy you send them, they'll mention it to their friends and customers. When you produce a paper, you're in the promo-tion business and you can't promote your paper too much or too often.

And for the sake of the revolution, get out to movement events and hawk or give them away. Get the thing down the road.

Press Services A press service is a group of newspapers who, through one central office, share their ideas, findings, and possibly exchange copies of their papers. The only such service we know of for high school underground papers is CHIPS, the Cooperative Highschool Independent Press Ser-vice. To join, you merely agree to send a certain number of copies of each of your issues to the CHIPS office in Houston. There is no fee involved. They, in turn, will take your copies with the copies from other papers around the country, and combine them into packets (containing one copy of each paper) and send these out to each member. So, in exchange for sending a certain number of copies of your paper, you will get copies of other high school undergrounds from which you, by the way, are free to print in your newspaper. Packets are mailed out monthly during the school year. Members also get other advantages; for example, CHIPS can sometimes help members get free or low-cost equipment and supplies. Other services of CHIPS are a semi-annual directory of high school undergrounds and literature for new groups. The CHIPS office is located at 1217 Wichita Street, Houston, Texas 77004. As of this writing there are 50 CHIPS members.

The Underground Press Service (UPS) is a much larger group and is intended for larger papers. It costs $25 to join. By joining, you agree to send a copy of each issue of your paper to all UPS members. If this seems too expensive, you might write to UPS, ask for a list of their members, and exchange with a few papers on an individual basis. To do that, simply send a copy of your paper with the word "exchange" written across the top. UPS can be reached at Box 26, Village P.O., New York 10024.

A news service consists of a group of correspondents who write on local news happenings and send that into a central office. The office will combine all the news stories, pictures, and graphics, etc., and send them out to subscribing newspapers, who are free to reprint it at will. FPS (the initials don't stand for anything in particular), a recently started news service for high school undergrounds, is operating in conjunction with CHIPS. FPS will send out packets every two weeks or so and the cost (for underground papers) is $3 or $4 depending on whether you contribute material for the publication. You can join FPS without joining CHIPS or you can join both of them.

There are several other news services for underground papers. The best known is the Liberation News Service (LNS) at 160 Claremont Ave., New York 10027. LNS sends out packets twice a week at a cost of $20 a month. Their packets are quite extensive, covering national and international news events in detail.

Subscriptions It is hardly worth the handling to sell subscriptions for less than one year, and two years is preferable. Since the paper could go out of business, most people realize that they are taking a risk when they subscribe. Even huge establishment magazines like *Saturday Evening Post* and *Look* have folded. Ultimately, probably the best bet for keeping track of subscriptions is a computer, with address labels automatically printed out on self-adhesive stickers. Another good way is by an Addressograph machine. Subscription services are often available, where they handle all the hassle for you; look in the Yellow Pages under Addressing Services. Once subscriptions start coming in, you should keep a record of who has paid and for how many issues. Also keep accurate records of addresses and zip codes. A good bookkeeping method is to type out addresses on labels as soon as the subs come in.

The Mails A bulk mailing permit can be obtained by simply paying a $35 fee. This allows you to mail at the rate of 3.6 cents per piece if the piece weighs less than 2.618 ounces, which most newspapers do. Otherwise it is 16 cents per pound, still much cheaper than first class. The $35 fee is good for one calendar year. An additional fee of $15 will obtain an indicia permit which eliminates the need for stamps. You just pay in cash at the time of mailing and you are issued a receipt.

Second class permits are available to publications that appear regularly and have paid circulation (subscriber and newstands) of at least 65 percent of the total number of copies released or greater than 75 percent advertising content. Many underground publications qualify for the permit. There is no fee, but clearance requires several months. Mailing costs can be cut considerably by mailing second class. The second class mail gets first class speed and handling, unlike third class.

Both second and third class bulk mail must be separated by zip code and the easiest way to do this is back on the mailing list or in the addressing plates. One cheap way to maintain mailing labels is to type up an original set, 33 to a page, then Xerox this master for each mailing. Addressograph machines are expensive, but ditto type addressing machines are considerably cheaper. Mail bags are free for the asking from the Post Office if you tell them you are a bulk mailer.

Regarding third class mail, if you use the notice RETURN POSTAGE GUARANTEED, you will get back your piece plus the new address of the addressee, if known. RETURN REQUESTED is obsolete language for third class mail.

First class mail is by far the best way to send your paper. It will cost 8¢ for each ounce. Delivery usually takes one or two days. If your paper weighs more than one ounce, consider third class mail. This will cost the same for the first ounce, but considerably less for each additional ounce. Third class mail can take from four days to forever to reach its destination. Packets of papers over two pounds may be mailed fourth class or parcel post. Rates are based on the packet's weight in pounds and the number of miles it must travel. If you can convince the postal clerk you're sending a book, you can mail your packet fourth class book rate, which is considerably cheaper than parcel post. Delivery time once again takes from days to never.

Always be sure to mark mail as to what class it is to be sent. Third class should also be marked "printed matter" if there is any doubt. If you are enclosing a written or typewritten note, add first class postage and mark "first class matter enclosed." If you can have your mail metered instead of using stamps, it should get to its destination earlier since the postmarking step will be bypassed. If your single copies can be folded to about 4 X 9 inches or smaller, they will almost surely get delivered faster than if they were bigger.

Communes

Here is a list of communes, organizations, groups—all with the fundamental purpose of achieving an alternate way of life in this country. Many welcome visitors, some are looking for new members; others would rather do their thing completely alone.

Our recommendation is this. If you intend to do some rural living, visit one of the reasonably hung-loose communes near you and see how it's done.

NOTE: Communes, at least some of them, have a short life span. Thus you may not find all of these still in existence. However, new ones form all the time, and if you look in areas where communing has been popular, you'll find them.

AHIMSA COMMUNITY, 320 Central, Parsons, Kan. 67351. 1965, 8 adults, no new members wanted. Visitors welcome on weekends. Buddhist.

ALTERNATIVES FOUNDATION, P.O. Box 1264, Berkeley, Calif. 94709. (Dick Fairfield) Communal living, total sexuality, peak experience training centers. Dedicated to the cybernated-tribal society.

ANANDA COOPERATIVE COMMUNITY, Allegheny Star Route, Nevada City, Calif. 95959.

ANY DAY NOW—Quaker Resistance House, 3611 Powelton Avenue, Philadelphia, Pa. 19104.

ASSOCIATION FOR SOCIAL DESIGN, 45 Rutland Square, Boston, Mass. 02118. (Dr. Matt Israel)—"Walden Two"-oriented, publish *ASD Forum*, sample $1.00.

BEAUMONT FOUNDATION, 640 Sandra Avenue, La Puente, Calif. 91746.

BHODAN CENTER OF INQUIRY, Sierra Route, Oakhurst, Calif. 93644 (209-683-4976). (Charles Davis) Seminars on human community, IC development on the land, 1934, 13 members. Trial period for new members. Visitors check in advance.

BIG STONE COLONY, Graceville, Minn. 54240. Christian, farming, about 100 people.

BRIDGE MOUNTAIN, Ben Lamond, Calif. Retreat center, esoteric-Oriental arts and "sensitivity" groups.

BROWN CAMPS, Box 800, Thornhill, Ontario, Canada. Services to disturbed children.

CAMP HILL VILLAGE, Copake, N.Y. 12516 (518-329-2744). 500 acres, 12 homes, community for the mentally handicapped, 150 members (30-40 staff included). New applicants need certain qualifications. Visitors welcome.

CATHOLIC WORKER FARM, Box 33, Tivoli, N.Y. 12583. Pacifist, service commune, 30 members.

CENTERS FOR CHANGE, 264 Flatbush Avenue, Brooklyn, N.Y. 11217 (c/o Blair Hamilton), (212-691-7369). 16 communal houses federated to develop educational environment, renovation, coffee house.

CHILDREN OF LIGHT COMMUNE, Box 35, Gila Bend, Ariz. 85337. Christian, 20 members.

CIRCLE PINES CENTER, Delton, Mich. 284 acres of forest and farmlands as camp for exploring cooperative living.

CITY OF LIGHT, Box 1904, Santa Fe, N.M. 87501. Esoteric, reincarnation, flying saucer religious community.

CLAN PAX (PEACE TRIBE), 3611 W. Iowa Street, Chicago, Ill. 60551.

CLOSE FARM, Meadville, Pa. 16335. Open 5 acres free to anyone.

COMMUNES FOR A NEW AGE, 1780 Daytona Road, Miami Beach, Fla. 33141. Helps new IC's get started.

COMMUNITY SERVICES, Box 243, Yellow Springs, Ohio 45387. (Dr. Arthur Morgan)

DROP CITY, Route 1, Box 125, Trinidad, Col. 81082. (1965), new members must meet specific criteria. Anarchist, artist, dome houses.

EARTH HOUSE, 129 Benefit Street, Providence, R.I. 02903. Community life center; mixed-media education.

EDUCATION AND TRAINING FOR COOPERATIVES, P.O. Box 3345, Jackson, Miss. 30207.

EVERDALE PLACE, RR 1, Hillsbury, Ontario, Canada. 1966, 7 adults, 40 children, school, dorms for students and houses for staff.

EXCHANGE, 715 Ashbury, San Francisco, Calif. 94117.

EXPANDED FAMILY, P.O. Box 415, New York, N.Y. 10032. Group marriage organizing for couples only. Newsletter, questionnaire, meetings, socials, outings.

FAMILY OF MYSTIC ARTS, Box 546, Sunny Valley, Ore. 97478.

FELLOWSHIP HOUSE AND FARM, 1512-23 W. Girard Avenue, Philadelphia, Pa. 19130. In North Philadelphia ghetto and country nearby.

FOREST RIVER COMMUNITY, Fordville, N.D. 58231. Hutterian, farming (Jos. H. Maedel, Business Manager), and stock-raising. Anabaptist.

GARDNER, TIM, 1310 7th Street, Des Moines, Iowa 50314. 1969, 10 adults. No new members wanted at present. Communal feeling and political commitment required. Visitors welcome.

GATE 5, Box 854, Sausalito, Calif. 94965. (c/o Piro Caro). Loose-knit, long-time (since WW II) community.

GOULD FARM, Great Barrington, Mass. 01230. (Harold Winchester) 1962, 15 adults, 50 children. Training for the mentally and emotionally handicapped. Visitors check in advance. Interdenominational.

GREENFEEL, Box 347, Barre, Vt. 05641. Joy-School, Community of Lovers.

GROW RESEARCH FOUNDATION, RR 1, Box 706, Veneta, Ore. 97487. Property in common, communal housing, 65-acre farm, 40 members.

HARRAD: Explorations in Interpersonal Relations, 145 Walden Street, Cambridge, Mass. 02122. (Randall Webb) Newsletter and social meetings for people interested in the Harrad idea.

HARRAD WEST, 2928 Derby Street, Berkeley, Calif. 94705. Urban-group, marriage-oriented commune, outside jobs.

HEAD, c/o Stone Age, 521½ Cedar, Minneapolis, Minn. 55404. "Hippie" commune.

HERE AND NOW COMMUNE, 1387 Haight Street, San Francisco, Calif. 94117. (Alan Noonan) Religious, mystical, flying saucer group.

HIDDEN SPRINGS, Route 4, Brantford, Ontario, Canada. Christian Rehabilitation Center/Community.

HIGHLANDER COMMUNITY, c/o John Perks, Paradox, N.Y. 12858.

HOSKINS, RR 2, Kiddville Road, Mount Sterling, Ky. 40353.

HOUSE OF THE 7TH ANGEL, Box 40, Route 1, Red Dog Road, Nevada City, Calif. 95959.

HURRLE, 1505 Fairchild, Manhattan, Kan. 66502.

HUTTERIAN BROTHERS, Expanola, Wash. 99010. Christian, farming, about 50 people.

IC., Box 5166, Seattle, Wash. 98107. Interested in group marriage, etc.

KERGUELEN ISLES, c/o Backus, 7400 R.I. Ave. #3, College Park, Md. 20740.

KERISTA-S.F., 128 Coleridge Street, San Francisco, Calif. 94110 (415-647-3908). (Jud & Joy Presmont & Dau) Free love organization.

KNOX BROTHERS COMMUNE, Pine Creek, Manitoba, Canada. Christian-Pentecostal, farming.

KUSHI, MICHIO, 216 Gardner Road, Brookline, Mass. 02167.

LAMA FOUNDATION, Box 444, San Cristobal, N.M. 87564.

LAND FELLOWSHIP, Smithsville, Ontario, Canada.

LAUGHING COYOTE MOUNTAIN, Black Hawk, Col. 80422. (c/o T. D. Linge) Pioneer, "adventure trails survival" school, etc.

LIBERTY HOUSE, Box 3193, Jackson, Miss. 39201.

LIPMAN, DALE, 4487 McPherson Avenue, St. Louis, Mo. 63108.

MAGIC MOUNTAIN FARM, Cave Junction, Ore. 97523. (c/o Westgate) Small farming community.

MAKEPEACE COLONY, Stephens Point, Wisc. 54481.

MAY VALLEY CO-OP, 10218 147 S.E., Renton, Wash. 92056. (John Affolter) Co-op residential separate family dwellings, common lands. Member of Puget Sound Consumers Cooperative.

MEETING SCHOOL, Rindge, N.H. 03461. 603-899-2872. 1957, community school, 25 members in summer, 65 in winter. Visitors check in advance.

MESSIAH'S WORLD COMMUNE, 1387 Oak Street, San Francisco, Calif. 94117. Share everything in common, health food restaurants, newspaper, band and chorus.

MORNINGSTAR RANCH, 12542 Graton Road, Sebastopol, Calif. 95472. (c/o Lou Gottlieb).

MORTON, CHESTER, 5003 S. Avon, Seattle, Wash. 98178. Community land $200 per acre.

NATURALISM, P.O. Box 8183, Chicago, Ill. 60620. (c/o George Peters) 1966, 14 adults, 1 child. Independent religion. New members must meet certain criteria. Visitors check in advance.

NEW ENGLAND CNVA FARM, RFD 1, Box 1978, Voluntown, Conn. 06384. Militant, pacifist.

NEW ROSEDALE COMMUNITY, Port La Prarie, Manitoba, Canada. Christian, farming, about 100 people.

NOAH'S ARK, Star Route, Monk Road, Harrison, Me. 04040. (c/o Peter & Rinda Aceves) Organically minded.

NOMADS, Box 5116, Santa Monica, Calif. 90401 (c/o Tom Murray)

OLYMPALI RANCH, Route 101, Novato, Calif. 94947. (c/o Don McCoy)

ORDER OF ST. MICHAEL, Route 7, Box 407D, Crown Point, Ind. 46307. Episcopalian only, singles and marrieds, 20 members.

PEACE ACTION FARM, Hicks Hill Road, Stanfordville, N.Y. 12581. (c/o Ammon Hennacy) 10 members (3 families).

PEACE HOUSE, 724 N. Marengo, Pasadena, Calif. 91103. (c/o Tod Friend) Free educational community.

PEOPLE OF THE LIVING GOD, 2101 Prytania Street, New Orleans, La. 70130. Christian, nonsectarian, about 85 members.

PORT CHICAGO VIGIL, P.O. Box 31055, San Francisco, Calif. 94107.

POWELTON NEIGHBORS, 3508 Hamilton, Philadelphia, Pa. 19104. Neighborhood housing, cooperative functions.

PREFORM, Box 5116, Santa Monica, Calif. 90405. (Tom Marshall) Newsletter.

RADICAL ACTION CO-OP, P.O. Box 226, New York, N.Y. 10028.

RESISTANCE, 2611 McGee Street, Berkeley, Calif. 94703.

RESISTANCE ACTION PROJECT, c/o AQAGM 20 S. 12th Street, Philadelphia, Pa. 19107.

RESURRECTION CITY USA, Route 1, Box 125A, Browns, Ala. 35724. (Cheryl Buswell) Developing a "city" opposed to capitalism, 16 miles from Selma, Ala., revolutionary, third world, 4 adults, 4 children. Visitors and new members welcome.

RYAN, JOE & HELEN, Route 1, Box 91, Franklin, N.H. 03235. 1964, 6 adults, 4 children, labor-trading orientation. Visitors check in advance.

SATURNA FREE SCHOOL, Saturna Island, B.C., Canada. 1968, 5 adults, 21 children, community oriented. New members on waiting list. Visitors check in advance.

SEDGEWICK COMMUNE, 3890 Sedgewick, Bronx, N.Y. 10463. Revolutionary.

SKY VIEW ACRES, Pomona, N.Y. 10970. (Jim Best) Religious pacifists.

SOCIETY FOR THE PRESERVATION OF EARLY AMERICAN STANDARDS, Rt. 2, Oxford, N.Y. 13830. 1961, 13 adults, back to the land movement. Trial period for new members meeting certain criteria. Visitors check in advance.

SOCIETY OF BROTHERS, Rifton, N.Y. 12471; Farmington, Pa. 15437; Norfolk, Conn. 06058. Christian, toy manufacturing.

SONS OF LEVI, SOUTH RANGE RANCH, Mansfield, Mo. 65704. (Mark Kelgore) Christian, farming, about 100 people.

SYNANON FOUNDATION, 1351 Ocean Front, Santa Monica, Calif. 90401 (also, Oakland, Calif.).

TANGUY HOMESTEADS, West Chester, Pa. 19380. Suburban, nonsectarian, co-op housing and community fellowship.

THELEME, Foot Road, Route 2, Akron, N.Y. 14001 c/o Skip Venneri (716-542-9027).

TRANS-LOVE ENERGIES, (Home of MC5), 1520 Hill Street, Ann Arbor, Mich. 48104 (313-761-3552).

TWIN OAKS, Route 4, Box 169, Louisa, Va. 23093 (703-294-2301). 1967, 123 acres, "Walden Two"-oriented, farming, 16 members. Visitors check in advance.

UNITY VILLAGE, Lees Summit, Mo. 64063. Religious, educational center, publication house for the UNITY movement.

USA, Box 155, Clawson, Mich. 48017. (c/o Wayne Clifton) 5 self-sustaining cities, 5,000 members, balanced production and distribution system, organic agriculture, craftsmen, factories. People with needed skills welcome, visitors not.

THE VALE, Route 1, Box 275, Yellow Springs, Ohio 45387. (c/o Griscom Morgan) 14 adults, 19 children, nonsectarian, pacifist, religious neighborhood group, land in common, school for first 3 grades and kinder-garten.

VILLAGE OF FREE SOULS, 3042 W. Wilson, Chicago, Ill. 60625. (Gene Kalin) Planning on a group of 50 to 100 people.

WELSH, MICHAEL T. 2707 8th Street, Minneapolis, Minn. 55406.

WHEELER RANCH, Occidental, Calif. 95465. Free land, drop-in, live-in center.

WHITFIELD, REV. N., JR., 245 W. 107th Street, New York, N.Y. 10025.

WOODSTOCK COMMUNE, RFD 2, Box 108, Sauger-ties, N.Y. 12477. Revolutionary.

WRETTE & SONS, Scregor, Manitoba, Canada. Christian, farming, 5 families.

YELLOW SUBMARINE COMMUNE, 2449 Floral Hill Drive, Eugene, Ore. 97403.

Thermal Springs of the Western United States

Here are some maps showing the location of more than 1,000 hot springs situated west of Denver.

If you've never visited a hot spring, you have a great experience ahead of you. Often it consists of a natural pool with the warm water bubbling up to keep it constantly fresh and clean. At other times hot water gushes out of the side of a mountain or hill and runs down to join a cooler stream.

Many hot springs have become resorts and these are mundane—full of concrete, asphalt parking lots, and demands for money. But with so many hot springs in the wilder regions of the West, you can find one for your own private use as long as you care to camp there. There is one in Idaho, for example, adjacent to a river. This spring falls in a steady stream over a rocky cliff, providing a delightful outdoor hot shower bath. Bring your soap—biodegradable, of course.

If that one's too out-of-sight for you, then try the one twenty-one miles north of Santa Barbara near the Pendola Ranger Station. It's listed as number 104 on the California map. It has been slightly developed by the forest service and has a concrete pool into which water at about 118°F. flows twenty-four hours a day all year long.

One final word ... hot springs are really dangerous because when you find one you never want to leave.

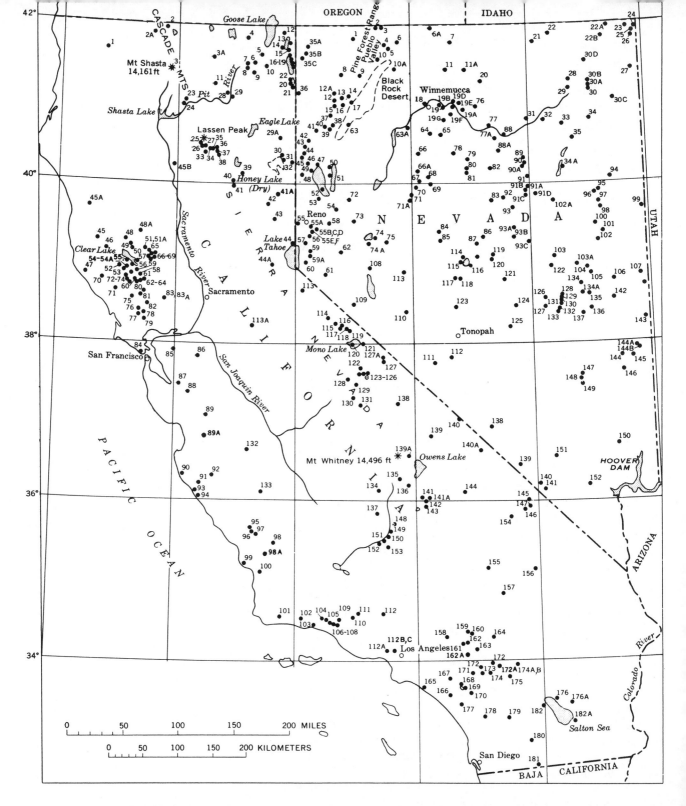

THERMAL SPRINGS OF CALIFORNIA AND NEVADA

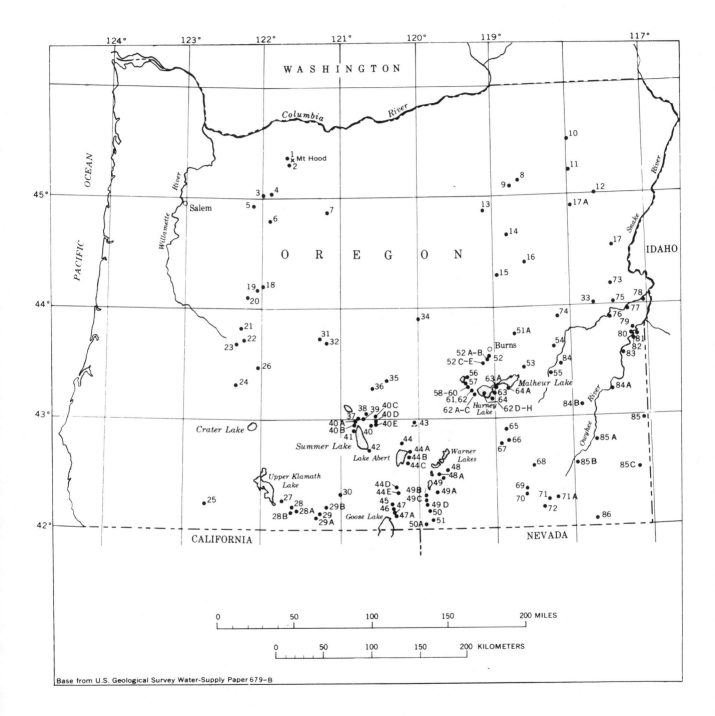

THERMAL SPRINGS OF OREGON 311

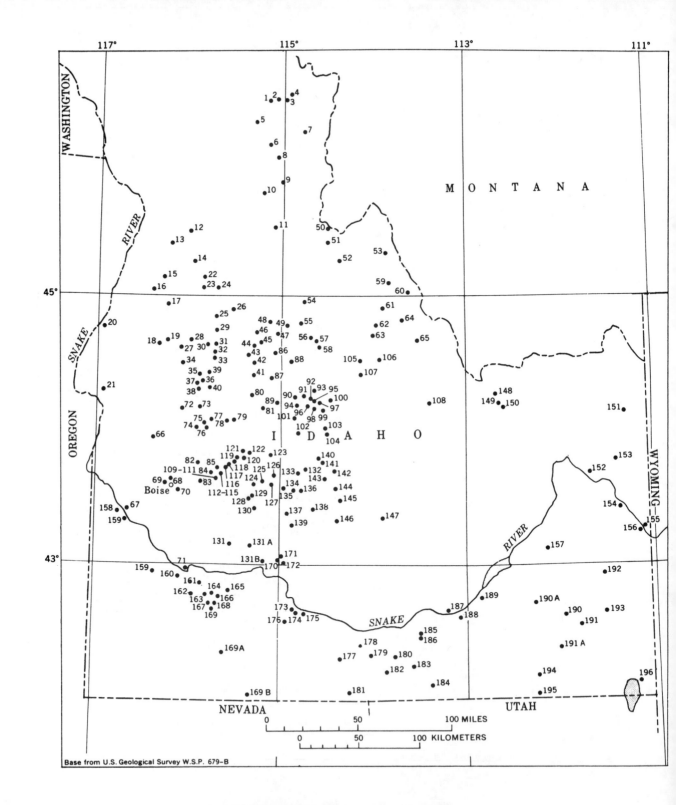

THERMAL SPRINGS OF IDAHO

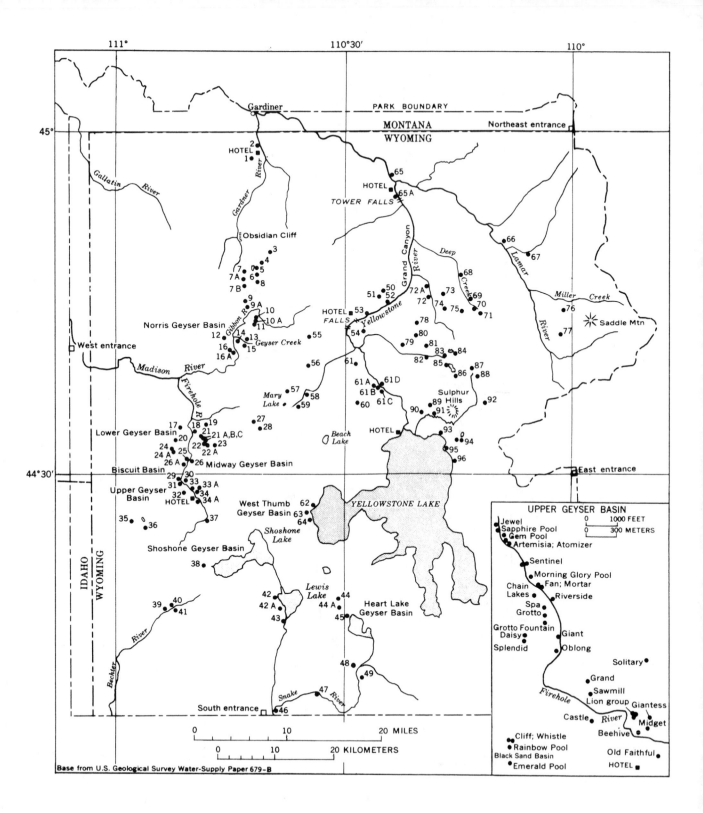

THERMAL SPRINGS OF YELLOWSTONE NATIONAL PARK, WYOMING

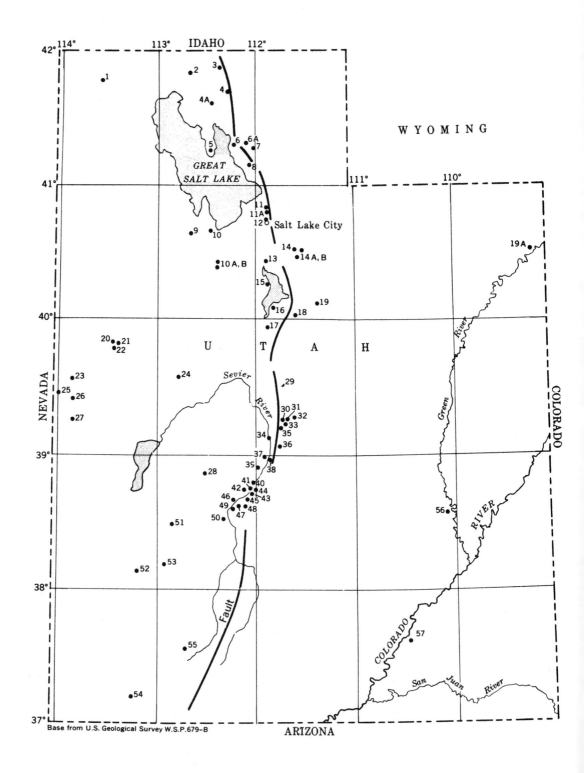

THERMAL SPRINGS OF UTAH

No. on figure	Name or location	Temperature of water (°F)	Flow (gallons per minute)	No. on figure	Name or location	Temperature of water (°F)	Flow (gallons per minute)

Arizona

No. on figure	Name or location	Temperature of water (°F)	Flow (gallons per minute)
1	Pakoon (Pahgun) Spring, on tributary of Grand Wash, 18 miles north of Colorado River.	100	----------
2	Sec. 23, T. 30 N., R. 23 E., 5 miles south of Hoover (Boulder) Dam.	Hot	----------
3	Lava Warm Springs, near Lava Falls Rapids in the Grand Canyon of the Colorado River.	89	6,700
4	Sec. 33, T. 18 N., R. 19 W., 25 miles southwest of Kingman.	Warm	----------
5	Sec. 32, T. 15 N., R. 6 E., 10 miles northeast of Camp Verde.	72	50
6	Verde Hot Springs, 0.5 mile northwest of Childs.	104	75
7	6 miles south of St. Johns	74	2
8	Castle (Monroe) Hot Springs, in sec. 3, T. 7 N., R. 1 W., on Castle Creek, 50 miles south of Prescott.	115–122	280
9	Salt Banks, in sec. 33, T. 6 N., R. 17 E., 30 miles west of Whiteriver.	Warm	----------
10	Soda Warm Spring, in sec. 13, T. 6 N., R. 19 E., 23 miles west of Whiteriver.	65	----------
11	Agua Caliente Springs, in sec. 19, T. 5 S., R. 10 W., 15 miles northeast of Palomas.	99–104	----------
12	Sec. 35, T. 5 S., R. 19 E., 3 miles north of Aravaipa.	90	6
13	Near Gila River, 3 miles north of Fort Thomas.	----------	----------
14	Indian Hot Springs, 8 miles northwest of Pima.	81–118	300
15	Near Bonito Creek, in T. 4 S., R. 27 E., 25 miles east of Fort Thomas.	Warm	----------
16	T. 4 S., R. 28 E., 10 miles west of Morenci	Hot	Small
17	Clifton Hot Springs	127–160	
18	Aguajito (Quitabaquito), near Mexican border.	Warm	----------
19	Hooker's Hot Springs, in sec. 6, T. 13 S., R. 21 E., 10 miles northeast of Cascabel.	130	40
20	Agua Caliente Spring, in sec. 13, T. 20 S., R. 13 E., 5 miles east of Amado.	90	50
21	Sec. 7, T. 18, S., R. 31 E., 6 miles southwest of Paradise.	----------	----------

California

No. on figure	Name or location	Temperature of water (°F)	Flow (gallons per minute)
1	Sec. 29, T. 15 N., R. 8 E., 14 miles southeast of Happy Camp.	90	2
2	Klamath Hot Springs (Shovel Creek Springs), 20 miles northeast of Ager.	100–152	25
2A	4.5 miles northeast of Ager	65–75	6
3	Near top of Mount Shasta, 11 miles northeast of Sisson.	150	5
3A	North of Big Glass Mountain	191	----------
4	Pothole Spring, 35 miles northwest of Alturas.	70	10
5	Near Rattlesnake Creek, 9 miles west to Alturas.	80	10
6	Essex Springs, in sec. 10, T. 42 N., R. 11 E.	80–92	700
7	Warm Spring Valley, 15 miles west of Alturas.	81	275
8	Kelly's Hot Spring, in sec. 29, T. 42 N., R. 10 E., 4 miles northeast of Canby.	204	325
9	Near Canyon Creek, 15 miles southwest of Alturas.	80	100
10	1.5 miles southeast of Alturas	72	1
11	Little Hot Spring Valley, 25 miles northwest of Bieber.	127; 170	225
12	Near Bidwell Creek, 1 mile northwest of Fort Bidwell.	97–108	75
13	Boyd Spring, on east side of Upper Lake, 12 miles southeast of Fort Bidwell.	70	1,000
14	Near southwest side of Upper Lake, 4 miles west of Lake City.	120–207	100
15	Near south end of Upper Lake, 12 miles northeast of Cedarville.	170–182	80
16	Sec. 12, T. 43 N., R. 18 E., near north end of Middle Lake, 12 miles northeast of Cedarville.	140–149	225
17	Leonard Springs, in sec. 7, T. 43 N., R. 17 E., 11 miles northeast of Cedarville.	150	50
18	Sec. 1, T. 42 N., R. 16 E., and sec. 6, T. 42 N., R. 17 E., 5 miles east-northeast of Cedarville.	130	500
18A	Cedar Plunge, 5 miles northeast of Cedarville.	180; 208	115
19	Benmac Hot Springs, in sec. 18, T. 42 N., R. 17 E., 5 miles east of Cedarville.	120	200
20	Menlo Warm Springs, in sec. 7, T. 39 N., R. 17 E., 5 miles south-southeast of Eagleville.	117–125	425
21	Near southwest side of Lower Lake, 8 miles south-southeast of Eagleville.	120	100
22	Bare Ranch, 12 miles southeast of Eagleville.	70	5
23	Kosk Creek, 65 miles northeast of Redding.	100	5
24	Big Bend Hot Springs, in sec. 36, T. 37 N., R. 1 W.	100–180	90
25	Upper Mill Creek, 1 mile northwest of Tophet Hot Springs (No. 26).	120–150	3
26	Tophet (Soupan, Suran) Hot Springs, on southwest side of Lassen Peak, 53 miles northeast of Red Bluff.	175 to boiling	5
27	Bumpas Hot Springs, on south side of Lassen Peak, 60 miles northeast of Red Bluff.	Boiling	100
28	Bassett Hot Springs, 2.5 miles east-northeast of Bieber.	173	175
29	Stonebreaker Hot Springs, 6 miles east-southeast of Bieber.	110–165	125
29A	Tipton Springs	70	925
30	Shaffer (Branbecks) Hot Springs, near north shore of Honey Lake.	160–204	250
31	Amedee Hot Springs, near Amedee railroad station.	178–204	700
32	Highrock Spring, 10 miles east-southeast of Amedee.	86	525
33	Morgan Hot Springs, 53 miles northeast of Red Bluff.	90–200	85
34	Devil's Kitchen, 1.5 miles west of Drake Hot Springs (No. 36).	150–205	50
35	Hot Spring Valley, 0.5 mile west of Drake Hot Springs (No. 36).	83	8
36	Drake Hot Springs, 6 miles southeast of Lassen Peak and 70 miles northeast of Red Bluff.	123–148	20
37	Boiling Spring (Tartarus) Lake, 1 mile south of Drake Hot Springs (No. 36).	170–190	Intermittent
38	Terminal Geyser, 3.5 miles southeast of Drake Hot Springs (No. 36).	120–205	8
39	Kruger Springs, 1 mile east of Greenville	90–106	8
40	Sec. 13, T. 25 N., R. 8 E., 2 miles northeast of Twain.	94	20
41	Sec. 14, T. 25 N., R. 8 E., on Indian Creek, 1 mile east of Twain.	80–98	35
41A	Marble Hot Wells, 5 miles south-southeast of Beckwourth.	125–161	350
42	McLear Sulphur Springs, 5 miles southwest of Beckwourth.	86	140
43	Campbell (Upper Soda, Freys) Hot Springs, 2 miles south of Sierraville.	65–111	80
44	Brockway (Carnelian) Hot Springs, on north shore of Lake Tahoe and 13 miles southeast of Truckee.	120–140	150
44A	Wentworth Springs	60–75	Small
45	Orrs Hot Springs, 16 miles northwest of Ukiah.	63–104	25
45A	0.5 mile north of Laytonville	70	200
45B	Tuscan (Lick) Springs	86	50
46	Vichy Springs, 3 miles northeast of Ukiah.	50–90	30
47	Point Arena Hot Springs, 15 miles southeast of Point Arena.	110–112	4.5
48	Crabtree Springs, 38 miles north-northeast of Lakeport.	68–105	15
48A	Fouts Springs	60–75	20
49	Sec. 35, T. 16 N., R. 8 W., 2 miles northwest of Bartlett (cold) Springs.	90	5
50	Newman (Soap Creek) Springs, 45 miles west of Williams.	70–92	25
51	Complexion Springs, 28 miles west of Williams.	74	1
51A	Chalk Mountain	67–70	3
52	Highland Springs, 6 miles southwest of Kelseyville.	52–82	20

No. on figure	Name or location	Temperature of water (°F)	Flow (gallons per minute)
		California—Continued	
53	England (Elliott) Springs, 8 miles south-southwest of Kelseyville.	56–76	8
54	Carlsbad Springs, 5 miles south of Kelseyville.	66–76	4
54A	Kelseyville	78	10
55	Soda Bay Springs, at base of Mount Konocti.	80–87	400
56	Near southwest shore of Clear Lake, 10 miles east of Kelseyville.	70–100	5
57	Sulphur Bank (Hot Bolata) Hot Springs, 10 miles north-northwest of Lower Lake.	83–120	----------
58	Howard Springs, 28 miles north-northwest of Calistoga.	48–110	135
59	Seigler Springs, 30 miles north-northwest of Calistoga.	58–126	35
60	Gordon Hot Spring, 28 miles north-north-west of Calistoga.	92	5
61	Spiers (Copsey) Springs, 24 miles north-northwest of Calistoga.	78; 84	15
62	Castle (Mills) Hot Springs, 25 miles north-northwest of Calistoga.	65; 164	----------
63	Anderson Springs, 22 miles north-north-west of Calistoga.	63–145	7
64	Harbin Springs, 20 miles north-northwest of Calistoga.	90–120	10
65	Deadshot Springs, 28 miles west-southwest of Williams.	65–79	11
66	Blancks Hot Springs, 27 miles southwest of Williams.	120	4
67	Jones Hot Springs, 26.5 miles southwest of Williams.	125	2
67A	Manzanita Quicksilver Mine	110–142	4
68	Wilbur (Simmons) Hot Springs, 26 miles southwest of Williams.	65–140	35
69	Elgin Quicksilver Mine, 30 miles west-southwest of Williams.	140–153	25
70	Hoods (Fairmount) Hot Springs, 15 miles west-northwest of Cloverdale.	100	5
71	Skagg's Hot Springs, 9 miles west-south-west of Geyserville.	120–135	15
72	The Geysers, 18 miles east-southeast of Cloverdale.	140 to boiling	30–50
73	Sulphur Creek, 21 miles southeast of Cloverdale.	120	5
74	Little Geysers, 22 miles east, southeast of Cloverdale.	110–160	8
75	Mark West Warm Springs, 7 miles northeast of Fulton.	60–82	30
76	Los Guilicos Warm Springs, 3.5 miles southwest of Glen Ellen.	78; 82	5
77	McEwan Ranch, 3 miles southwest of Kenwood.	80	50
78	Eldridge State Home, 6 miles north-north-west of Sonoma.	72	10
79	Ohms and Boyes Hot Springs, 2 miles northwest of Sonoma.	114–118	----------
79	Fetters Hot Springs, 2.75 miles northwest of Sonoma.	100	----------
79	Agua Caliente (Aqua Rica) Springs, 3 miles northwest of Sonoma.	97–115	10
80	Aetna Springs, 17 miles north of St. Helena.	63–92	20
81	Calistoga Hot Springs, 225 yds. east of depot.	126–173	8
82	St. Helena White Sulphur Springs, 2 miles southwest of St. Helena.	69–90	6
83	Napa Rock (Priest) Soda Springs, 15 miles east-northeast of St. Helena.	79	15
83A	Phillips Soda Springs	68; 76	10
84	Rocky Point Spring, 6 miles northeast of Point Bonita.	100	5
85	Sulphur Springs, 2 miles northeast of Walnut Creek (town).	75–81	5
86	Byron Hot Springs, 2 miles south of Byron.	72–120	15
87	Warm Springs, 2 miles northeast of Warm Springs (town).	85–90	15
88	Alum Rock Park Springs, 7 miles north-west of San Jose.	62–87	15
89	Gilroy Hot Spring, 14 miles northeast of Gilroy.	110	15
89A	San Benito Mineral Well, 4 miles southeast of Hollister.	75	----------
90	North Fork of Little Sur River, 30 miles (by road) south of Monterey.	103; 114	----------
91	Tassajara Hot Springs, in sec. 32, T. 19 S., R. 4 E.	100–140	100
92	Paraiso Hot Springs, 8 miles south-south-west of Soledad.	65–111	10
93	Slate's Hot Springs, in sec. 9, T. 21 S., R. 3 E.	100–121	50
94	Dolan's Hot Springs, 7 miles from Slate's Hot Springs.	100	5
95	Paso de Robles Mud Bath Springs, 2.5 miles north of Paso Robles.	55–118	100
96	Paso de Robles Hot Springs, in southwest part of Paso Robles.	105	1,700
97	Santa Ysabel Springs, 4 miles southeast of Paso Robles.	94	150
98	Cameta Warm Spring, 30 miles southeast of Paso Robles.	74	3
98A	San Luis (Sycamore) Hot Spring, 8 miles south-southwest of San Luis Obispo.	107	50
99	Pecho Warm Springs, 15 miles southwest of San Luis Obispo.	72; 95	17
100	Newsom's Arroyo Grande Warm Springs, 2.5 miles east of Arroyo Grande.	98	15
101	Las Cruces Hot Springs, 4 miles north of Gaviota station.	67–97	50
102	San Marcos (Mountain Glen, Cuyama) Hot Springs, 20 miles northwest of Santa Barbara.	89–108	45
103	Montecito (Santa Barbara) Hot Springs, 6 miles northeast of Santa Barbara.	111–118	50
104	Sec. 4, T. 5 N., R. 25 W., 1 mile east of Mono Creek and 12 miles northeast of Santa Barbara.	90	15
105	Sec. 1, T. 5 N., R. 25 W., 4 miles north of Santa Ynez River and 15 miles north-east of Santa Barbara.	90	10
106	Vicker's Hot Springs, in Matilija Canyon, 9 miles northwest of Nordhoff.	118	5
107	Stingley's Hot Springs, 8.5 miles north-west of Nordhoff.	76; 100	4
108	Matilija Hot Springs, 6 miles northwest of Nordhoff.	65–116	45
109	Wheeler's Hot Springs, 7.5 miles north-northwest of Nordhoff.	62–102	40
110	Willett Hot Spring, in sec. 31, T. 6 N., R. 20 W., 24 miles north-northwest of Fillmore.	120	50
111	Sespe Hot Springs, in sec. 21, T. 6 N., R. 20 W., 22 miles north-northwest of Fillmore.	97–191	125
112	Elizabeth Lake Canyon, 13 miles northeast of Castiac station.	100	5
112A	Encino Ranch (Seminole) Hot Springs	85	5
112B	Radium Sulphur Spring, in northwestern part of Los Angeles.	80	----------
112C	Bimini Hot Spring, in northern part of Los Angeles.	104	100
113	Grover's Hot Springs, 4 miles west of Markleeville.	128–146	100
113A	Valley Springs	75	1
114	Fales' Hot Springs, in sec. 24, T. 6 N., R. 23 E., 13 miles northwest of Bridgeport.	97–141	300
115	Buckeye Hot Spring, in sec. 3, T. 4 N., R. 24 E., 5.5 miles west-southwest of Bridgeport.	140	25
116	Sec. 27, T. 5 N., R. 25 E., 1.5 miles south-east of Bridgeport.	121–148	10
117	1.5 miles south-southeast of Bridgeport	70–105	25
118	Warm Springs Flat, 5 miles southeast of Bridgeport.	100	5
119	Sec. 20, T. 4 N., R. 26 E., near Mormon Creek, 7 miles southeast of Bridgeport.	100	5
120	Paoha Island in Mono Lake	176	100
121	Mono Basin Warm Spring, on east edge of Mono Lake.	90	10
122	Sec. 13, T. 3 S., R. 28 E., 5 miles northeast of Casa Diablo Hot Springs (No. 123).	170	5

California—Continued

No. on figure	Name or location	Temperature of water (°F)	Flow (gallons per minute)	No. on figure	Name or location	Temperature of water (°F)	Flow (gallons per minute)
123	Casa Diablo Hot Springs, in sec. 32, T. 3 S., R. 28 E., on U.S. Highway 395.	115–194	35	155	Paradise Springs, 25 miles north of Daggett.	85–106.5	30
124	Casa Diablo Hot Pool, in sec. 35, T. 3 S., R. 28 E., 3 miles northeast of Casa Diablo.	180	Intermittent	156	Soda Station Springs, in sec. 14, T. 12 N., R. 8 E.	75	30
125	The Geysers, in sec. 30, T. 3 S., R. 29 E.	120–202	500	157	Newberry Spring, in sec. 32, T. 9 N., R. 3 E., 600 yd south of Newberry railroad station.	77	300
126	Whitmore Warm Springs, in sec. 18, T. 4 S., R. 29 E.	90	306	158	Tylers Bath Springs, in Lytle Canyon, 15 miles northwest of San Bernardino.	92	5
127	Benton Hot Springs, in sec. 2, T. 2 S., R. 31 E., 300 yd northwest of Benton post office.	135	400	159	Sec. 15, T. 3 N., R. 3 W., in Deep Creek Canyon, 16 miles southeast of Victorville.	80–100	5
127A	Bertrand Ranch	70	100	160	Sec. 14, T. 3 N., R. 3 W., in Deep Creek Canyon, 15 miles southeast of Victorville.	80–100	5
128	Reds Meadows Hot Springs, 10 miles southwest of Mineral Park.	90–120	10	161	Harlem Hot Spring, 5 miles north-north-east of San Bernardino.	120	
129	Fish Creek Hot Springs, in sec. 9, T. 5 S., R. 27 E., at head of Fish Valley.	110	5	162	Waterman Hot Springs, 6.5 miles north-northeast of San Bernardino.	123	5
130	Sec. 16, T. 7 S., R. 27 E., on South Fork of San Joaquin River.	100–112	25	162	Arrowhead Hot Springs, 7 miles north-northeast of San Bernardino.	110–187	50
131	Blaney Meadows Hot Springs, in sec. 10, T. 8 S., R. 28 E.	100–110	40	162A	Urbita Hot Springs, 1 mile south of San Bernardino.	80–106	250
132	Mercey Hot Springs, 25 miles south of Dos Palos.	79–109	6	163	Sec. 34, T. 1 N., R. 2 W., in Santa Ana Canyon, 12 miles east-northeast of San Bernardino.	90	3
133	Fresno Hot Springs, on branch of Waltham Creek, 18 miles west of Coalinga.	88–97	20	164	Near Baldwin Lake, 40 miles southeast of Victorville.	88	5
134	South Fork of the Middle Fork of Tule River, 27.5 miles east-northeast of Portersville.	77	25	165	Fairview Hot Spring, 7 miles southwest of Santa Ana.	96	15
135	Jordan Hot Springs, 65 miles north of Kernville.	95–123	75	166	San Juan Capistrano Hot Springs, 13 miles northeast of San Juan Capistrano.	121–124	35
136	Monache Meadows, 14 miles southwest of Olancha.	100	2	167	Glen Ivy (Temescal) Hot Spring, 11 miles south-southeast of Corona.	102	15
137	California (Deer Creek) Hot Springs	105–126	50	168	Wrenden (Bundys Elsinore) Hot Springs, 25 yd north of Elsinore depot.	118	
138	Keough Hot Springs, 8 miles south of Bishop.	130	825	169	Elsinore Hot Springs, 50 yd north of Elsinore depot.	125	
139	Saline Valley, 10 miles northeast of Saline Valley Borax Mine.	100	5	170	Murrieta Hot Springs, 4 miles east-north-east of Murrieta.	134–136	75
139A	Skinner Ranch	Warm	10	171	Pilares Hot Spring, 8 miles northeast of Perris.	100	3
140	Staininger Ranch (Grapevine) Springs, in Grapevine Canyon, 50 miles northeast of Keeler.	75	30	172	Eden Hot Springs, 9 miles southwest of Beaumont.	90–110	30
140A	Keene Wonder Spring, at west base of Funeral Range. Nevares and Texas springs are farther south.	80–93	30	172A	Highland Springs	112 (max)	
141	14 miles southeast of Haiwee	150–203	Small	173	Gilman (San Jacinto, Relief) Hot Springs, 6 miles northwest of San Jacinto.	83–116	20
141A	Devil's Kitchen, 2 miles northeast of Coso Hot Springs (No. 142).	180 to boiling	Small	174	Soboba (Ritchey) Hot Springs, 2.5 miles northeast of San Jacinto.	70–111	25
142	Coso Hot Springs, 20 miles northeast of Little Lake.	140 to boiling	Small	174A	Desert, in sec. 30, T. 2 S., R. 5 E.	112–116	
143	Near Little Lake, 18 miles south of Haiwee.	80	1	174B	Lucky Seven, 2 miles southeast of Desert.	200	
144	Panamint Valley, 4 miles north of Ballarat.	80	1	175	Palm Springs, 6 miles south of Palm Springs station.	100	5
145	Yeoman Hot Springs, in sec. 1, T. 21 N., R. 7 E., 5 miles northeast of Zabriskie.	80	100	176	Dos Palmas Spring, on northeast side of Salton Sink, 6 miles east of Salton railroad station.	80	25
146	2 miles north of Tecopa	108; 109	225	176A	Hot Mineral Well	186	900
147	Resting Spring, 5.5 miles northeast of Tecopa.	80	260	177	Deluz Warm Springs, 20 miles north-northeast of Oceanside.	84–88	5
148	2 miles northeast of Kernville	98; 113	4	178	Agua Tibia Spring, 30 miles northeast of Oceanside.	92	10
149	Neills Hot Spring (Agua Caliente), 7 miles south-southwest of Kernville.	131	115	179	Warner (Las Aguas Calientes) Hot Springs, in sec. 36, T. 10 S., R. 3 E.	131–139	150
150	Clear Creek (Hobo) Hot Springs, in sec. 25, T. 27 S., R. 32 E.	119	20	180	Agua Caliente, in secs. 18 and 19, and 19, T. 14 S., R. 7 E.	90	20
151	Delonegha Springs, 45 miles northeast of Bakersfield.	104–112	25	181	Jacumba Springs, in secs. 7 and 8, T. 18 S., R. 8 E.	94; 96	15
152	Democrat Springs, 40 miles northeast of Bakersfield.	100–115	25	182	Fish Springs, on west side of Salton Sea, 13 miles south of Mecca.	90	280
153	Williams Hot Springs, 16 miles northeast of Caliente.	60–100	20	182A	Salton volcanoes	100 to boiling	Small
154	Saratoga Springs, 15 miles west of Sperry railroad station.	82	125				

Colorado

No.	Name or location	Temperature of water (°F)	Flow (gallons per minute)	No.	Name or location	Temperature of water (°F)	Flow (gallons per minute)
1	Juniper Hot Springs, in sec. 16, T. 6 N., R. 94 W.	102–105	25	4	Moffat (Eldorado) Spring, 12 miles southwest of Boulder.	70	10
2	Routt Hot Springs, 7 miles north of Steamboat Springs (No. 2A).	148–150	130	5	Hot Soda Springs at Idaho Springs.	98–108	50
2A	Steamboat Springs	103–150	2,000	6	Glenwood Springs	106–150	3,000
3	Hot Sulphur Springs	90–118	40				

No. on figure	Name or location	Temperature of water (°F)	Flow (gallons per minute)	No. on figure	Name or location	Temperature of water (°F)	Flow (gallons per minute)
	**Colorado—Continued**						

Colorado—Continued

No. on figure	Name or location	Temperature of water (°F)	Flow (gallons per minute)	No. on figure	Name or location	Temperature of water (°F)	Flow (gallons per minute)
7	Big Dotsero Spring, on north bank of Colorado River 1.5 miles downstream from Dotsero.	84	400	24	Valley View (Orient) Hot Springs, in sec. 31, T. 46 N., R. 10 E., 7 miles southeast of Villa Grove.	72–99	200
8	Avalanche Springs, near Avalanche	112–134	200	25	Red Creek (Siloam, Parnassus) Springs, 12 miles southwest of Pueblo.	59–73	5
9	Conundrum Spring, 16 miles south of Aspen.	100	25	26	Geyser Warm Spring, at Placerville	94	5
10	Alkali Springs, near north end of bridge over the Gunnison River at Austin.	72	5	27	Orvis (Ridgway, Uncompahgre) Hot Spring, 2 miles southeast of Ridgway.	132	300
11	Sec. 21, T. 13 S., R. 89 W., 10 miles east of Somerset.	90	3	28	Ouray Hot Springs	100–158	200
12	Ranger (Cement Creek) Spring, 1.5 miles above mouth of Cement Creek.	83	350	29	Sec. 33, T. 41 N., R. 11 W., 200 yd southeast of Dunton Store.	110	20
13	Sec. 18, T. 14 S., R. 84 W., 2.5 miles above mouth of Cement Creek.	100	1,800	30	Iron Spring, 0.75 mile north of Rico	82	30
14	Waunita (Tomichi) Hot Springs, on Hot Springs Creek, 28 miles east of Gunnison.	140–160	1,000	31	Wagon Wheel Gap Springs	132–150	100
15	Cebolla (Powderhorn) Hot Springs (Ojo de los Caballos), 6 miles south of Powderhorn.	79–114	100	32	Sec. 26, T. 38 N., R. 1 W., 26 miles northeast of Pagosa Springs.	100;120	50
16	Rhodes Spring, 8 miles southwest of Fairplay.	79	300	33	Shaw's Spring, 6 miles north of Del Norte	88	10
17	Hartsell Hot Springs, 25 miles east of Leadville.	105–134	10	34	Pinkerton Springs, in sec. 26, T. 37 N., R. 9 W., 14 miles north of Durango.	87–95	8
18	Mound Soda (Currant Creek) Spring, 20 miles northwest of Parkdale.	68	----------	35	Tripp Springs, 10 miles north of Durango	90–95	50
19	Cottonwood (Buena Vista Hot) Springs, 6 miles west of Buena Vista.	120–144	150	36	Trimble Springs, 9 miles north of Durango.	90–110	50
20	Mount Princeton (Heywood Hot, Chalk Creek Hot) Springs, 3 miles west of Nathrop.	98–150	50	37	Sec. 8, T. 35 N., R. 4 W., 30 miles west of Pagosa Springs (town).	120	3
21	Poncha Springs	80–168	500	38	12 miles northeast of Pagosa Springs (town).	78	----------
22	Wellsville Warm Spring, 5 miles northwest of Howard.	94	150	39	Pagosa Springs (town):		
22A	Canon City:				Pagosa Hot Springs	110–160	600
	Near east end of Royal Gorge of Arkansas River.	101	----------		Well	140	100
	Fremont Natatorium	100	140	40	3 miles southeast of Pagosa Springs (town)	120	Small
23	Chamberlain (Mineral) Hot Springs, in sec. 12, T. 45 N., R. 9 E., 6 miles south of Villa Grove.	116–133	50	41	Warm Sulphur Spring, on the South Fork of the Navajo River, 7 miles east of Chromo.	80	Small
				42	Agua Caliente Spring, in T. 35 N., R. 8 E., 2 miles southwest of Capulin.	90	50
				43	McIntyre (Los Ojos) Warm Springs, in sec. 13, T. 35 N., R. 10 E., 8 miles east of La Jara.	62	100
				44	Dexter Spring, in sec. 9, T. 35 N., R. 11 E., 12 miles east of La Jara.	71	5

Idaho

No. on figure	Name or location	Temperature of water (°F)	Flow (gallons per minute)	No. on figure	Name or location	Temperature of water (°F)	Flow (gallons per minute)
1	Wier Creek Hot Springs, in sec. 13, T. 36 N., R. 11 E.	Hot	5	17	Sec. 22, T. 19 N., R. 2 E., 3 miles northeast of Meadows.	100	50
2	Colgate Springs, in sec. 9, T. 36 N., R. 12 E.	105–120	20	18	Sec. 2, T. 15 N., R. 1 E., 1.25 miles north of mouth of Warm Spring Creek.	Hot	100
3	Jerry Johnson's Hot Springs, in sec. 7, T. 36 N., R. 13 E.	100–130	450	19	Sec. 33, T. 16 N., R. 2 E., 15 miles east of Cottonwood.	Hot	25
4	Horse Creek, 4 miles southeast of Jerry Johnson's Hot Springs.	80	200	20	T. 17 N., R. 5 W., in Snake River Canyon upstream from mouth of Brownlee Creek.	Hot	----------
5	Stanley Hot Spring, in sec. 6, T. 34 N., R. 10 E., near Boulder Creek 4 miles upstream from junction with Lochsa River.	Hot	2	21	T. 11 N., R. 5 W., on Monroe Creek 6 miles northeast of Weiser.	Warm	----------
6	Stuart Hot Spring, in sec. 4, T. 32 N., R. 11 E., on Link Creek 5 miles upstream from junction with Selway River.	Hot	35	22	Sec. 11, T. 21 N., R. 5 E., 12 miles west of Shiefers.	Hot	100
7	Sec. 4, T. 33 N., R. 14 E., 11 miles southwest of Elk Summit ranger station.	Warm	40	23	Sec. 15, T. 20 N., R. 5 E., 15 miles southwest of Shiefers.	Warm	5
8	Martin Creek Hot Springs, in sec. 25, T. 31 N., R. 11 E., 3.5 miles west of Wylies Peak.	Hot	15	24	Sec. 35, T. 20 N., R 7 E., on South Fork of Salmon River 7 miles south of Shiefers.	90–136	100
9	Sec. 14, T. 29 N., R. 12 E., 2 miles south of Grouse Peak.	Hot	10	25	Sec. 25, T. 18 N., R. 6 E., on South Fork of Salmon River 25 miles north of Knox.	Hot	15
10	Red River Hot Springs, in sec. 10, T. 28 N., R. 10 E., 10 miles northeast of Red River ranger station.	120	15	26	Sec. 17, T. 18 N., R. 8 E., near mouth of Riordan Creek.	90	2
11	Barht's Hot Springs, in sec. 13, T. 25 N., R. 11 E., on Salmon River 200 yds below mouth of Hot Springs Creek.	Hot	200	27	T. 15 N., R. 3 E., 10 miles north of Cascade.	Hot	----------
12	Sec. 7, T. 24 N., R. 4 E., 2 miles north of Salmon River.	110	10	28	T. 16 N., R. 4E., on Gold Fork River 25 miles north of Cascade.	Hot	----------
13	Riggins Hot Spring, in sec. 13, T. 24 N., R. 2 E., 10 miles east of Riggins.	Hot	----------	29	Sec. 1, T. 16 N., R. 6 E., on South Fork of Salmon River 15 miles north of Knox.	Hot	2
14	Burgdorf Hot Spring, in sec. 1, T. 22 N., R. 4 E.	113	150	30	Sec. 17, T. 15 N., R. 6 E., 6 miles north of Knox.	Hot	100
15	Sec. 13, T. 21 N., R. 1 E., on east side of Little Salmon River 3 miles north of Round Valley.	Hot	----------	31	Sec. 14, T. 15 N., R. 6 E., 6 miles northeast of Knox.	Hot	250
16	Yoghann Hot Sulphur Spring, in sec. 26, T. 20 N., R. 1 E., on west side of Little Salmon River 10 miles northwest of Meadows.	Hot	----------	32	Sec. 11, T. 14 N., R. 6 E., 4 miles east of Knox.	Hot	450
				33	Sec. 14, T. 14 N., R. 6 E., 4 miles southeast of Knox.	Hot	100
				34	T. 14 N., R. 3 E., 0.25 mile from Cascade	Hot	20
				35	Sec. 2, T. 12 N., R. 5 E., on Middle Fork of Payette River 12 miles east of Alpha.	Hot	35
				36	Sec. 11, T. 12 N., R. 5 E., near Middle Fork of Payette River.	100	15

No. on figure	Name or location	Temperature of water (°F)	Flow (gallons per minute)	No. on figure	Name or location	Temperature of water (°F)	Flow (gallons per minute)

Idaho—Continued

No. on figure	Name or location	Temperature of water (°F)	Flow (gallons per minute)	No. on figure	Name or location	Temperature of water (°F)	Flow (gallons per minute)
37	Sec. 15, T. 12 N., R. 5 E., near Middle Fork of Payette River.	90	15	81	Sacajawea Hot Springs, in sec. 30, T. 10 N., R. 11 E., near mouth of Bear Creek.	100	200
38	Boiling Springs, in sec. 22, T. 12 N., R. 5 E., near Middle Fork of Payette River.	Hot	150	82	T. 5 N., R. 5 E., 6 miles southwest of Idaho City.	110–115	900
39	Sec. 28, R. 13 N., R. 6 E., near Bull Creek 15 miles east of Alpha.	Hot	15	83	Nevin Spring, sec. 1, T. 3 N., R. 5 E., near mouth of Cottonwood Creek.	Hot	200
40	Sec. 31, T. 12 N., R. 6 E., near Silver Creek 15 miles southeast of Alpha.	90	250	84	Twin Springs, on north side of Middle Fork of Boise River downstream from mouth of Browns Creek.	Hot	350
41	Sec. 23, T. 13 N., R. 10 E., 0.5 mile southwest of mouth of Bear Valley Creek.	Hot	10	85	Bassett Hot Spring, upstream from Logging Gulch, on north side of Middle Fork of Boise River.	Hot	30
42	Sec. 30, T. 14 N., R. 10E., 0.25 mile from mouth of Dagger Creek.	Warm	2	86	Sec. 1, T. 14 N., R. 11 E., 2 miles northwest of Greyhound.	Warm	4
43	Sec. 13, T. 14 N., R. 9 E., on Sulphur Creek.	80–110	7	87	Sec. 2, T. 12 N., R. 13 E., 6 miles east of Cape Horn.	Warm	200
44	Sec. 34, T. 15 N., R. 10 E., near mouth of Sulphur Creek.	Hot	25	88	Sec. 33, T. 14 N., R. 13 E., 10 miles southwest of Casto.	Warm	3
45	Sec. 23, T. 15 N., R. 10 E., near Middle Fork of Salmon River.	Hot	3	89	Sec. 15, T. 10 N., R. 12 E., near Stanley___	Hot	200
46	Sec. 17, T. 16 N., R. 10 E., on branch of Indian Creek near Chinook Mountain.	Hot	10	90	Sec. 36, T. 11 N., R. 13 E., near mouth of Yankee Fork of Salmon River.	Hot	250
47	Sec. 20, T. 16 N., R. 12 E., 10 miles north of Greyhound.	Hot	40	91	Sec. 20, T. 11 N., R. 14 E., 4 miles east of mouth of Yankee Fork of Salmon River.	Hot	200
48	Sec. 15, T. 17 N., R. 11 E., 8 miles south of Roosevelt.	Hot	50	92	Secs. 22 and 27, T. 11 N., R. 14 E., 6 miles east of mouth of Yankee Fork of Salmon River.	Warm	5
49	Sec. 28, T. 17 N., R. 13 E., on Middle Fork of Salmon River, 2 miles upstream from mouth of White Creek.	Hot	10	93	Sec. 19, T. 11 N., R. 15 E., on Salmon River 1 mile upstream from Sunbeam Dam.	168	200
50	Sec. 17, T. 25 N., R. 17 E., on Horse Creek 25 miles northwest of Shoup.	110	10	94	Sec. 3, T. 10 N., R. 13 E., 2 miles south of mouth of Yankee Fork of Salmon River.	Warm	400
51	Sec. 32, T. 24 N., R. 17 E., 17 miles west of Shoup.	Warm	25	95	Robinson Bar Ranch Hot Springs, in sec. 34, T. 11 N., R. 15 E., at mouth of Warm Spring Creek.	130	40
52	T. 22 N., R. 18 E., on west side of Copper King Mountain.	Hot	----------	96	T. 10 N., R. 15 E., near mouth of Hot Creek.	134–147	----------
53	Sec. 22, T. 23 N., R. 22 E., 5 miles north of Carmen.	Hot	80	97	Loon Creek Hot Springs, in T. 11 N., R. 15 E.	115–136	700
54	Sec. 26, T. 19 N., R. 14 E., 1 mile east of Mormon Ranch.	Hot	40	98	T. 10 N., R. 15 E., near head of Loon Creek.	Hot	----------
55	Sec. 19, T. 17 N., R. 14 E., near Cache Creek 4 miles upstream from its mouth.	Warm	10	99	Sec. 19, T. 10 N., R. 16 E., on Slate Creek 6 miles upstream from its mouth.	Hot	200
56	Sec. 10, T. 15 N., R. 14 E., on Warm Spring Creek.	80–190	400	100	Sullivan Hot Springs, in sec. 27, T. 11 N., R. 17 E., on Sullivan Creek 3 miles west of Clayton.	107	5,000
57	Sec. 1, T. 15 N., R. 15 E., 5 miles northwest of Parker Mountain.	Warm	75	101	Sec. 18, T. 9 N., R. 14 E., on the Salmon River.	105	150
58	Sec. 15, T. 15 N., R. 16 E., near Parker Mountain.	Hot	200	102	Pierson Hot Spring, in sec. 27, T. 8 N., R. 14 E.	120	300
59	Salmon Hot Springs, in sec. 3, T. 20 N., R. 22 E., 7 miles south of Salmon.	Warm	400	103	Secs. 30 and 31, T. 8 N., R. 17 E., on East Fork of Salmon River.	70–120	450
60	Sec. 34, T. 20 N., R. 24 E., 7 miles northeast of Tendoy.	Hot	200	104	Sec. 6, T. 7 N., R. 17 E., on East Fork of Salmon River.	75–110	300
61	T. 18 N., R. 22 E., 27 miles south of Salmon.	Hot	200	105	Beardsley Hot Springs, in sec. 23, T. 14 N., R. 19 E., on east bank of Salmon River.	123 (max)	1,500
62	T. 17 N., R. 21 E., in Kronk Canyon of Salmon River 40 miles south of Salmon.	Hot	100	106	Sulphur Creek Spring, in sec. 26, T. 14 N., R. 21 E., 15 miles northwest of Goldberg.	57	1,500
63	Sec. 18, T. 16 N., R. 21 E., at upper end of Kronk Canyon of Salmon River 3 miles downstream from mouth of Pahsimeroi River.	Hot	100	107	T. 13 N., R. 20 E., on Warm Springs Creek 10 miles southeast of Challis.	Warm	100
64	Warm Spring Creek, 4 miles southwest of Lemhi Indian Agency.	Warm	----------	108	T. 9 N., R. 27 E., in Little Lost River Valley.	80	----------
65	Sec. 4, T. 15 N., R. 25 E., 10 miles west of Leadore.	87	3	109	South side of Middle Fork of Boise River, 0.25 mile downstream from mouth of Sheep Creek.	Hot	200
66	Sec. 9, T. 7 N., R. 1 E., 1 mile southwest of Sweet.	Hot	----------	110	Sheep Creek Bridge Spring, on Middle Fork of Boise River at Sheep Creek Bridge.	Hot	100
67	T. 1 N., R. 3 W., on east side of Snake River 1 mile east of Enterprise.	67	----------	111	Reed Spring, on Sheep Creek near its mouth.	Hot	----------
68	T. 4 N., R. 2 E., on west bank of Squaw Creek 3 miles north of Boise.	Hot	Large	112	Smith Cabin Springs, on both sides of Middle Fork of Boise River upstream from junction with North Fork.	Hot	900
69	T. 3 N., R. 2 E., on Cottonwood Creek 1 mile west of Boise.	Warm	----------	113	Loftus Spring, on north side of Middle Fork of Boise River downstream from mouth of Loftus Creek.	Hot	100
70	Boise Hot Springs, in T. 3 N., R. 2 E., 4.5 miles southeast of Boise.	90–140	255	114	Crevice Spring, on north side of Middle Fork of Boise River downstream from mouth of Vaughn Creek.	Hot	20
71	Sec. 29, T. 5 S., R. 4 E., near Grand View__	109	100	115	Vaughn Spring, on south side of Middle Fork of Boise River upstream from mouth of Vaughn Creek.	Hot	200
72	Sec. 20, T. 10 N., R. 3 E., 14 miles north of McNish ranger station.	Warm	30	116	Ninemeyer Springs, on south side of Middle Fork of Boise River downstream from mouth of Big Five Creek.	Hot	900
73	Sec. 32, T. 10 N., R. 4 E., 3 miles northwest of Garden Valley.	Hot	----------	117	Pool Creek Spring, on north side of Middle Fork of Boise River upstream from mouth of Pool Creek.	Warm	50
74	Sec. 6, T. 8 N., R. 5 E., on South Fork of Payette River 10 miles east of Garden Valley.	Hot	20	118	South side of Middle Fork of Boise River upstream from mouth of Straight Creek.	Hot	180
75	Sec. 2, T. 8 N., R. 5 E., 0.5 mile west of Danskin Creek.	Hot	8	119	Dutch Frank's Springs, on south side of Middle Fork of Boise River downstream from mouth of Dutch Frank's Creek.	Hot	1,800
76	Sec. 11, T. 8 N., R. 5 E., 1.5 miles east of Boston & Idaho power plant.	Hot	15				
77	Sec. 31, T. 9 N., R. 6 E., 0.25 mile west of Pine Flat.	Hot	30				
78	Sec. 31, T. 9 N., R. 8 E., on north side of South Fork of Payette River.	Warm	40				
79	Kirkham Hot Springs, in sec. 32, T. 9 N., R. 8 E., on South Fork of Payette River.	90	150				
80	Bonneville Hot Springs, in sec. 31, T. 10 N., R. 10 E., on Warm Spring Creek.	100	200				

No. on figure	Name or location	Temperature of water (°F)	Flow (gallons per minute)	No. on figure	Name or location	Temperature of water (°F)	Flow (gallons per minute)
			Idaho—Continued				
120	Granite Creek Springs, on Middle Fork of Boise River, in sec. 4, T. 5 N., R. 9 E., 8 miles east of Narton.	130 (max)	50	156	Secs. 13 and 24, T. 2 S., R. 45 E., on west side of South Fork of Snake River 3 miles southwest of Blowout.	88–144	----
121	T. 5 N., R. 9 E., on both sides of Middle Fork of Boise River, 0.25 mile upstream from mouth of Granite Creek.	Hot	200	157	Lincoln Valley Warm Springs, in sec. 36, T. 3 S., R. 37 E., 3 miles south of old Fort Hall.	69–87	----
122	Sec. 36, T. 6 N., R. 9 E., on south side of Middle Fork of Boise River, 0.5 mile downstream from mouth of Granite Creek.	130 (max)	30	158	Enterprise, in T. 1 N., R. 3 W.	128	3,000
123	Sec. 32, T. 6 N., R. 12 E., 2 miles east of Atlanta.	100–130	50	159	Given's Hot Springs, in T. 1 S., R. 3 W., on south side of Snake River near mouth of Reynolds Creek.	98	35
124	Sec. 10, T. 3 N., R. 10 E., 0.5 mile northeast of Featherville.	Warm	45	159A	Toy Ranch, in sec. 29, T. 5 S., R. 1 E.	115–120	50
125	Sec. 9, T. 3 N., R. 11 E., 7 miles east of Featherville.	Warm	Small	160	Sec. 14, T. 6 S., R. 3 E., on Shoofly Creek near Grand View.	Warm	300
126	Sec. 24, T. 4 N., R. 11 E., on Willow Creek, 10 miles northeast of Featherville.	Hot	45	161	Rosebrier Spring, in sec. 32, T. 6 S., R. 5 E., on Little Valley Creek 10 miles southeast of Comet.	68	Small
127	Sec. 13, T. 3 N., R. 11 E., on South Fork of Boise River 10 miles east of Featherville.	Hot	30	162	Sec. 24, T. 7 S., R. 4 E., near head of Little Valley Creek.	99	135
128	Sec. 5, T. 2 N., R. 10 E., 6 miles south of Featherville.	Hot	50	163	Bruneau Hot Spring, in sec. 21, T. 7 S., R. 6 E., near Hot Springs post office on west side of Bruneau Valley.	105	1,200
129	Sec. 33, T. 3 N., R. 10 E., 4.5 miles south of Featherville.	128	45	164	Sec. 22, T. 7 S., R. 6 E., in Bruneau Valley.	111	35
130	Sec. 5, T. 1 N., R. 10 E., north of Fishing Falls.	164 (max)	----	165	Trammel's Hot Springs, in sec. 22, T. 7 S., R. 6 E., in Bruneau Valley.	114	1,000
131	Hot (Ranch) Springs, in sec. 16, T. 3 S., R. 8 E., 10 miles east of Mountain Home.	103–167	900	166	Sec. 35, T. 7 S., R. 6 E., on east bank of Bruneau River.	Warm	Large
131A	Daugherty's (Lattie's) Hot Spring, 15 miles north of Glenns Ferry.	146	500	167	Hot Creek Springs, in sec. 3, T. 8 S., R. 6 E., 11 miles south of Bruneau.	94–98.5	1,800
131B	Hot Spring, 1 mile east of King Hill.	125	20	168	Sec. 3, T. 8 S., R. 6 E., in Bruneau Valley downstream from mouth of Hot Creek.	100	----
132	Sec. 1, T. 4 N., R. 14 E., on Big Smoky Creek 8 miles north of Carrietown.	Warm	10	169	Sec. 29, T. 8 S., R. 7 E., 100 yd downstream from Buckaroo diversion dam in Bruneau Valley.	105	----
133	Sec. 32, T. 4 N., R. 14 E., on Big Smoky Creek 8 miles northwest of Carrietown.	Hot	20	169A	Indian (Bat) Hot Springs, in sec. 33, T. 12 S., R. 7 E., on West Fork of Bruneau River.	145–158	2,000
134	Sec. 18, T. 3 N., R. 13 E., on South Fork of Boise River near mouth of Bear Creek.	Warm	15	169B	Kitty's Hot Hole, 10 miles southwest of Three Creek.	Hot	Small
135	Sec. 30, T. 3 N., R. 14 E., on Little Smoky Creek 8 miles southwest of Carrietown.	Warm	10	170	White Arrow Hot Springs, in sec. 31, T. 4 S., R. 13 E., near Blanche.	149	1,200
136	Wasewick Hot Springs, in sec. 28, T. 3 N., R. 14 E., 6 miles southwest of Carrietown.	125–150	250	171	Blanche Crater Warm Springs, 1.5 miles northeast of White Arrow Hot Springs (no. 170).	80	Small
137	Wardrop Hot Springs, in sec. 29, T. 1 N., R. 13 E., on Corral Creek 2 miles north of Corral.	Hot	100	172	Tschannen Warm Springs, 2 miles southeast of White Arrow Hot Springs (no. 170).	110	Small
138	Sec. 14, T. 1 N., R. 15 E., 5 miles north of Blaine.	Warm	15	173	Sec. 30, T. 8 S., R. 14 E., on island in Salmon Falls Creek near Austin.	130	5
139	Sec. 34, T. 1 S., R. 13 E., 5 miles south of Corral.	Hot	25	174	Ring's Hot Spring, in sec. 31, T. 8 S., R. 14 E., on south side of Snake River.	125	200
140	Russian John Hot Springs, in sec. 33, T. 6 N., R. 16 E., near Wood River 18 miles northwest of Ketchum.	102	50	175	Banbury Hot Springs, in sec. 33, T. 8 S., R. 14 E., on south bank of Snake River 4 miles upstream from mouth of Salmon River.	131	600
141	Easly Warm Springs, in sec. 11, T. 5 N., R. 16 E., on south side of Wood River 16 miles northwest of Ketchum.	99	100	176	Poison Spring, in T. 9 S., R. 13 E., in canyon of Salmon River 8 miles upstream from mouth of river.	Warm	Small
142	Guyer Hot Springs, in sec. 15, T. 4 N., R. 17 E., 2.5 miles west of Ketchem.	160	450	177	Sec 10, T. 13 S., R. 18 E., on Rock Creek 10 miles north of Stricker.	90	1,300
143	Sec. 36, T. 4 N., R. 16 E., on Warm Spring Creek 11 miles southwest of Ketchum.	Hot	450	178	Artesian City Hot Springs, in sec. 6, T. 12 S., R. 20 E.	100	Small
144	Clarendon Hot Springs, in sec. 26, T. 3 N., R. 17 E., on Deer Creek 6 miles west of Hailey.	125–150	100	179	Poulton Warm Spring, in sec. 6, T. 13 S., R. 21 E., 9 miles northwest of Oakley.	72	----
145	Hailey Hot Springs, in sec. 18, T. 2 N., R. 18 E., 2.5 miles southwest of Hailey.	146	50	180	Land Spring, in sec. 7, T. 13 S., R. 23 E., 6 miles northeast of Oakley.	60	2,000
146	Lava Creek Hot Spring, in sec. 24, T. 1 S., R. 17 E., near Magic Reservoir.	96	130	181	Thoroughbred Springs, in sec. 21, T. 16 S., R. 19 E.	69	200
147	Condie Hot Springs, in sec. 14, T. 1 S., R. 21 E., near Carey.	124	450	182	Oakley Warm Spring, in sec. 27, T. 14 S., R. 22 E., 5 miles south of Oakley.	114	10
148	Sec. 25, T. 11 N., R. 32 E., 10 miles south of Edie.	80	3,000	183	Sec. 6, T. 14 S., R. 25 E., 1 mile southwest of Elba.	Warm	----
149	Sec. 34, T. 10 N., R. 33 E., 18 miles west of Dubois.	Hot	----	184	Frazier Hot Spring, in sec. 23, T. 15 S., R. 26 E., 5 miles southwest of Bridge.	204	120
150	Lidy Hot Springs, in sec. 2, T. 9 N., R. 33 E., 16 miles west of Dubois.	124	300	185	Bridger Hot Spring, in sec. 25, T. 15 S., R. 25 E., 6 miles northeast of Albion.	120	4
151	Sec. 6, T. 9 N., R. 44 E., near Warm River.	Warm	50	186	Sec. 22, T. 11 S., R. 25 E., 4 miles northeast of Albion.	100	3
152	Heise Hot Spring, in sec. 25, T. 4 N., R. 40 E., on South Fork of Snake River at Heise.	120	400	187	Sec. 19, T. 9 S., R. 28 E., near Lake Walcott.	70	700
153	Pincock (Lime Kiln) Hot Spring, in sec. 6, T. 5 N., R. 43 E., 6 miles south of Canyon City.	Hot	65	188	Fall Creek Warm Springs, in sec. 29, T. 9 S., R. 29 E., 8 miles northeast of Yale.	62	9,000
154	Sec. 29, T. 1 N., R. 43 E., on Fall Creek 4 miles northwest of Irwin.	Warm	----	189	Indian Hot Springs, in sec. 19, T. 8 S., R. 31 E., on south side of Snake River.	140	1,000
155	Alpine Hot Springs, in secs. 18 and 19, T. 2 S., R. 46 E., on east side of South Fork of Snake River 5 miles northwest of Alpine.	120–150	25	190	Lava Hot Springs, in T. 9 S., R. 38 E., on both sides of Portneuf River 2 miles south of Lava.	100–144	4,200
				190A	6 miles northwest of McCammon.	Warm	Small

No. on figure	Name or location	Temperature of water (°F)	Flow (gallons per minute)	No. on figure	Name or location	Temperature of water (°F)	Flow (gallons per minute)
			Idaho—Continued				
191	T. 10 S., R. 40 E., on west side of Bear River at south end of Gentile Valley.	125	----------	194	T. 14 S., R. 36 E., 2 miles southwest of Malad.	85	----------
191A	Downata Hot Springs, 4 miles southeast of Downey.	112	470	195	T. 16 S., R. 36 E., 12 miles southeast of Malad.	Warm	----------
192	T. 6 S., R. 42 E., in canyon of Blackfoot River.	82	Small	196	Bear Lake Hot Springs, near northeast shore of Bear Lake and 16 miles south of Montpelier.	83–134	150
193	Bear River Soda (Beer) Springs, in T. 9 S., R. 42 E.	76–88	----------				
			Montana				
1	Camas Hot Springs, in sec. 3, T. 21 N., R. 24 W.	110–114	----------	22A	Big Spring, on east bank of Missouri River 4 miles southeast of Toston.	59	29,000
2	Sec. 4, T. 21 N., R. 24 W., 1 mile west of Camas.	Warm	----------	23	Plunket's (Mockel, Nave's Warm) Spring, at head of Warm Creek, 10 miles southwest of Toston.	62	4,000
3	Sec. 9, T. 18 N., R. 25 W., 4 miles south of Paradise.	114	20	24	White Sulphur (Brewer's) Springs........	95–125	500
4	Granite (Lolo) Hot Springs, 8 miles southwest of Woodson.	135	25	25	Big Hole Hot Springs, at Jackson..........	132 (max)	1,500
5	Warm Springs Creek, 6 miles north of Garrison.	Warm	----------	26	Elkhorn Hot Springs, in sec. 29, T. 4 S., R. 12 W., on Miller Creek 6 miles north of Polaris.	120–150	110
6	Sun River (Medicine) Hot Springs, on North Fork of Sun River 30 miles by road west of Augusta.	84	500	27	Ziegler Hot Springs, near Apex...........	Hot	----------
7	Helena Hot Springs, 2 miles west of Helena.	122;141	30	28	Lovell Springs, in sec. 21, T. 8 S., R. 9 W., 9 miles southwest of Dillon.	72	1,125
8	Big Warm Springs, in sec. 24, T. 26 N., R. 25 E., 6 miles south of Lodgepole.	72–86	10,000	29	Brown (Ryan Canyon) Springs, in sec. 30, T. 8 S., R. 9 W., 11 miles southwest of Dillon.	72	360
9	Little Warm Springs, in sec. 32, T. 26 N., R. 26 E., 9 miles south of Lodgepole.	Warm	3,500	30	Barkel's Hot Springs, at Silverstar........	Hot	50
10	Warm Spring, in sec. 19, T. 17 N., R. 18 E., on Warm Spring Creek 12 miles north of Lewistown.	68	80,000	31	Clark's Warm (Potosi Hot) Springs, on south branch of Willow Creek, 5 miles south of Pony.	100–120	550
11	Sec. 19, T. 12 N., R. 23 E., on Durphy Creek, 3 miles south of Tyler.	71	15,000	32	Hapgood (Norris) Hot Springs, on Hot Spring Creek near Norris.	80–122	50
12	Medicine Rock (Weeping Child) Hot Springs, on Weeping Child Creek, 15 miles southeast of Hamilton.	Hot	4,500	33	Puller's Hot Springs, on upper Ruby Creek, 10 miles northwest of Virginia City.	95; 108	150
13	Sec. 31, T. 1 S., R. 22 W., 4 miles east of Slate Creek station.	Warm	330	34	Sec. 18, T. 12 S., R. 1 E., 3 miles southwest of Cliff Lake.	Warm	100
14	Gallogly (Ross' Hole, Medicine) Hot Springs, in sec. 15, T. 1 S., R. 19 W., 4 miles south of Camp Creek station.	110–125	150	35	Bozeman (Ferris, Matthews) Hot Springs, on West Gallatin River, 7 miles west of Bozeman.	137	250
15	Warm Springs, near Warm Springs railroad station, 10 miles northeast of Anaconda.	Warm	----------	36	Hunter's Hot Springs, 20 miles northeast of Livingston.	148–168	1,500
16	Anaconda Hot Springs, 3 miles east of Anaconda.	Warm	----------	37	Emigrant Gulch Warm Springs (Chico Spring), on Emigrant Creek near Chico.	102	240
17	Gregson Hot Springs, 15 miles west of Butte.	----------	----------	38	Corwin Hot Springs, in sec. 25, T. 8 S., R. 7 E.	[1] 120 (max)	----------
18	Alhambra Hot Springs, 17 miles south of Helena.	90–134	----------	39	Bear Creek Springs, in sec. 19, T. 9 S., R. 9 E., 3 miles south of Gardiner.	90	30
19	Boulder Hot Springs, 3 miles southeast of Boulder.	125–187	Large	40	Anderson's Spring, in sec. 29, T. 3 S., R. 13 E., near Boulder Creek 3 miles southwest of Hubble.	70	90
20	Pipestone Springs, 20 miles southeast of Butte.	Hot	----------				
21	Bedford Springs, on north side of Indian Creek 3.5 miles northwest of Townsend.	74	1,400				
22	Kimpton (Warner) Warm Springs, on branch of Crow Creek, 7 miles west of Toston.	65	100				
			Nevada				
1	T. 46 N., R. 27 E., 12 miles west of Pine Forest Range.	108	Small	11	T. 41 N., R. 41 E., on bank of Little Humboldt River, 12 miles southeast of Paradise Valley post office.	130	----------
2	Bog Ranch Hot Springs, on north side of Thousand Creek Valley 6 miles southwest of Denio, Oregon.	130; 190	20	11A	Near North and South Forks of Little Humboldt River, 25 miles east of Paradise Valley.	Hot	Small
3	T. 47 N., R. 31 E., south of Steens Mountain.	178	----------	12	Double Hot Springs, in T. 37 N., R. 24 E., on west flank of Black Rock Range.	165–191	5
4	T. 45 N., R. 32 E., 12 miles north of Mason's Crossing of Quinn River.	118	Small	12A	Near base of west flank of Black Rock Range.	130–150	3
5	T. 45 N., R. 32 E., 11 miles north of Quinn River (town).	130	150	13	T. 37 N., R. 25 E., on southeast side of Black Rock Range.	Hot	----------
6	T. 45 N., R. 33 E., on west side of King River valley.	76; 80	----------	14	T. 37 N., R. 26 E., in arm of Black Rock Desert.	Hot	----------
6A	Cordero Mine....................	118; 138	----------	15	Van Riper, in T. 36 N., R. 24 E., on southwest side of Black Rock Range.	145	50
7	T. 45 N., R. 41 E., at head of North Fork of Little Humboldt River.	Hot	----------	16	T. 36 N., R. 25 E., at south end of Black Rock Range, 10 miles southeast of Division Peak.	Hot	----------
8	T. 40 N., R. 25 E., at Soldier Meadows, 15 miles south of old Camp McGarry.	Hot	----------	17	Secs. 16, 21, 24, 34, T. 36 N., R. 26 E., on west border of Black Rock Desert.	Hot	----------
9	T. 40 N., R. 28 E., west of sink of Quinn River, at west edge of Black Rock Desert.	60	----------	18	2 miles north of Winnemucca......	Hot	Small
10	T. 43 N., R. 31 E., 7 miles west of Mason's Crossing of Quinn River.	155	----------	19	Golconda Hot Springs, in T. 36 N., R. 40 E.	120–150	250
10A	Near south bank of Quinn River...........	Warm	Small				

No. on figure	Name or location	Temperature of water (°F)	Flow (gallons per minute)	No. on figure	Name or location	Temperature of water (°F)	Flow (gallons per minute)
				Nevada—Continued			
19A	Blossom Hot Spring, in sec. 10, T. 35 N., R. 43 E., 8 miles north of Valmy.	107	70	48	Fish Spring, in T. 26 N., R. 19 E., 10 miles northwest of Pyramid railroad station.	Warm	
19B				49	T. 26 N., R. 20 E., on northwest side of Pyramid Lake.	206–208	
19C							
19D	Humboldt River Valley	Warm	Small	50	T. 27 N., R. 23 E., on northwest shore of Winnemucca Lake.	Warm	
19E							
19F				51	T. 26 N., R. 23 E., on west shore of Winnemucca Lake.	Warm	
19G							
20	T. 39 N., R. 40 E., at head of South Fork of Little Humboldt River.	Hot	Small	52	T. 24 N., R. 22 E., on Anaho Island in Pyramid Lake.	120	
21	Sec. 30, T. 45 N., R. 54 E., 5 miles southeast of Mountain City.	104–106	20	53	Cottonwood Spring, in sec. 26, T. 23 N., R. 21 E., in Warm Spring Valley 3 miles south of Dewey.	Warm	
22	Sec. 23, T. 46 N., R. 56 E., 15 miles east of Mountain City.	104	55	54	T. 21 N., R. 24 E., in Dead Ox Canyon 12 miles south of Dixon.	Warm	
22A	1.5 miles north of Contact.	133	5	55	Lawton Hot Springs, 6 miles west of Reno.	120	250
22B	Mineral (San Jacinto) Spring.	78–126	1,200	55A	Moana Springs, 2 miles south of Reno.	100–200	
23	Sec. 22, T. 47 N., R. 68 E., on west side of Goose Creek.	57	850	55B	Huffaker Springs, 5 miles southeast of Moana bathing resort.	79–81	10
24	Nile Spring, in sec. 30, T. 47 N., R. 70 E., on east side of Goose Creek.	106	6	55C	Zoleggi Springs, 3 miles southwest of Huffaker Springs (no. 55B).	103	125
25	Gamble's Hole, in sec. 10, T. 46 N., R. 69 E., on east side of Goose Creek.	103	8	55D	Da Monte Springs, 1.5 miles east of Zoleggi Springs.	130	40
26	Sec. 26, T. 46 N., R. 69 E., at head of main fork of Spring Creek.	62	200	55E	Mount Rose, 10 miles south of Reno.	Hot	
27	T. 41 N., R. 69 E., at south end of Thousand Springs Valley.	Boiling		55F	Reno Hot Springs, 10.5 miles south of Reno.	Hot	
28	Hot Creek mining district in T. 39 N., R. 60 E., on Marys River 15 miles north of Deeth.	110–122	30	56	Steamboat Springs, in sec. 33, T. 18 N., R. 20 E., 11 miles south of Reno.	167–203	300
29	Cress Ranch, in sec. 14, T. 38 N., R. 59 E., 8 miles north of Deeth.	Hot	Small	57	Bowers Mansion (Franktown Hot) Spring; 10 miles north of Carson City.	115–118	75
30	Sec. 21, T. 38 N., R. 62 E., in Emigrant Canyon, 4.2 miles north of Wells.	98	50	58	T. 19 N., R. 23 E., 10 miles southwest of Wadsworth.	73	
30A	5.5 miles north of Wells.	113–122	10	59	Carson (Swift's, Shaw's) Hot Springs, 2 miles north of Carson City.	120	75
30B	Metropolis.	102	800	59A	Nevada State Prison.	Warm	
				60	Walley's (Genoa) Hot Springs, 6 miles northwest of Minden.	136–160	Large
30C	Johnson Ranch.	73	30	61	Hind's Hot Springs, in sec. 16, T. 12 N., R. 23 E., near Simpson.	60–143	550
30D	H. D. Ranch.	142–154	600	62	Wabuska Springs, in T. 15 N., R. 25 E., 1 mile north of Wabuska.	138–162	
31	Hot Sulphur Springs, T. 33 N., R. 53 E., 9 miles northwest of Carlin.	98	15	63	Butte Spring, in T. 33 N., R. 26 E., at north end of Hot Springs Butte, 25 miles southwest of Sulphur.	182	20
32	Elko Hot Springs, in T. 34 N., R. 55 E., 1 mile west of Elko.	192		63A	Near Humboldt River, 2 miles north of Mill City.	Warm	Small
33	T. 33 N., R. 58 E., 8 miles southwest of Fort Halleck.	Warm		64	Leach's (Pleasant Valley) Hot Springs in sec. 35, T. 32 N., R. 38 E., in Grass Valley 29 miles south of Winnemucca.	158–202	200
34	T. 34 N., R. 62 E., near Warm Creek in Independence Valley.	Warm	250	65	Guthrie (Nelson) Springs, in sec. 36, T. 32 N., R. 38 E., 25 miles south of Winnemucca.	139–204	250
34A	Near east side of Ruby Lake.	Hot	Small				
35	Miller's Hot Springs, in T. 30 N., R. 59 E., at northeast end of Franklin Lake.	170		66	Kyle's Hot Springs, in sec. 2, T. 39 N., R. 36 E., 25 miles southeast of Humboldt.	100–160	Small
35A	Hill's Warm Spring, in sec. 18, T. 44 N., R. 20 E., 10 miles north of Vya.	83	10	66A	Miller Ranch.	58–61	900
35B	Hill's Spring, in sec. 11, T. 43 N., R. 19 E., 5 miles north of Vya.	66	8	67	Sec. 1, T. 25 N., R. 36 E., near north end of Salt Marsh (Osobb) Valley.	Hot	
35C	Twin Springs, in sec. 4, T. 42 N., R. 19 E., at Vya.	70	200	68	Sou (Gilbert's) Hot Springs, in sec. 29, T. 26 N., R. 38 E., near north end of Salt Marsh (Osobb) Valley.	160–185	
36	T. 38 N., R. 18 E., at south end of Surprise Valley.	Hot		69	Cone Spring, in sec. 26, T. 25 N., R. 38 E., in Salt Marsh (Osobb) Valley.	125	Small
37	Wards' (Fly Ranch) Hot Springs, in T. 34 N., R. 23 E., at northwest end of Alkali Flat and 5 miles northeast of Granite Peak.	69 to boiling		69	Sec. 35, T. 25 N., R. 38 E., 0.25 mile from Cone Spring, in Salt Marsh (Osobb) Valley.		
38	Gerlach Hot Springs, 1 mile northwest of Gerlach.	188–194		70	T. 24 N., R. 36 E., on northwest side of Salt Marsh (Osobb) Valley.	Warm	Small
39	Mud Springs, 2 miles west of Gerlach.	Hot		71	T. 23 N., R. 35 E., on northeast side of Pah Ute Mountains.	Hot	Small
40	Deep Hole Spring, in sec. 25, T. 33 N., R. 22 E., at north end of Smoke Creek Desert.	62	30	71A	5 miles south-southwest of spring No. 71.	Warm	Small
41	Wall Spring, in sec. 3, T. 32 N., R. 21 E., on northwest side of Smoke Creek Desert.	Warm		72	Springer's (Brady's, Fernley) Hot Springs, in sec. 12, T. 22 N., R. 26 E., on U.S. Highway 40.	158–209	50
42	Buffalo Spring, in T. 31 N., R. 20 E., on west side of Smoke Creek Desert.	Warm		73	Eagle Salt Works Springs, in T. 20 N., R. 27 E., 15 miles northwest of Fallon.		
43	Buckbrush Spring, in T. 29 N., R. 19 E., on west side of Smoke Creek Desert.	Warm		74	Borax Spring, in T. 17 N., R. 30 E., 3 miles east of South Carson Lake.	178	
44	Rotten Egg Spring, in T. 29 N., R. 19 E., on southwest side of Smoke Creek Desert.	92	10	74A	Lee Springs, 18 miles south of Fallon.	172	25
45	Round Hole Spring, in sec. 31, T. 29 N., R. 19 E., on southwest side of Smoke Creek Desert.	Warm		75	Sec. 6, T. 16 N., R. 32 E., 20 miles southeast of Fallon.	Hot	
46	Ross Spring, in T. 28 N., R. 20 E., at south end of Smoke Creek Desert.	Hot		76	Izzenhood Ranch Springs, in T. 36 N., R. 45 E., 25 miles north of Battle Mountain.	83	1,000
47	T. 28 N., R. 21 E., near north end of Pyramid Lake.	Hot		77	White River Springs, in sec. 8, T. 33 N., R. 47 E., 2 miles west of Rock Creek.	Warm	
				77A	Beowawe Geysers, in sec. 5, T. 31 N., R.	120 to	100

Nevada—Continued

No. on figure	Name or location	Temperature of water (°F)	Flow (gallons per minute)
	48 E., in Whirlwind Valley 8 miles west of Beowawe.	boiling	
78	Sec. 24, T. 29 N., R. 41 E., in Buffalo Valley 25 miles southwest of Battle Mountain (town).	130	5
79	Mound Spring, in sec. 7, T. 28 N., R. 44 E., in Reese River valley 25 miles south of Battle Mountain (town).	110	3
80	Sec. 23, T. 27 N., R. 43 E., 1 mile north of Hot Spring Ranch in Reese River valley.	124	450
81	Sec. 26, T. 27 N., R. 43 E., at Hot Spring Ranch.	122	50
82	T. 27 N., R. 47 E., 10 miles south of Lander.	Hot	
83	T. 22 N., R. 47 E., near north end of Grass Valley.	181	
84	T. 18 N., R. 39 E., in Smith Creek valley 6 miles north of Hot Springs.	Warm	Small
85	Sec. 25, T. 17 N., R. 40 E., on west side of Smith Creek valley.	Hot	
86	Spencer Hot Springs, in T. 17 N., R. 46 E., 18 miles southeast of Austin.	117-144	6
87	Sec. 14, T. 16 N., R. 45 E., 20 miles southeast of Austin.	Hot	5
88	Horseshoe Ranch Springs, 1 mile northeast of Beowawe.	125-132	30
88A	Sec. 2, T. 29 N., R. 48 E., in Crescent Valley 12 miles south of Beowawe.	122	40
89	Sec. 12, T. 28 N., R. 52 E., at head of Hot Creek, 14 miles north of Mineral.	84	5,900
90	Carlotti Ranch Springs, in sec. 24, T. 28 N., R. 52 E., 10 miles north of Mineral.	95; 102	100
99A	Bruffey's (Mineral Hill) Hot Springs, in sec. 14, T. 27 N., R. 52 E., 7 miles northeast of Mineral.	108-152	50
91	Flynn Ranch Springs, in sec. 5, T. 25 N., R. 53 E., in Diamond Valley.	69-78	10
91A	Siri Ranch Spring, in sec. 6, T. 24 N., R. 53 E., in Diamond Valley.	87	300
91B	Sadler (Big Shipley) Springs, in sec. 23, T. 24 N., R. 52 E., in Diamond Valley.	103-106	5,000
91C	Sulphur Springs, in sec. 36, T. 23 N., R. 52 E., on Sulphur Springs Ranch in Diamond Valley.	74	20
91D	Jacobson Ranch Springs, on east side of Diamond Valley.	71-75	900
92	Sec. 15, T. 24 N., R. 47 E., on west side of Grass Valley.	Hot	Small
93	Sec. 33, T. 24 N., R. 48 E., on east side of Grass Valley.	Hot	Small
93A	Bartine Hot Springs, in sec. 5, T. 19 N., R. 50 E., in Antelope Valley 35 miles west of Eureka.	105; 108	10
93B	Clobe Hot Spring, in sec. 28, T. 18 N., R. 50 E., in Antelope Valley, 45 miles southwest of Eureka.	142	100
93C	Sara Ranch Springs, in sec. 7, T. 16 N., R. 53 E., at head of Fish Creek.	66	4,000
94	Collar and Elbow Spring, in sec. 27, T. 26 N., R. 65 E., near north end of Steptoe Valley.	92	20
95	Cherry Creek (Young's) Hot Springs, in T. 23 N., R. 63 E., 1.2 miles southwest of Cherry Creek (town) in Steptoe Valley.	118-135	40
96	Shellbourne Hot Springs, in T. 23 N., R. 63 E., about 100 ft from Cherry Creek (Young's) Hot Springs (No. 95).	124; 135	
97	Borchert John Spring, in sec. 16, T. 22 N., R. 63 E., in Steptoe Valley.	66	800
98	Monte Neva (Goodrich, Melvin) Hot Springs, in secs. 24, T. 21 N., R. 63 E., 1 mile northwest of Warm Springs railroad station in Steptoe Valley.	173-193	625
99	T. 21 N., R. 70 E., at east base of Kern Mountains.	Warm	
100	Sec. 5, T. 19 N., R. 63 E., 10 miles northwest of McGill.	58-76	200
101	McGill Warm Springs, in sec. 21, T. 18 N., R. 64 E., 0.75 mile west of McGill.	76-84	450
102	Ely Warm Spring, in sec. 10, T. 16 N., R. 63 E., 1.5 miles northeast of Ely.	85	23
102A	Moore's Ranch Springs, in T. 23 N., R. 56 E., in Newark Valley.	65-70	200
103	Big Blue Spring, in sec. 23, T. 14 N., R. 56 E., near the north end of White Pine Valley.	Warm	
103A	Williams Hot Springs, in sec. 33, T. 13 N., R. 60 E., 12 miles northwest of Preston.	124; 128	185
104	Preston Springs, in sec. 1, T., 12 N., R. 61 E.	72	5,700
105	Lund Spring, in sec. 33, T. 12 N., R. 62 E.	66	2,400
106	Warm Sulphur Springs, in T. 11 N., R. 65 E., at head of Warm Creek.	Warm	972
107	Big Spring, in T. 11 N., R. 69 E., in Snake Valley, 15 miles south of Baker.	64	8,000, 12,000
107A	Sec. 30, T. 10 N., R. 70 E., at head of Big Springs Creek.	Warm	2,000
108	Double Spring, in sec. 13, T. 13 N., R. 29 E., 3 miles north of Walker Lake.	Warm	
109	Sec. 4, T. 7 N., R. 27 E., on East Walker River, 20 miles west of Hawthorne.	Hot	
110	T. 6 N., R. 35 E., at Sodaville.	80-101	100
111	Waterworks Springs, in sec. 22, T. 2 S., R. 39 E., at Silver Peak.	69-118	500
112	Alkali Spring, in sec. 26, T. 1 S., R. 41 E., 11 miles northwest of Goldfield.	120-140	50
113	Wedell Springs, in sec. 7, T. 12 N., R. 34 E., 12 miles southeast of Rawhide.	129; 144	60
114	T. 14 N., R. 43 E., 1 mile east of McLeod's Ranch in Big Smoky Valley.	Hot	
115	Gendron Spring, in T. 14 N., R. 43 E., near Millett in Big Smoky Valley.	61	10
116	Charnock (Big Blue) Springs, in T. 13 N., R. 44 E., near Charnock Ranch.	80	450
117	Sec. 14, T. 11 N., R. 42 E., in Big Smoky Valley, 14 miles south of Millett.	Boiling	600
118	Darrough Hot Springs, in sec. 17, T. 11 N., R. 43 E., on Darrough Ranch in Big Smoky Valley.	160-207	200
119	Sec. 1, T. 14 N., R. 47 E., 2 miles southeast of Potts.	Warm	
120	Diana's Punch Bowl, in sec. 22, T. 14 N., R. 47 E., 5 miles south of Potts.	Hot	Small
121	Fish Springs, in secs. 26 and 35, T. 11 N., R. 49 E., in Fish Creek valley.	Warm	
122	Sec. 32, T. 13 N., R. 56 E., 5 miles north of Duckwater.	Warm	Large
123	Indian Springs, in T. 7 N., R. 42 E., near San Antonio.	Warm	
124	T. 7 N., R. 51 E., on Hot Creek 8 miles northeast of Tybo.	Warm	
125	T. 4 N., R. 50 E., near south end of Hot Creek valley.	Boiling	
126	Lock's Springs, in sec. 15, T. 8 N., R. 55 E., on west side of Railroad Valley 20 miles southwest of Currant.	93-99	2,000
127	Chimney Springs, in sec. 16, T. 7 N., R. 55 E., in Railroad Valley 6 miles south of Lock's Springs (No. 126).	130-160	100
128	Blue Eagle Springs, in sec. 11, T. 8 N., R. 57 E., on east side of Railroad Valley 18 miles south of Currant.	82	1,385
129	Kate Spring, in sec. 14, T. 8 N., R. 57 E., 0.75 mile south of Blue Eagle Springs (No. 128).	73	14
130	Butterfield Springs, in sec. 27, T. 8 N., R. 57 E., on east side of Railroad Valley.	64	227
131	Bacon Springs, in sec. 34, T. 8 N., R. 57 E., on east side of Railroad Valley.	57	2
132	Bullwhacker Spring, in sec. 28, T. 7 N., R. 57 E., on east side of Railroad Valley.	59	10
133	Willow Springs, in sec. 5, T. 6 N., R. 57 E., on east side of Railroad Valley.	60	30
134	Mormon Springs, in sec. 33, T. 9 N., R. 61 E., 5 miles west of White River.	100	100
134A	Moon River Springs.	92	900
135	Riordan Ranch (Emigrant), Springs, in T. 9 N., R. 62 E., near White River.	70	200
136	White River Valley (Flag, Sunnyside) Springs, in secs. 28, 31, and 32, T. 7 N., R. 62 E., on Whipple and Hendricks Ranches.	65-75	2,000
137	Hot Creek Ranch Springs, in sec. 18, T. 6 N., R. 61 E., in White River valley 8 miles southwest of Sunnyside.	85-90	5,000
138	Hicks Hot Springs, in T. 11 S., R. 47 E., 5 miles north of Beatty.	110	40
139	Ash Meadow Springs, in sec. 22, T. 17 S., R. 50 E.	76-94	450
140	Pahrump Springs, in sec. 14, T. 20 S., R. 53 E., on Pahrump Ranch.	77	2,200
141	Manse Springs, in sec. 3, T. 21 S., R. 54 E., on Manse Ranch.	75	1,500
142	Geyser Ranch Springs, in T. 8 N., R. 65 E., 5 miles east of Patterson.	65-70	50
143	T. 5 N., R. 70 E., on Hammond Ranch.	84	
144	Bennetts Springs, in T. 2 S., R. 66 E., 9 miles west of Panaca.	70	Small

No. on figure	Name or location	Temperature of water (°F)	Flow (gallons per minute)
	Nevada—Continued		
144A	Delmue's Springs, 10 miles north of Panaca	70	200
144B	Flatnose Ranch	70	100
145	Panaca Spring, in sec. 4, T. 2 S., R. 68 E.	85–88	2,500
146	Caliente Hot Spring, in T. 4 S., R. 67 E., 0.25 mile north of Caliente.	110	
147	Hiko Spring, in sec. 22, T. 4 S., R. 60 E.	90	4,000
148	Crystal Spring, 1 mile northwest of Hiko.	90	9,000
149	Ash (Alamo) Spring, 4 miles south of Hiko.	90–97	9,000
150	T. 14 S., R. 65 E., 3 miles west of Moapa	90	
151	Indian Spring, in sec. 16, T. 16 S., R. 56 E., 1 mile south of Indian Spring railroad station.	78	410
152	Las Vegas Springs, in T. 20 S., R. 61 E., 2 miles west of Las Vegas.	73	2,600
	New Mexico		
1	Sec. 32, T. 11 N., R. 2 W., 10 miles south of Shiprock.	68	3
2	Sec. 8, T. 7 N., R. 2 W., 5 miles north of Newcomb.	65	3
3	Sec. 16, T. 7 N., R. 2 W., 4 miles north of Newcomb.	67	7
4	Sec. 23, T. 25 N., R. 8 E., 0.75 mile northwest of La Madera.	80	10
5	Sec. 24, T. 25 N., R. 8 E., 1 mile northeast of La Madera.	100	5
6	Sec. 25, T. 25 N., R. 8 E., 0.25 mile north of La Madera.	90	15
7	Sec. 35, T. 25 N., R. 8 E., 1 mile southwest of La Madera.	100	5
8	Ojo Caliente Springs, 12 miles northwest of Barranca.	98–113	350
9	Togay Springs, in sec. 33, T. 19 N., R. 15 W., 20 miles east of Tohatchie.	65	65
10	Murray Spring, in sec. 29, T. 20 N., R. 3 E., 15 miles north of Jemez Springs (town).	130	150
11	San Antonio Springs, in sec. 7, T. 20 N., R. 4 E., on San Antonio Creek 20 miles north of Jemez Springs (town).	120	50
12	Sulphur Springs, in sec. 3, T. 19 N., R. 3 E., 12 miles north of Jemez Springs (town).	76–167	500
13	Soda Dam Springs, in sec. 15, T. 18 N., R. 2 E., in Canyon de San Diego, 2 miles north of Jemez Hot Springs (No. 15).	75–105	10
14	McCauley Spring, in sec. 4, T. 18 N., R. 3 E., 7 miles north of Jemez Springs (town).	100	110
15	Jemez Hot Springs (Ojos Calientes), in sec. 22, T. 18 N., R. 2 E., 12 miles north of Jemez (pueblo).	94–168	200
16	Phillips Springs, in T. 16 N., R. 1 W., 10 miles west of Jemez (pueblo) and 1 mile northeast of Rio Salado.	70	Small
17	Indian (Jemez) Springs, in T. 16 N., R. 2 E., 2 miles north of San Ysidro.	120	
18	San Ysidro Hot Springs, in sec. 8, T. 15 N., R. 1 E., 7 miles southwest of San Ysidro.	86 (max)	
19	San Ysidro Warm Springs, in secs. 3, 9, 10, T. 15 N., R. 1 E.	68	Small
20	Las Vegas Hot Springs, 6 miles northwest of Las Vegas.	80–140	100
21	Ojo Caliente Springs, in sec. 21, T. 8 N., R. 20 W., 12 miles southwest of Zuni.	80	500
22	Quelites Mineral Spring, in T. 8 N., R. 2 W., on north side of San Jose River 2 miles northwest of Quelites.	80	3
23	Socorro Warm Springs, 1.5 miles southwest of Socorro.	93	500
24	Ojo Caliente, in sec. 31, T. 8 S., R. 7 W., 15 miles northwest of Monticello.	85	1,200
25	Sec. 23, T. 12 S., R. 20 W., 1 mile south of Pleasanton.	80–124	50
26	Sec. 30, T. 11 S., R. 12 W., 1 mile south of DD Bar Ranch.	80	50
27	Sec. 19, T. 12 S., R. 13 W., on Diamond Creek near its mouth.	151	30
28	Sec. 26, T. 13 S., R. 16 W., near Turkey Creek.	80	20
29	Sec. 3, T. 14 S., R. 16 W., on Turkey Creek 3 miles above its confluence with the Gila River.	Hot	20
30	Gila Hot Springs, in sec. 5, T. 13 S., R. 13 W., on the Gila River near Diamond Creek.	90–100	900
31	Sec. 3, T. 13 S., R. 13 W., on the Gila River.	Hot	30
32	Sec. 20, T. 13 W., R. 13 W., on the Gila River.	Hot	30
33	Sec. 16, T. 14 S., R. 14 W., on the Gila River.	Hot	20
34	Hudson's Hot Springs, 4 miles northwest of Mimbres.	142	
35	Apache Tejo Warm Springs, 7 miles north of Whitewater.	97	2,000
36	Faywood Hot Springs, in T. 20 S., R. 11 W., 6 miles northeast of Faywood.	142	120
37	Hot Springs (Palomas), near Truth or Consequences.	90–105	10
38	Radium Hot Springs, near Radium Springs railway station 17 miles north of Las Cruces.	165; 185	Small
	Oregon		
1	Sec. 29, T. 2 S., R. 9 E., in crater of Mount Hood.	120–194	
2	Mount Hood Warm Springs, in sec. 24, T. 3 S., R. 8½ E., on south side of Mount Hood.	60–80	25
3	Sec. 25, T. 6 S., R. 6 E., on the Clackamas River.	188 (max)	
4	Carey (Austin) Hot Springs, in sec. 30, T. 6 S., R. 7 E., on the Clackamas River.	176–196	
5	Bagsby Hot Springs, in sec. 26, T. 7 S., R. 5 E., on Hot Springs Creek 4 miles south of Thunder Mountain.	Hot	50
6	Breitenbush Hot Springs, in sec. 20, T. 9 S., R. 7 E., on the Breitenbush River.	140–198	900
7	Warm Springs, in secs. 19 and 20, T. 8 S., R. 13 E., on Warm Springs River 9 miles north-northeast of Warm Springs Indian Agency.	138–145	Large
8	Lehman Hot Springs, in sec. 1, T. 5 S., R. 33 E., on Camas Creek.	Hot	75
9	Hideaway Springs, in T. 5 S., R. 33 E., 7 miles southwest of Lehman Hot Springs (No. 8).	Hot	
10	Sec. 6, T. 1 S., R. 39 E., 2 miles northeast of Summerville.	Warm	
11	Hot Lake, in T. 4 S., R. 39 E., 10 miles southeast of La Grande.	180	175
12	Medical Springs, in sec. 24, T. 6 S., R. 41 E., 20 miles north-northeast of Baker.	140	50
13	Ritter (McDuffee) Hot Spring, sec. 8, T. 8 S., R. 30 E., on north bank of Middle Fork of John Day River.	110	35
14	Hot Sulphur Spring, in sec. 35, T. 10 S., R. 32 E., on Camp Creek 6 miles south of Susanville.	120	
15	Bear Gulch Spring, in sec. 11, T. 15 S., R. 31 E., near Canyon Creek 10 miles south of Canyon City.	Warm	2
16	Blue Mountain Hot Springs, in sec. 13, T. 14 S., R. 34 E., near mouth of Reynolds Creek 10 miles south of Prairie City.	Hot	
17	Sam-O Mineral Springs, in sec. 2, T. 12 S., R. 43 E., 4 miles southeast of Durkee.	80	
17A	Radium Hot Spring, in sec. 28, T. 7 S., R. 39 E., 10 miles northeast of Baker.	135	Small
17B	Sam-O Spring, in sec. 16, T. 9 S., R. 40 E., near Baker.	80	400
18	Belknap Hot Springs, in sec. 11, T. 16 S., R. 6 E., 6 miles east of McKenzie Bridge.	147–180	75

Oregon—Continued

No. on figure	Name or location	Temperature of water (°F)	Flow (gallons per minute)
19	Foley Springs, in sec. 28, T. 16 S., R. 6 E., 4.5 miles southeast of McKenzie Bridge.	162–174	25
20	Sec. 7, T. 17 S., R. 5 E., on the South Fork of McKenzie River, 8 miles southwest of McKenzie Bridge.	130 (max)	60
21	Wall Creek Hot Springs, in sec. 26, T. 20 S., R. 4 E., 10.5 miles northeast of Oakridge.	98	3
22	Winino (McCredie) Springs, in sec. 36, T. 21 S., R. 4 E., 11 miles east of Oakridge.	Hot	20
23	Kitson Springs, in sec. 6, T. 22 S., R. 4 E., 8 miles southeast of Oakridge.	114	35
24	Umpqua Warm Spring, in sec. 20, T. 26 S., R. 4 E., on Umpqua River 5 miles south of Potter Mountain.	105	5
25	Jackson (Bybee) Hot Springs, 2 miles northwest of Ashland.	104 (max)	70
26	Sec. 31, T. 24 S., R. 5½ E., in Summit Lake Valley.	Warm	----------
27	Klamath Hot Springs, at Klamath Falls.	185	150
28	0.5 mile northeast of Olene	130	8
28A	Taylor Warm Spring, 2 miles east of Olene	75	500
28B	Crystal Springs, 1 mile south of Olene	76	1,350
29	Oregon (Turner) Hot Springs, in sec. 10, T. 40 S., R. 13 E., 10 miles southeast of Bonanza.	148	35
29A	Smith's Hot Spring, in sec. 10, T. 40 S., R. 13 E., 9.5 miles southeast of Bonanza.	146	5
30	Wilkerson's Warm Springs, in sec. 6, T. 40 S., R. 14 E., 13 miles southeast of Bonanza.	76	20
31	Robertson's Springs, in sec. 18, T. 38 S., R. 15 E., in Horsefly Valley 8 miles south of Bly.	Hot	----------
32	Paulina Springs, in sec. 26, T. 21 S., R. 12 E., near north shore of Paulina Lake.	65; 70	10
33	East Lake Hot Springs, in sec. 29, T. 21 S., R. 13 E., on south shore of East Lake.	110–141	----------
34	Sec. 36, T. 19 S., R. 32 E., near Twelve-mile Creek 20 miles southwest of Paulina.	60–87	----------
35	Sand Springs, in sec. 35, T. 25 S., R. 19 E., 5 miles northeast of Fossil Lake.	62	30
36	Sec. 32, T. 26 S., R. 18 E., on west shore of Christmas Lake.	62	3
37	Ana River Springs, in sec. 6, T. 30 S., R. 17 E., 7 miles north of Summer Lake post office.	66	48,000–75,000
38	Buckhorn Creek Springs, in sec. 5, T. 30 S., R. 17 E., 9 miles north of Summer Lake Post Office.	68	1,000
39	Johnson Creek Springs, in sec. 34, T. 29 S., R. 17 E., 12 miles northeast of Summer Lake post office.	56	9,000
40	Thousand Springs, in sec. 19, T. 30 S., R. 18 E., on east side of Summer Lake Valley.	66	200
40A	R. C. Foster's Spring, 2 miles southwest of Ana River.	66	2,500
40B	W. O. Grisel's Spring	60.5	10
40C	Russell Emery's Spring	64.5	2
40D	J. G. Foster's Spring	65	50
40E	Lost Cabin Spring	67.5	100
41	Pardon Warm Spring, in sec. 35, T. 30 S., R. 16 E.	76	40
42	Summer Lake (Woodward; J. W. Farleigh's) Hot Spring, in sec. 11, T. 33 S., R. 17 E.	116	21
43	Sec. 12, T. 30 S., R. 22 E., on west shore of Alkali Lake.	59	25
44	Sec. 22, T. 32 S., R. 21 E., on XL Ranch 3 miles north of Abert Lake.	63	10
44A	Northeast shore of Abert Lake	65	20
44B	East shore of Abert Lake	68	10
44C	Southeast shore of Abert Lake	80	30
44D	White Rock Ranch Springs, 10 miles north of Lakeview.	63; 71	10
44E	Russell Bean's Spring	69	Small
45	Hunters Hot Springs, 2 miles north of Lakeview.	128–162	600
46	Leo Hank's (Leitnead, Joyland Plunge, Lakeview) Hot Spring, 1.5 miles south of Lakeview.	157	50
47	Gus Allen's (Barry Ranch, Down's, Lakeview) Hot Springs, 2 miles south of Lakeview.	175–185	50
47A	F. S. Longfellow's Spring	63	20
48	Sec. 16, T. 35 S., R. 26 E., on upper Rock Creek 4 miles east of North Warner Lake.	105–115	50
48A	Antelope Spring	104	30
49	Hart Mountain Hot Spring, in sec. 7, T. 36 S., R. 26 E., on the north side of Hart Mountain about 200 ft below crest.	Hot	Small
49A	Fisher's Spring	144	20
49B	W. D. Moss Ranch, on west side of South Warner Lake.	72; 83	500; 30
49C	Charles Crump's Spring	104	5
49D	Warner Valley Ranch	98; 107; 164	20; 2; 10
50	Adel Hot Spring, in sec. 23, T. 39 S., R. 24 E., 1 mile east of Adel post office.	160	10
50A	Pat Hallinan's Spring, 1 mile southwest of Houston Spring (No. 51).	1.3	20
51	Houston Hot Springs, in sec. 27, T. 40 S., R. 24 E., 3 miles east of Warner Lake post office.	160	5
51A	Sec. 14, T. 22 S., R. 32½ E., 17 miles northeast of Burns.	72	225
52	Millpond Spring and other springs in secs. 35 and 36, T. 23 S., R. 30 E.	73–80	1,200
52A	0.75 mile south of Millpond Spring (No. 52).	78	300
52B	Goodman Spring, 1 mile south of Millpond Spring (No. 52).	Warm	300
52C	3.5 miles southwest of Millpond Spring (No. 52).	64	75
52D	1.5 miles east of spring No. 52C	72	485
52E	Baker Spring, 1.5 miles southeast of spring No. 52D.	62–70	50
53	Crane Hot Spring, in sec. 34, T. 24 S., R. 33 E., near Crane Creek Gap 4 miles northwest of Crane.	122–126	180
54	Sec. 23, T. 22 S., R. 36 E., on the west side of Middle Fork of Malheur River 8 miles northwest of Riverside.	138–144	90
55	Sec. 16, T. 25 S., R. 36 E., on the west side of South Fork of Malheur River 8 miles north of Venator.	104–108	300
56	Sec. 12, T. 26 S., R. 27 E., near south shore of Silver Lake.	68	45
57	Sec. 33, T. 26 S., R. 28 E., 3.5 miles east of Iron Mountain.	68	10
58	Double-O Spring, in sec. 34, T. 26 S., R. 28 E., 1.5 miles west of Double-O Ranch.	74	5,350
59	Double-O Barnyard Spring, in sec. 33, T. 26 S., R. 28 E., on Double-O Ranch.	72	1,750
60	Basque (East Double-O) Springs, in sec. 31, T. 26 S., R. 29 E., 1 mile southeast of Double-O Ranch.	67–74	1,800
61	Johnson Springs, in sec. 5, T. 27 S., R. 29 E., 2.5 miles southeast of Double-O Ranch.	72	900
62	Hughet (Crane Creek) Spring, in sec. 8, T. 27 S., R. 29 E., 3 miles southeast of Double-O Ranch.	68	5,900
62A	Sizemore Upper Spring, in sec. 9, T. 27 S., R. 29 E., 5 miles southeast of Double-O Ranch.	67	1,160
62B	Sizemore Lower Spring, in sec. 15, T. 27 S., R. 29 E., 0.5 mile southeast of Sizemore Upper Spring (No. 62A).	66	410
62C	Hurlburt Spring, in sec. 15, T. 27 S., R. 29 E., 1 mile southeast of Sizemore Lower Spring (No. 62B).	Warm	25
62D	Between high- and low-water boundaries of Harney Lake.	66–108	30
63	Lynch Spring, in sec. 8, T. 27 S., R. 30 E.	65	25
63A	Dunn Spring, in sec. 4, T. 27 S., R. 30 E., on south side of Mud Lake.	65; 70	10; 25
64	Sec. 36, T. 27 S., R. 29½ E., 0.5 mile from southeast shore of Harney Lake.	154	180

Oregon—Continued

No. on figure	Name or location	Temperature of water (°F)	Flow (gallons per minute)
64A	Sodhouse (Springer) Spring	54	1,800–5,200
65	Hoghouse Spring, in sec. 13, T. 31 S., R. 32 E., on west side of Donner and Blitzen River valley.	78–80	1,800
66	Sec. 5, T. 32 S., R. 32½ E., 1 mile northeast of P Ranch.	83	100
67	Sec. 12, T. 32 S., R. 32 E., 1 mile southwest of P Ranch.	89	500
68	Sec. 33, T. 34 S., R. 34 E., on west border of the Alvord Desert 6 miles south of Alvord Ranch.	168–177	135
69	Sec. 15, T. 37 S., R. 33 E., 2 miles south of Alvord Lake.	160	6
70	Sec. 15, T. 37 S., R. 33 E., at old borax works 2.5 miles south of Alvord Lake.	97	900
71	Sec. 24, T. 38 S., R. 37 E., 5 miles northeast of Flagstaff Butte.	96–100	30
71A	5 miles southwest of Whitehorse Ranch	114	10
72	Sec. 16, T. 39 S., R. 37 E., on north side of Trout Creek 0.5 mile downstream from mouth of Little Trout Creek.	128	45
73	Sec. 4, T. 16 S., R. 43 E., near Willow Creek 20 miles northwest of Vale.	Hot	----
74	Sec. 11, T. 19 S., R. 37 E., in Warm Creek valley near Beulah.	185	Small
75	Neal Hot Spring, sec. 9, T. 18 S., R. 43 E., 12 miles northwest of Vale.	168	24
76	Sec. 18, T. 19 S., R. 43 E., on the Malheur River 15 miles southwest of Vale.	Hot	----
77	Vale Hot Springs, in sec. 20, T. 18 S., R. 45 E., on the south side of the Malheur River 0.5 mile east of Vale.	198	20
78	Sec. 31, T. 17 S., R. 47 E., on the Malheur River 3 miles west of Ontario.	164	----
79	Mitchell Butte Hot Springs, in sec. 12, T. 21 S., R. 45 E., on the Owyhee River.	122–141	----
80	Deer Butte Hot Spring, in sec. 14, T. 21 S., R. 45 E., on the Owyhee River.	115	----
81	North Black Willow Spring, in sec. 25, T. 21 S., R. 45 E., on the Owyhee River near Snively's Ranch.	67	----
82	South Black Willow Spring, in sec. 35, T. 21 S., R. 45 E., on the Owyhee River.	71	----
83	Sec. 10, T. 23 S., R. 44 E., on the Owyhee River 2 miles downstream from mouth of Dry Creek.	Hot	----
84	Sec. 20, T. 24 S., R. 37 E., near South Fork of Malheur River 5 miles south of Riverside.	106–143	60
84A	Sec. 18, T. 27 S., R. 43 E., on the Owyhee River 30 miles northwest of Jordan Valley.	Hot	Large
84B	Near north end of Saddle Mountain 25 miles northwest of Rome.	Warm	Small
85	Canter's Hot Springs, in sec. 2, T. 30 S., R. 46 E., 0.5 mile west of Jordan Valley.	120	10
85A	Scott's Springs, 6 miles southwest of Rome.	68	5,000
85B	Tudor's Springs, 24 miles southwest of Rome.	68	6,000
85C	South Fork of Owyhee River, 40 miles south of Jordan Valley.	88–95	1,000
86	Sec. 36, T. 40 S., R. 42 E., 6 miles north of McDermitt, Nev.	130	200

Texas

No. on figure	Name or location	Temperature of water (°F)	Flow (gallons per minute)
1	Near bank of the Rio Grande, at south end of Quitman Mountain.	100	----
2	Near bank of the Rio Grande, 2 miles east of the south end of Quitman Mountain.	118	----
3	Hot Spring Creek, 5 miles east of the Rio Grande and 7 miles northeast of Ruidosa.	114	45

Utah

No. on figure	Name or location	Temperature of water (°F)	Flow (gallons per minute)
1	Warm Springs in sec. 20, T. 12 N., R. 15 W., 17 miles north-northwest of Terrace railroad station.	Warm	900
2	Blue (Honeyville) Springs, in T. 13 N., R. 5 W., 18 miles southeast of Snowville.	86	----
3	Udy's Hot Springs, near the Malad River 2 miles southwest of Plymouth.	90–122	3,500
4	Crystal Springs, in T. 11 N., R. 2 W., 12 miles north of Brigham City.	121–134	----
4A	Near south end of Little Mountain, 7 miles west-northwest of Corinne.	Warm	Small
5	T. 6 N., R. 5 W., on east side of Promontory Point.	84	----
6	Utah (Bear River) Hot Springs, in T. 7 N., R 2 W., 8 miles northwest of Ogden.	131–144	110
6A	Clay's Hot Springs, 10 miles north of Ogden.	140	50
7	Patio Spring, 12 miles northeast of Ogden.	68	200
8	Ogden Hot Springs, in T. 6 N., R. 1 W., at mouth of Ogden Canyon.	121; 150	Small
9	Big Springs, in T. 2 S., R. 8 W., on the west side of Stansbury Range.	74	----
10	Grantsville Warm Springs, 5 miles northwest of Grantsville.	74–91	50
10A	Morgan's Warm Springs, 4 miles southwest of Stockton.	80	500
10B	Russell's Warm Springs, 4.5 miles southwest of Stockton.	90	200
11	Beck's Hot Springs, 4 miles north of Salt Lake City.	128	----
11A	Warm Springs, 2 miles north of Salt Lake City.	118	350
12	Wasatch Springs, in the northwestern part of Salt Lake City.	130	350
13	Crystal Springs, in T. 4 S., R. 1 W., 4 miles southwest of Draper.	70	----
14	Schneitter's Hot Pots, 4.5 miles northwest of Heber.	85–116	20
14A	Luke's Hot Pots, 4 miles northwest of Heber.	78–110	30
44B	Buhler's Springs, 3.5 miles northwest of Heber.	80–108	10
15	Saratoga Springs, on northwest shore of Utah Lake.	111	211
16	T. 8 S., R. 1 E., on south shore of Utah Lake 8 miles northwest of Payson.	88	200
17	T. 10 S., R. 1 E., near the north end of Long Ridge 2 miles east of Goshen.	70	2,000
18	Castilla Mineral Springs, in T. 9 S., R. 3 E., in Spanish Fork Canyon 15 miles south of Provo.	111; 145	----
19	Sec. 14, T. 8 S., R. 5 E., on Diamond Creek 15 miles east of Springville.	Warm	700
19A	12 miles northeast of Jensen, in canyon of Green River.	90	10
20	Hot Springs, in T. 11 S., R. 14 W., at north end of Fish Springs Mountains and 3 miles north-northeast of Fish Springs (town).	74–78	----
21	Big Spring, in T. 11 S., R. 14 W., 1 mile southeast of Hot Springs (No. 20).	85	----
22	Fish Springs, in T. 11 S., R. 14 W., 4 miles southeast of Hot Springs (No. 20) and 3 miles east of Fish Springs (town).	80–140	----
23	Sec. 33, T. 14 S., R. 18 W., on Miller's Ranch 8 miles south of Trout Creek.	64	500
24	Abraham Springs in T. 14 S., R. 8 W., on Fumarole Butte, 19 miles north-northwest of Delta.	100–205	1,200
25	Sec. 31, T. 15 S., R. 19 W., in Snake Valley 1 mile west of Gandy.	82	Large
26	Sec. 9, T. 16 S., R. 18 W., in Snake Valley 2 miles south of Foote's Ranch.	68	1,000
27	Knoll Springs, in sec. 11, T. 18 S., R. 18 W., in Snake Valley 12 miles southeast of Smithville.	68–71	----
28	Sec. 24, T. 22 S., R. 6 W., 3 miles northwest of Hatton.	94	Large
29	Brewer's Springs, in secs. 13 and 24, T. 15 S., R. 2 E., 1 mile northwest of Wales.	57–62	400

No. on figure	Name or location	Temperature of water (°F)	Flow (gallons per minute)	No. on figure	Name or location	Temperature of water (°F)	Flow (gallons per minute)
			Utah—Continued				
30	Lowry's Spring and Squires' Spring, in sec. 23, T. 18 S., R. 2 E., 3 miles south of Manti.	59; 62	40	45	Sec. 25, T. 24 S. R. 3 W., 6 miles south of Richfield.	59	25
31	Livingston Warm Springs, in sec. 13, T. 18 S., R. 2 E., 1 mile south of Manti.	62; 73	285	46	Jericho Spring, in sec. 6, T. 25 S., R. 3 W., 2 miles northeast of Joseph.	65	700
32	Manti Springs, in sec. 17, T. 18 S., R. 3 E., 2 miles southeast of Manti.	59; 65	30	47	Johnson Spring, in sec. 27, T. 25 S., R. 3 W., 2 miles southeast of Monroe.	80	200
33	Morrison Spring, in sec. 35, T. 18 S., R. 2 E., 2 miles northeast of Sterling.	61	2,500	48	Cooper Hot Springs, in sec. 15, T. 25 S., R. 3 W., 0.5 mile east of Monroe.	144–156	100
34	Gunnison Spring, in sec. 18, T. 19 S., R. 1 E.	61	8	49	Joseph Hot Springs, in sec. 23, T. 25 S., R. 4 W., 1 mile southeast of Joseph.	135–146	30
35	Ninemile Warm Spring, in sec. 4, T. 19 S., R. 2 E.	72	900	50	Sevier Spring, in sec. 32, T. 25 S., R. 4 W.	59	100
36	Sec. 32, T. 20 S., R. 2 E., 8 miles northeast of Redmond.	58	15	51	Roosevelt (McKean's) Hot Spring, in T. 27 S., R. 9 W., on west slope of Mineral Mountains 15 miles northeast of Milford.	192	10
37	Redmond Springs, in secs. 11 and 12, T. 21 S., R. 1 W., near Redmond.	70	6,000	52	Warm Springs, secs. 21 and 28, T. 30 S., R. 12 W., 2 miles south-southwest of Thermo railroad siding.	90–175	20
38	Salt Spring, in sec. 17, T. 21 S., R. 1 E., 2 miles northeast of Salina.	72	2	53	Radium (Dotson's) Warm Springs, in sec. 7, T. 30 S., R. 9 W., 1 mile east of Minersville.	97	57
39	Oak Spring and Christianson Spring, in sec. 1, T. 22 S., R. 2 W., 2 miles west of Aurora.	60	20	54	La Verkin Hot Springs, on Rio Virgin 2 miles north of Hurricane.	108–132	1,000
40	Herrin's Hole Spring, in sec. 23, T. 23 S., R. 2 W., 1 mile north of Glenwood.	63	450	55	T. 37 S., R. 7 W., 25 miles southwest of Panguitch.	Warm	----------
41	Cove Springs, in sec. 27, T. 23 S., R. 2 W., 1 mile west of Glenwood.	60	4,000	56	Undine Springs, in T. 25 S., R. 17 E., in Labyrinth Canyon of the Green River.	Warm	----------
42	Richfield Hot Springs, in sec. 26, T. 23 S., R. 3 W.	74	1,500	57	Warm Spring Canyon near its junction with "Narrow Canyon" or "Dark Canyon" of the Colorado River.	91	----------
43	Indian Spring and Parcel Creek Spring, in sec. 25, T. 23 S., R. 2 W., near Glenwood.	60	130				
44	Sec. 5, T. 24 S., R. 2 W., 2 miles southeast of Richfield.	52–61	4,500				
			Washington				
1	Baker Hot Spring, in sec. 30, T. 38 N., R. 9 E., on east side of Mount Baker.	108	7	9	Hot Springs, in sec. 21, T. 20 N., R. 9 E., at Hot Springs railroad station.	120–122	----------
2	Sol Duc Hot Springs, in sec. 32, T. 29 N., R. 9 W., 14 miles (by road) southwest of Crescent Lake.	100–132	50	10	Clerf Spring, in sec. 5, T. 17 N., R. 20 E., 8 miles east of Ellensburg.	68	1,100
3	Olympic Hot Springs, in sec. 27, T. 29 N., R. 8 W., 11.5 miles (by trail) southwest of Elwha post office.	120–125	135	11	Ohanapecosh Hot Springs, in sec. 4, T. 14 N., R. 10 E., near south base of Mount Rainier.	109–120	60
4	Sulphur Creek Spring, in sec. 30, T. 32 N., R. 12 E., 1 mile north of Sulphur Creek Shelter.	98	4	12	Sec. 9, T. 11 N., R. 15 E., on the North Fork of Simcoe Creek.	90	40
5	White Chuck Hot Springs, in sec. 1, T. 30 N., R. 12 E., near the White Chuck River.	100–110	30	12A	North slope of Mount St. Helens.	142–190	----------
				12B	Crater of Mount Adams.	Hot	----------
6	San Juan Hot Springs, in sec. 25, T. 28 N., R. 11 E., on the North Fork of Skykomish River 5 miles east of Galena.	100	25	13	Nicolai Spring, in sec. 15, T. 11 N., R. 23 E., 10 miles north of Sunnyside.	66	300
7	Scenic (Great Northern) Hot Springs, in sec. 28, T. 26 N., R. 13 E., 5 miles west of Scenic.	122	30	14	Sec. 16, T. 6 N., R. 13 E., 5 miles southeast of Glenwood.	76	Large
8	McDaniels Hot Springs, in sec. 15, T. 23 N., R. 11 E.	114–127	30	15	Blockhouse Mineral Springs, in sec 12, T. 4 N., R. 14 E., 8 miles west of Goldendale.	67	50
				16	Cascade Warm (Moffet's Hot) Springs, in sec. 16, T. 2 N., R. 7 E., near Cascade.	96	20
			Wyoming				
1	Boiling (Hot) River, 0.8 mile north-northeast of Yellowstone Park Headquarters.	----------	10,000	9A	Fryingpan Springs, 2 miles northwest of Norris Junction.	----------	----------
2	Mammoth (White Mountain) Hot springs, 0.5 mile southwest of Yellowstone Park Headquarters.	160 (max)	225–1,152	10	Congress Pool, 0.3 mile southwest of Norris Junction.	----------	----------
				10A	Crater of Monarch Geyser, near Congress Pool (No. 10).	----------	----------
3	3 miles east of Obsidian Cliff.	----------	Small	11	Geysers in Norris Geyser Basin:		
4	Northeast base of The Landmark.	----------	Small		Ebony Geyser.	----------	----------
5	Near east side of Lake of the Woods.	----------	Small		Echinus Geyser.	----------	----------
6	0.5 mile southeast of Lake of the Woods.	----------	Small		Emerald Spring.	----------	----------
7	Amphitheater Springs, 0.8 mile west of Lake of the Woods.	135–196	----------		Fan Geyser.	----------	----------
7A	Clearwater Springs, 1 mile southwest of Amphitheater Springs (No. 7) and 0.5 mile northwest of Roaring Mountain.	178–198	----------		Ledge Geyser.	----------	----------
7B	Pool in crater of Semi-Centennial Geyser, near Obsidian Creek 0.6 mile south of Clearwater Springs (No. 7A).	Hot	----------		Mud Geyser.	----------	----------
8	Whiterock Springs, 1 mile south-southeast of Lake of the Woods.	149–156	Small		Steamboat Geyser.	----------	----------
9	Bijah Spring, 0.4 mile northwest of Fryingpan Springs (No. 10).	184	58.5		Valentine Geyser.	----------	----------
					100 ft northwest of Valentine Geyser.	----------	----------

Wyoming—Continued

No. on figure	Name or location	Temperature of water (°F)	Flow (gallons per minute)
	Vixen Geyser		
	Whirligig Geyser		
12	Sylvan Springs, in Gibbon Meadows 3.5 miles southwest of Norris Junction.	190 (max)	Small
13	Gibbon Hill Geyser, near east side of Gibbon Meadows at foot of southwest side of Gibbon Hill.	188–198	
14	Artists Paintpots, at foot of northwest side of Paintpot Hill.	178–199	149
15	Geyser Springs, at foot of east side of Paintpot Hill.		
16	Monument Geyser in Monument Geyser Basin 1 mile west-southwest of Painpot Hill.	197	5,400
16A	Beryl Spring, 1.5 miles north of Gibbon Falls.	197	54
17	Queen's Laundry (Red Terrace) Spring, 1.5 miles southwest of Fountain Ranger Station.	160	
18	River Group Springs, on both sides of Firehole River 1.5 miles south of Fountain Ranger Station.	119–203	
19	Morning Mist Springs, near Nez Perce Creek 1.2 miles east-southeast of Fountain Ranger Station.	201 (max)	Small
20	Fairy Springs, 2.7 miles south-southwest of Fountain Ranger Station.	184–202	
21	Fountain Paintpot		
21A	Clepsydra Geyser		
21B	Fountain Geyser, 2.2 miles southeast of Fountain Ranger Station.		
21C	Morning Geyser, near Fountain Geyser (No. 21B).		
22	Great Fountain Geyser, 1 mile south-southeast of Fountain Geyser (No. 21B).	204	22
22A	Pink Cone Geyser		
23	White Dome Geyser, 0.8 mile south of Fountain Geyser (No. 21B).		
24	Spray Geyser, at base of south end of Twin Buttes 4 miles southwest of Fountain Ranger Station.		72
24A	Pool in crater of Imperial Geyser, 0.2 mile west of Spray Geyser.		690
25	Prismatic Lake in crater of Excelsior Geyser, about midway between Upper Basin Ranger Station and Fountain Ranger Station.	146	2,700
26	Flood Geyser, 0.5 mile southeast of Prismatic Lake (No. 25).	201	18
26A	Rabbit Creek area, 1 mile east-southeast of Prismatic Lake (No. 25).	201 (max)	
27	Tributary of Juniper Creek, 6.5 miles east of Fountain Ranger Station.		
28	Juniper Creek Springs, 1.1 miles southeast of No. 27.		
29	Biscuit Basin, 2.2 miles northwest of Old Faithful Inn:		
	Jewel Geyser	190	
	Sapphire Pool (Soda Geyser)	201	
30	1.7 miles northwest of Old Faithful Inn, on northeast side of Firehole River:		
	Gem Pool		
	Artemisia Geyser		
	Atomizer Geyser		
30A	1.2 miles northwest of Old Faithful Inn, on northeast side of Firehole River:		
	Sentinel Geysers	201	
	Morning Glory Pool	171	
	Fan Geyser	198	
	Mortar Geyser	198	
	Riverside Geyser		
31	1 mile northwest of Old Faithful Inn, on southwest side of Firehole River:		
	Chain Lakes (Bottomless Pit) Geyser		
	Spa Geyser		
	Grotto Geyser		
	Grotto Fountain		
	Daisy Geyser	198	
	Splendid Geyser	200	
	Giant Geyser	205	
	Oblong Geyser	202	
32	0.5 mile north-northwest of Old Faithful Inn, on northeast side of Firehole River:		
	Grand Geyser		
	Turban Geyser		
	Sawmill Geyser		
32A	0.3 mile north of Old Faithful Inn, on northeast side of Firehole River:		
	Lion (Niobe) Geyser	201	
	Lioness Geyser	203	
	Big Cub Geyser	201	
	Little Cub Geyser		
	Giantess Geyser	202	
	Midget Geyser		
	Beehive Geyser		
32B	Solitary Geyser, 0.6 mile north of Old Faithful Inn.	200	
33	Black Sand Basin, 0.8 mile west of Old Faithful Inn:		
	Cliff Geyser	190	
	Whistle Geyser	149	
	Rainbow Pool	151	
	Sunset Lake	169	
	Emerald Pool	158	
33A	Castle Geyser, 0.4 mile northwest of Old Faithful Inn.		
34	Old Faithful Geyser, near Old Faithful Inn.		
34A	Pipeline Creek Springs, 0.5 mile southeast of Old Faithful Inn.		
35	1 mile west of Summit Lake and 7 miles west-southwest of Old Faithful Inn.		
36	0.5 mile south-southeast of Summit Lake.		
37	Lone Star Geyser, 2.7 miles south-southeast of Old Faithful Inn.		
38	Shoshone Geyser Basin, 7.5 miles south-southeast of Old Faithful Inn:		
	Bead Geyser		
	Lion Geyser		
	Little Giant Geyser		
	Minute Man Geyser		
	Union Geyser		
39	Bechter River Springs, 12.5 miles south-southwest of Old Faithful Inn.		

No. on figure	Name or location	Temperature of water (°F)	Flow (gallons per minute)
Wyoming—Continued			
40	Three River Junction Springs, near confluence of Phillips, Littles, and Ferris Forks of Bechler River.		
41	Tendoy Falls Springs, on Ferris Fork of the Bechler River.		
42	Near northwest shore of Lewis Lake	Hot	
42A	0.5 mile west of west shore of Lewis Lake	190–198	Small
43	Near south outlet of Lewis Lake	154 (max)	Small
44	Deluge Geyser, near Witch Creek in Heart Lake Geyser Basin.		
44A	Spike Geyser, near Witch Creek in Heart Lake Geyser Basin.		
45	Rustic Geyser, 0.25 mile west of north end of Heart Lake.	201	
46	Near confluence of Snake and Lewis Rivers, 0.5 mile north-northeast of South Entrance to Yellowstone National Park.	158 (max)	
47	Snake Hot Springs, near the Snake River 5 miles upstream from confluence with Lewis River.	120–163	
48	Near mouth of Basin Creek, 3 miles south of Heart Lake.		
49	Near Snake River, 0.5 mile downstream from mouth of Basin Creek.		
50	Washburn Hot Springs, 1.8 miles southeast of Dunraven Pass Ranger Station.	178–198	
51	Sulphur Creek Springs, 1.3 miles upstream from mouth of Sulphur Creek and 2 miles south-southeast of Dunraven Pass Ranger Station.		
52	Near mouth of Sulphur Creek, 3 miles south-southeast of Dunraven Pass Ranger Station.		
53	0.5 mile northeast of Inspiration Point, on both sides of Yellowstone River.		
54	Forest Springs, 1.2 miles east-southeast of Canyon Lodge at the Yellowstone River Falls.		
55	0.5 mile south of Norris-Canyon Road and 4 miles west-southwest of Canyon Ranger Station.		
56	Violet Springs, on tributary of Alum Creek 6 miles southwest of Canyon Ranger Station.	Hot	740
57	Highland Hot Springs, on tributary of Alum Creek 3.5 miles southwest of Violet Springs (No. 56) and 1.1 miles north-northeast of Mary Lake.		
58	Alum Creek Springs, 2 miles east of Highland Hot Springs (No. 57).	194 (max)	Large
59	1 mile southeast of Highland Hot Springs (No. 57) and 1 mile northeast of Mary Lake.		
60	Elk Antler Creek Springs.		
61	Sulphur Spring (Crater Hills Geyser), 1 mile west of Yellowstone River and 4 miles south of Canyon Ranger Station.	194	Small
61A	Crater Hills Mudpots, on Lake-Canyon Road near mouth of Elk Antler Creek.		
61B	Dragon's Mouth Spring, on Lake-Canyon Road 6 miles (by road) northwest of Fishing Bridge.	160	
61C	Mud Volcano, near Dragon's Mouth Spring (No. 61B). / Mud Geyser.	185 (max)	
61D	Sulphur Caldron, on northeast side of Yellowstone River nearly opposite Dragon's Mouth Spring (No. 61B).		
62	Near west shore of West Thumb of Yellowstone Lake, 2 miles north of Thumb Ranger Station.		
63	Near west shore of West Thumb of Yellowstone Lake, 1.5 miles north-northwest of Thumb Ranger Station.	200	
64	Near Thumb Ranger Station, on west shore of West Thumb of Yellowstone Lake:		
	Thumb Paintpots	200 (max)	
	King Geyser		
	Lakeshore Geyser		
	Occasional Geyser		
	Twin Geysers		
	Fishing Cone Spring, offshore from Thumb Paintpots.		
65	Near Yellowstone River, 1 mile downstream from mouth of Lamar River.		
65A	Calcite Springs, in canyon of Yellowstone River 1 mile downstream from mouth of Tower Creek.	156–01	
66	Near Lamar River, 1 mile north-northwest of mouth of Cache Creek.		
67	Wahb Springs, in Death Gulch 2.2 miles upstream from mouth of Cache Creek.		
68	Near Deep Creek, 0.4 mile upstream from mouth of Shallow Creek.	Hot	100
69	Near Deep Creek, 3 miles upstream from mouth of Shallow Creek.		
70	Near Deep Creek, 4 miles upstream from mouth of Shallow Creek.		
71	Near Deep Creek, 5 miles upstream from mouth of Shallow Creek.		
72	Whistler Geyser, near west bank of Broad Creek 3 miles upstream from its mouth. / Joseph's Coat Springs.	198 / Hot	
73	Near head of tributary to Broad Creek, 1.5 miles east of Whistler Geyser and Joseph's Coat Springs (No. 72).		
74	Near head of tributary to Broad Creek, 2 miles southeast of Whistler Geyser and Joseph's Coat Springs (No. 72).		
75	Hot Springs Basin, 1.5 miles north of Wapiti Lake.		
76	Near tributary of Miller Creek, 2.7 miles northwest of Saddle Mountain.		
77	Near tributary of Lamar River, 2.6 miles west-southwest of Saddle Mountain.		
78	Near head of Moss Creek, 3 miles south-southwest of Whistler Geyser and Joseph's Coat Springs (No. 72).		
79	Bog Creek Springs, near head of Bog Creek, a tributary of Sour Creek.		
80	Head of unnamed tributary of Sour Creek, 1.5 miles northeast of Bog Creek Springs (No. 79).		
81	Along unnamed tributary of Sour Creek, 2 miles east of Bog Creek Springs (No. 79).		
82	Sour Creek Springs, 2.3 miles west of Fern Lake.		
83	Ponuntpa Springs, 0.6 mile southwest of Fern Lake.	113–180	
84	Near east end of Fern Lake.		Small
85	Near northwest end of White Lake.	Warm	Small
86	Near southeast end of White Lake.	Warm	Small
87	The Mudkettles, near Pelican Creek 1.5 miles east of southeast end of White Lake.		
88	The Mushpots, 1 mile southeast of the Mudkettles (No. 87).		
89	Near west end of Sulphur Hills, 1.8 miles south of Stonetop Mountain.	196	
90	Ebro Springs, 2.5 miles south-southwest of Stonetop Mountain.		
91	Vermilion Springs, near Pelican Creek, 2.3 miles south of Stonetop Mountain.		
92	Pelican Springs, at confluence of Pelican and Raven Creeks.		
93	Beach Springs, on shore of Mary Bay of Yellowstone Lake.		
94	Turbid Springs, near south end of Turbid Lake.	Hot	Small
95	Steamboat Springs, on northeast shore of Yellowstone Lake at Steamboat Point.	186–198	
96	Butte Springs, on northeast shore of Yellowstone Lake, 1.5 miles southeast of Steamboat Point.	190 (max)	10
97	DeMaris (Cody) Hot Springs, 4 miles southwest of Cody.	76–100	
98	T. 55 N., R. 94 W., in Sheep Canyon of the Bighorn River near mouth of Five Springs Creek.	Warm	
99	T. 53 N., R. 94 W., near upper end of Black Canyon of the Bighorn River.	Warm	Small
100	Sec. 8, T. 48 N., R. 115 W., near the Snake River 2 miles south of boundary of Yellowstone National Park.	Hot	100
101	T. 39 N., R. 116 W., near the Snake River 4 miles downstream from mouth of Hobak River.	94	100
102	Granite Hot Springs, in sec. 6, T. 39 N., R. 113 W.	110	360
103	Near west bank of Salt River, 2.5 miles north of Auburn.	68–140	38
104	Sec. 2, T. 38 N., R. 110 W., on the Green River near Wells.	Warm	Large

No. on figure	Name or location	Tempera-ture of water (°F)	Flow (gallons per minute)	No. Assoc. on figure	Name or location	Tempera-ture of water (°F)	Flow (gallons per minute)
					Wyoming—Continued		
105	T. 32 N., R. 107 W., near Fremont Butte.	Hot	Small	111A	3.5 miles northwest of Thermopolis, near sulfur deposits.	Hot	Small
106	Near Warm Spring Creek 4 miles north-west of Dubois.	84 (max)	----------	112	Sec. 35, T. 32 N., R. 86 W., on Horse Creek near Independence.	Warm	Large
107	Near mouth of Little Warm Spring Creek, 3 miles southwest of Dubois.	68	----------	113	Alcova Hot Springs, in T. 30 N., R. 83 W., in Fremont Canyon of the North Platte River.	139	75
108	Fort Washakie Hot Springs, in sec. 2, T. 1S., R. 1 W., 24 miles west of Riverton.	110	2,000	114	T. 31 N., R. 71 W., near the North Platte River 9 miles south of Douglas.	Warm	----------
109	T. 30 N., R. 97 W., 4 miles southwest of Hailey.	100–120	100	115	Saratoga Hot Springs, in T. 17 N., R. 84 W.	120	10
110	T. 29 N., R. 96 W., near Sweetwater River 12 miles southwest of Myersville.	Warm	----------	116	10 miles northwest of Laramie.	74	----------
111	Big Horn (Thermopolis) Hot Springs, on the Bighorn River at Thermopolis.	135	>12,600				

13 Sources

We've come to the end of the book, but it's really just the beginning. Here are a number of books, booklets, catalogs, pamphlets, newspapers, and magazines. They're from the straight world, the movement, and the underground. Many of them were pre-selected by the godfather of most of these efforts, the famous *Whole Earth Catalog*. We are much indebted to Stewart Brand for his creativity in pointing the way.

So now we'd like to do Stewart a favor and suggest that you try his Whole Earth Catalog Store for any of these books before you buy them elsewhere. The store's address is 558 Santa Cruz Ave., Menlo Park, California 94025. Just tell them that Wild Bill sent you.

GOOD HUNTING!

Clothing
Do clothes really make the man? Walk through the Pentagon with four stars on your shoulder; then try it with a tin one on a stick.

Basketry
F. S. Christopher
1952; 108 pages, $1.25
Dover Publications, Inc.
180 Varick Street
New York, N.Y. 10014

The Illustrated Hassle-Free
Make Your Own Clothes Book
Sharon Rosenburg, Joan Wiener
1971; 154 pages (and 1972, paperback), $1.95
Straight Arrow
World Publishing Co.

331

110 E. 59th Street
New York, N.Y. 10002

Coats and Clark's Sewing Book
1967; 224 pages, $3.95
Golden Press, Inc.
850 Third Avenue
New York, N.Y. 10022

Successful Sewing: A Modern Guide
Nesta Hollis
1969; 206 pages, $8.75
Taplinger Publishing Co., Inc.
29 East Tenth Street
New York, N.Y. 10003

The Standard Book of Quilt Making and Collecting
Marguerite Ickis
1949, 1959; 273 pages, $3.00
Dover Publications, Inc.
180 Varick Street
New York, N.Y. 10014

How to Start a Community Newspaper,
How to Sustain a G.I. Underground Paper
$.25 each
Vocations for Social Change
Canyon, Calif. 94516

How to Start a High School Underground Paper
$.25
CHIPS
520 N. Brainard Street
Naperville, Ill. 60540

Home Tanning and Leather Making Guide
A. B. Farnham
1950; 176 pages, $1.50
Harding's Books
2878 E. Main Street
Columbus, Ohio 43209

Craft Manual of North American Footwear
George M. White
1966; 71 pages, $1.95
Mission Valley News
St. Ignatius, Mont. 59865

How to Make Cowboy Horse Gear
Bruce Grant
1957; 186 pages, $3.50
Corness Maritime Press
Box 109
Cambridge, Md. 21613

Complete Book of Progressive Knitting
Ida Riley Duncan
1966; 386 pages, $2.75
Liveright Publishing Corporation
386 Park Avenue South
New York, N.Y. 10016

Communications

If I wanted a message, I'd send for a Western Union boy.
SAM GOLDWYN

How to Start an Underground Paper
Send postage to
Underground Press Syndicate
Box 26, Village P.O.
New York, N.Y. 10014

Printing as a Hobby
J. Ben Lieberman
1963; 128 pages, $.95
Signet-New American Library
1301 Avenue of the Americas
New York, N.Y. 10019

Doing It

Every man feels instinctively that all the beautiful sentiments in the world weigh less than a single lovely action.
LOWELL

300 Ways to Moonlight
Jerry Le Blanc
1969; 176 pages, $.75
Paperback Library
315 Park Avenue
New York, N.Y. 10010

Wildcrafters World
$1 per year
Homesteader and Landcrafters Newsletter
$2 per year (6 issues)
. . . and assorted manuals, $1.00
Wildcrafters Publications
R.R. 3, Box 118
Rockville, Ind. 47872

Guerrilla Warfare
"Yank" Berk Levy
1964; 119 pages, $2.00
Paladin Press
Box 1307
Boulder, Col. 80302

Minimanual of the Urban Guerrilla
Carlos Marighella
1969; 40 pages, $1.25
British Tricontinental Organization
15 Lawn Road
London N.W. 3, England

Riot and Disaster Control (FM19-15)
1967; 230 pages, $3.00
Normount Armament Co.
Box 217
Forest Grove, Ore. 97116

150 Questions for Guerrillas
General Alberto Bayo
1963; 86 pages, $2.00
Paladin Press
Box 1307
Boulder, Col. 80302

We Shall Fight in the Streets
Captain S. J. Cuthbert
$2.00
Paladin Press
Box 1307
Boulder, Col. 80302

Military Materials (TM-1910/TO 11A-1-34)
350 pages, $6.00
Normount Armament Co.
Box 217
Forest Grove, Ore. 97116

Total Resistance
Major H. von Dach Bern
1965; 173 pages, $6.50
Paladin Press
Box 1307
Boulder, Col. 80302

Guerrilla Warfare
Ché Guevara
1961; 133 pages, $1.65
Paladin Press
Box 1307
Boulder, Col. 80302

*How to Defend Yourself, Your Family,
and Your Home*
George Hunter
1970; 307 pages, $6.95
David McKay Co., Inc.
750 Third Avenue
New York, N.Y. 10017

The Book of Pistols and Revolvers
W. H. B. Smith
$14.95
Stackpole Books
Cameron & Kelker Streets
Harrisburg, Pa. 17105

Small Arms of the World
W. H. B. Smith
$16.95
Stackpole Books
Cameron & Kelker Streets
Harrisburg, Pa. 17105

*Basic Pistol Marksmanship;
Basic Rifle Marksmanship;* and
Basic Shotgun Marksmanship
$.25 each
National Rifle Association
1600 Rhode Island Avenue, N.W.
Washington, D.C. 20036

Special Forces Foreign Weapons Handbook
SGM Frank A. Mayer
Paladin Press
Box 1307
Boulder, Col. 80302

First Book of Stage, Costume and Make-up
Barbara Berk
1954; $1.95
Franklin Watts, Inc.
Subsidiary of Grolier
575 Lexington Avenue
New York, N.Y. 10022

Stage Makeup
Richard Carson
$7.50
Meredith Press
250 Park Avenue
New York, N.Y. 10017

*How to Avoid Electronic Eavesdropping
and Privacy Invasion*
$2.98
Investigator Information Service
806 Robertson Boulevard
Los Angeles, Calif. 90035

Locksmithing
Locksmithing Institute
Little Falls, N.J. 07424

Subminiature Electronic Devices Catalog
Ace Electronics
11500 BN W. Seventh Avenue
Miami, Fla. 33168

Shooter's Bible
1970; 576 pages, $3.95
Follett Publishing Co.
1010 W. Washington Boulevard
Chicago, Ill. 62221

The Drug Bust
John Dominick
1970; 95 pages, $1.95
The Light Company
259 W. 15th Street
New York, N.Y. 10011

How to Live on Nothing
Joan Ranson Shortney
1961; 336 pages, $.95
Pocket Books
630 Fifth Avenue
New York, N.Y. 10020

Champagne Living on a Beer Budget
Mike and Marilyn Ferguson
1968; 247 pages, $1.75
G. P. Putnam's Sons
200 Madison Avenue
New York, N.Y. 10016

Consumer Reports
$8 per year
Consumers Union
Mount Vernon, N.Y. 10550

Kibbutz: Venture in Utopia
Melford E. Spiro
1956, 1963; 266 pages, $2.25
Schocken Books, Inc.
67 Park Avenue
New York, N.Y. 10016

Education

Learn as if you were to live forever; live as if you were
to die tomorrow.

Catalog of Free Teaching Materials
Gordon Salisbury
1970; 392 pages, $2.50
P.O. Box 1075
Ventura, Calif. 93001

Educator's Guide to Free Films
1968; 784 pages, 49,443 films, $10.75

Educator's Progress Service
Randolph, Wisc. 53956

Big Rock Candy Mountain
$8 per year
Portola Institute, Inc.
1115 Merrill Street
Menlo Park, Calif. 94025

Start Your Own Skool
$1.00
New Directions Community School
445 Tenth Street
Richmond, Calif. 94801

Outside the Net
John D. Vanden Brink, Thomas P. Wilbur, Eds.
$2 per year (3-4 a year)
Outside the Net
Box 184
Lansing, Mich. 48901

Free and Inexpensive Educational Aids
J. Pepe Thomas
1962; $1.75
Dover Publications, Inc.
180 Varick Street
New York, N.Y. 10014

Whole Earth Catalog
$8 per year: 2 big catalogs,
4 $1-catalogs (Jan., March, July, Sept.
Last one is $5 and worth it.)
558 Santa Cruz Avenue
Menlo Park, Calif. 94025

Guide to Correspondence Study in Colleges and Universities
1970; free
University of California Extension Service
2223 Fulton Street
Berkeley, Calif. 94720

Penn State Correspondence School Catalog
Free
Correspondence Courses
The Pennsylvania State University
202 Agricultural Education Building
University Park, Pa. 16802

Free Material for Earth Science Teachers
W. Matthews, R. Bartholomew
1964; $1.50
Prentice-Hall, Inc.
Englewood Cliffs, N.J. 07632

New Schools Exchange
2840 Hidden Valley
Santa Barbara, Calif. 93103
(Information on free schools)

Where to Get and How to Use Free and Inexpensive Teaching Aids
$1.95
Atherton Press
70 5th Avenue
New York, N.Y. 10011

New Schools Manual
$1.00
New Directions Community School
445 Tenth Street
Richmond, Calif. 94801

Farming, Gardening, and Making It Back to the Land

When the fox preaches, beware of your geese.

The Encyclopedia of Organic Gardening
J. I. Rodale and staff
1968; 1145 pages, $10.00
Rodale Books, Inc.
33 E. Minor Street
Emmaus, Pa. 18049

How to Grow Vegetables and Fruits by the Organic Method
J. I. Rodale
1961; 926 pages, $10.00
Rodale Books, Inc.

33 E. Minor Street
Emmaus, Pa. 18049

How to Make It on the Land
Ray Cohan
1972; $5.00 (paperback)
Prentice-Hall, Inc.
Englewood Cliffs, N.J. 07632

The Ex-urbanite's Complete and Illustrated Easy-Does-It First Time Farmer's Guide
Bill Kaysing

1971; 320 pages, $7.95
Straight Arrow Books
625 Third Street
San Francisco, Calif. 94107

Wood Heat Quarterly
$3 per year (4 issues)
Lowther Press
R.D. 1
Wolcott, Vt. 05680

The Green Revolution
$4 per year, monthly
Route 1, Box 129
Freeland, Md. 21053

Make It
Write for current price and availability
Box 526
Old Chelsea Station
New York, N.Y. 10011

Natural Life Styles
$3 per year
53 Main
New Paltz, N.Y. 12561

The Mother Earth News
$5 per year (6 issues)
P.O. Box 38
Madison, Ohio 44057

Leisure Camping
1969; 53 pages, $3.95
Camping Enterprises
923 Dodd Road
St. Paul, Minn. 55118

Monomatic Toilet
$195 approximately, from
Monogram Industries, Inc.
10131 National Boulevard
Los Angeles, Calif. 90034

Nasco Farm and Ranch Catalog
Nasco
Fort Atkinson, Wisc. 53538

or
Nasco West
Box 3837
Modesto, Calif. 95352

Direct Use of Sun's Energy
Farrington Daniels
1964; 374 pages, $10.00
Yale University Press
149 York Street
New Haven, Conn. 06511

Three pamphlets on wind generator
equipment from:
Quirk's Victory Light Co.
33 Fairweather Street
Bellevue Hill, N.S.W. 2023,
Australia

Bucknell Engineering Co.
10717 E. Rush Street
South El Monte, Calif.

Dyna Technology, Inc.
P.O. Box 3263
Sioux City, Iowa

Prospecting and Operating Small Gold Placers
William F. Boericke
1933; 145 pages, $5.95
John Wiley & Sons, Inc.
605 Third Avenue
New York, N.Y. 10016

Miners Catalog
42 pages, free
Miners and Prospectors Supply
177 Main Street
Newcastle, Calif. 95658

*Ben Meadows Forestry
and Engineering Supplies Catalog*
536 pages, $3.00
Ben Meadows Company
P.O. Box 8377
Atlanta, Ga. 30306

Chainsaws, information free from
Homelite
A Textron Division
Port Chester, N.Y. 10573

Food

Hey, get a loaf of bread to go with that wine.

*Wild Edible Plants of the
Western United States*
Donald and Janice Kirk
1970; 307 pages, $3.95
Naturegraph Publishers
Heraldsburg, Calif. 95448

*An Essay on Brewing, Vintage and Distillation,
Together with Selected Remedies for
Hangover Melancholia or How to Make Booze*
John F. Adams
1970; 108 pages, $.95
Doubleday and Company, Inc.
501 Franklin Avenue
Garden City, New York 11531

Dome Cookbook
Steve Baer
1968; 40 pages, $1.00
Lama Cookbook Fund
Corrales, N.M. 87048

Grow Your Own
Jeanie Darlington
1970; 87 pages, $1.75
The Bookworks
1611 San Pablo Avenue
Berkeley, Calif. 94702

Gourmet Cooking for Free
Bradford Angier
1970; 190 pages, $4.95
Stackpole Books
Cameron and Kelker Streets
Harrisburg, Pa. 17105

Cooking Good Foods
34 pages, $1.50
The Order of the Universe Publishers
Box 203
Prudential Center Station
Boston, Mass. 02199

Cooking with Grains and Vegetables Plus
29 pages, $1.00
The Order of the Universe Publishers
Box 203
Prudential Center Station
Boston, Mass. 02199

Stalking the Wild Asparagus
Euell Gibbons
1962; 303 pages, $2.95
David McKay Co.
750 Third Avenue
New York, N.Y. 10017

The Money in the Bank Cookbook
Marie Roberson Hamm
1969; 250 pages, $1.25
The Macmillan Company
866 Third Avenue
New York, N.Y. 10022

*The Impoverished Student's Book of Cookery,
Drinkery, and Housekeepery*
Jay F. Rosenburg
1965; 148 pages, $1.50
Doubleday and Company, Inc.
501 Franklin Avenue
Garden City, N.Y. 11531

Let's Cook It Right
Adelle Davis
1947, 1970; 576 pages, $1.50
New American Library, Inc.
1301 Avenue of the Americas
New York, N.Y. 10019

The Grub Bag
Ita Jones
March 1971; 258 pages, $1.95
Random House
Westminster, Md. 21157

Zen Macrobiotic Cooking
$1.25
Avon Books
959 Eighth Avenue
New York, N.Y. 10019

The Soybean Cookbook
Dorothea Van Gundy Jones
1963; 240 pages, $1.45
Arc Books
219 Park Avenue South
New York, N.Y. 10003

Guide to Organic Food Shopping and Living
Jerome Goldstein and M. C. Goldman, Eds.
1970; 116 pages, $1.00
Rodale Press, Inc.
Emmaus, Pa. 18049

Meals for Millions
Modern Protein Food (Brochure and information)
Free
1800 Olympia Boulevard
Santa Monica, Calif. 90404

Quantity Recipes
Marion A. Wood and Katherine W. Harris

1945, 1966; 233 pages, $1.00
Cornell Home Economics Extension
New York State College of Human Ecology
Building 7, Research Park
Cornell University
Ithaca, N.Y. 14850

The Tassajara Bread Book
Edward Espe Brown
1970; 146 pages, $2.95
Shambala Publications, Inc.
2010 Seventh Street
Berkeley, Calif. 94710

Natural Foods Cook Book
Beatrice Trum Hunter
1961; 368 pages, $.95
Pyramid Publications, Inc.
444 Madison Avenue
New York, N.Y. 10022

Gypsy Life in New America

The east and west are mine and the north and south.
— "OPEN ROAD," WHITMAN

The American Boys Handbook
D. C. Beard
1882; 391 pages, $3.95
Charles E. Tuttle Company, Inc.
Rutland, Vt. 05701

Indian Crafts and Lore
W. Ben Hunt
1954; 112 pages, $4.50
Golden Press, Inc.
Western Publishing Company
1220 Mound Avenue
Racine, Wisc. 53404

Catalog of Indian Books
$1.00
The Ceremonial Indian Book Service
P.O. Box 1029
Gallup, N.M. 87301

How to Travel Without Being Rich
Norman D. Ford
1969; 179 pages, $2.50

Grosset and Dunlap, Inc.
51 Madison Avenue
New York, N.Y. 10010

White Water Handbook for Canoe and Kayak
John T. Urban
1969; 76 pages, $1.50
Appalachian Mountain Club
5 Joy Street
Boston, Mass. 02108

Cruising Under Sail
Eric C. Hiscock
1950, 1965; 468 pages, $12.75
Oxford University Press, Inc.
200 Madison Avenue
New York, N.Y. 10016

Ferro-Cement Boat Construction
Jack R. Whitener
1971; 128 pages, $10.00
Cornell Maritime Press, Inc.
Box 109
Cambridge, Md. 21613

The Explorers Trademart Log
$3 per year (bimonthly)
Explorers Trademart
P.O. 1630
Annapolis, Md. 21404

Professional Guide's Manual
George Leanard Herter and Jacques P. Herter
1966; 98 pages, $.45
Herter's, Inc.
Waseca, Minn. 56093

Pole, Paddle, and Portage
Bill Riviere
1969; 255 pages, $6.95
Van Nostrand-Reinhold
450 West 33rd Street
New York, N.Y. 10001

Survival Evasion and Escape
1957, 1965, 1969; 430 pages, $3.50
Superintendent of Documents
U.S. Government Printing Office
Washington, D.C. 20402

Survival Equipment Company
Division of Victor Tool Company
Free catalog
Oley, Pa. 19547

Shotgun News
$4 per year (biweekly)
Shotgun News
Box 878
Columbus, Neb. 68601

Wildwood Wisdom
Ellsworth Jaeger
1945, 1969; 491 pages, $6.95
The Macmillan Company
866 Third Avenue
New York, N.Y. 10022

The Golden Book of Camping
William Hill Court
1971; 104 pages, $3.95
Golden Press, Inc.
850 Third Avenue
New York, N.Y. 10022

At Home in the Wilderness
Sun Bear

1968; 90 pages, $3.00
Naturegraph Publishers
8339 W. Dry Creek Road
Healdsburg, Calif. 95448

The Book of Survival
Anthony Greenbank
1967; 223 pages, $.95
New American Library, Inc.
1301 Avenue of the Americas
New York, N.Y. 10019

The Survival Book
Paul Nesbitt, Alonzo Pond, and William Allen
1959; 338 pages, $1.95
Funk and Wagnalls
c/o Thomas Y. Crowell
201 Park Avenue South
New York, N.Y. 10003

Light Weight Camping Equipment
Gerry Cunningham, Margret Hansson
1959; 130 pages, $2.50
Colorado Outdoor Sports Corporation
5450 North Valley
Denver, Col. 80216

Handbook for the Alaskan Prospector
Ernest Wolf
1969; 460 pages, $6.00
The Mineral Industry Research Laboratory
University Of Alaska
College, Alaska 99701

Camping and Woodcraft
Horace Kephart
1917, 1921, 1967; 479 pages, $6.95
The Macmillan Company
Front and Brown Streets
Riverside, N.J. 08075

Skills for Training the Wilds
Bradford Angier
1967; 280 pages, $6.95
Stackpole Books
Harrisburg, Pa. 17105

Anybody's Bike Book
Tom Cuthbertson
1971, $3.00

339

Ten Speed Press
2510 Bancroft Way
Berkeley, Calif. 94704

The Complete Book of Bicycling
Eugene A. Sloan
1970; 342 pages, $9.95
Trident Press
c/o Simon and Schuster
1 W. 39th Street
New York, N.Y. 10018

The Complete Walker
Colin Fletcher
1969; 353 pages, $8.18
Alfred A. Knopf, Inc.

33 West 60th Street
New York, N.Y. 10023

Horses: Their Selection, Care, and Handling
Margret Cabell Self
1943; 170 pages, $5.95
A. S. Barnes and Company
Box 421
Cranbury, N.J. 08312

Practical Western Training
Dave Jones
1968; 176 pages, $5.95
Van Nostrand-Reinhold
45 East 33rd Street
New York, N.Y. 10001

"Home Sweet Home"

*Low-Cost Wood Homes for Rural America—
Construction Manual*
1969; 112 pages, $1.00
Superintendent of Documents
U.S. Government Printing Office
Washington, D.C. 20402

Adobe Construction Methods
1964; 35 pages, $.25
Agricultural Publications
207 University Hall
University of California
Berkeley, Calif. 94720

Domestic Water Supply and Sewage Disposal
Edwin P. Anderson
1960; 440 pages, $4.50
Theodore Audel and Co.
A Division of Bobbs-Merrill
4300 W. 62nd Street
Indianapolis, Ind. 46268

How to Build Your Home in the Wood
Bradford Angier
1952; 310 pages, $2.45
Hart Publishing Co., Inc.
510 Avenue of the Americas
New York, N.Y. 10011

How to Stay Alive in the Woods
Bradford Angier

1956; 285 pages; $.95
The Macmillan Company
866 Third Avenue
New York, N.Y. 10022

Wilderness Cabin
Calvin Rustrum
1961; 169 pages, $5.95
The Macmillan Company
Front and Brown Streets
Riverside, N.J. 08075

Soil-Cement—Its Use in Building
United Nations
1964; 85 pages, $1.50
U.N. Sales Section
New York, N.Y. 10017

Handbook for Building Homes of Earth
$3.00
U.S. Department of Commerce
Clearinghouse for Federal
    Scientific & Technical Information
Springfield, Va. 22151

The Indian Tipi
Reginald and Gladys Laubin
1957; 208 pages, $4.95
University of Oklahoma Press
Faculty Exchange
Norman, Okla. 73069

Village Technology Handbook
1970; 400 pages, $7.00
VITA
College Campus
Schenectady, N.Y. 12308

Making Buildings with the CINVA-Ram Block Press:
A Supervisors Manual
1966; 21 pages, $.45
VITA
College Campus
Schenectady, N.Y. 12308

Wiring Simplified
H. P. Richter
1968; 143 pages, $1.25
Park Publishing Company
Box 8527
Lake Street Station
Minneapolis, Minn. 55408

Electrical Code for One- and Two-Family Dwellings
1969; 133 pages, $1.75
National Fire Protection Association
60 Battermarch Street
Boston, Mass. 02110

The Forgotten Art of Building a Good Fireplace
Vest Orton
1969; 60 pages, $2.00
Yankee, Inc.
Dublin, N.H. 03444

Manual of Individual Water Supply Systems
U.S. Department of Health, Education, and Welfare
$.60
Superintendent of Documents
U.S. Government Printing Office
Washington, D.C. 20402

Japanese Homes and Their Surroundings
Edward S. Morse
1886, 1961; 372 pages, $2.50
Dover Publications Inc.
180 Varick Street
New York, N.Y. 10014

Culture Breakers, Alternatives, and Other Numbers
Ken Isaacs

$5
MSS Educational Publishing Co., Inc.
19 E. 48th Street
New York, N.Y. 10017

Flexible Skin Material (for tent domes)
from
Security Parachute Co.
P.O. Box 3096
San Leandro, Calif. 94578

The Way Things Work
1967; 590 pages, $9.95
Simon and Schuster
630 Fifth Avenue
New York, N.Y. 10020

Introduction to Engineering Design
Thomas T. Woodson
1966; 434 pages, $9.95
McGraw-Hill Book Company
Princeton Road
Hightstown, N.J. 08520
or
Manchester Road
Manchester, Mo. 63062
or
8171 Redwood Highway
Novato, Calif. 94947

Handbook for Building Homes of Earth—PB 179 327
$3.00
Superintendent of Documents
U.S. Government Printing Office
Washington, D.C. 20402

Cinva-Ram Block Press
Bellows—Valvair
200 W. Exchange Street
Akron, Ohio 44309

Stone Shelters
Edward Allen
1969; 199 pages, $13.50
The M.I.T. Press
50 Ames Street
Cambridge, Mass. 02142

Concrete and Masonry, U.S. Army TM5—742
1970; 200 pages, $1.00
Division of Public Documents

U.S. Government Printing Office
Washington, D.C. 20402

Wood Uses
National Forest Product Association
1619 Massachusetts Avenue, N.W.
Washington, D.C. 20036

Tipis
Goodwin-Cole Co.
1315 Alhambra Boulevard
Sacramento, Calif. 95816

Nomadics Tipi
Nomadics
Star Route
Box 41
Cloverdale, Ore. 97112

Building a Log House
1914, 1965; 43 pages, $.50
Cooperative Extension Service
University of Alaska
Box 1109
Juneau, Alaska 99801

Yurt Construction Plan
$3 from
Bill Coperthwaite
Bucks Harbor, Me. 04618

Earth for Homes:
Ideas and Methods
Exchange PB 188918
$3.00
Superintendent of Documents
U.S. Government Printing Office
Washington, D.C. 20402

Solar Devices, Stills, Heaters, Cookers, Etc.
Brace Research Institute
Agricultural Engineering Building
MacDonald College
McGill University
Montreal, Quebec, Canada

Excreta Disposal for Rural Areas and Small Counties
E.G. Wagner and J.N. Lanoix
1958; 187 pages, $5.00
The American Public Health Association

1740 Broadway
New York, N.Y. 10019

Water Supply for Rural Areas and Small Counties
E. G. Wagner and J. N. Lanoix
1959; 340 pages
The American Public Health Association
1740 Broadway
New York, N.Y. 10019

Sanitation Manual for Isolated Regions
1967; 64 pages, free
Department of National Health and Welfare
Ottawa, Ontario, Canada

Well Drilling Operations,
Army and Air Force Technical Manual
TM 5-297 AFM 85-23
1965; 249 pages, $1.00
U.S. Government Printing Office
Division of Public Documents
Washington, D.C. 20402

Dempster Windmills and Pumps
Dempster Industries Inc.
P.O. Box 848
Beatrice, Neb. 68310

Domebook Two
1971; 128 pages, $4.20
Pacific Domes
General Delivery
Bolinas, Calif. 94924

The Owner-Built Home
and Preliminary House Design
(send sketch, etc.)
Ken Kern
1961; 300 pages, $10
(without preliminary design, $5.00)
Ken Kern
Sierra Route
Oakhurst, Calif. 93644

Your Engineered House
Rex Roberts
1964; 237 pages, $8.95
J. P. Lippincott Company
East Washington Square
Philadelphia, Pa. 19105

Canadian Wood-frame House Construction
197 pages, free
Canadian Central Mortgage
and Housing Corporation
650 Lawrence Avenue West
Toronto 7, Ontario, Canada

Land

He that plants trees in the earth loves others better than
himself.

Living with Your Land
John Vosburgh
1968; 191 pages, $6.95
Charles Scribner's Sons
597 Fifth Avenue
New York, N.Y. 10017

National Park Guide
Michael Frome
1970; 176 pages, $2.95
Rand McNally and Co.
405 Park Avenue
New York, N.Y. 10022

Guidebook to Campgrounds
1970; 303 pages, $3.95
Rand McNally and Co.

Be Your Own Legal Eagle

. . . we know the law.

Up Against the Law
Jean Strouse
1970; 269 pages, $.95
Signet
New American Library, Inc.
1301 Avenue of the Americas
New York, N.Y. 10019

Movement Legal Defense
$.50
International Liberation School
1925 Grove Street
Berkeley, Calif. 94704

The Draftees Guide
Robert S. Rukin
1970; 38 pages, $1.75

FHA Pole House Construction
Free
U.S. Department of Housing
and Urban Development
Federal Housing Administration
Washington, D.C. 20410

405 Park Avenue
New York, N.Y. 10022

Status of Aerial Photography
free
U.S. Geological Survey
Denver, Col. 80225
or
Washington, D.C. 20242

Where It Is Still Pleasant to Live in the USA
$1.00
Garden Way Research Associates
Charlotte, Vt. 05445

Grove Press, Inc.
214 Mercer Street
New York, N.Y. 10012

Rules for Radicals
Saul D. Alinsky
1971; 196 pages, $6.95
Random House
Westminster, Md. 21157

IV-F, A Guide to Draft Exemption
David Suttler
1970; 121 pages, $1.50

343

Grove Press, Inc.
214 Mercer Street
New York, N.Y. 10012

Handbook for Conscientious Objectors
Arlo Tatum
1968; 110 pages, $1.00
World Without War Council
1730 Grove Street
Berkeley, Calif. 94709

Face to Face with Your Draft Board
Allan Blackman
1969; 90 pages, $.95
World Without War Council
1730 Grove Street
Berkeley, Calif. 94709

Revolution for the Hell of It
1968; 271 pages, $1.25
Pocket Books
630 Fifth Avenue
New York, N.Y. 10020

Guerrilla Street Theatre
Send 25¢ and large stamped envelope to
Henry Lesnick
915 West End Avenue, Apt. 8F
New York, N.Y. 10025

Sometimes a Great Notion
Ken Kesey
1964; 599 pages, $1.25
Bantam Books, Inc.
666 Fifth Avenue
New York, N.Y. 10019

Police badges, I.D. cards, tech manuals, black light
equipment, bug directors, pin tumbler
lock-picking gun, police radio monitors, miniature
cameras, recorders, etc. from
International Police Equipment Co.

The Bust Book
Boudin, Glick, Raskin, and Reichbach
1970; 159 pages, $1.25
Grove Press, Inc.
214 Mercer Street
New York, N.Y. 10012

The Draft Physical
1970; 12 pages, $1.00
Brooklyn Bridge Press
P.O. Box 1894
Brooklyn, N.Y. 11202

1001 Ways to Beat the Draft
Kupferberg and Bashlow
1967; $.75
Grove Press, Inc.
214 Mercer Street
New York, N.Y. 10012

The Lucky Bag
Aboard ships, a locker is reserved for all those items which
have no regular place. It is called the Lucky Bag.

906 Robertson Boulevard
Los Angeles, Calif. 90035

Encyclopedia of U.S. Government Benefits
$10.00
William H. Wise & Co., Inc.
336 Mountain Road
Union City, N.J. 07087

The Foundation Directory
Marianna O. Lewis, Ed.
1967; 1,198 pages, $12.00
Russell Sage Foundation
230 Park Avenue
New York, N.Y. 10017

Understanding Foundations
J. Richard Taft
1967; 205 pages, $2.95
McGraw-Hill Book Company
Princeton Road
Hightstown, N.J. 08520

Birth certificates
Customized forms printed,
$15 first one; regular price after, 2 for $1.00
1,400 standardized forms, 2 for $1.00

Form Distributors
P.O. Box 893
League City, Tex. 77573

The Selling of the President
Joe McGinniss
1970; 278 pages, $1.25
Pocket Books
630 Fifth Avenue
New York, N.Y. 10020

Mechanical Bride
Marshall McLuhan
1961; 239 pages, $2.95
Beacon Press
25 Beacon Street
Boston, Mass. 02108

Medical and Dental

Birth Control Handbook
McGill Students' Society
$.10
Students' Society of McGill University
3480 McTavish Street
Montreal, Quebec, Canada

Dear Doctor Hippocrates
Eugene Schoenfeld
1968; 112 pages, $.95
Grove Press, Inc.
214 Mercer Street
New York, N.Y. 10012

Current Diagnosis and Treatment
H. Brainard
$9.50
Lange Medical Publications
Drawer L
Los Altos, Calif. 94022

Medical Cadre
$.25
ILS
1925 Grove Street
Berkeley, Calif. 94709

Handbook of Surgery
J. L. Wilson
$6.00

Understanding Media: The Extensions of Man
Marshall McLuhan
1965; 346 pages, $1.95
McGraw-Hill Book Company
330 W. 42nd Street
New York, N.Y. 10036

Vocations for Social Change
Send a donation for this newsletter
printed bimonthly from
Canyon, Calif. 94516

The Canyon Collective (tabloid)
1970; 24 pages, $.05
P.O. Box 78
Canyon, Calif. 94516

Lange Medical Publications
Drawer L
Los Altos, Calif. 94022

Abortion
Lawrence Lader
1966; 264 pages, $1.95
Beacon Paperback (try *Whole Earth Catalog*)
558 Santa Cruz
Menlo Park, Calif. 94025

Emergency Medical Guide
John Henderson, M.D.
1963, 1969; 556 pages, $3.95
McGraw-Hill Book Company
Princeton Road
Hightstown, N.J. 08520

The Home Medical Handbook
E. Russel Kodet and Bradford Angier
1970; 224 pages, $4.95
Association Press
291 Broadway
New York, N.Y. 10007

First Aid
American National Red Cross
1933, 1937, 1945, 1957; 249 pages, $.75
Doubleday and Company, Inc.
277 Park Avenue
New York, N.Y. 10017

The Complete Home Medical Encyclopedia
Harold T. Hyman, M.D.
1963, 1965; 832 pages, $1.65
Avon Books
959 Eighth Avenue
New York, N.Y. 10019

Preparation for Childbirth
1963, 1969; 47 pages, free or cheap
Maternity Center Association
48 E. 92nd Street
New York, N.Y. 10028

How to Keep Your Volkswagen Alive
John Muir
1969; 242 pages, $5.50
John Muir Publications
Box 613
Santa Fe, N.M. 87501

Volkswagen Owners' Handbook of Maintenance and Repair
$3.00
Floyd Clymer
222 North Virgil Avenue
Los Angeles, Calif. 90004

Basic Auto Repair Manual No. 3
1971; 384 pages, $3.95
Peterson Publishing Company
8490 Sunset Boulevard
Los Angeles, Calif. 90069

Auto Engines and Electrical Systems
$9.95
Motor

A Manual of Simple Burial
Ernest Morgan
1968; 64 pages, $1.00
The Celo Press
Burnsville, N.C. 28714

Handy Medical Guide for Seafarers
R. W. Scott
1969; 86 pages, $2.40
International Marine Publications
Camden, Me. 04843

Your Teeth
D. A. Collins, D.D.S.
1967; 224 pages, about $4.50
Doubleday and Company, Inc.
277 Park Avenue
New York, N.Y. 10017

Moving On

The most important thing in my life right now is getting this bearing to fit.

THE GRAPES OF WRATH, JOHN STEINBECK

250 W. 55th Street
New York, N.Y. 10019

Modern Motorcycle Mechanics
J. B. Nicholson
1942, 1969; 702 pages, $8.00
Nicholson Brothers Motorcycles Ltd.
225 Third Avenue North
Saskatoon, Saskatchewan, Canada

Hitch-Hiking in Europe
Ed Buryn
1969; 72 pages, $1.75
Hannah Associates
721 Bryant
San Francisco, Calif. 94107

Traveler's Directory
Peter Kocalanos
1970; 56 pages, $3.00
Peter Kocalanos
51-02 39th Avenue
Woodside, N.Y. 11377

**Things to Make or, How to Let the Devil
Put Your Idle Hands to Work**

How to Manual: Posters
$1.25
Agitprop Literature Programme
160 N. Gower Street
London N.W. 1, England

Street Theatre, local journal,
printing, leaflets, films, press
publicity, Power Research Guide
$.25 each
Agitprop Literature Programme
160 N. Gower Street
London N.W. 1, England

Bottle cutter
$3.00
Fleming Bottle and Jug Cutter
2110 S.W. 173rd Place
Seattle, Wash. 98166

How to Work with Tools and Wood
Robert Campbell
1967; 448 pages, $.75
Pocket Books
630 Fifth Avenue
New York, N.Y. 10020

Carpentry for Beginners
Charles H. Hayward
1969; $4.50
Emerson Books, Inc.
251 W. 19th Street
New York, N.Y. 10011

Hand Woodworking Tools
Leo P. McDonnell
1962; 294 pages, $5.00
Delmar Publishers, Inc.
Box 5087
Albany, N.Y. 12205

Practical House Carpentry
John D. Wilson
1957; $2.95
McGraw-Hill Book Company
330 W. 42nd Street
New York, N.Y. 10036

Index

Vinyl repair:
   publications on, 19
VITA, 136
Vocations for Social Change, (VSC), 266-
   68, 332, 345
   list of contacts for, 267-68
Volkswagen, insurance on, 72
Von Hilsheimer, George, 72
VSC (Vocations for Social Change), 266-
   68, 332, 345
   list of contacts for, 267-68

Wagons, sheep, 232, 34
Walden Pond, 115
Wall construction of log cabin, 126
Wanderjahr, 243
Warfare, unconventional, 248, 256
Wash and wear fabrics, 145-46
Water living, 138-40, 239-43
   publications on, 338, 339
   See also Houseboats
Water mill construction, 83
Water sports
   as job, 20
   as recreation, 83
Water supply, nomadic vehicles and, 219-
   20, 225, 230-32

Water supplies, publications on, 119, 340,
   341, 342
Water tanks as housing, 137
Waterfalls as housing, 136
Weapons, publications on, 248, 333, 334
Weather maps and climate descriptions,
   sources of, 58-59
Weathermen (political group), 249
Weaving, 156
Welding, as job, 29-30
Well-drilling, manuals on, 342
Wenatchee (Washington), 10-11
Whole wheat
   bread, 101
   cost of, 90, 92, 100
   source of, 89
   uses for, 90-91, 98, 101, 110, 113
White Pine County (Nevada), 11
Whitman, Walt, 338
Whole Earth Catalog, The, 3, 285
Whole Earth Catalog Store, 285, 331
Wholesale foods, 104-6
Wilcock, John, 217, 219
Wild plants, edible, 7
   publications on, 337
Willamette Valley (Oregon), 11
Wind generator, publications on, 336
Windmills, publications on, 342

Window construction in log cabin, 126
Window frame construction in log cabin,
   126
Window shutter construction in log cabin,
   126
Winemaking, 18
Wiring, publications on, 341
Wood, sale of as job, 31-32
Wood housing, publications on, 120, 122,
   123, 340, 343, 347
Woodcrafts, publications on, 339, 342
Woodward, Joe, 264
Woodworking, publications on, 347
Wool, 144, 145, 153
   protecting from moths, 157
Wright, Frank Lloyd, 136
Writing
   apprenticeship in, 202-3
   as job, 30
   publications on, 30

Yeager, Philip B., 255
Yeast, baking, 95
Yellowstone National Park (Wyoming),
   thermal springs of, 313
Yogurt, natural, 96

Zen macrobiotics, publication on, 337